Palgrave Studies in (Re)Presenting Gender

Series Editor
Emma Rees, Director, Institute of Gender Studies, University of
Chester, Chester, UK

The focus of Palgrave Studies in (Re)Presenting Gender is on gender and representation. The 'arts' in their broadest sense – TV, music, film, dance, and performance – and media re-present (where 'to represent' is taken in its literal sense of 'to present again', or 'to give back') gender globally. How this re-presentation might be understood is core to the series.

In re-presenting gendered bodies, the contributing authors can shift the spotlight to focus on marginalised individuals' negotiations of gender and identity. In this way, minority genders, subcultural genders, and gender inscribed on, in, and by queer bodies, take centre stage. When the 'self' must participate in and interact with the world through the body, how that body's gender is talked about – and side-lined or embraced by hegemonic forces – becomes paramount. These processes of representation – how cultures 'give back' gender to the individual – are at the heart of this series.

More information about this series at
https://link.springer.com/bookseries/16541

Carmen Dexl · Silvia Gerlsbeck
Editors

The Male Body in Representation

Returning to Matter

Editors

Carmen Dexl
American Studies
University of Regensburg
Regensburg, Germany

Silvia Gerlsbeck
English Studies: Literature
and Culture
Friedrich-Alexander-Universität
Erlangen-Nürnberg
Erlangen, Germany

ISSN 2662-9364   ISSN 2662-9372   (electronic)
Palgrave Studies in (Re)Presenting Gender
ISBN 978-3-030-88603-5   ISBN 978-3-030-88604-2   (eBook)
https://doi.org/10.1007/978-3-030-88604-2

PREFACE

The drawing from Michelangelo's *Studies for the Libyan Sibyl* (ca. 1510–1511) portrays Sibyl, the priestess of the Oracle of Zeus-Ammon. While this sketch, one out of a series, might be familiar to us, it is also profoundly defamiliarizing: What exactly do we see here? What is portrayed? We see the rear view of a part of a body, the figure's head slightly tilted, eyes looking downward, the facial features soft, almost delicate, with a slim nose and high cheekbones, and braided hair. The viewer's eye is immediately drawn to the muscular back and equally sinewy arms, the clearly visible overall high muscle tone of the figure's body. Drawn with red chalk, which was especially suited for the particularized, highly naturalistic study of anatomical detail, the powerful muscular body and soft delicate face that converge in this figure challenge the categorization of the figure in terms of sex and gender. We might be familiar with the finished painting on the ceiling of the Sistine Chapel in Vatican City for which these sketches laid the ground, yet the story of the studies on which the sketches are based is intriguing: While some of the drawings portray softer anatomical forms, which the Metropolitan Museum of Art (Met) in New York City describes as "feminine",[1] this sketch is based on a young

---

[1] The image and quote stem from the website of the Metropolitan Museum of Art, which owns the drawings: https://www.metmuseum.org/art/collection/search/337497. Last accessed July 27, 2021.

male model posing for Michelangelo in his studio and presents us with—as the Met puts it—a more "masculine" body. This de-entanglement of notions of sex and gender from the body seems a fitting way to open our volume, as it underscores these concepts' characteristic "conceptual fuzziness". This book is thus motivated by inquiring into how more nuanced understandings of and insights into these concepts can be gained from analyzing the male body as it emerges in representation.

Regensburg, Germany   Carmen Dexl
Erlangen, Germany   Silvia Gerlsbeck

CONTENTS

NOTES ON CONTRIBUTORS

Jonathan A. Allan is a Canada Research Chair in Men and Masculinities at Brandon University in Canada. He teaches in the Department of English, Drama, and Creative Writing and the Gender and Women's Studies Program. He is the author of *Men, Masculinities, and Popular Romance* (Routledge, 2020) and *Reading from Behind: A Cultural Analysis of the Anus* (University of Regina Press/Zed Books, 2016). His forthcoming book is titled *Men, Masculinities, and Infertilities*. He is the co-editor of the *Journal of Bodies, Sexualities, and Masculinities* (Berghahn) and Vice President of the American Men's Studies Association (AMSA).

Carmen Dexl is an assistant professor in American Studies at the University of Regensburg, Germany. She is currently working on her second book project about negotiations of aging in modern and postmodern dance, which is located at the intersection of Performance Studies, Age Studies, and Body Studies. Her Ph.D. thesis, which she completed at Friedrich-Alexander-Universität Erlangen-Nürnberg in 2017, was placed in the fields of Literary Studies, African American Studies, and Masculinity Studies. As a co-coordinator of the CITAS-funded research network "Knowledge Infrastructures" at the University of Regensburg, she pursues a project on Black modernist entertainment culture and the circulation of embodied knowledge. Her publications center on African American fiction, dance and cultural performance, and processes of transnational and intercultural exchange.

Sandra Dinter is a postdoctoral researcher in English Literature and Culture at Friedrich-Alexander-Universität Erlangen-Nürnberg in Germany. Her research interests include literary representations of gender and space, mobility studies, (neo-)Victorian Studies, and narrative fiction about and for children. She is the author of *Childhood in the Contemporary English Novel* (Routledge, 2019) and co-editor of *Transdisciplinary Perspectives on Childhood in Contemporary Britain: Literature, Media and Society* (Routledge, 2018). Currently, she is working on a book-length study on female pedestrians in nineteenth-century British culture and literature and co-editing the collection *Medicine and Mobility in Nineteenth-Century British Literature, History, and Culture* (Palgrave, 2022).

John Finkelberg is a Ph.D. candidate in History at the University of Michigan and an Eisenberg Graduate Student Fellow at the Eisenberg Institute for Historical Studies. He is also the co-author of "Fashion in the Life of George Sand" published in *Fashion Theory: The Journal of Dress, Body, and Culture* (2020). His Ph.D. thesis, titled *Becoming a Man in the Age of Fashion: Gender and Menswear in Nineteenth-Century France*, traces the production, sale, use, and representation of menswear in France from the July Revolution of 1830 to the collapse of the Second French Empire in 1870.

Silvia Gerlsbeck is a research associate and doctoral candidate in English Literature and Culture at Friedrich-Alexander-Universität Erlangen-Nürnberg, Germany, where she is currently completing her dissertation on constructions of authorship and masculinity in Anglo-Caribbean artist novels. Her research interests and teaching activities include Black British and Caribbean literature, Masculinity and Sexuality Studies, theories and representations of authorship, Body Studies, and posthumanism. Current and forthcoming publications center on the work of George Lamming, Samuel Selvon, and David Dabydeen.

rl goldberg is a Junior Fellow in the Society of Fellows at Dartmouth College, US. Their work has been published in *Transgender Studies Quarterly*, *The Paris Review*, *The Los Angeles Review of Books*, *ASAP/J*, and elsewhere. They are currently working on their first monograph, based on their dissertation, which they conducted in the Department of English at Princeton University. Titled *I Changed My Sex! Pedagogy and Trans*

Narrative, the book is a phenomenological account of trans self-writing and interrogates the ways in which trans texts are received as pedagogy.

Melanie Haller is a research assistant at the Institute of Music, Art, and Textile at the University of Paderborn in Germany. She received her Ph.D. in 2012 with a thesis on intersubjectivity in Argentine tango. From 2004 to 2015, she worked at the Institute of Human Movement Science at the University of Hamburg and, from 2019 to 2020, she was a visiting professor in the Department of Design at the Hamburg University of Applied Sciences (HAW). Her research interests and publications focus on the sociology and materiality of fashion, fashion-bodies, fashion and diversity, and Gender Studies, and involve qualitative methods. Her work benefits from her critical perspective as a body sociologist and her education as a tailor. Her most recent publications include *Mode–Sport–Körper: Vom zeitgenössischen Phänomen zur historischen Betrachtung* (2017) and her co-edited volume titled *Der Tod und das Ding. Textile Materialitäten im Kontext von Vergänglichkeit* (Waxmann, 2020).

Christian Krug is a senior lecturer in English Literary and Cultural Studies at Friedrich-Alexander-Universität Erlangen-Nürnberg in Germany. His research and teaching focuses on popular culture and its historicity, with a focus on the "structures of feeling", the libidinal investments, the desires and fantasies underlying the cultural practices of social groups at specific moments in time—and how these are profoundly ideological (his Ph.D. thesis on nineteenth century British melodrama was published in 2001, the co-edited collection *The Popular and the Past* in 2016). He also works on "icons" of popular culture and their ideological functions, such as James Bond (he co-edited *The Cultures of James Bond* in 2011). As a member of the Global Sentimentality Network (https://www.sentimental.phil.fau.de), he is currently researching the role sentimentality plays in British popular culture.

Martina Kübler is a postdoctoral researcher at the English Department at Ludwig Maximilian University of Munich in Munich, Germany. In 2020, she completed her doctoral dissertation on disability and masculinity in the novels of D. H. Lawrence, Ernest Hemingway, and William Faulkner. She is a member of the research groups "Globalization and Literature" and "Philology of Adventure" at LMU Munich. Her research interests include gender, sexuality, and queer studies, disability studies, globalization, and modernism.

Jay McCauley Bowstead lectures Cultural and Historical Studies at London College of Fashion (University of the Arts London, UK). He is a co-convener of the university's Masculinities Research Hub, where he organized the conference "Globalising Men's Style" in 2020, together with Charlie Athill. Jay McCauley Bowstead's scholarly work focuses on gender, design, and materiality, with recent publications including the monograph *Menswear Revolution* (Bloomsbury, 2018), a co-authored article on designer Charles Jeffrey with Fenella Hitchcock (2020), and a chapter on cultural hybridity in the anthology *Dandy Style*, edited by Shaun Cole and Giles Lambert (2021). In addition, his research interests include the relationship between ethics, fashion production, and public policy discourses.

Michael McMillan is a London-based writer, playwright, artist/curator, and academic, known for his critically acclaimed installation-based exhibition *The West Indian Front Room*, curated at the Geffrye Museum (2005–2006). It was iterated in The Netherlands, Curaçao, Johannesburg, and France, and was the basis of both the *BBC4* documentary *Tales from the Front Room* (2007) and his book *The Front Room: Migrant Aesthetics in the Home* (2009). Forthcoming works in 2021 include a permanent 1970s' period room of his work *The Front Room*, and a triptych film installation of *Waiting for Myself to Appear*, his one-woman-site responsive performance piece (Geffrye Museum, 2019) at the renamed Museum of the Home. He is currently an associate lecturer in Cultural and Historical Studies at London College of Fashion (University of the Arts London, UK) and a research associate with the Visual Identities in Arts & Design Research Centre (University of Johannesburg, South Africa).

Alla Myzelev is an associate professor of Art History and Museum Studies at the State University of New York at Geneseo where she teaches courses in modern and contemporary visual culture. She has published on gender representation in the arts, activism, and material culture. She is currently writing a monograph on masculinity and fashion in the Soviet Union and is the author of *Architecture, Design and Craft in Toronto 1900–1940: Creating Modern Living* (Ashgate, 2016). Her edited collection of articles *Exhibiting Craft and Design: Transgressing the White Cube Paradigm, 1930–Present* was published by Routledge (2017). Her research interests revolve around gender and contemporary culture. She published on and curated DIY culture, fiber art, and digital environments, including a yearly exhibition of Feminist Art in Toronto (2014–2019).

David Patrick is a postdoctoral research fellow in the International Studies Group at the University of the Free State in South Africa. Being the author of *Reporting Genocide: Media, Mass Violence and Human Rights* (I.B. Tauris, 2017), he received his Ph.D. in History from the University of Sheffield in 2013. He is currently working toward the completion of his second monograph, which will detail press coverage of the 2014 Scottish independence referendum. With journal articles appearing in *International Politics* and *Scottish Affairs*, his research interests include genocide and mass violence, the media framing of historical events, and the sociocultural aspects of professional boxing.

Ana Stevenson is a lecturer at the University of Southern Queensland in Australia, and a research associate in the International Studies Group at the University of the Free State in South Africa. Her research is primarily concerned with women and transnational social movements, as demonstrated in her first book *The Woman as Slave in Nineteenth-Century American Social Movements* (Palgrave Macmillan, 2019), the co-edited collection *Gender Violence in Australia: Historical Perspectives* (Monash University Publishing, 2019), and journal articles in the *Women's History Review*, Cultural & Social History, and the *Pacific Historical Review*. Her broader research interests include Gender Studies, Fashion History, and Media History.

LIST OF FIGURES

CHAPTER 1

Returning to Matter: New Perspectives on the Male Body in Representation

Carmen Dexl and Silvia Gerlsbeck

WHY BODIES MATTER

The 'male body' is a fit, healthy, and mostly white body—at least that is what a look at photographs and sports-related advertising on social media platforms featuring images of men posing shirtless on the beach or at the gym and showing off their well-trained, toned, and muscular

C. Dexl
American Studies, University of Regensburg, Regensburg, Germany
e-mail: carmen.dexl@ur.de

S. Gerlsbeck (✉)
English Studies: Literature and Culture, Friedrich-Alexander-Universität
Erlangen-Nürnberg, Erlangen, Germany
e-mail: silvia.gerlsbeck@fau.de

bodies suggests.[1] Representations of idealized male physiques tied to Western-centric notions proliferate—despite attempts at diversification[2]—and render bodies subject to a variety of disciplinary techniques, such as dieting, tattooing, working out, or plastic surgery. The current media landscape thus evidences an increasing commodification of male bodies: While the objectification of bodies has for a long time extended to women only, men are more and more becoming 'bodily objects' in contemporary consumer culture and their bodies, too, a "negotiable commodity" (Dworkin and Wachs 2009, 7–8). This coalesces with a growing visibility of bodies that do *not* correspond to such ideal imaginings under the banner of body positivity. Both constructions of bodies, however, must be understood within broader neo-liberal tendencies that 'sell' the ideal of investing into one's own body as a form of investing into one's health, physical and mental wellbeing, and success. This kind of body politics, connected to the cult of individualism, has of late come under scrutiny.

Focusing on representations of the male body and related gender constructions in a broad variety of cultural contexts, the contributions in this volume of international and multidisciplinary scope tackle the various cultural sign systems, discourses, and ideological interpellations that bodies are embedded in and constitutive of. They engage with the subject from different disciplinary and critical perspectives, including Literary Studies, Media Studies, Performance Studies, Art History, Historical Studies, Fashion Studies, Body Sociology, and Queer and Transgender Studies, and focus their analyses on various cultural contexts, such as Russia, France, Great Britain, the Caribbean, North America, or Japan, as well as on a wide variety of cultural productions and cultural formats.[3]

[1] We would like to thank Claudia Hachenberger for her valuable assistance in editing the manuscript and creating the index. We would also like to thank Catharina Kriesl, Marie Kluge, Vanessa Goß, Anna Alkofer, and the Office of Equality and Diversity for their support.

[2] See Sarah Gee and Steven Jackson's study *Sport, Promotional Culture and the Crisis of Masculinity* (2017) on this topic.

[3] We see the bandwidth of Cultural Studies scholarship as one of the field's benefits as it allows us to rethink the male body in the intersection between materiality, social practice, and representation, look at a wide array of cultural formats, and frame the contributions assembled here productively. All inquiries build on an extended notion of 'text', exploring literary, visual, and other cultural texts.

In its full scope, *The Male Body in Representation: Returning to Matter* thus acknowledges the plurality of gendered experiences and the diversity of male bodies as they are negotiated, revisited, and potentially reshaped through representation. It aims to add to Cultural Studies scholarship interested in the significance of the body and gender in general and contribute to the fields of Masculinity and Body Studies in particular.

Donna Haraway's statement that "[i]t matters what matters we use to think other matters with" (2016b, 12) poignantly summarizes the overall concerns of our book and hints at the intriguing ambiguity of 'matter': In our reading, it, on the one hand, points to how 'matter', meaning bodies, serves to make sense of the matters of the world and how 'matter', meaning the world as we perceive it, is in turn reproduced in bodies. On the other hand, it allows us to discuss scholarly 'matters', i.e., the methods and theories we use to think through the matter of male bodies and their representation. This includes, as will become clear in this introduction, the following three aspects: First, conceptualizing 'the male body' in the intersection between constructivist and different traditions of materialist thought; second, building on and contributing to the existing research on masculinities and 'male bodies'; and third, embracing paranoid and reparative lenses of reading to approach cultural representations. This entails attending to the signifying potential that representation ascribes to the body, the conception of its embeddedness in symbolic sign systems, that is, its discursive nature, its own textuality, at the same time as it allows for extrapolating the role that representation accords to often neglected material aspects of the body. With this focus, this introduction aims to frame the contributions assembled in this book in theoretical and methodological terms, while it also constitutes a contribution to scholarship in itself by situating, theorizing, and discussing 'the male body' within existing fields of research.

LOCATING THE 'MALE BODY'

Locating the 'male body' in the fields of Masculinity and Body Studies as well as in the context of representation first of all requires a short reflection on the terminology used. When the contributions in this volume speak of the 'male body', this is not be understood as referring to a biological essence—as indicated, for instance, by the 'presence' of genitalia or hormones. It rather works as a term that refers to the discursive ascription of a 'male sex' onto the body, which is predicated on the *interpretation* of material aspects as 'male'—i.e., the body that is, by means of its biological features, shape, or form *read* as 'male'.[4] The term 'masculine', which can converge with or diverge from the male body, here, refers to the social construction of gender that is subject to discursive production and evocative of historically and culturally specific idea(l)s of masculinity.[5] That is to say, there is no neat trajectory from male (sex) to masculine (gender), as, at the latest, poststructuralist interventions in the field have shown. A 'female body', too, can be read as masculine, and vice versa, or transition to or identify as a 'male body', as some of the contributions herein show. Similarly, the term 'body' in this context designates not a concept 'before' sex or gender, but is understood as the materialization of a discursively constructed category onto which sexed and gendered notions are mapped and which has agency in constituting and expressing gender concepts. The body as such then emerges as discursively formed matter, accessible through representation, which makes it available for different (re-)readings and, by implication, different re-materializations.

Any discussion of the 'male body' cannot proceed without sketching the broader historical and disciplinary contexts in which the subject

---

[4] This is in line with scholarship that, in the wake of Judith Butler, conceives of sex as a discursively produced category. Our conception of the 'male body' builds on this discursive notion of sex but moves on to place it in dialogue with new materialist positions that stress the relevance of matter, as this introduction to the topic and our attempt at a definition of the 'male body' illustrate.

[5] Jeff Hearn, for instance, has distinguished concepts of 'male', 'men', and 'masculinities' and explained their interrelations and implications; see, for instance Hearn (2012), where he uses the term 'gex' to refer to the intersection of gender and sex, or Hearn (2011). Closely attending to the implications of 'male', 'masculine', and 'men', he points towards the different significations of 'male' and traces its use from a mere biological perspective to account for the social, political, and other embodied experiences of men (2011, 206–207). By now, even biologists, for instance, have started to acknowledge that 'sex' is not to be defined as a binary category, but rather as a spectrum (cf. for instance Ainsworth 2015), thus opening the 'male sex' for a more social definition.

matter is located and to which this volume aims to contribute. Scholarship in the fields of Masculinity[6] and Body Studies[7] have contributed to de-essentializing both masculinity and the body and to recognizing these concepts in their diversity. Kevin Floyd and Stefan Horlacher, for example, poignantly claim that "'masculinity' is, in a sense, a misnomer; there are only 'masculinities', the field insists, in the plural" (2017, 1). Emerging in the wake of feminist movements in the 1980s in Europe, particularly England, the Netherlands, Germany, and Scandinavian countries, and the United States (Seidler 2006, 1), the field of Masculinity Studies, initially shaped by sociological perspectives, has by now diffused and diversified. To fully outline the vast work on masculinities is beyond the scope of this introduction, but it aims to map out the status of 'matter' in the field.

Fashionings of male bodies in relation to culturally and historically specific hierarchical models of masculinity are often conceived through the frame of 'hegemonic masculinity'. Coined by R.W. Connell, it is one of the pioneering concepts in Masculinity Studies and has enabled the analysis of the relationality and dynamics of masculinities in different settings. As the dominant position within a certain order of social hierarchies that also includes subordinate, complicit, and marginalized positions (2005, 76–86), it embodies and reflects "the currently accepted answer to the problem of the legitimacy of patriarchy, which guarantees (or is taken to guarantee) the dominant position of men and the subordination of women" (77). While Connell's concept has by now become 'hegemonic' itself and also been contested for its shortcomings, its influence on the study of men and masculinities cannot be overstated, as the

---

[6] In grappling with this by now highly differentiated field, one must point to the seminal work by Harry Brod, R.W. Connell, Jeff Hearn, Michael Kimmel, Todd W. Reeser, bell hooks, Cynthia Cockburn, or Stephen M. Whitehead, among many others. Many of their findings are by now unquestioned prerequisites for the study of masculinities. This includes assumptions that 'masculinity' needs to be conceived in the plural and as relational, socially constructed, produced, and reproduced, as well as historically variable.

[7] Body Studies, which has flourished particularly since the 1990s, is by now often used as an umbrella term for scholarly inquiries into aspects of embodiment, self-fashioning, identity, and body practices and techniques. Introductions to this field that often but not exclusively deploy a sociological point of view include the *Routledge Handbook of Body Studies* edited by Bryan S. Turner (2012) and Margo DeMello's *Body Studies: An Introduction* (2014).

contributions herein, which to some extent also reflect on forms of relationality between men, show. Notions of hegemony take on additional meaning in the context of transcultural fashionings of masculinities, and the theoretical premises and critical concerns of research on the concept of 'global masculinities', for example, have contributed to the contestation and diversification of dominant paradigms. Thus, the notion of cultural difference within studies of men and masculinities and with it 'non-Western' masculinities have come into focus.[8] Ronald L. Jackson II and Murali Balaji have in their studies put emphasis on "the representations and assumed practices of black masculinity" (2011, 21) within existing paradigms of Masculinity Studies.[9] Some contributions in this volume take up negotiations of masculinity in a global context by focusing on fashionings of male bodies in concordance with or opposition to hegemonic paradigms, or inquire into the specific position of 'othered' masculinities.

With the proliferation of inter- and multidisciplinary publications in Masculinity Studies in the past few years, including studies such as *Performing Masculinity* (2010), edited by Rainer Emig and Antony Rowland, Sarah Gee and Steven Jackson's *Sport, Promotional Culture and the Crisis of Masculinity* (2017), Anna Hickey-Moody's *Deleuze and Masculinity* (2019), or Eric Louis Russell's *Alpha Masculinity* (2021), the field has witnessed an oftentimes implicit, yet increasing turn towards considering the body as an epistemological category in its own right. Historically, for the most part, the body has been a central subject of analysis in the disciplines of the natural sciences, due to its allegedly natural materiality, and of philosophy, where it, however, became marginalized in the wake of Humanist traditions and Cartesian dualism. René Descartes's

---

[8] 'Global masculinities' emerged in the late 1980s and early 1990s through seminal work like David D. Gilmore's *Manhood in the Making* (1990) and was further developed through a *Global Masculinities* series by London-based Zed publisher, which also featured Bob Pease and Keith Pringle's *A Man's World? Changing Men's Practices in a Globalized World* (2001), or Ronald L. Jackson II and Murali Balaji's *Global Masculinities and Manhood* (2011). A more recent *Global Masculinities* series started by Palgrave in 2011 is concerned with the role of intersectionality, diversity, and cultural specificity for constructions of masculinity and the (tense) relation of the global and local in the formation of gender, thus inviting both comparative and transnational perspectives on the topic.

[9] Horlacher and Floyd's collection *Post-World War II Masculinities in British and American Literature and Culture* (2013) also offers scholarship on comparative masculinity studies.

separation of mind and body, as epitomized by his oft-quoted 1637 statement that reason is "the only thing that makes us men and distinguishes us from the beasts" (2001, 4), not only entailed a privileging of the mind as instrument of rational thought, seemingly available to what was normatively construed as the white *male* human subject only, but also led to a neglect of the body's role for generating knowledge (Wolfe 2009, xiv, xvi–xvii).

Scholarly literature on the body typically traces the genealogy of its renaissance back to different—partly contrasting, yet also interrelated—traditions that have revaluated the body and made it 'legible' after the centuries-long dominance of Cartesian dualism.[10] Phenomenological accounts of the body, for instance, as indebted to the work of mostly Continental philosophers such as Edmund Husserl, Maurice Merleau-Ponty, or Jean-Paul Sartre, have shifted the focus to embodiment and brought the significance of the experiencing body into focus (MacMullan 2002, 2). Indebted to Martin Heidegger's notion of *Dasein* and Marcel Mauss's 'techniques of the body', Merleau-Ponty, most prominently, has as early as in the 1940s emphasized how reality comes into being via 'perceptive awareness', which is tied to the body, its material condition, and related positioning in the world: "[I]n order to be able to affirm a truth, the actual subject must first have a world or be in the world" (2012, 131). The body thus emerges as the prime vehicle for human experience.[11] At the same time, the body for Merleau-Ponty "is much more than an instrument or a means; it is our expression in the world, the visible form of our intentions" (1964, 5), i.e., it allows for plural forms of self-fashioning, stylizations, and identifications. The possible strategies used for expressing the self are subject to specific historical and cultural conditions, in which

---

[10] The attempt to correct the Cartesian neglect of the body is at the center of what Maxine Sheets-Johnstone termed the 'corporeal turn' in her 1990 study *The Roots of Thinking*. She also responds critically to the privilege given to textuality and language for the production of social experience in light of an earlier, the linguistic, turn. Sheets-Johnstone's concern with the body, specifically the lived body in movement, is paradigmatic of the wave of scholarship in the Humanities and Social Sciences that was published between the mid-1980s and mid-1990s.

[11] The work of Husserl, Merleau-Ponty, or Sartre has also influenced the sociology of embodiment, e.g., Pierre Bourdieu's conception of bodily dispositions (habitus) as an incorporation of social forces (Lane 2000, 100–102).

they acquire social meanings, and hence are not only *produced* by them but also "reproducing" them (Butler 1988, 521).

While phenomenological approaches brought the body into focus, they (implicitly) posit the *male* body as universal and *only* body. Poststructuralist approaches, indebted to the work of Michel Foucault or Jacques Derrida, for instance, offer relevant alterations to these accounts of (male) embodiment. Foucault's theories explain how the workings of power and discourse generate the body. While Foucault, as Nikki Sullivan states, nowhere in his work offers a concise theory of the body (2012, 106), his studies pertaining to the 'docile' body, biopower, or the history of sexuality lend themselves to observations of how bodies are subjected to but also become productive within discourse. Implied in this process are various disciplinary techniques and institutions, such as medicine, the law, or the military, for instance.[12] While Foucault, too, never explicitly discusses the *male* body, rendering the body "gender-neutral and broadly applicable" (Bordo 1997, 198),[13] the male body as an implicit 'locus' of patriarchal—and state—power can be considered central to his work. It is particularly with an eye on difference and its political ramifications that poststructuralist perspectives show their merits: As differential categories that distinguish bodies from another—such as gender, sexuality, race, class, or ability—are no longer conceived as 'natural' essence of bodies but rather as discursively created, they are also opened up to deconstructive analysis and ideological critique. In the 1980s and 1990s, scholars like Jane Gallop, Cynthia Cockburn, or Elizabeth Grosz have exposed patriarchal ideologies and bodily normativity in regard to masculine identity formation, thus making visible the specificities of male embodiment. In

---

[12] In *The History of Sexuality*, for example, Foucault elaborates on the production of 'new' sexual identities, such as homosexuality, through the workings of discourse and power; similarly, his study *Discipline and Punish* includes the example of the 'body of the condemned', which conceptualizes the body as a locus of discipline. In *Society Must Be Defended: Lectures at the Collège de France, 1975–76,* he expands his theoretical reflections, making an argument for how the rise of the modern nation-state and its reliance on new technologies of 'biopower' that enabled the state to take control over life and death contributed to increased sovereign power and aimed at generating docile, productive bodies.

[13] Susan Bordo draws attention to the paradoxical status of the male body even within poststructuralist thinking: While the female body continues to be viewed under "the sign of her Otherness", the male body becomes "the Body proper" while "*as* male body [it] disappears completely, *its* concrete specificity submerged in its collapse into the universal" (1997, 198; emphasis in original).

this vein, some of the contributions herein look at inscriptions of power structures on the body and explore how this can be reasserted by subjects in order to claim authority, others are motivated by feminist or queer lenses that illustrate how bodies can dismantle the myth of the phallus and rework the disciplinary functioning of patriarchal discourse.

A central figure regarding the intersection of these traditions is, of course, Judith Butler: Having provided differentiated accounts of corpo-reality and gender performativity, scholarship from various disciplines has benefited immensely from her work that draws on Foucault's concepts of discourse and its regulatory power as well as theories of constituting acts, based on phenomenological and theatrical models, to define the body in the intersection of constructivism and materiality. As Butler states in *Bodies that Matter*, the "matter of bodies" is inextricably intertwined with "regulatory norms that govern their materialization and the signification of those material effects" (2014, 2). She stresses that the materialization of bodies needs to be considered as part of a constantly evolving process that is always incomplete and hence allows for rearticulation and rematerialization (2–4). The same is true for gender that, constituting a performative social category, is created by and creates what it describes through perpetually repeated and reiterated acts of social behavior. This suggests that masculinity gains relevance as a signifying code through a constant and "compulsory repetition of prior [acts] and subjectivating norms, [...] which work, animate, and constrain the gendered subject, and which are also the resources from which resistance, subversion, displacement are to be forged" (2013, 22).[14] The performativity of iden-tity categories—extending next to sex and gender also to class, race, or ability—is a central theme in many of this volume's articles that look at different bodily practices, stylizations, or 'constitutive acts'.

[14] Butler's thinking has paved the way to differentiated models of masculinity, as repre-sented, for example, by what Halberstam termed 'female masculinity' as well as what has been identified as 'male femininity'. By disassociating masculinity from the male body in *Female Masculinity* (1998) and attending to various possible forms of gender expression, such as drag-king performances, Halberstam offers directions for how to read the male body without preconfiguring it as basis for expressions of masculinity. Halberstam's work is in line with feminist theory that brings the male body into focus as a sexed and gendered body, a specific rather than a universal body, and is particularly relevant for theorizing trans* embodiments.

Dissatisfied with the poststructuralist paradigm due to its supposed exhaustion and taking their cue from Gilles Deleuze's materialist philosophy, feminist and new materialist scholars like Elizabeth Grosz, Donna Haraway, Karen Barad, Rosi Braidotti, or Jane Bennett seek to move beyond the insights of the linguistic turn. Without abandoning its premises, they specifically consider how 'matter' (human and non-human) contributes to the formation of subjectivity and particularly inquire into the limits of language to reckon with the body's materiality and embodied experience. Works like Karen Barad's "Posthuman Performativity" find fault with the focus on language and culture, which still also structures Butler's insights, and a concomitant neglect of (bodily) matter: "Language matters. Discourse matters. Culture matters. There is an important sense in which the only thing that does not seem to matter anymore is matter" (2003, 120). While this has been—reductively—interpreted as a rejection of the linguistic altogether (e.g., Ahmed 2008) and might seem to pose a conflict for a book that focuses on representations, we understand Barad's intervention as a call to attempt analyses that attest to the *interconnectedness* of matter and discourse for bodies as they are represented in cultural productions. Similarly, scholars like Braidotti call not for abandoning, but for "[r]ethinking the embodied structure of human subjectivity after Foucault" (2000, 158). A challenging and appealing facet of this field is the mutual constitution of language and matter: "[B]iology is culturally mediated as much as culture is materialistically constructed" (Ferrando 2013, 31).[15] Some contributions explore how the resistant materiality of the body—or instances where, as Jean-Luc Nancy phrases it, the body becomes "the end of the signifier" (2008, 75)—surfaces in representation, for instance, through the evocation of moments of intense pleasure, pain, or shock, where matter cannot be 'spoken', or through textual gaps, where the linguistic mediation of bodily experience is deliberately left open, or through portrayals of bodies that disturb or subvert readers' expectations. In this way, the insistence of

---

[15] The recent decades in particular have witnessed a surge in new materialist thinking, mirrored in a plethora of publications that engage notions of anti-anthropocentrism, the agency of matter, and relationships between human and non-human matter in a variety of disciplines, see, for instance, Stacy Alaimo and Susan Hekman's *Material Feminisms* (2008) or Diana Coole and Samantha Frost's *New Materialisms: Ontology, Agency, and Politics* (2010). Kai Merten's edited volume *Diffractive Reading* has sought to combine insights from new materialism, particularly Barad's notion of 'diffraction', with new reading practices (2021).

matter constitutes an impasse to the discursive, and representation adopts specific means to illustrate the epistemological limits that matter presents.

In light of these theoretical reflections, the conception of the male body now warrants a more nuanced definition: first, it is a material entity that is itself subject to interpellations into discourses and systems. Second, it is not conceived of as an entity 'before' masculinity or as the natural counterpart to the social, but rather as a locus where models of 'doing' not only gender, but also race, age, ability, class, and sexuality are created and, due to their malleability, constantly renegotiated. Third, the focus on the discursive and performative does not imply that matter itself has no agency. Rather, moments of resistance to signification or the ambivalence of matter are also legible in representations of bodies. Cultural productions here provide a space for imagining, playing with, and challenging concepts of embodiment and constructions of masculinity; in this way, they contribute to generating more differentiated and potentially more plural visions of the body.

Representing and Reading Bodies

In tracing these lines of thought, this book shifts the focus towards representation. It explores not only figurations of the body within the field of cultural representation—aware that representations of male bodies are themselves subject to ideological interpellation—but also inquires into the implications that representation might have for the social perception of 'bodily matter' and 'how bodies matter'. The play on the dual meaning of the term 'to matter' as '"to materialize' and 'to mean'" (Butler 2014, 32) and, one could add, to 'matter in its own right', is intentional here, as it signals our interest in how representation engages with the 'matter' of bodies, their materialization, and the social meanings and the social status they acquire in specific contexts. The focus on representation is decisive here, as it offers a realm of imagining and exploring facets of 'our' being in the world. As a social and cultural practice, representation shapes and reshapes our understanding of the body and its place in the world, thus constituting a central cultural 'agent' (Felski 2015) for generating insights into the specific social experience of gendered, sexed, classed, racialized, or dis/abled male bodies. The contributions assembled in this collection subscribe to this understanding of representations as co-constituents of social reality.

The critical approaches that predominate in readings of masculinity and corporeality in all disciplines are of a deconstructive nature. In this context, the body is often read as a metaphoric site on which "the dominant political concerns and anxieties of society tend to be translated into disrupted, disjointed and disturbed images of the body", thus rendering "[o]ur sense of social order [...] in terms of the balance or imbalance of the body" (Turner 2012, 4). That is to say that deconstructive readings scrutinize representations of the body to identify larger social and political problems raised through this form of representation. In these readings, the notions of 'crisis' or 'masculinity at risk' that long dominated the field of Masculinity Studies still resonate. While this volume also features paranoid perspectives on representations of 'bodies in crisis' with a focus on the societal and ideological underpinnings of such diagnoses, the volume is—in its overall thrust—complemented by a practice of reading that supplements the crisis narrative with an ameliorative one. Building on the critical research that has validated the benefits of deconstructive readings, this volume wishes to enrich the existing scholarship on men and masculinities by additionally offering a reparative account.

Eve Kosofsky Sedgwick, responding to Melanie Klein's 'paranoid position', criticizes the predominancy of a hermeneutics of suspicion and exposure, which has been coined by Paul Ricoeur, as a style of reading committed to unmasking the workings of ideology and claiming an oppositional stance (1997, 4–9). She formulates an additional practice of reading, derived from queer experiences, that can be helpful for generating new perspectives. She terms this a reparative reading practice, i.e., a method of analysis where the fixation on crisis, anxiety, and other negative affects is surpassed by a deliberate seeking of pleasure, an embracing of insecurities, anxieties, or surprises, and a creative energy that helps to reorganize existing possibilities of being or to generate new ones (22–25). In doing so, applying a reparative perspective can put forward ameliorative models of thought. As Sedgwick explains in her introduction to *Novel Gazing*, "Paranoid and Reparative Reading, Or, You're So Paranoid, You Probably Think This Introduction is About You",

> the reparative reading position undertakes a different range of affects, ambitions, and risks. What we can best learn from such practices are, perhaps, the many ways selves and communities succeed in extracting sustenance from the objects of a culture – even of a culture whose avowed desire has often been not to sustain them. (35)

We acknowledge that Sedgwick's definition of 'reparative reading' is neither fixed and finite, nor is it—due to its emergence from and enmeshment with the 'paranoid'—innocent; rather, it presents an impulse for different readings as collected in this volume. In combining these approaches, we do not set them against each other, recalling that Sedgwick also does not conceive of these reading practices as mutually exclusive but equally valid, as her usage of the term "and" in the title of her meditations on paranoid and reparative readings suggests.[16]

As part of this volume's methodological framing, the selected contributions variously draw on paranoid and reparative perspectives to (re-)read representations of the male body and constructions of gender. They are structured into four major sections revolving around representations of what we termed 'non/conforming', 'fashionable', 'passing', and 'pioneering' bodies. We consider these categorizations not as finite designations to classify representations of bodies but rather as unstable references to both the qualities and cultural potentials these representations have, especially for critically interrogating and/or creatively reworking concepts of the male body and gender expressions.

The first section of this collected volume revolves around "Non/Conforming Bodies" in three articles that focus on constructions of black men's embodiment in the UK, images of the 'ideal male physique' in US sporting magazines, and representations of 'unruly white men' in British film. Within hegemonic contexts, these bodies are either non-conforming or conforming or oscillating on a spectrum of these concepts in different ways. Some of the male bodies analyzed in this section are variously faced with experiences of precarity, stereotypification and marginalization, or forms of discrimination; as bodies that cannot or do not (want to) conform they fulfill critical, subversive functions by negotiating, revising, or challenging the concept of 'hegemonic masculinity'. By contrast, other bodies this section foregrounds are highly complicit with reasserting hegemonic notions of gender, especially at moments of crisis, and thus serve to demarcate 'appropriate' from 'inappropriate' masculinities as well as constructions of conformity and non-conformity.

The article by **Michael McMillan** opening this section looks at conceptualizations of black men's embodiments that specifically negotiate

---

[16] For elaborations on Sedgwick's title, particularly the conjunctions 'and' and 'or' and their significations, see Berlant and Edelman (2014, 43–44).

categories of sexuality, gender, and fatherhood and reflect the need to work through traumata against the backdrop of colonial history and diasporic experiences. It sets these ongoing explorations in relation to the artist's 1996 performance piece *Brother to Brother* that is revisited and reviewed in a process of critical self-reflection. Drawing on Stuart Hall's 'reconstruction work' and Christina Sharpe's 'wake work', McMillan comes to conceive of performance not only in bell hooks's terms as 'a site of opposition' to limiting stereotypical figurations of the black body but also as what he calls a 'safe space' for black men, allowing them to express vulnerability and become agents in constructing black masculinities and performing black corporeality. Reciprocally, the relevance of embodied consciousness is explored for the part it plays in creating and revising McMillan's own work. The article thus comprises paranoid and reparative perspectives on what it means to engage in embodied performance practice and to form subject positions for black men in the UK.

Shifting the focus towards hegemonic concepts of bodies, the next contribution by **Ana Stevenson** and **David Patrick** examines the perpetuation of images of the 'ideal male body' in selected US-based boxing and wrestling magazines from the 1950s and 1960s by centering on the bodybuilder physique as emblematic embodiment of masculine ideals. Tracing this ideal's historical origin back to the nineteenth century, the authors explore how the advertisements that sought to appeal to readers-as-consumers with representations of hard, muscular, sporty bodies collapse images of the white male citizen's body with an imaginary US national body in line with the era's conservatism and thus echo then prevailing cultural values and social norms. The paranoid perspective adopted by Stevenson and Patrick exposes the magazines' complicity in reasserting hegemonic masculinity at a time when the exclusiveness of this concept was challenged by (demands for) the representation of black bodies in the cultural as well as political arena.

The concluding article in this section by **Christian Krug** picks up on the notion of conflicting and yet interrelating notions of masculinity in his analysis of the British 'Social Problem film' *Violent Playground* (1958). Krug argues that the film showcases competing but relational models of masculinity in its exploration of working-class juvenile delinquency. These include a performative model, tied to the material body and potentially transgressive, and a conformist one which is more aligned with the requirements of a larger social body and the object of social discipline. Scrutinizing *Violent Playground*'s 'sentimental politics', which works at the intersection of ideology and affective corporeality, Krug's critical reading foregrounds the film's attempts to emotionally interpellate the audience by teaching it to 'feel right' about its unruly males. Dominant masculinities are posited but remain ideological vanishing points, however, and the film also features other, contingent, bodies that complicate visions of an affluent and consensual British post-World War II society.

Section II, "Fashionable Bodies", looks at fashion as a symbolic system that "constructs and reproduces the body in its genre determination, by virtue of signs on the body, to which the community attributes qualities and values as 'masculine' or 'feminine'" (Calefato 2021, 45). It can turn them into stereotypes, but also deform and invent new signs (45). Spanning different periods and cultures, this section analyzes fashioned and fashionable male bodies as implicated in and constitutive of social and political paradigm shifts and conceives of fashion as expressive—and constitutive—of particular 'structures of feeling'. Within this context, all contributions map out diverging concepts of bodies that oscillate between conforming to and subverting dominant ideologies.

The opening article in this section by **Jay McCauley Bowstead** accesses the fashionable body from a contemporary perspective and explores two divergent fashionable male physiques—the 'spornosexual' and the 'waif'—as constructed by and signifying within fashion discourses and lifestyle media. Since the turn of the millennium, luxury menswear has promoted an aesthetic of slenderness while, in recent years, a simultaneously highly-muscular and carefully groomed male body has reemerged in reality television and social media. Though these differing corporeal ideals are associated with discrete markets and manifest of differing ideals of masculinity, both point to the increasing 'spectacularization' of the male physique in visual culture as mapped out at the beginning of this introduction. McCauley Bowstead places these 'new' ideals in a larger social, cultural, economic, and class context and connects the desirable body and notions of self-fashioning and self-branding to a neo-liberal rhetoric of self-improvement. He thereby illuminates how dominant economic paradigms manifest themselves in image making and bodily practices, and how men navigate these forces by refashioning their physiques.

From a similar critical perspective, **John Finkelberg**'s contribution analyzes transnational visual and textual imagery of the dandy in the contexts of July Monarchy France and Victorian England and their implication in creating and fostering particular forms of masculinity in intersection with and as a reaction to the periods' specific political idea(l)s. It conceives representations of the 'dandified' body as multi-layered systems of signification. On the one hand, cultural representations of the dandy served to encourage viewers' participation in an expanding consumer society. On the other hand, however, they created and employed a discourse of 'over-styling' the body and thus compromising one's masculinity. This discourse served the didactic purpose of furthering appropriate middle-class behavior and thus of advancing and upholding hegemonic norms of masculinity in France and England during the first half of the nineteenth century. Drawing on a variety of texts and illustrations, Finkelberg's contribution shows that the language of dandyism was as malleable as the concept of masculinity itself.

The final contribution in this section by **Alla Myzelev** continues the exploration into intersecting discourses of fashionable bodies and politics. Analyzing representations of *Stiliagi*, a post-war Soviet countercultural movement that emerged in the 1940s—at the same time as the French *Zazous*, the English Teddy Boys, or the German Swing Kids—in various media and life-writing, Myzelev inquires into the *Stiliagi* body as contradictorily inscribed and signifying: Cherished and imitated by the post-war urban youth and denigrated by the Soviet cadres for its supposed corruption of masculine norms, the *Stiliagi* body stands at the threshold of a 'traditionally Soviet', i.e., a war-experienced and heroized concept of manhood *vis-à-vis* a younger, 'Western-inspired', and more internationally oriented ideal of manliness. Yet while the *Stiliagi*'s fashion choices to some extent allowed for more flexible forms of gender expression, Myzelev's contribution also shows that this did not extend to *sexual* plurality, as the 'specter of homoeroticism' that haunts this—mostly male—counter-movement is consistently sublimated in all forms of *Stiliagi* representations.

The third section revolves around "Passing Bodies", i.e., bodies that in our understanding (attempt to) undertake different acts of transition and border crossings. In their various efforts of passing, these bodies attest to the performativity of identity categories, to use Butler's term here, with reference to not only gender and sexuality but also race and ability and, in this way, point towards the fluidity and mobility of bodily matter and identity categories. The 'passing body' can therefore—in line with Marjorie Garber's elaborations on 'the transvestite'—be considered a "disruptive element that intervenes" and signals not just a crisis of social boundaries that thus become destabilized but also a "crisis of category itself" (1992, 17). While this puts emphasis on the possible subversive qualities of passing and underscores the epistemic crisis that such challenges to social expectations and crossings of allegedly fixed social borders can signal, passing can also reinforce existing power relations and social hierarchies, as the three contributions assembled in this section explain.

Sandra Dinter's article analyzes autobiographical works by the three European women authors Flora Tristan, George Sand, and Vita Sackville-West with a focus on their attempts to claim male corporeality and its privileges by walking publicly in masculine disguise. She shows that these representations of cross-dressing lend themselves well to paranoid and reparative readings, arguing that they not only expose how female mobility has been oppressed in urban spaces—which privilege male, upper-class, white, and able bodies – but also constitute exciting and plea-surable adventures for the women who are either passing or not passing successfully for male *flâneurs*. Dinter explains that her failed passing allows Tristan to stage herself as a woman who spectacularly disrupts the patriarchal order, while Sand portrays herself as a writer who secretly subverts but ultimately leaves intact such norms. Finally, Sackville-West's memoir reinstates patriarchal norms even more resolutely.

The contribution by **rl goldberg** continues the focus on 'passing' from female to male with an analysis of Clarissa Sligh's photography project *Wrongly Bodied* (2009), a book that sets two contextually and perceptually different gender transitions in relation with one another: that of Jake McBee, a transgender man who transitioned in Texas, and that of Ellen Craft, who passed as a white disabled man to escape from slavery. The article draws on theories of the archive to argue that the book constitutes a creative revisionary project whereby the nineteenth-century story of racial passing and a twenty-first-century story of trans 'passing' complement and illuminate each other. Pondering points of convergence and divergence between the acts of passing represented in *Wrongly Bodied*, goldberg suggests that the incorporation of these two (different) archives in the book complicates the line between paranoid and reparative perspectives and produces new understandings of trans materiality and the workings of the archive.

In the concluding article of this section, **Jonathan A. Allan** shifts the focus towards representations of bodies that blur the boundaries between 'disability' and 'ability'. Focusing specifically on the portrayal of disabled male heroes in the popular romance novel, Allan contrasts paranoid and reparative readings of these books' central characters and the narratives they are embedded in. He shows how selected examples of the popular romance, a traditionally gendered popular cultural genre, construct their protagonists as desirable heroes, and is careful to elaborate on the pitfalls of an exclusive embrace of a reparative perspective in this regard, as that would construe the romance novel as a possible site for 'recovering' the disabled body and thus run the risk of reinstating normative concepts of and rigid lines between 'ability' and 'disability'. Against this background, the article outlines possible limits of this reader-oriented approach and argues for complementing it with a critical, paranoid position.

The focus on 'passing' bodies in section III already indicates a movement towards more flexible notions of identity and points towards alternative forms of embodiment, which now move center stage in section IV titled "Pioneering Bodies?". All bodies represented in this section share qualities that might be identified as 'pioneering' for how they, at the specific historical moments of their formation, seem to anticipate new body concepts and allow for more diverse expressions of masculinity, while simultaneously raising critical questions concerning the historical trajectory underlying these corporeal formations. All contributions assembled in this section approach their topic with a more decidedly reparative take, which increases as the section progresses. The male body in this section then emerges as an open-ended signifier that critically negotiates historical experiences of marginalization, exclusion, or hegemonic complicity and at the same time, in a reparative turn to the future, envisions a pluralization of body concepts. The fact that the section questions the 'pioneering' status of these bodies points to the inherent interminability of the potentials they anticipate.

The opening article of this section by **Carmen Dexl** and **Silvia Gerlsbeck** continues the concern with crossing categories of the previous section and opens up critical perspectives on pioneering bodies by exploring posthuman imaginations in Caribbean Speculative Fiction. Based on two short story collections, the authors argue that the male body in particular is figured as a nexus where conflicting views of an increasingly technologized age manifest: For once, its cyborgian status can be called 'pioneering', as it evokes hopes for a "postgender world" (Haraway 2016a, 8) and for overcoming 'category purism'; at the same time, however, the texts use it to criticize the Western- and androcentric notions that underlie beliefs in transhuman development and formulate a larger criticism of humanist thought. Beyond offering a critical reading of how the texts represent the disciplinary workings of technology under conditions of racial capitalism, Dexl and Gerlsbeck also trace the cyborg's 'reparative' potential in the analyzed texts, which, rather than in incorporating 'otherness', lies in 'de-naturalizing' bodies and fusing cultural traditions of knowledge.

The second article in this section by **Melanie Haller** continues the focus on transcultural knowledge exchange in a discussion of the 'pioneering' status that a contemporary fashion phenomenon, the 'meggings', might claim for the formation of more diverse body images and constructions of masculine subjectivities. This contribution thus explicates the relevancy of cultural formations for the making of social realities. Taking a diachronic approach from within the field of body sociology and Fashion Theory, she traces the emergence of the 'meggings' within the larger field of (men's) fashion and relates it to shifting notions of (hegemonic) masculinity at different historical and cultural moments. As her contribution shows, tight-fitting legwear for men has undergone a shift in signification and, since the twentieth century, been associated with anti-fashion discourses and 'othered' forms of masculinity, thus counter-hegemonically oriented and indicative of 'new' methods of fashioning the male body. By situating the meggings within a transcultural framework, with a particular focus on the influential role of different style cultures on its recent popularization, Haller's fashion-sociological approach provides an important addition to this volume's interest in the mediating power of cultural phenomena.

The final contribution in this section by **Martina Kübler** stems from the field of Literary Studies and explores two figurations of disabled white men in classical texts of the literary canon. Reading disability through the lens of queer theory and attending to the disabled body's multilayered signification, Kübler focuses her analysis not only on the subversive, but particularly on the productive ways in which impairment can work: While disability registers as a metaphor for 'masculinity in crisis' and has served to question hegemonic notions of masculinity, the texts by Hemingway and Lawrence she focuses on transcend this connection and show how the material effects of impairment, such as impotence, also serve to imagine non-normative ways of knowing, being, and experiencing the world by posing a challenge to constructions of the 'normal', the 'heterosexual', and the 'masculine'. From a reparative point of view, representations of disability can thus serve to inspire more creative ways of navigating the world and of imagining new, *queer* ways of being (masculine)—and claim 'pioneering status' in this regard.

All contributions connect to and expand the existing scholarship as outlined above by drawing upon a multitude of theories and central concepts in their analysis of specific case studies. They often implicitly, sometimes also explicitly, reflect on the relation between representation and social practice, and the meanings and forms of identity construction that emerge in this interstice: some contributions focus, for instance, on the historical significance of representations of (fashionably dressed) men in visual culture and explore their ability to 'speak' to ways in which men were either expected or not expected to dress. Attending to what parts of the body clothing covers and how exactly it covers them serves to uncover how masculinity was constructed in specific contexts. In the twenty-first century, the relationship between representations of the male physique and the ways in which individuals shape, style, and groom their bodies has become more complex as user-generated content has come to the fore. While images of idealized bodies disseminated through the media have always been received, decoded, understood, and negotiated in a variety of ways by audiences, in the context of social media, these representations have become more pervasive and the boundaries between audience and media producers more porous.

Other articles foreground the intricate interconnection between (literary) writing and social practice, particularly the mediating effects of representation for the co-constitution of social experience and social meanings of bodies and gender. Still others make an argument for the different cultural functions of journalistic endeavors, e.g., press articles, magazines and ads, or satire, that either articulate social criticism or foster complicity with existing gender norms, images of men, and power relations. In this way, representation is both shaped by and, in turn, (re-) shapes social practice, a fact that the coda to this volume also foregrounds.

The coda closing *The Male Body in Representation: Returning to Matter* understands itself as a reverse introduction: It maps out yet different lines of convergences between the articles assembled here, presents access points to the volume and the topic in its breadth, and sketches larger methodological and theoretical approaches to the 'male body'. In this vein, this collection is part of an ongoing interrogation of epistemologies of the male body, their cultural negotiations, and the interconnection with and potentials for gender politics.

REFERENCES

Ahmed, Sara. "Open Forum Imaginary Prohibitions: Some Preliminary Remarks on the Founding Gestures of the 'New Materialism'." *European Journal of Women's Studies* 15, no. 1 (2008): 23–39.

Ainsworth, Claire. "Sex Redefined." *Nature* 518 (2015): 288–291.

Alaimo, Stacy, and Susan Hekman. *Material Feminisms.* Bloomington and Indianapolis: Indiana UP, 2008.

Barad, Karen. "Posthumanist Performativity: Toward an Understanding of How Matter Comes to Matter." *Signs: Journal of Women in Culture and Society* 28, no. 3 (2003): 801–831.

Berlant, Lauren, and Lee Edelman. *Sex, Or the Unbearable.* Durham: Duke UP, 2014.

Bordo, Susan. *Twilight Zones: The Hidden Life of Cultural Images from Plato to O.J.* Berkeley: U of California P, 1997.

Braidotti, Rosi. "Teratologies." In *Deleuze and Feminist Theory*, edited by Ian Buchanan and Claire Colebrook, 156–172. Edinburgh: Edinburgh UP, 2000.

Butler, Judith. "Performative Acts and Gender Constitution: An Essay in Phenomenology and Feminist Theory." *Theatre Journal* 40, no. 4 (1988): 519–531.

———. "Critically Queer." In *The Routledge Queer Studies Reader*, edited by Donald E. Hall and Annamarie Jagose, 18–31. Abingdon: Routledge, 2013.

———. *Bodies That Matter: On the Discursive Limits of Sex.* Hoboken: Taylor and Francis, 2014 [1993].

Calefato, Patrizia. *Fashion as Cultural Translation: Signs, Images, Narratives.* London: Anthem Press, 2021.

Connell, Raewyn. *Masculinities.* 2nd ed. Cambridge: Polity Press, 2005.

Coole, Diana, and Samantha Frost, eds. *New Materialisms: Ontology, Agency, and Politics.* Durham and London: Duke UP, 2010.

DeMello, Margo. *Body Studies: An Introduction.* London and New York: Routledge, 2014.

Descartes, René. *Discourse on Method, Optics, Geometry, and Meteorology.* Revised ed. Indianapolis and Cambridge: Hackett, 2001 [1637].

Dworkin, Shari L., and Faye Linda Wachs. *Body Panic: Gender, Health, and the Selling of Fitness.* New York and London: New York UP, 2009.

Emig, Rainer, and Antony Rowland, eds. *Performing Masculinity.* London: Palgrave Macmillan, 2010.

Felski, Rita. *The Limits of Critique.* Chicago: Chicago UP, 2015.

Ferrando, Francesca. "Posthumanism, Transhumanism, Antihumanism, Metahumanism, and New Materialisms: Differences and Relations." *Existenz* 8, no. 2 (2013): 26–32.

Floyd, Kevin, and Stefan Horlacher. "Contemporary Masculinities in the UK and the US: Between Bodies and Systems." In *Contemporary Masculinities in the*

UK and the US: Between Bodies and Systems, edited by Stefan Horlacher and Kevin Floyd, 1–18. Cham: Palgrave Macmillan, 2017.

Foucault, Michel. *The History of Sexuality: Volume 1: An Introduction*. Translated by Robert Hurley. New York: Vintage Books, 1990 [1976].

———. *Society Must Be Defended: Lectures at the Collège de France, 1975–76*. Edited by Mauro Bertani and Alessandro Fontana, translated by David Macey. New York: Picador, 2003 [1976].

———. *Discipline and Punish: The Birth of the Prison*. New York: Random House, 2012 [1975].

Garber, Marjorie. *Vested Interests: Cross-Dressing and Cultural Anxiety*. New York: Routledge, 1992.

Gee, Sarah, and Steven Jackson. *Sport, Promotional Culture and the Crisis of Masculinity*. London: Palgrave Macmillan, 2017.

Gilmore, David D. *Manhood in the Making: Cultural Concepts of Masculinity*. New Haven and London: Yale UP, 1990.

Halberstam, J. Jack. *Female Masculinity*. Durham: Duke UP, 1998.

Haraway, Donna. "A Cyborg Manifesto." In *Manifestly Haraway*, edited by Donna Haraway, 3–90. Minneapolis and London: U of Minnesota P, 2016[a].

———. *Staying with the Trouble. Making Kin in the Chthulucene*. Durham and London: Duke UP, 2016[b].

Hearn, Jeff. "The Materiality of Men, Bodies, and Towards the Abolition of 'Men'." In *Männlichkeiten denken: Aktuelle Perspektiven der kulturwissenschaftlichen Masculinity Studies*, edited by Martina Läubli and Sabrina Sahli, 195–215. Bielefeld: Transcript, 2011.

———. "Male Bodies, Masculine Bodies, Men's Bodies: The Need for a Concept of Gex." In *The Routledge Handbook of Body Studies*, edited by Bryan S. Turner, 307–320. London and New York: Routledge, 2012.

Hickey-Moody, Anna. *Deleuze and Masculinity*. London: Palgrave Macmillan, 2019.

Horlacher, Stefan, and Kevin Floyd, eds. *Post-World War II Masculinities in British and American Literature and Culture: Towards Comparative Masculinity Studies*. London and New York: Routledge, 2013.

Jackson II, Ronald L., and Murali Balaji. "Introduction." In *Global Masculinities and Manhood*, edited by Ronald L. Jackson II and Murali Balaji, 17–30. Urbana: U of Illinois P, 2011.

Lane, Jeremy F. *Pierre Bourdieu. A Critical Introduction*. London and Sterling, VA: Pluto Press, 2000.

MacMullan, Terrance. "Introduction: What Is Male Embodiment?" In *Revealing Male Bodies*, edited by Nancy Tuana et al., 1–16. Bloomington: Indiana UP, 2002.

Merleau-Ponty, Maurice. *The Primacy of Perception: And Other Essays on Phenomenological Psychology, the Philosophy of Art, History and Politics*. Edited by James M. Edie. Evanston, IL: Northwestern UP, 1964.

———. *Phenomenology of Perception*. Abingdon: Routledge, 2012 [1945].

Merten, Kai, ed. *Diffractive Reading: New Materialism, Theory, Critique*. Lanham: Rowman & Littlefield, 2021.

Nancy, Jean-Luc. *Corpus*. Translated by Richard A. Rand. New York: Fordham UP, 2008.

Pease, Bob, and Keith Pringle, eds. *A Man's World? Changing Men's Practices in a Globalized World*. London: Zed, 2001.

Russell, Eric Louis. *Alpha Masculinity: Hegemony in Language and Discourse*. London: Palgrave Macmillan, 2021.

Sedgwick, Eve Kosofsky. "Paranoid Reading and Reparative Reading, or, You're So Paranoid, You Probably Think This Introduction is About You." In *Novel Gazing: Queer Readings in Fiction*, edited by Eve Kosofsky Sedgwick, 1–37. Durham and London: Duke UP, 1997.

Seidler, Vic. *Transforming Masculinities: Men, Cultures, Bodies, Power, Sex and Love*. Abingdon: Routledge, 2006.

Sheets-Johnstone, Maxine. *The Roots of Thinking*. Philadelphia: Temple UP, 1990.

Sullivan, Nikki. "Foucault's Body." In *The Routledge Handbook of Body Studies*, edited by Bryan S. Turner, 106–116. London and New York: Routledge, 2012.

Turner, Bryan S. "Introduction: The Turn of the Body." In *The Routledge Handbook of Body Studies*, edited by Bryan S. Turner, 1–17. London and New York: Routledge, 2012.

Wolfe, Cary. *What is Posthumanism?* Minneapolis, MN: University of Minnesota Press, 2009.

PART I

Non/Conforming Bodies

CHAPTER 2

Brother to Brother: A Rereading of Black Masculinities in Embodied Performance

Michael Mcmillan

But this experience of, as it were, experiencing oneself as both subject and object, of encountering oneself from the outside, as another—an other—sort of person next door, is uncanny. (Hall 2007, 269; emphasis in original).

"It Looks to Me Like You the Envy of the World"[1]

When my son was five years old, I witnessed how a white female teacher's body froze with fear when she met him. It was a flashing moment that

[1] Morrison (1973, 3–4).

M. Mcmillan (✉)
London College of Fashion, University of the Arts London, London, United Kingdom
e-mail: m.mcmillan62@btinternet.com

Visual Identities in Art & Design Research Centre (VIAD), University of Johannesburg, Johannesburg, South Africa

C. Dexl and S. Gerlsbeck (eds.), *The Male Body in Representation*, Palgrave Studies in (Re)Presenting Gender, https://doi.org/10.1007/978-3-030-88604-2_2

one could easily miss and dismiss as mere unconscious bias, like Frantz Fanon's famous recounting of his interpellation by a white boy in the streets of Lyon with the call of "tiens, un Nègre!" [look, a Negro!] (1967, 111). My son was completely unaware of what was being projected onto his small body, just as I had been unaware as a child of how Black boys were routinely labelled. But as he grew up into the body of a young man, his mother and I had to have 'the talk' that most Black parents dread, but accept that they must have with their boys to make them aware that they will be perceived and treated in society in a way that has nothing to do with their personality and character, but everything to do with their bodies as young Black men. What is the experience, in Stuart Hall's words quoted above, "of experiencing oneself as both subject and object" and "as another – *an other*", where the 'uncanny' lies in a terrifying familiar recycling of a colonial phantasy based on fear of and desire for the Black male body? Race placed Black men at the intersection of male privilege and racial subjugation, where they have been celebrated, exoticized, and feared by white men and women alike. Black men are the "envy of the world", as Sula, the eponymous protagonist expresses in Toni Morrison's novel (1973, 3–4). That is, there is a craving for what Black men are perceived to possess, and this ravenous hunger for Black male flesh is also registered in other contexts, for instance, in another gangster flick, a 16-bar verse, the football premier league, 'stop and search', soul murder in school, on camera as he pleads: "I can't breathe".

There is a conjuncture in the symbolism of George Floyd's dying words "I can't breathe", the words of a Black man choked to death by a white policeman's knee on his neck, and the need to breathe of COVID-19 patients hooked on ventilators: these, too, are more often men than women, with mortality four times greater in Black and Brown communities than in white ones (Public Health England 2020). In this conjuncture that the COVID-19 pandemic has exposed, "I can't breathe" has become a metonym for the Black Lives Matter movement in global protests against the ongoing suffocation through structural racism and the vulnerability of Black men's bodies in the face of racist violence. Another uncanny paradox is that the majority of frontline health and care sector workers comes from working-class Black and Brown communities with limited access to proper health care, who experience systemic racism daily in their workplace while trying to save lives, and are dying disproportionately from the lack of personal protective equipment (PPE), as if they are expendable. In Britain, they are also often part of the Windrush genera-tion of post-war Caribbean immigrants and their descendants, who have found themselves treated as illegal immigrants and subsequently incar-cerated in detention centers, deported, and denied medical treatment by the NHS with the effect that they are disproportionally dying from the trauma of this Kafkaesque nightmare.

In his seminal essay "Reconstruction Work" (1984), Hall looks at images of post-war Black settlement, as in *Picture Post*'s 1956 pictorial essay "Thirty Thousand Colour Problems" about Caribbean migration to Britain. In the mode of documentary realism, the Black subjects are portrayed as 'social problems' in these images, which in the British popular imaginary would be a code for the racial problem of immigra-tion in the post-war years and which echoes the racist discourse of Brexit today. Born in England in 1962, and having grown up and lived as a Black man in Britain, I stand symbolically for one of those 'social problems' and negotiate this experience in my own work of embodied performance. On a self-reflexive level, Hall's 'reconstruction work' engages with what Mary Louise Pratt calls an 'autoethnographic' text:

> [I]f ethnographic texts are those in which European metropolitan subjects represent to themselves their others (usually their conquered others), autoethnographic texts are representations that the so-defined others construct *in response to* or in dialogue with those texts. (1991, 35; emphasis in original)

A critical practice that can be linked to autoethnographic reconstruction is offered by Christina Sharpe's *In the Wake: On Blackness and Being* (2016). In the monograph, she meditates on her personal loss where the wake or 'Nine Night'[2] no longer signifies the event of mourning after death, but the wake in the wave of a moving slave ship, of contempo-rary Black life framed by close proximity to death. In the afterlife of the transatlantic slave trade, there is trauma in the wake of social and physical

---

[2] Based on the African belief that the spirits of the dead live on and following a Caribbean cultural practice after the death of a loved one, African-Caribbean families in the UK will for nine nights create a space for mourners to come and celebrate the deceased in the family home. On the final night of the funeral, a wake is held, which includes food, drinks, music, and even dancing to give the deceased spirit 'a good send-off' into the next world.

death. Sharpe advocates 'wake work' as a critical practice of experimentation where the distinction between art and theory becomes blurred: "It is my particular hope that the praxis of the wake and wake work, the theory and performance of the wake and the wake work, as modes of attending to Black life and Black suffering, are imagined and performed here" (22).

In exploring how diasporic Black masculinities are embodied, this article conjoins the decoloniality of Sharpe's 'wake work' as a critical praxis with the criticality of Hall's 'reconstruction work' to revisit, as an autoethnographic return, the creative process of making my devised performance piece *Brother to Brother* (McMillan 1996). This article also provides an opportunity to reconsider my earlier writing on Black masculinity, namely "'What happened to you today that reminded you that you were a Black man?' The process of exploring Black masculinities in performance" (McMillan 2004). In addition, it offers a rereading of *Brother to Brother*'s (McMillan 1996) creative process that is supplemented by comments from Douglas Russell, one of the workshop participants. In this self-reflexive invocation, the wake work on Black masculine 'being' and 'becoming' construes "performance practice as a site of opposition" (hooks 1995, 210). This article argues that performance can provide a safe space for Black men to work through trauma and express often repressed feelings of anger, hurt, fear, and vulnerability towards discovering a new embodied consciousness in the healing of self. Performance thus empowers wake work in terms of practicing and performing Black corporeality in a highly affirmative way.

Diasporic Black Bodies

Diaspora as a term is used here metaphorically, not literally:

> [D]iaspora does not refer us to those scattered tribes whose identity can only be secured in relation to some sacred homeland to which they must at all costs return. [...] [It is not defined] by essence or purity, but by the recognition of a necessary heterogeneity and diversity: by a conception of 'identity' which lives with and through, not despite, difference; *hybridity*. (Hall 1993, 400; emphasis in original)

Therefore, the symbolic journeys that the diasporic Black subject took, Hall suggests, were a 'process' of 'becoming' as well as of 'being', which belongs to the future as much as to the past. Diasporic identity is, therefore, continually being negotiated through a "complex historical process of appropriation, compromise, subversion, masking, invention and revival" (401). The multiplicity of these subject positions resonates with W. E. B. Du Bois's idea of a 'double consciousness' as postulated in his 1903 essay "Of Our Spiritual Strivings", which correlates with Stuart Hall's notion of alterity in the being and becoming of a Black man: "[...] this experience of, as it were, experiencing oneself as both subject and object, of encountering oneself from the outside, as another— *an other*—sort of person next door, is uncanny (2007, 269; emphasis in original). But what is often overlooked is how the intersection of race and gender with class and sexuality reveals the insidious trauma of racism, patriarchy, homophobia, and poverty as social texts of everyday life. And the following extract from *Brother to Brother* (McMillan 1996) speaks to the wakeness of that embodied trauma:

BLUE: This could have been my brother.
PURPLE: This could have been my son.
BLUE: This could have been my father.
PURPLE: This could have been me.
CHANT: I speak in the voice of a dead man
      I speak in the voice of a dead man
      I speak in the voice of a dead man
RED: I speak in the voice of a dead man
      a sad voice
      a vibrant voice
      a joyous voice
      an indignant voice
      a damaged voice
      an assassin's voice
      a pained voice
      a violent voice
      a fucked up voice.
PURPLE: I speak in the voice of a dead man
      a suffering voice
      a depressed voice
      a poetic voice
      an oppressed voice

a choking voice
a polluted voice
a stringent voice
a victorious voice
a punished voice.
CHANT: You're gonna get your fucking head kicked in.
BLUE: I speak in the voice of a dead man
a murderous voice
a violated voice
a child's voice
a son's voice
a father's voice
a slave's voice
a suicidal voice
a lynched voice
a brother's voice
a dead man's voice. (McMillan 1996)

Wake work unveils the historic pattern that underlies the racial violence Black subjects experience, which demands 'being woke', in the sense of being aware of social and racial injustice in the twenty-first century. Strikingly, the police killing of Breonna Taylor in the USA did not mobilize the same community protest as the killing of George Floyd and reminds us that the intersectionality of racism and sexism that Black women experience often goes unrecognized or remains less acknowledged.

In addition, there are forms of vulnerability among Black men that tend not to mobilize any community protest, much less debate. This form of vulnerability, emerging from the intersection of race, gender, and sexuality—and class to some extent—, is eloquently explored in Barry Jenkins's Oscar award-winning film *Moonlight* (2016). The film presents three stages in the life of the main character Chiron: his youth as 'Little', adolescence as 'Chiron', and early adult life as 'Black'. It explores the difficulties he faces with his sexuality and identity, including the physical and emotional abuse he endures growing up. Masculinity is portrayed as rigid and aggressive, as the behavior of young Black men in Chiron's teenage peer group, for instance, suggests. A key theme in the film is how hypermasculinity among Black men is associated with peer acceptance and community, where being gay is perceived as being weak or effeminate and therefore puts one at the risk of being faced with social alienation and homophobic judgement. Chiron is caught within this double-conscious divide—of being a Black gay man and embodying a hypermasculine posture for survival. In the third scene, Chiron recognizes the need to conform to a heteronormative ideal of Black masculinity and remakes himself as a man named 'Black' who embraces stereotypes of race and gender by becoming muscular and a drug-dealer. In a moving scene at the end, Black becomes Chiron again and leans his head on Kevin, his friend from his teenage years, after sharing his sense of vulnerability with him. For co-writer Tarell Alvin McCraney, *Moonlight* is a semi-autobiographical reworking of his play *In Moonlight Black Boys Look Blue* (2003), which he created to cope with his mother's death from AIDS. He argues that communities without privilege or power seek to gain it in other ways, such as enhancing masculine identity, knowing that this often provides a means to gain social control in a patriarchal society (*BBC Newsnight* 2017). *Moonlight* explores how Black men cope with feeling powerless by overstating their masculinity, which in becoming toxic leads them to no longer wanting to be "caressed, or nurtured, or gentle" ("Moonlight's Tarell Alvin McCraney" 2017, n.pag.).

This 'structure of feeling' (Williams 1953) in the "architexture of Black masculinity", to use Jeffrey Q. McCune's phrase, "illuminates how space (the physical frame) and the texture of the space (ideological frames of gender) can create a vernacular understanding of what constitutes appropriate gender presentation and sexual behavior" (2014, 16). McCune's work on the 'down-low', where African-American men have sex with other men while maintaining a heterosexual lifestyle in public, illustrates how narrow scripts of gender performance for Black men complicate their intimacies. Javon Johnson asks a pertinent question here: "What if we restructure the 'architexture of Black masculinity' in the wake to allow for free and openly vulnerable, intimate, and connected Black masculinities?" (2019, 47). This is the question that motivated my work in *Brother to Brother*, as the following section explains.

BROTHER TO BROTHER—AN AUTOETHNOGRAPHIC RETURN

The wake work and reconstruction work that Johnson's proposal requires involves rethinking Black masculine identity "as a work-in-process, a disappearing act, a performance", to echo the critic Julie MacDougall (qtd. in hooks 1995, 213). In this context, as a playwright, performance writer, and director, ethnography for me, like for MacDougall, is an "open and infinite semiotic chain, an ongoing activity rather than a stable definition" (213). This implies a concern with "the act of doing, rather than the immobile quality contained in the lexeme 'ethnography'" (213). This "critical ethnography" of "performance practice as a site of opposition", to cite bell hooks again, uses "polyphonic strategies to convey specific aspects of Black experience" (214), "a kind of truth", as Toni Morrison puts it (1995, 95).

In the being and becoming of Black masculinity, for me, there is also a "conjuncture" (Hall 1997, 51) in the ways that Black artists began responding to cultural political events that signified the intersection of race, gender, class, and sexuality as recurring themes. The Black feminist and queer movements offer a theoretical framework to navigate some of these issues and questions through activism and creative agency.[3] Essex Hemphill's *Brother to Brother: New Writings by Black Gay Men* (1991) provided a vocabulary for me to explore the feminine side of masculinity. The term 'Brother to Brother' was further popularized in Marlon Riggs's film *Tongues Untied* (1989) that was concerned with the lack of dialogue between Black men, who formed erotic relationships with one another. This work did not limit itself to a Black gay agenda, but poetically and discursively engaged with the state of Black masculinity as challenged by the experience of 'faggotry'. Within this context, Black men loving Black men was a revolutionary act.

Becoming a father in the late 1980s, I relooked at my relationship with my father in how I was parented to inform my own parenting. This process included reconnecting with my own childhood vulnerability, so as to have an emotionally expressive relationship with my son, which I lacked with my father. This also meant embracing the feminist mantra that 'the personal is political' as 'work-in-process' in my lived experience, but also in my critical praxis as an arts practitioner. In a community of practice, I was interpellated by and organically drawn to the work of artist peers exploring similar questions I was concerned with at this moment.

---

[3] Some notable Black female representatives here include activists Angela Davis, Olive Morris, Kimberlé Williams Crenshaw; novelists Toni Morrison, Alice Walker, Octavia E. Butler; poets Audre Lorde, Maya Angelou, Sonia Sanchez; visual artists Sonia Boyce, Faith Ringgold, Lorna Simpson; and film makers Julie Dash, Euzhan Palcy, or Martina Attille. Films like Isaac Julien's *Looking for Langston* (1989), Marlon Riggs's *Tongues Untied* (1989), and Jennie Livingston's *Paris is Burning* (1990) also valorized Black queer identities in the era of HIV/AIDS and created a space to rethink other forms of masculinities coming into being.

While in New York, the African-American playwright George C. Wolfe[4] showed me a video of Pomo Afro Homos (Post-Modern African-American Homosexuals),[5] and I was struck by their feistiness. They were three Black gay men from the North American West Coast and through dramatic tableau, song, dance, and some serious snapping and voguing, their performance piece *Fierce Love* challenged heteronormative representations of the struggles of Black gay men and queer people, redefining their communities and sexuality in finding their way home (McMillan 1995). Pomo Afro Homos, like Essex Hemphill in *Brother to Brother* (1991), advocated an inclusive approach towards Black masculinity. Brian Freeman of Pomo Afro Homos argued for Black theatre to embrace performance as a genre and a need to re-educate ourselves about the diversity and differences amongst our practices, cultural political as well as personal agendas.[6] There is a notion that the work of Black performance (live art) artists tends to be too avant-garde, experimental, and inaccessible for Black audiences, especially if they include themes of sexuality. Consequently, Black theatre companies in the USA chose to deny Pomo Afro Homos's existence in banning them from attending the 1991 National Black Theatre Festival in Winston-Salem, North Carolina. I invited them to perform their piece *Dark Fruit* as part of the North East HIV/AIDS Festival (Pomo Afro Homos 1992), a multi-event program that I coordinated with photographer-in-residence Nick Lowe as part of our joint year-long residencies.

As writer-in-residence, I worked with people infected and affected by HIV/AIDS in Newcastle and North East England, which intersected sexual politics, sexuality, race, illness, and death, and affected me on a creative and personal level, as people I had been collaborating with passed away. In the UK during the 1990s, the heterosexual experience of HIV/AIDS was largely silenced, because it was stigmatized as a 'gay

---

[4] George C. Wolfe's award-winning work as a playwright includes *The Colored Museum* (1986), *Spunk* (1990), *Jelly's Last Jam* (1991), and, as a director, Tony Kushner's *Angels in America: Millennium Approaches* (1993). From 1993 to 2004, he was artistic director and producer of the New York Shakespeare Festival/Public Theatre.

[5] Pomo Afro Homos was founded in San Francisco by choreographer-dancer Djola Bernard Branner, actor Brian Freeman, and singer, dancer, and actor Eric Gupton. Later, Marvin K. White joined the group.

[6] This statement stems from an interview with Brian Freeman, conducted by Michael McMillan at Drill Hall Arts Centre, London, 1993.

plague' and therefore ignited homophobic anxieties about being labelled gay. Moreover, homophobia in the Black communities has a legacy in the criminalization of homosexuality under British colonialism, and as this legislation still exists in former colonies across the African diaspora, it continues to bolster a Christianized discourse about appropriate forms of sexuality. Black British community-based HIV/AIDS initiatives were beginning at this moment, but in Newcastle, the Black communities were largely invisible in the city's cultural industries, and without access to discrete community networks, it was difficult to find a local Black person who had grown up and lived there and felt brave enough to talk about being infected or affected by HIV/AIDS. Coming from London, which in Newcastle was viewed as a world away, I was probably perceived as an outsider interloper, who, while having empathy with the local Black experience of race, was there only temporary, because I would disappear after the residency was over. That said, I did eventually collaborate with outsiders like myself: Black and white female students at the University of Newcastle, a white male artist, and Patrick Williams, a Canadian Black gay man, whose glory was being a drag queen in Newcastle's gay clubs. Together, we created *The Last Blind Date Show* (McMillan 1992), a performance piece that parodied Cilla Black's popular heteronormative TV game show *Blind Date* (1983–2003). The residency culminated in the publication of *Living Proof: Views of a World Living with HIV & AIDS—Photography & Writings* (McMillan and Lowe 1992).

Inscribed in the cultural politics of this work are various discourses surrounding health and illness that have stigmatized and hurt the Black body: For once, the narrative that in Africa heterosexual intercourse was a mode of transmission of HIV/AIDS and would eventually spread throughout the world was intimately linked to colonial ideas of 'Africa' and the Black body as the site of hypersexuality and disease in the white Western imagination. In this neo-colonial fantasy, HIV infection and deaths from AIDS in Africa and diasporic Black communities could therefore be justified, because to 'exterminate all the brutes' after Joseph Conrad (2006, 50) is the historical continuity of colonialism in racial capitalism. In the wake of COVID-19, Black and Brown female health workers have been portrayed in the liberal media as heroes who have given up their lives to save ours, rather than acknowledging that they were often forced into that position because of institutionalized racism in the NHS. Similarly, the Black male taxi driver, Trevor Belle, and Black female transport worker, Belly Mujinga, who both died from the virus after being spat upon by passengers, are treated as individual tragedies rather than a consequence of the raced, classed, and gendered lived experience of Black female and male transport and health workers who have been treated as 'social problems' since the 1950s. On the other hand, in 2018, Terence Barber, a Black male bus driver in Florida, who assaulted a white passenger for racially abusing and spitting at him, is sacked. Barber becomes an aggressor rather than a victim of racism, which is often how Black people—especially men—are portrayed when they exercise their human rights to fight against racism. It is the fear of being stigmatized as the aggressive Black man and subsequently losing their status and position, if not their life, that prompts many Black men to strategically acquiesce in the face of racism, especially the micro-aggressive form. I think about my father here, and like my mother's, his silence as an Othered immigrant in the face of racism was a survival strategy, which is often attributed to the resilience of the Windrush generation, but this ignores how the trauma of swallowing anger affected their mental wellbeing and health in later life. It is this myth of indestructible flesh written on the Black male body that I sought to disrupt and get behind to understand how Black masculinity is embodied in performance practice.

Other artistic encounters that informed the wake work and creation of safe spaces of performance through which new modes of embodied consciousness could emerge included seeing *OJ Othello* by the Netherlands-based multicultural performance ensemble Made in Da Shade (1999). Rather than commenting on the guilt or innocence of African-American football celebrity OJ Simpson, accused of killing his wife Nicole Brown Simpson and her friend Ron Goldman, their multimedia piece made an analogy with Shakespeare's Black general Othello, whose toxic jealousy drives him to murder his wife Desdemona. But before *OJ Othello*, I was transformed by seeing *The Undersiege Stories* by The Hittite Empire, a performance ensemble of African-American men from Santa Monica (The Hittite Empire 1994). Their use of improvisation to explore the brutal, yet tender layers of Black masculinity affected me profoundly in terms of beginning to actualize my desire to explore Black masculinities in a British context through performance. The Hittite Empire would go on to create *Man in the Belly of a Slave Ship* (1997), a site-specific responsive performance installation in the bowels of a ship in Liverpool's dockyard, which symbolized how the city became prosperous through the transatlantic slave trade. As artistic director of the Double Edge Theatre, I subsequently invited The Hittite Empire to lead a one-day Black-men-only creative workshop, which I took part in.[7] This was a safe space which conceptually, one could argue, emerged from the feminist movement and its creation of spaces for, about, with, and by women. Discourses of gender, race, and sexuality intersected in spaces open only to Black women and LGBTQIA artists, providing similar safety for participants. Led by writer, performance poet, and The Hittite Empire director Keith Antar Mason, the workshop used a series of exercises to create a safe space that empowered participants to begin unmasking themselves and thus to deconstruct the discourses inscribed onto their bodies, which is echoed in Clyde Taylor's comment that "[b]lack men are densely mythogenic, the object of layered fictions produced by others. [...] And like other mythogenic people, Black men are, as if in self-defense, prolific generators of self-descriptive legends" (1994, 169). In one memorable exercise, each participant was lifted aloft by the group and carried around the room while their names were chanted aloud. As a trust-based exercise, it enabled us to celebrate each other as Black men, which we rarely experience in our everyday lived experience. It was evident from what was shared during the workshop process that there was an urgent need for other Black-men-only safe spaces in the UK. There are local community projects that focus, for instance, on gun and knife crime, but these initiatives, often dependent on the vagaries of funding, are fragmented, and in focusing on problematic Black male youth reinscribe the dominant trope of their own racialized oppression. As a consequence, older men, i.e., their fathers, tend to be overlooked even though they need their own safe spaces, where transgenerational conversations with their sons can be built. To maintain the safe space that The Hittite Empire had created, participants who lived locally were subsequently invited to a series of follow-up sessions, where apart from creative outputs, attendance was therapeutic and cathartic.

These workshops that I led also provided an opportunity to experiment with creative exercises. In that context, I began recruiting other Black men, such as arts administrator Douglas Russell and live artist Ronald Fraser-Munro, who I collaborated with to develop what would become the performance workshop project *Brother to Brother* (McMillan 1996). Eventually, Arts Council funding provided the resources to develop the production and hire three male actors of African-Caribbean heritage:

---

[7] Black-men-only workshop. London: Double Edge Theatre, summer 1994.

Benji Reid, Michael Mannash-Daniels, and Ekundayo (aka Anthony Lennon). They had previously collaborated with Denise Wong, Artistic Director of the Black Mime Theatre Ensemble (BMT), who used a devised workshop process to develop a new form of mime that emphasized visual rather than verbal skills, drawing on styles and methods of prominent white 1980s dance and physical theatre companies, such as DV8, Moving Picture Mime Show, and Théâtre de Complicité. They also drew on Black vernacular culture, cartoons, comic strips, and popular culture to create avant-garde, yet popular work that reflected the concerns of Black British people, such as *Drowning* (1991), *EDR—Earliest Date of Release* (1993), *Dirty Reality II* (1995), or *Mourning Song* (1996). These artistic encounters provided examples of creative exercises, performance techniques, poetic monologues as non-linear narratives, as well as an attitude towards beginning to unpack the embodiment of Black masculinity through an oppositional performance practice.

Towards Performing Alternative Embodied Selves: *Brother to Brother*'s Workshop Performance Practice

Brother to Brother employed a similar collaboratively devised workshop process, which, as critical praxis, also embraced Michel Foucault's notion that power consists of being able to act, and to act on the action of others (1978, 3–13). As a social intervention, individuals and groups were empowered to move from being the object into being the subjects of their own history. This radical and transformative practice resonates with Augusto Boal's *Theatre of the Oppressed* (1974) that shows how theatre action can be placed at the service of the oppressed (or dispossessed) for their own expression, and with a new language and mode of action, they can discover new forms of self-expression. In his 'forum theatre', spectators are invited to challenge the role of the acting protagonist and change the course of dramatic action. The improvisational technique called 'cop in the head', a drama exercise where 'actor-spectators' create symbolic images by using their bodies to unearth notions of oppression or so-called 'cops', that have been internalized and influence our actions, was derived from 'forum theatre'. In developing *Brother to Brother*, 'cop in the head' served as a workshop exercise to reveal the ramifications of 'double consciousness' towards understanding the repressive and seductive process of 'osmosis', as Boal describes it (1990, 93), i.e., the internalization of dominant social norms, values, and ideals. It aimed to explore how through performance, a new body consciousness can be promoted in the potential recovery of self. It allowed us to accept and understand our 'structures of feeling' as Black men and consequently work through our own embodied trauma and vulnerabilities. Performance provided a space for the wake work of practicing and performing a Black masculine corporeality that was expressed through the self-love of our being and becoming. Towards telling stories of our everyday lived experience, we began each morning of our intensive workshop process with Benji, Michael, Ekundayo, and myself asking each other the same question: "What happened to you today that reminded you that you were a Black man?" (McMillan 2004). Douglas Russell, who participated in some of the workshop exercises, shares his reflections on the process as follows:

> I was a little anxious of coming into a process of developing an intimate piece with men I did not know very well or did not know. After the first meeting, however, my anxiety subsided, as the other players, though different from me, had a scope of experience I could relate too. I also felt there was more of my experience they could relate to than I had imagined.[8]

Rather than characters, Benji, Michael, and Ekundayo became the personas *Red*, *Blue*, and *Purple*, which alluded to Ntozake Shange's choreo-poem *For Colored Girls Who Have Considered Suicide/When the Rainbow Is Enuf*, which first premiered in 1976 (Shange 1978). In this multi-media performance piece that fused music, dance, and poetry, seven women perform as embodied colors of the rainbow and enact stories of love, self-doubt, foolishness, and the terror of facing sexism and racism. As an interdisciplinary, non-linear, fragmented piece that used vernacular culture, *For Colored Girls*—like the work of BMT—were exemplars of performance practice as a site of oppositional practice. Drawing on Fanon's work, this critical praxis is eloquently expressed by Claire MacDonald:

---

[8] This statement stems from an interview with Douglas Russell, conducted by Michael McMillan, London, 2021.

Writing what I call 'texts for the theatre' has in my experience been a much more eloquent form to discuss cultural identities and difference than the play text. This is because 'the play' is perceived to be dependent on character, whilst the 'text' can explore persona or personae in all their strangeness and complexity. Fanon's insight into the colonised psyche, having to intimately know the heart and the mind of the master better than the master knows those things himself, finds its bitter truth in the text for performance [...]. Persona literally means the masks through which we speak. For those of us who negotiate the everyday by using many voices, many guises and strategies because we have to, the performance text in the hybrid form can transgress the traditions and conventions of the play and give voice to our experience of the contemporary world – with all its mixed messages. (qtd. in McMillan 1998b, 30–31)

The personas of *Red, Blue*, and *Purple* symbolized passion, vulnerability, and romance in the spectrum of Black masculine subjectivity, which provided Benji, Michael, and Ekundayo with strategic masks behind which they could perform "a kind of truth" (Morrison 1995, 95) of their own lived experience, whilst simultaneously enabling a Brechtian distance and interaction with rhetorical and direct questions to the audience. From improvisations, recurring themes began to congeal around shared narratives of childhood vulnerabilities, emotional illiteracy, familial relationships, anger and rage, the joy and pain of love, and the fear of failure. As Joshua Bennett points out, "[t]enderness is the substrate of Black male life. It is what the world refuses (in) us" (2019, 30). The process was reminiscent of the blues aesthetic, in that we had to go through the pain to reach the beauty, and begin forgiving and loving ourselves, in order to be able to love someone else. This is exemplified in the following testimony from Russell:

The development of the piece was organic. I felt able to bring myself to the process and I think the others did, too. Michael was key to this process. He did not sit and observe, he participated, he was right there with us. I did not pick this up in the beginning, but Michael was gluing the stories together through his participation.

As the piece developed, I observed parts of myself in each of the other players and we built a team spirit and a rapport that enabled safety for each of us as individuals, collectively in that space and in the performance.

Michael weaved the different stories into one performance without losing the individual elements of each story.

We remembered the deferred dreams of our Caribbean migrant parents, their puritanical discipline, and how their flesh was separated from their bodies to survive in a racist society. Alluding to Alice Walker's *In Search of Mother's Gardens* (1983), searching for our fathers became a theme about being fathers ourselves, and the fear of failure in patriarchal terms to be 'men', faithful partners, reliable enough to hold our families together:

PURPLE: Dad don't read the newspaper,
    I'm talking to you.
    Dad turn off the TV.
    Dad turn off the radio,
    this is not cricket dad.
    It's me.
    Remember that time
    when I came second in a competition.
    I came home with a trophy
    about the same size as your own.
    I put it down with the certificate
    on the TV,
    you made a cup of tea
    and decided to put it on my certificate.
    Remember that dad.
    Remember that big brown stain
    right over my name.
    Next day my face was in the newspaper
    you got to the centre page,
    all the family was waiting for you,
    we'd all seen it,
    but you skipped over it like there was nothing there.
    Remember
    like you were frightened to see it.
    It's the same paper,
    go to the middle page,
    look at it,
    if you can,
    that's me
    that's your son.
    I'm your legacy. (McMillan 1996)

From audio recordings of these sessions, I developed a performance text that included short ensemble vignettes, poetic monologues, and multimedia projections, as well as a layered soundscape. This included a moving tube train as a site of performance, and the sound of tube trains going through tunnels. These visual and sonic motifs alluded to Clay, the Black male, and Lula, the white female character on a subway train in LeRoi Jones's (aka Amiri Baraka) play *Dutchman* (1964) and the British Rail where many Caribbean migrants were invited to come and work on. Other references included Harriet Tubman escorting runaway slaves to freedom from Southern to Northern states of America in her 'underground railway' and trains as symbols of spiritual rites of passage and transcendence in gospel and spiritual hymns.

Black love stories in popular music and culture are, as Paul Gilroy suggests, "narratives of love and loss [that] transcode other forms of yearning and mourning associated with histories of dispersal and exile" (1993, 201). In this spirit, the soundscape also included manipulated samples of Stevie Wonder, Marvin Gaye and Diana Ross, and Curtis Mayfield. There were also subversive mutated jungle versions of the British national anthem, William Blake's hymn *Jerusalem*, and sound bites of an interview with the British Home Secretary, Michael Howard (1993–1997), defending the statement by the Metropolitan Police Commissioner, Sir Paul Condon, that during the 1990s, 80 percent of muggings in London were committed by Black people.

The only prop we used was a custom-made 2 × 3 m Union Jack flag, which in red, gold, and green transgressively alluded to Gilroy's *There Ain't No Black in the Union Jack* (1987) and the Rastafarian colors. It was also versatile as a burial wrap to memorialize the murder or suicide of an unknown Black man, or a rope to hang from a tree, or the placenta in a birth ritual.

Brother to Brother toured to venues across the UK,[9] where marketing, as with other Black theatre productions, included intensive outreach to local Black communities, with publicity placed in hairdressers and barber shops, eateries, community organizations as well as dissemination via local private and mainstream radio stations. Eventually, the audiences were predominantly Black women and some Black men dragged along by their spouses and partners.

A similar intensive outreach and networking approach was utilized to recruit participants for local Black-men-only workshops that complemented performances in each venue. Many 'talked the talk' about the value of and need for Black-men-only safe spaces, but very few actually 'walked the walk' in attending. Nevertheless, for participants that did attend, there was an opportunity to begin exploring in a safe space with other Black men issues, feelings, and experiences they rarely, if ever, were able to express before.

Self-reflexively, the first production of *Brother to Brother* as a momentary instantiation did not adequately address how the representation of Black male sexuality is constructed and enacted. One critique at the time said that the show verged on the homophobic. Indeed, sexuality was a contested theme during *Brother to Brother*'s devised workshop process, where it was easier to engage with stereotypical representations of Black male heterosexuality, rather than other forms of sexuality, sexual identities, and practices. As a consequence, we unintentionally subscribed to the 'scripts' of "appropriate gender presentation and sexual behaviour", as echoed in McCune's "architexture of Black masculinity" (2014, 16) and the film *Moonlight* (Jenkins 2016). In this hegemonic heteronormative rhetoric, the discourse of homophobic paranoia can also mask latent homoerotic, if not homosexual, desire to echo McCune's work on the 'down low'. As Cheryl Clarke demonstrates in her essay "The Failure to

---

[9] Tour venues included: The Green Room, Manchester; Afro-Caribbean Family and Friends (ACFF), Nottingham; Kuumba Arts Centre, Bristol; West Yorkshire Playhouse, Leeds; Spring Gardens Arts Centre, High Wycombe; and Yaa Asanatewa Arts Centre, London (October 1996). The workshop performance practice that was developed in *Brother to Brother* also informed a series of workshops I led with Black prisoners in HM Prison The Mount and co-led workshops with young Black boys at Crofton Secondary School. It further formed the basis of the *Brother 2 Brother* workshop project (McMillan 2001–2002) that was developed in collaboration with the NHS based community development organization Young People's Sexual Health Project. Over a year, we explored relationships between older and younger Black men through a program of intensive workshops that culminated in an ensemble presentation with workshop participants at The Albany Empire, Deptford, in 2003.

Transform", the issue of homophobia in Black communities cannot be ignored any longer (1983, 199). It was important for me to learn from cultural politics inscribed in the creative process while making *Brother to Brother*. In its second production with Talawa Theatre (McMillan 1998a), the character *Blue*'s text was rewritten, even though some in the original cast did not accept this. Being a Black gay man was now incidental to the character, as illustrated in the following extract:

> *BLUE*: We met a year before we met
> that was the year before I met you
> that's when I met you.
> I saw you in the distance.
> Damn!
> I gotta have piece of that.
> You were a dancer
> so I waltzed over.
> Pleased to meet you.
> My name's Blue.
> I saw your show today,
> you danced very well.
> Oh you weren't in the show!
> Are you sure?
> Well I really wanted to speak to you.
> You smiled.
> I see you again two weeks later.
> I try to speak to you,
> but you give me the cold shoulder.
> No problem!
> But there is a problem,
> because I'm feeling hurt,
> feeling rejected,
> like someone stabbed me.
> I play the game.
> I pick on somebody that you love,
> that I know I can get to you through.
> So I pick on your friend Tom.
> Tom's bisexual,
> great guy.
> We laughed,
> we joked
> and you'd say leave him alone.
> I'd leave him alone.

I'd leave you two alone.
At an after-show party,
I'm drinking champagne.
You haven't got a drink,
but take my glass and drink from it.
You give it back, I look at you
and take a drink where your lips were.
Where to now?
We go to a club,
we're drinking,
music in the background,
reggae and soul music.
I look at you.
I look in your eyes.
I look at your body,
you're beautiful.
I've been thinking.
Nah
What?
Nah it's alright I'll be taking liberties.
What?
I'd like to kiss your lips.
That kiss was sweet.
What are you doing after?
Nothing.
Come back to my place?
Only for a drink.
We go back to your place.
Excuse me I've got to do something.
I'll be here,
I hear the shower,
blissful.
He was half Maori,
half Fiji,
his name was Lee,
L.E.E. (McMillan 1998a)

Brother to Brother was also part of a corpus that shared an exploration of embodied Black masculinities through performance techniques, including choreographed movement and, in one instance, dance. This included *Invisible* (McMillan 1993), based on the prologue from Ralph Ellison's seminal novel *Invisible Man* (1952), which revolves around a young Black man who experiences painful lessons about race in his search for identity while migrating from the US South to the US North. The prologue to *Invisible Man* begins where the novel ends: the main protagonist, alienated from the reality of his existence, escapes into a manhole. He makes the cavernous Black hole his home, listening to Louis Armstrong's "(What Did I Do to Be So) Black and Blue" (1929), and wires the ceiling and walls with 1369 lights. Light symbolizes truth, hope, and happiness, which he has been searching for, but was previously blinded to. This surreal world lends itself to the *mise-en-scène* of *Invisible* which had a solo male performer stripped down to his pants, performing rituals with water in a Beckettian pit of sand, while images are being projected onto a screen above him. The piece thus underlines the search for identity constructions in the face of the racialization of Black men's bodies.[10]

Along with performance/live artists Ronald Fraser-Munro, Mem Morrison, Kevin Johnson, Max Alder, and Dinesh Allirajah, I was invited by the performance poet SuAndi, cultural director of the Manchester-based National Black Arts Alliance, to lead a series of workshops that retold embodied stories of fathers as sons and as fathers with local Black men from the Greater Manchester area. The outcome was a performance piece that fused short dramatic sketches, poetic monologue, movement, mixed audio-visual media, and 20 drummers for an ensemble performance at the Contact Theatre in Manchester (National Black Arts Alliance 2001).

[10] Another piece which negotiates the racialization of the Black male body is *Master Juba* (McMillan 2006), which is based on the nineteenth-century young Black male dancer, William Henry Lane aka Master Juba from New York, who was famous for fusing African dance styles with the Irish jig as a basis for tap dance. This was also the era of blackface minstrelsy where white performers began blackening up and grotesquely caricaturing Black vernacular culture, especially in terms of orality, music, and dance, which later fostered the rise of Vaudeville on both sides of the Atlantic, and the appropriation and commodification of Black performance. In competing for work, many Black performers wore blackface minstrelsy as well, bizarrely imitating—and in some cases parodying, such as Bert Williams later—a white man imitating a Black man.

"NOTHING IN THE WORLD LOVES A BLACK
MAN MORE THAN ANOTHER BLACK MAN"[11]

Twenty-five years ago, when *Brother to Brother* was created, Black masculinities and the social realities of Black embodiment were largely unexplored in UK-based performance and theatre, and using a devised workshop process made it even more novel and experimental. Therefore, in the reconstruction work of rereading *Brother to Brother*'s creative process, I have tried to present it as exemplary of what performance practice can do: on the one hand, it constitutes a site of opposition that embraces decoloniality towards critical praxis, and on the other, I have attempted to show in some small measure how the corporeality of Black masculinity is mediated by multiple vulnerabilities as embodied trauma. For *Brother to Brother* to serve as a model of 'wake work' for safe Black-men-only spaces, there are lessons to be learnt from the process, because it is evident from the struggle to reconnect with all those involved, now in our fifties, that it affected us in different ways. Russell had a positive experience:

> The process gave me confidence, as well as the opportunity to relate to the other players, two of which I knew of, but did not really know. I learned just how common my, our experience was, and it was enriching to learn how others managed their experiences. The most profound element for me was having the opportunity to openly share – initially with other Black men and then on a wider basis with our audience.

> The clue was/is in the name of the piece. It is all about love.

For others, their experience has been more complex, and life course, mental health, and emotional wellbeing has made reconnecting challenging. For myself, my approach would be different now. I would take a more ethical approach towards creating a safe space that would include an aftercare space, where workshop participants could breathe and reflect on their experience of the process. Clearly, Black masculinity is a process of becoming, and wake work in this area is urgently needed given the multiple intersectional vulnerabilities and trauma of Black male lived experience. In this context, metaphors can provide conceptual bridges to lived

---

[11] Morrison (1973, 3–4).

experience. Audre Lorde provides such a bridge in her essay "The Uses of the Erotic" (1984). In reclaiming its patriarchal confusion with the pornographic, the 'erotic' is, for Lorde, "a measure between the beginning of our sense of self and the chaos of our strongest feelings" (88). In this locus of sensation, joy and pleasure are valorized as sources of women's erotic power in the everyday, where the 'true knowledge' for understanding the self reconnects the spiritual (psychic and emotional) with the political. Lorde's metaphor of the erotic can provide a conceptual bridge to 'rediscover' the feminine in the masculine for Black men, where there is joy, pleasure, but also pain, anger, and fear in being vulnerable on the road of becoming. In the end, we return to where we began, because as an adult, my son recently told me that he was grateful that I showed him an alternative masculinity in parenting him. I was relieved, because as a parent, I do not believe we possess a road map to how we parent our children, except that we hope they become emotionally grounded individuals, who know who they are. My son's statement gave me confidence that he is on the path to knowing who he is.

References

Bennett, Joshua. "Buck Theory." *The Black Scholar* 49, no. 2 (2019): 27–37.

Boal, Augusto. *Theatre of the Oppressed*. Translated by Charles A. and Maria-Odilia Leal McBride. New York: Theatre Communication Group, 1974.

———. "The Cop in the Head: Three Hypotheses." Translated by Susana Epstein. *Theatre Drama Review* 34, no. 3 (1990): 35–42.

Clarke, Cheryl. "The Failure to Transform: Homophobia in the Black Community." In *Home Girls: A Black Feminist Anthology*, edited by Barbara Smith Latham, 197–208. New York: Kitchen Table: Women of Color Press, 1983.

Conrad, Joseph. *Heart of Darkness*. Edited by Paul B. Armstrong. 4th ed. New York and London: Norton, 2006 [1899].

Du Bois, W. E. B. "Of Our Spiritual Strivings." In *The Souls of Black Folk*, 1–15. Chicago: A. C. McClurg & Co, first edition [1903].

Ellison, Ralph. *Invisible Man*. New York: Random House, 1952.

Fanon, Frantz. *Black Skin, White Masks*. London: Grove Press, 1967 [1952].

Foucault, Michel. *The History of Sexuality, Vol. 1*. London: Allen Lane, 1978.

Gilroy, Paul. *There Ain't No Black in the Union Jack: The Cultural Politics of Race and Nation*. London: Hutchinson, 1987.

———. *The Black Atlantic: Modernity and Double Consciousness*. London: Verso, 1993.

Hall, Stuart. "Reconstruction Work." *Ten-8*, no. 16 (1984): 2–9.

———. "Cultural Identity and Diaspora." In *Colonial Discourse and Post-Colonial Theory: A Reader*, edited by Patrick Williams and Laura Chrisman, 392–401. London: Harvester Wheatsheaf, 1993.

———. *Representation: Cultural Representations and Signifying Practices*. Milton Keynes: The Open University, 1997.

———. "Epilogue: Through the Prism of Intellectual Life." In *Culture, Politics, Race and Diaspora: The Thought of Stuart Hall*, edited by Brian Meeks, 269–291. London: Lawrence and Wishart, 2007.

Hemphill, Essex, ed. *Brother to Brother: New Writings by Black Gay Men*. Boston: Alyson Publications, 1991.

hooks, bell. "Performance Practice as a Site of Opposition." In *Let's Get It on: The Politics of Black Performance*, edited by Catherine Ugwu, 210–221. London and Seattle: ICA/Bay Press, 1995.

Johnson, Javon. "Reflections: On Black Masculinity and Bereavement." *The Black Scholar* 49, no. 2 (2019): 44–49.

Jones, LeRoi. *Dutchman and the Slave: Two Plays*. New York: HarperCollins, 1964.

Lorde, Audre. "The Uses of the Erotic: The Erotic as Power." In *Sister Outsider: Essays and Speeches*, 53–59. Freedom, CA: The Crossing Press, 1984.

McCune, Jeffrey Q. *Sexual Discretion: Black Masculinity and the Politics of Passing*. Chicago: U of Chicago P, 2014.

McMillan, Michael. *The Last Blind Date Show*. Earl Grey Square, Newcastle, *North East AIDS Week*, Artists Agency, 1992.

———. *Invisible*. Performed by Chris Tajah. Directed by Topher Campbell. London: Double Edge Theatre, 1993.

———. "Fishing for a New Religion (for Lynford French)." In *Let's Get It on: The Politics of Black Performance*, edited by Catherine Ugwu, 190–209. London and Seattle: ICA/Bay Press, 1995.

———. *Brother to Brother*. Performance Piece Devised in Collaboration with Benji Reid, Michael Mannash-Daniels, and Ekundayo. Produced and directed by Michael McMillan. UK tour, 1996.

———. *Brother to Brother*. Performed by David Carr, Cornel John, and Anthony Lennon (Ekundayo). Directed by Michael Buffong. London: Talawa Theatre, Lyric Studio Theatre, Hammersmith, 1998a.

———. *Livewriting: Explorations in Training-Research*. Manchester: The Manchester Metropolitan U, 1998b.

———. *Brother 2 Brother*. Lewisham: Young People's Sexual Health Project, 2001–2002.

———. "What Happened to You Today That Reminded You That You Were a Black Man? The Process of Exploring Black Masculinities in Performance." In *Theatre and Empowerment: Community Drama on the World Stage*, edited by Richard Boon and Jane Plastow, 60–93. New York: Cambridge UP, 2004.

———. *Master Juba*. Directed by Stuart Mullins. Theatre Is & GLYPT South East England Tour, 2006.

McMillan, Michael, and Nick Lowe. *Living Proof: Views of a World Living with HIV & AIDS—Photography & Writings*. Newcastle: Artists Agency, 1992.

Moonlight. Dir. Barry Jenkins, Miami: A 24, Plan B Entertainment, Pastel Productions, 2016.

"Moonlight's Tarell Alvin McCraney: 'I'm Still That Vulnerable Boy'." *BBC Newsnight*, February 18, 2017. https://www.bbc.co.uk/programmes/p04 t3zbq. Accessed May 18, 2020.

Morrison, Toni. *Sula*. New York: Alfred A. Knopf, 1973.

———. "The Site of Memory." In *Inventing the Truth: The Art and Craft of Memoir*, edited by Russell Baker and William Knowlton Zinsser, 83–102. 2nd ed. Boston and New York: Houghton Miffin, 1995.

National Black Arts Alliance. *In My Father's House*. Manchester: Contact Theatre, 2001.

Pomo Afro Homos. *Dark Fruit*. North East HIV/AIDS Festival. Newcastle: Artists Agency, 1992.

Pratt, Mary Louise. "Arts of the Contact Zone." *Profession* (1991), 33–40.

Public Health England. *Disparities in the Risk and Outcomes of COVID-19*. London: PHE, 2020.

Shange, Ntozake. *For Colored Girls Who Have Considered Suicide/When the Rainbow Is Enuf*. London: Methuen, 1978.

Sharpe, Christina. *In the Wake: On Blackness and Being*. Durham: Duke UP, 2016.

Taylor, Clyde. "The Game." In *Black Male: Representations of Masculinity in Contemporary American Art*, edited by Thelma Golden, 167–174. New York: Whitney Museum of American Art, 1994.

The Hittite Empire. *The Undersiege Stories: The Punic Wars*. London: ICA, 1994.

———. *Man in the Belly of a Slave Ship: Walk the Plank, Floating Theatre Ship at Salford Quays 1315*. Keith Antar Mason, Gerard Williams, Kirk Washington Junior, and UK Artists: Douglas Russell, Joseph Jones, and Delroy Williams. Manchester: Black Arts Alliance, 1997.

Walker, Alice. *In Search of Our Mother's Gardens*. San Diego: Harcourt, 1983.

Williams, Raymond. "The Idea of Culture." *Essays in Criticism: A Quarterly Journal of Literary Criticism* 3, no. 3 (1953): 239–266.

CHAPTER 3

'You're a Real Man After All': Fashioning the Male Physique in Twentieth-Century Boxing and Wrestling Magazines

Ana Stevenson and David Patrick

INTRODUCTION

Across the twentieth century, sporting magazines increasingly shaped ideas about the male physique. This article analyzes advertisements in boxing and wrestling magazines of the 1950s and 1960s that were published in the United States.[1] What motivated the vast majority of these

---

[1] Boxing and wrestling's historical emergence from transatlantic sporting culture has been elaborated by Gorn (1986), Sammons (1990), Rickard (1999), and Boddy (2008).

A. Stevenson (✉)
University of Southern Queensland, QLD Toowoomba, Australia
e-mail: Ana.Stevenson@usq.edu.au

D. Patrick
University of the Free State, Bloemfontein, South Africa

© The Author(s), under exclusive license to Springer Nature
Switzerland AG 2022
C. Dexl and S. Gerlsbeck (eds.), *The Male Body in Representation*,
Palgrave Studies in (Re)Presenting Gender,
https://doi.org/10.1007/978-3-030-88604-2_3

53

advertisements was the assumption that most men's bodies were neither big enough nor strong enough and were not properly proportioned. The featured representations linked such physical shortcomings to perceived failures of character and, thus, of manliness. Primarily through advertisements for fitness-based consumer products, such as free-weights, chest-expanders, or home exercise regimens, boxing and wrestling magazines confronted their male readership with visual and rhetorical conceptions of an ideal male physique. The 'ideal' manly body, however, remained indistinct, as the magazines frequently featured bodybuilders as models *par excellence* and neglected each sport's different physical requirements.

Magazines dedicated to boxing and wrestling enjoyed significant circulation throughout the Anglophone world. Of the many produced in the United States, this article focuses on three that enjoyed particular popularity during the 1950s and 1960s: Nat Fleischer's *The Ring* (1922–), Joe Weider's *Boxing and Wrestling* (1952–1966), and Stanley Weston's (later Abe Glick's) *Boxing Illustrated Wrestling News* (1958–1967). These magazines expanded their readership during the shift towards a white-collar economy in the United States at the time as a growing post-war fitness culture tacitly acknowledges that a man's musculature would no longer be guaranteed through his labor. All primary sources were compiled in original hard copy from a personal collection, with 150 separate editions accessed across a representative and multi-year study which allowed for the analysis of significant strategies of constructing, representing, and envisioning the male body. Through distinctive advertising patterns related to fitness and muscle-building products, these magazines both shaped and reinforced notions of 'what makes a man'.

This article will examine ideas of manliness, constructions of masculinity, and the ideal physique as inspired by the bodybuilder's body in twentieth-century boxing and wrestling magazines. These concepts are historically contingent, socially constructed, and changed over time; however, manliness generally encapsulates the ideas about what it means to be a man (Bederman 1995; Kimmel 2005; Hogg 2012), while masculinity refers more directly to ideas about gender (Connell 1995). This article analyzes the emergence of cultural ideals surrounding manliness as they evolved in the nineteenth century, particularly the ideal of a 'muscular Christianity', and formed the background to these later representations. It then situates their later evolution in boxing and wrestling magazine advertisements at a moment when sports and physical fitness became increasingly central to self-perception for the US-American body politic. Offering what Eve Kosofsky Sedgwick describes as a paranoid reading (1997), this article critically interrogates the ideologies that underlay the physical fashioning in boxing and wrestling magazines. Advertisements interpellated their readers into buying into an idealized body image premised on increasingly huge muscularity. This, they suggested, would influence a man's economic success, his ability to prevail in violent physical confrontations, and his realization of heterosexual romance. Accordingly, the advertisements in boxing and wrestling magazines espoused that men and boys could only hope to become 'a real man after all' if they, as individuals, succeeded in cultivating what was venerated as the ideal manly physique.

'MUSCULAR CHRISTIANITY', THE IDEAL 'MANLY' PHYSIQUE, AND THE US-AMERICAN BODY POLITIC

The historical phenomenon of 'muscular Christianity' emerged as a cultural ideal during the nineteenth century. Christian socialism inspired a new genre of literature which promoted unity and patriotism across the British Empire by prioritizing sports such as boxing in the education of boys (Howarth 1973, 27–33). Literary scholar Donald E. Hall describes 'muscular Christianity' as "an association between physical strength, religious certainty, and the ability to shape and control the world around oneself" (1994, 7).[2] Thus, this idealized Christian manliness developed out of a literary project of "writing the male body" in line with discourses of colonial and imperial expansion, as representations of diverse and sometimes contending corporeal imaginings sought to construct systems of meaning and social hierarchies which privileged hegemonic masculinities and guaranteed their claims of power (4–7).

This cultural milieu idealized a manly physique based upon the ancient Greek and Roman classical inheritance. The eighteenth century's European classical revival resonated with enlightenment theories about biological difference and racial hierarchy (Painter 2010). Hence, it privileged whiteness, and especially the facial and physical features thought to have characterized the men of antiquity (Hogg 2012, 125;

---

[2] The term 'muscular Christianity' first appeared in *Saturday Review*, specifically in T. C. Sandars's book review of Charles Kingsley's provincial novel *Two Years Ago* (1857) (Hall 1994, 7).

Blom 2015, 165–166, 370). Territorial expansion through settler colonialism enabled British men to affirm their own sense of racial superiority, particularly in opposition to imperialist ideas about the inferiority of indigenous masculinities (Hogg 2012, 121–125). Since boxing, too, enjoyed a popular revival during this same era, cultural commentators often compared the bodies of athletes with the beauty of classical statues (Boddy 2008, 20, 32–34). An appreciation for boxing and personal excellence in the sport was gradually framed as the product of an Anglo-Saxon heritage.

Ideas about manliness have repeatedly faced perceived moments of 'crisis'. It has been suggested that one such crisis stemmed from the shift from an agrarian to a market economy during the nineteenth century in the United States. As middle-class men entered an increasingly competitive urban marketplace, one school of thought suggested that economic success would follow if they could gain control over themselves and their bodies. The interior experience of one's own manhood—that is, "a sense of security that radiated outward from the virtuous self into a sturdy and muscular frame that had taken shape from years of hard physical labor" (Kimmel 2005, 45)—could, by the 1870s, be transformed into a series of physical characteristics obtainable through hard training in the gymnasium (37–45). The muscular body thus emerged as an anxious response to these tumultuous economic developments and shifts in the labor market, with parallels in later historical epochs.

Historian Gail Bederman charts the concurrent shift in what constituted the ideal male body across these decades, from the lean, wiry form that had dominated in the 1860s to the bulk and muscularity that emerged during the 1890s. Long considered a pastime for working-class men, boxing and prizefighting newly captured the interest of men of the more privileged classes. This generated an US-American ideal which lionized the "powerful, large male body of the heavyweight prizefighter" (1995, 8) over the middleweight or welterweight's smaller body "as the epitome of manhood" (8). Theodore Roosevelt famously cultivated a physical transformation from a sickly, asthmatic childhood to a barrel-chested adventurer. What amounted to a "new fascination with muscularity" amongst middle-class men also enabled strongmen such as the Prussian-born Eugen Sandow and the US-American Bernarr Macfadden to exploit new marketing opportunities for fame and fortune (15). These strongmen sparked a muscular, manly ideal which would permeate US American popular culture—from the illusionist Harry Houdini to the novelist Edgar Rice Burroughs's *Tarzan* book series, published between 1912 and 1965 (Kasson 2001). The growing popularity of boxing and wrestling in the United States at the turn of the twentieth century reflected what Bederman describes as an obsession with the connection between manhood, civilization, and Anglo-Saxon dominance. Indeed, westward territorial expansion enabled white men to construct and perform cultural ideals about their supremacy in an imperial sphere (1995, 4, 20–23). Yet the connections between civilization, white manhood, and sporting prowess were not always reflected in popular culture. Although boxing gained popularity in the United States on account of matches between Irish and English immigrants, African-American men had also been some of the first pugilists (Boddy 2008, 44–46, 78, 166). In 1908, Jack Johnson became the first non-white heavyweight champion. When Jim Jeffries, a previously undefeated heavyweight champion, came out of retirement to fight Johnson in 1910, Johnson's victory triggered deep anxieties about the state of white masculinity (Bederman 1995, 1–10; Boddy 2008, 181–202). This high-profile boxing challenge may rank as one of the most controversial sporting events in US-American history.

The first decades of the twentieth century also witnessed physical culture movements emerge across Europe and the United States (Martschukat 2011). Although many working-class men continued to perform physically demanding manual labor, World War I offered unprecedented insight into the ill-health of the male population in Britain and the United States (Winter 1980). When confronted with statistical evidence revealing the effects of poverty, malnutrition, and unhealthful working conditions, this data caused political apprehension (Silbey 2004; Linker 2007). The influence of Social Darwinism and the rise of eugenics during the 1920s caused further unease in relation to the average man's physique.[3] Against this background, sports and physical fitness became increasingly central to an individual's self-perception within the US-American body politic. Shelly McKenzie describes how "fitness

---

[3] The most pernicious connections between white manhood and racial dominance were taken to their logical extension in Nazi Germany, where physical fitness became deeply enmeshed with fascism and National Socialism. Indeed, Adolf Hitler was deeply displeased when the African-American runner Jesse Owens prevailed at the 1936 Olympic Games (Blom 2015, 162–172, 355–372), as Owens's multiple gold medal wins publicly undermined entrenched and widely propagated Nazi ideas concerning white superiority and fitness.

entrepreneurs" began to promote a new type of physical culture based on the "belief that a regular regimen of physical activity could improve one's ability to find employment, be successful, attract a partner, and enjoy life" (2013, 5). Fitness entrepreneurs cultivated a fitness culture in which men as well as women could reshape their bodies. The politicians and cultural commentators of the 1950s observed the degree to which suburbanization was leading to more sedentary lifestyles. The physical consequences of these economic shifts and geographic trends generated significant cultural anxieties. In response to a Cold War ethos, government officials asserted that physically fit bodies needed to be cultivated so that US-American citizens—men and women, adults, and children—could assert national superiority (McKenzie 2013). Many US-Americans also enjoyed an improved standard of living, together with an increased disposable income and leisure time to devote their bodies to fitness regimes.

In the decades after World War II, this fitness ethos would reverberate through boxing and wrestling magazines. Against the gradual decline of heavy industry and occupations that relied on physical strength and endurance, the United States also witnessed the expansion of suburbia and an evolution towards a white-collar economy. The GI Bill offered opportunities for young, white veterans to embark upon higher education and white-collar careers that distinguished their economic circumstances from those of their forefathers. Amongst these middle-class men living in suburbia, boxing and wrestling magazines gained popularity as a product of the era's increased consumerism.

ADVERTISING THE 'MANLY BODY' IN BOXING AND WRESTLING MAGAZINES

Boxing and wrestling magazines gained immense popularity during the twentieth century. According to journalism historian Bruce J. Evensen, Pierce Egan's column *Boxiana* (1813–1824) had been famous in both Britain and the United States, while sporting magazines such as John Stuart Skinner's *American Turf Register and Sporting Magazine* (1829–1844) emerged in Jacksonian America. The era during which bare-knuckle boxing became prevalent mirrored the rise of the sports section in major newspapers, from the *New York World* (1860–1931) to the *San Francisco Examiner* (1863–). The increasing popularity of boxing and wrestling in the first decades of the twentieth century then coincided with the trend towards specialty magazines. In the fifty years following *The Ring*'s founding in 1922, "the magazine published more than forty million words on boxing, making *Ring* the Bible of boxing" (Evensen 2008, 60–63).

Historically associated with the circus or fairground, boxing and wrestling are performative sports that share certain congruences and divergences. Boxing involves competitors aiming to "injure or exhaust" their opponent through punching (Boddy 2008, 15). The sport usually favors leaner, smoother muscles to improve performance and avoid susceptibility to early fatigue, so pugilists usually train in the gymnasium to develop power, speed, and endurance. In contrast, a higher degree of physical contact meant wrestling would become ever more concerned with the "drama of the male body" (Rickard 1999, 136). As professional wrestlers began to develop larger, more robust physiques, training sought to balance aesthetics with functional strength and agility; with the physical size of individual competitors being a professional necessity. Bodybuilding, however, evolved to become the "public display of aesthetic muscularity for its own sake" (Dutton and Laura 1989, 28). Its proponents emphasize their size, definition, and symmetry of musculature for aesthetic purposes rather than athletic prowess. A specific type of musculature and physique therefore became associated with dedicated bodybuilders—one that does not necessarily make the most capable pugilist or wrestler. Although there are overlaps between regimes, these differences meant that each sport also developed specific athletic and training techniques for increasingly distinctive physical development.

These points of distinction generated a conceptual disconnect in twentieth-century boxing and wrestling magazines. Although the journalism in boxing and wrestling magazines was largely concerned with these sports, their advertisements did not always depict what was considered to be the ideal physique for either sport during the 1950s and 1960s. They often featured famous bodybuilders, especially Charles Atlas (1892–1972). The long-term publisher and editorial director of *Boxing and Wrestling*, Canadian bodybuilder Joe Weider (1919–2013), also exhibited a pivotal cultural influence on a changing culture of muscularity and fitness, including a focus on bodybuilding (Shurley and Todd 2012). Although professional wrestlers tended to be larger than the average boxer below the heavyweight divisions, there remained key distinctions between these standards and the ideal to which bodybuilders increasingly aspired. Thus, many of the advertisements in boxing and wrestling magazines would promote and idealize a physical transformation that particularly resonated with the bodybuilding fraternity.

Restoring the 'Most Perfectly Developed Man'

The popularity and circulation of boxing and wrestling magazines ensured a broad readership for advertisers. Primarily aimed at young men and teenagers, these magazines shaped ideas about what constituted the most socially desirable man in both body and mind. Classical antiquity had established the connection between a boxer's "moral virtues—his discipline, courage, modesty and self-control" (Boddy 2008, 19)—and his physical beauty, a comparison which again emerged during the sport's eighteenth-century revival (14–20). Many twentieth-century boxing and wrestling magazines inverted this paradigm to equate a man's physical shortcomings with his perceived moral inadequacies to cultivate particular personal anxieties and insecurities. As print commercials became more prominent, advertisers shamed and demeaned men with underdeveloped musculature.

Advertisements in boxing and wrestling magazines became increasingly pervasive between the 1930s and the 1950s, with promotions transforming from about one-sixth to a full page. In an effort to sell products and systems related to muscular development, magazines mobilized the sense of personal shame and humiliation thought to result from an underdeveloped body. H & H Associates used this approach to promote *Vitatone*, a weight-gain supplement, describing their product as ideal for men who were "ashamed to wear a bathing suit" and were "skinny and embarrassed when [they] undress[ed] because of [their] scrawny body, thighs, arms and legs". This advertisement in *Boxing Illustrated Wrestling News* even invoked the advice of medical professionals to testify to the effects of *Vitatone*: "Your doctor may also tell you that [being] underweight can make you feel embarrassed, sensitive and ashamed [...] That you may be feeling 'gawky' and ill at ease, because you are so thin" (*Boxing Illustrated Wrestling News*, Vol. 1 (12), December 1959, 28). This was not health advice per se; instead, doctors emphasized that emotional and psychological wellbeing could be achieved through increased physical musculature.

Famous bodybuilders became exemplars for a man's capacity to achieve this desired physical transformation. Charles Atlas had been a celebrated bodybuilding and fitness icon for the better part of two decades by the

1950s. Born Angelo Siciliano in Calabria, Italy, his 'Dynamic-Tension' method focused on building strength through resistance by pitting one muscle group against another. What distinguished Atlas's method from most other contemporary exercise formulae was its lack of reliance on athletic equipment. Further, as Jacqueline Reich observes, earlier exercise regimes—including those promoted by Bernarr Macfadden—had been directed towards both men and women. Atlas, however, addressed himself to men alone. Founded in 1929, the Charles Atlas Ltd. mail-order fitness course aimed to improve a man's body and mind through a series of twelve lessons which "targeted the chest, abs, arms, spine, back, shoulders-thighs-legs, upper arms, calves, wrists, and fingers" (2010, 455), or advocated certain nutritional and lifestyle changes (448–449, 454–455). Several decades after his professional and physical peak, a 1963 advertisement in *Boxing and Wrestling* continued to boast of how Atlas had used his own method to transform himself "from a scrawny, 97-pound weakling into 'The World's Most Perfectly Developed Man'" (*Boxing and Wrestling*, Vol. 3 (1), November 1963, 84).

The advertising industry routinely used testimonials from experts and consumers during the 1950s and 1960s. Testimonial advertising is said to represent a "*consumer experience*, giving prospective purchasers an opportunity to hear directly from their predecessors in the marketplace" (Moskowitz and Schweitzer 2009, 3; emphasis in original). In relation to their use in marketing muscle-building products, Dominique Padurano describes how the template for the bodybuilding testimonial began some sixty years earlier when Eugen Sandow emerged as an international bodybuilding celebrity during the 1890s. Both Sandow and Macfadden chronicled sickly childhoods, followed by an exercise epiphany that cultivated a physical metamorphosis. Founded by Macfadden, the magazine *Physical Culture* (1899–1955) relied on testimonial advertising and aimed to assure readers that their physical improvements would be meritocratic and derived from one's own tenacity. When, in 1921, Atlas was awarded first prize in the magazine's 'World's Most Handsome Man' contest, an accompanying article in *Physical Culture* diverged from the Sandow and Macfadden template insofar as Atlas described enjoying a healthy childhood. Yet doubt may be cast upon the veracity of the famous bodybuilder's testimonial narratives; indeed, Padurano observes crucial differences between this 1921 account and two subsequent accounts, which appeared 21 years later. In January 1942, Atlas told the *New*

Yorker that his health had degenerated after he and his mother immigrated from Italy to Brooklyn. Only a month later, he recounted to the *Saturday Evening Post* that his childhood had always been defined by sickliness and physical weakness. Through this process of "re-crafting [...] his own autobiography" (2009, 186), Padurano argues that Atlas had completed his own personal metamorphosis into a savvy American businessman and entrepreneur (173–186). This again spoke to a series of individual and cultural anxieties, in which physical strength became ideologically connected to the possibility of a man securing economic success.

Regardless of whether bodybuilders' testimonies had any substantial basis in reality, the use of testimonial advertising worked to evoke physical change as eminently desirable for men. Testimonials reiterated the sense of shame, awkwardness, or humiliation that a man admitted to feeling before he embarked on a fitness system which would eventually earn him a larger, more robust physique. The typical bodybuilding testimonial used a 'before-and-after' format in which upwardly mobile young men achieved an idealized masculine body and identity, which Charles Atlas Ltd. then decided to commodify (Padurano 2009, 175–177).[4] Other companies persisted with this format across the subsequent decades. As one *Boxing and Wrestling* testimonial reflected: "Just look at my 'before' and 'after' pictures on this page. Today I'm a bodybuilding champion instead of a physical wreck to be ridiculed and pushed around" (1956, 5). To highlight a 'weakened' start in life, however, was to invariably present a narrative of physical redemption—a personal narrative that echoes cultural narratives of discipline, hard labor, and success in line with the myth of the American Dream. Countless entrepreneurs would embrace an approach that became prevalent in the Weider companies' advertisements, which routinely shared the results of success stories: "...100 pounds of skin and bones! What a rundown wreck! [...] Truly [I was] a pathetic case of weakness before he mailed me this coupon!" (*Boxing and Wrestling* 1962, 7).

The possibility of transforming from a 'rundown wreck' to a 'HE-MAN' highlighted the degree of physical metamorphosis an individual might hope to achieve. According to cinema historian Liz Clarke,

---

[4] Interestingly, by relying on a pattern of 'before' and 'after', the typical bodybuilding testimonial of the 1950s can be read as precursor of contemporary representations in social media.

the term 'HE-MAN' gained prominence following World War I as "a specifically American description of masculinity denoting virile, rugged, muscular strength" (2015, 174). Many war films of the 1920s depict men who abandoned the traits of 'civilized' masculinity to instead embrace a rugged 'uncivilized' masculinity, which also extended to advertisements about physical fitness. The valorization of an 'uncivilized' masculinity operated in juxtaposition to the connection between constructions of white manhood and claims of civilization that had been established in earlier decades; however, as a cultural ideal, the 'HE-MAN' also asserted that all white men had the potential for heroism, especially in wartime, if only they could harness it (173–175).

The 'HE-MAN' emerged in boxing and wrestling magazines as a shorthand for the personal transformation and muscular physique that these publications promised their male readership. One 1954 comic strip in *Boxing and Wrestling* portrayed Bob, who is skinny, attempting to win the affections of Alice, the daughter of a man who owns a timber company. US-American lumberjacks had long been associated with a masculine world of work, representative of the archetype of the 'HE-MAN' (Tomczik 2008). In this advertisement, Alice asks: "Bob, why can't you be like Dad's men? They're tough with terrific stamina!" By the comic's final panel, Bob has developed into a muscular, strong-jawed specimen who, while also having become notably taller somehow, takes the adoring Alice into his arms and declares: "Alice! Come here! You've got yourself a *man!*" (*Boxing and Wrestling* (British Edition), Vol. 2 (8), April 1954, 56; emphasis in original). This comic positioned the lumber-jack profession as a bastion of outdoor masculinity amidst a society in which men increasingly worked indoors, behind a desk. The 'HE-MAN' also emerged in advertisements featuring Atlas himself:

Take a good honest look at yourself! Are you proud of your body or are you satisfied to go through life being just 'half the man' you could be? NO MATTER how ashamed of your present physical condition you may be – how old or young you are – you have the DORMANT muscle power in your God-given body to be a real HE-MAN. Believe me, I know because I was once a 97-pound HALF-ALIVE weakling. (*Boxing and Wrestling*, Vol. 2 (8), February 1963, 5)

Regardless of his profession, these advertisements suggested that any man could hope to harness the latent potential of his 'God-given body' in a manner that evoked the muscular Christianity of the Victorian era.

The transformation to a 'HE-MAN' also mirrored the language that had dominated news reports of the discoveries made at the Nazi concentration camps, which had been liberated within living memory. The revelation of these atrocities created media outrage across April and May 1945, which often focused on the skeletal appearance of camp victims and survivors. The accompanying reports, images, and newsreels were so shocking that they became a cultural reference point for that generation (Patrick 2018, 9–58). Thus, not only did the advertisements in boxing and wrestling magazines highlight young men's perceived physical deficiencies; they also captured the persistent anxieties about white manhood and racial fitness. "My friends called me a human skeleton" (*Boxing and Wrestling* (British Edition), Vol. 2 (11), July 1954, 34), one Weider promotion maintained, quoting a satisfied user of the product. These advertisements promised that a man could avoid the shame of a weak, skeletal physique and enjoy a better life by utilizing a certain fitness product or system.

Almost uniformly, boxing and wrestling magazines featured testimony and celebrity endorsement from white men. However, rare advertisements did feature tips and techniques from professional African-American athletes. The champion boxer Joe Louis, for example, was featured in a Weider advertisement: "No one will dare push you around. You'll gain courage and self-confidence as Gus Lesnevich teaches you how a 2-inch shift of your feet will turn a 'powder puff' punch into an explosive KO blow" (*Boxing and Wrestling*, Vol. 6 (4), December 1955, 6). This advertisement appeared in 1955, a decade after his war record had established Louis as an US-American cultural icon. The positioning of the 'Brown Bomber' was notable insofar as *Boxing and Wrestling* marketed the former champion's knowledge and expertise as a boxer, rather than his physique alone. But this representation diverged from emerging trends on the magazines' covers, within feature articles, and in wider sports journalism. While black boxers had gained increasing visibility as early as the 1930s and had the chance to gain fame, as the case of Louis illustrates most prominently, advertisers nonetheless preferred to foster communities of self-identification among white men. A critical, 'paranoid' reading of the magazines therefore suggests that the 1950s may have offered new possibilities for black men in the arena of boxing and wrestling, yet continued—in line with the era's conservatism—to exclude African-American men from concepts of 'US-American manliness', which was predicated on the bodies of white men. Notions of the US national body thus merged with idealized notions of the white male citizen's body.

The bodily ideal promoted in boxing and wrestling magazines offered white men the chance to regain what was perceived to be a 'lost' masculinity. Across the 1950s, this sense of loss resulted from the cultural and economic shifts which emerged in conjunction with the decade's ongoing deindustrialization and suburbanization. Consequently, advertisers exploited the cultural anxiety that a man might fear being mocked for a small, skeletal frame to promote the desirability of an increasingly muscular ideal.

FASHIONING MALE VIOLENCE IN THE PUBLIC SPHERE

These advertisements employed an ideological discourse of a 'lost' masculinity that needed to be regained in order to sell consumer-oriented fitness products. But their cultural function lay in exploiting the fears and anxieties that might result from a failure to prevail in confrontations between men. Physical appearance has long been connected to ideas about men's honor, a tradition maintained culturally through acts of violence (Spierenburg 1998).[5] Strikingly, the advertisements in these magazines routinely portrayed scenarios in which smaller men were rendered vulnerable to intimidation and attack from bigger, more manly men.

Boxing and wrestling magazines implied that a man's desire to command respect and avoid bullying could be achieved by appropriately fashioning his physique. To emphasize a sense of shared victimhood, often through personal testimony, individuals recollected the suffering of themselves and other men. An advertisement for Atlas's muscle-building guide described the incident which, he claimed, was the catalyst for his physical transformation, under the capitalized sub-heading: "A 'BEATING-UP' TURNED THIS WEAKLING INTO A CHAMP!'":

[5] These representations followed logics of class. Indeed, economic success—they suggested—could preclude the allegedly inherent manly tendency to resort to violent behavior.

One night a frail 97-lb., 15-year-old youth was making his way home …
Suddenly, without warning, a brutal hoodlum loomed out of the dark and
beat him senseless. That night the young man made a solemn vow: '*Never
will I let any man hurt me again.*' (*Boxing and Wrestling*, Vol. 5 (8),
March 1966, 5; emphasis in original)

If, as John Archer argues, violence between men often occurs as a result
of perceived violations of social rules (1994, 121–140), then these advertising scenarios often represented the transgression of social rules as bodily
violations. Not being big enough was, quite literally, believed to invite
physical attack. But these scenarios drew on more than just the imagination. The bodybuilding testimonial narratives of Atlas and Weider
recalled how their newly developed muscles had enabled them to prevail
in the face of unprovoked male aggression (Shurley and Todd 2012, 6–7).
These advertisements did not seek to challenge male violence; rather, they
recognized and endorsed it in order to make its enactment possible. As
Major League Suppliers asserted: "You owe it to yourself to keep FIT,
HEALTHY and to FEAR NO ONE!" (*Boxing and Wrestling*, Vol. 5
(10), May 1955, 59). By thus evoking scenarios of male-on-male aggression and violence and appealing to male readers' 'obligation' to succeed,
boxing and wrestling magazines reinforced traditional notions of male
honor and chivalry and sought to sell their fitness products and body
ideals to a wider population.

The most aggressive advertising scenarios featured young women as
onlookers and were staged at the beach. While beach culture gained
great popularity across the twentieth century, Elsa Devienne argues that
postwar urban regeneration inculcated new modes of social exclusion
aimed at the working classes and racialized communities. Los Angeles
specifically used urban renewal projects to transform its coastline into a
space that would appeal to 'respectable', upwardly mobile white families (2016, 32–33). During the 1950s, the beach also became the site of
emerging sporting and leisure cultures. At Santa Monica's Muscle Beach,
locals could newly enjoy the spectacle of "beautiful, tanned, and muscular
bodies" (Devienne 2018, 335). Against this backdrop and in order to sell
their fitness products, boxing and wrestling magazines depicted beachside
scenes in which the male bodies that did not live up to the physical ideal
were constructed as undesirable.

Boxing and Wrestling engaged with these ideologies of manhood. One
advertisement featured an illustration of an emaciated teenager on the

beach, accompanied by the headline: "The Insult That Made Me a HE-MAN!" The teenager finds himself pushed in the face by a much larger and more muscular assailant, who holds the waist of a young woman in a bathing suit. This advertisement explicitly emphasized the social stigma which men were thought to face if they were not capable of defending themselves physically: "The big muscular bully snarled, 'Get lost, you skinny runt', then gave me a shove and walked off with the girl I wanted to impress. It happened right on the beach, in sight of everybody. People laughed…I nearly cried with shame!" (*Boxing and Wrestling* (British Edition), Vol. 5 (11), September 1957, 52).

Some advertisements went a step further to evoke the far more sinister specter of a criminal attack. Promising to teach *The Ring*'s male readership methods for overcoming "any Jiu-Jitsu fiend or knife thrower", the Andrew Publishing Company maintained that even "You may be a lightweight but you can overpower the biggest bully!" (*The Ring* (British Edition), Vol. 31 (5), June 1952, 3). A man's desire to defend himself against would-be attackers also extended to family and friends. *Boxing and Wrestling* invoked the ideal of the manly protector to add immediacy to the fear of being incapable of fighting off attackers: "You owe it to your own piece of mind – to your loved ones – to be able to defend yourself in these days when attack may come at any time from hoodlums, criminals and 'wiseguys'" (1963, 71). Little, if any, of this language was accompanied by racialized illustrations. Advertisers routinely depicted the criminals as white men; the main distinction was the aggressor's physically enormity in comparison to his diminutive victims. Nonetheless, references to 'hoodlums' and 'wiseguys' do have racial undertones and thus also play into racist cultural imaginaries of these decades.

Bodybuilders particularly emphasized that their consumer fitness products would offer men the physical capabilities to combat such violence. Mike Marvel promised customers a "lean taut rock-solid punch-proof midsection" (*Boxing and Wrestling*, Vol. 2 (7), January 1963, 84), while Atlas asserted that doing his course for only fifteen minutes per day would lead to "sledge hammer fists" and a "battering ram punch" (*Boxing and Wrestling*, Vol. 2 (8), February 1963, 5). The promise of improved martial prowess also invoked language and behaviors which ranged from tame to violent. The Apollon Institute claimed—in an advertisement entitled "BE A GIANT AMONGST MEN!!"—to offer "the kind of HE-MAN sinews that can snap a steel chain or bring a bully to his knees" (*Boxing and Wrestling*, (British Edition), Vol. 3 (2), October 1954, 56).

The Andrew Publishing Company was even more forthright. Alongside a picture of a man disarming a knife-wielding assailant, it featured the prominent headline: "I broke his hand like a MATCH!" This self-defense course essentially condoned and even promoted this degree of violence, further claiming alongside an illustration: "IT WAS EASY! He was helpless. He howled with pain! I was amazed how quickly I turned the tables on the thug with this simple bone-smashing hold!" (*The Ring* (British Edition), Vol. 31 (5), June 1952, 3).

The fitness and muscle-building advertisements in boxing and wrestling magazines promised, often explicitly, that being more muscular and thus more durable would result in customers being less at risk of confrontations with other men. This suggested that by following certain training and fitness regimes, men could avoid any potentially shaming incidents, ranging from social embarrassment in front of women at the beach to deadly criminal threats. Stylizing the male body became not only a means of preparing one's body for intimidation or violence, but also a precursor to physical desirability.

Fashioning the Sexually Attractive Male Body

Boxing and wrestling magazines also counselled that an underdeveloped physique would be unattractive to women. Kasia Boddy describes how the idea that boxing might bring a young man romantic success was promoted as early as the eighteenth century. After the champion John Broughton, to whom the first rules of prizefighting were attributed in 1743, secured the patronage of the Duke of Cumberland, he began promoting bareknuckle fights at his Amphitheatre in London. Broughton also inaugurated a boxing academy which offered tuition to upper-class men, promising his pupils that the pursuit would instill greater success with women. A correlation between these sports and heterosexual romance emerged again during the twentieth century, especially once it became fashionable for women to attend boxing matches.

Increasingly, boxing and wrestling magazines positioned muscular bodies as the apex of sexual selection. Women had periodically participated in eighteenth-century boxing as participants and spectators, but their presence gradually waned as it morphed into a male-coded sporting culture (Boddy 2008, 28–31). By the late nineteenth century, women again began to emerge as spectators of these sports. The literature and films of the 1920s and 1930s, especially by women writers, emphasized the boxing champion's 'sexual lure', thus subscribing to an image of manhood that casts male boxers as 'sex symbols' (29–35, 218–224). The sport's renewed popularity also mirrored the rise of Social Darwinism across the early decades of the twentieth century. Cultural commentators opined that men, and then women, "became interested in boxing as a subject matter within which to explore the mechanisms of sexual selection, the 'struggle between the males for possession of the females'" (158–159). Fitness celebrities and bodybuilding testimonials perpetuated Darwinist rationales for building a manly physique. Weider's own physical transformation had changed how women and men alike perceived him; one of his earliest magazines, *Your Physique* (1940–1953), thus offered its readership information about "weightlifting *and* building a better physique" (Shurley and Todd 2012, 8; emphasis in original).[6]

Accordingly, *Boxing and Wrestling* routinely promised men that a better body would ensure that "[p]opularity, romance, admiration will be yours" (*Boxing and Wrestling*, Vol. 7 (1), September 1956, 5). Advertisements featured photographs, illustrations, and cartoons which portrayed men and women who embodied the era's most attractive ideals. With a stage name that evoked a classical inheritance (Reich 2010, 445–446), Charles Atlas promoted a method which promised "the kind of body men respect and women admire!" (*The Ring*, Vol. 30 (11), December 1951, 66). Joe Weider, too, offered men the prospect of "that Adonis look women admire and men envy" (*Boxing and Wrestling*, Vol. 8 (5), January 1958, 83). Invariably small and slender, the women in these advertisements often wore only bathing suits and looked adoringly upon the huge male models. Women routinely made physical contact with men, often holding their biceps. The Better Health Institute featured a young woman squeezing the arm of a flexing male model, asking: "DO YOU HAVE THE PHYSIQUE SHE CAN'T RESIST?" (*Boxing Illustrated Wrestling News*, Vol. 4 (7), July 1962, 63). Boxing and wrestling magazines implied that women would not seek out men who failed to reach an appropriate degree of muscular development. Each commercial venture promised greater romantic rewards to those men who purchased specific health and fitness products or systems. *Boxing and Wrestling*, for example, used testimony from an 'F.S.' from Chicago to claim: "Only three weeks,

---

[6] This magazine was later renamed *Muscle Builder* (1953–1980) and then *Muscle & Fitness* (1980–).

and I have more dates than I can handle!" (*Boxing and Wrestling*, Vol. 2 (7), January 1963, 84).

Although boxing and wrestling magazines consistently idealized heterosexual romance, the association between these sports and homosexuality would also intensify during the 1950s. Across the early twentieth century, an excess of highly developed musculature had come to be associated with homosexuality, especially amongst bodybuilders (Alvarez 2008). This association increased in conjunction with the sexual connotations relating to the experience of training (Richardson 2004, 58–59). [7] These homosexual sporting subcultures also presented new commercial opportunities during the 1950s. David K. Johnson describes the commercial success and cultural and activist influence of 'physique entrepreneurs,' including Bob Mizer's *Physique Pictorial* (1951–1990) as well as Irv Johnson's *Tomorrow's Man* (1953–1969) and *MANual* (1962–1967), which featured men's bodybuilding in photographs and illustrations with a clear erotic subtext. The queer readership of these 'physique magazines' understood the characteristics which distinguished such publications from their mainstream boxing, wrestling, and bodybuilding counterparts (Johnson 2019, 23–52). At the same time, the athletes on Santa Monica's Muscle Beach actively disassociated themselves from homosexuality by cultivating what Devienne describes as a "heterosexual glamour", a trend which was reversed when the beach became the site of a heterosexual sex crime panic in 1958 (2018, 330).

Boxing and wrestling magazines appear to have largely sidestepped any moral panic about homosexuality by promoting what might be described as a parallel heterosexual glamour. Indeed, these magazines had long been at pains to emphasize their respectability across previous decades. During the fifty-year period when Fleischer edited *The Ring*, its back cover consistently included the following disclaimer:

> *The Ring* is a magazine which a man may take home with him. He may leave it on his library table safe in the knowledge that it does not contain one line of matter either in the text or the advertisements which would be

---

[7] Kenneth R. Dutton suggests that assumptions about the relationship between muscularity and homosexuality may operate more at the level of cultural idea than reality, insofar as same-sex desire may be no more statistically prevalent amongst bodybuilders than in the community at large (2014, 221–222).

offensive. The publisher of *The Ring* guards this reputation of his magazine jealously. It is entertaining, and it is clean.

The boxing and wrestling magazines of the 1950s and 1960s were actively constructing women as the primary observers and beneficiaries of the muscular, manly physique. Almost without exception, advertisers depicted well-developed male models either alone or alongside women, rather than picturing two male models together.

Just as physique magazines creatively addressed their queer readership, mainstream boxing and wrestling magazines subtly distanced themselves from homosexual sporting subcultures. The advertisements aimed to give more men the opportunity to successfully protect and defend themselves and others, with romantic rewards. However, the byproduct of such patriarchal and heterosexist cultural norms was a tacit acceptance of a masculine culture of violence, with potential consequences for violence against women and homosexual men.

CONCLUSION

Boxing and wrestling magazines idealized a heavy, bulky, and muscular physique which became the epitome of manliness during the 1950s and 1960s. Preying upon men's cultural anxieties and insecurities to promote product-based consumerism, advertisers instructed that the purchase of various consumer products would enable men to implement new fitness regimes that would transform their perceived physical shortcomings and lead to success. Yet these consumer ideologies were infused with cultural ideologies about manliness and masculinity. Being too small or too skinny was thought to render a man economically unsuccessful, vulnerable to assault or intimidation from other men, and unattractive to women. These advertisements subtly and progressively privileged the size and stature of the bodybuilding physique, despite being published in boxing and wrestling magazines. The concept of being a 'real man after all' was increasingly premised on huge muscularity, physical strength, and aesthetic appeal in a manner which continues to be negotiated in the fitness and muscle-building advertisements in twenty-first century print and digital cultures.

REFERENCES

Alvarez, Erick. *Muscle Boys: Gay Gym Culture*. New York: Routledge, 2008.
Archer, John. "Violence between Men." In *Male Violence*, edited by John Archer, 121–140. London: Routledge, 1994.
Bederman, Gail. *Manliness and Civilization: A Cultural History of Gender and Race in the United States, 1880–1917*. Chicago: U of Chicago P, 1995.
Blom, Philipp. *Fracture: Life and Culture in the West, 1918–1938*. London: Atlantic Books, 2015.
Boddy, Kasia. *Boxing: A Cultural History*. London: Reaktion Books, 2008.
Boxing and Wrestling. Edited by Joe Weider, vols. 1–13 (1952–1966).
Boxing Illustrated Wrestling News. Edited by Stanley Weston (later Abe Glick), vols. 1–9 (1958–1967).
Clarke, Liz. "Ladies Last: Masculinization of the American War Film in the 1920s." *Journal of Popular Film and Television* 43, no. 4 (2015): 171–187.
Connell, R.W. *Masculinities*. 2nd ed. Cambridge: Polity Press, 1995.
Devienne, Elsa. "The Right to the Beach? Urban Renewal, Public Space Policing and the Definition of a Beach Public in Postwar Los Angeles, 1940s–1960s." *Revue Française d'Études Américaines* no. 3 (2016): 31–51.
———. "The Life, Death, and Rebirth of Muscle Beach: Reassessing the Muscular Physique in Postwar America, 1940s–1980s." *Southern California Quarterly* 100, no. 3 (2018): 324–367.
Dutton, Kenneth R. "Sexuality and the Muscular Male Body." In *Routledge Handbook of Sport, Gender and Sexuality*, edited by Jennifer Hargreaves and Eric Anderson, 218–225. London: Routledge, 2014.
Dutton, Kenneth R., and Ronald S. Laura. "Towards a History of Body-building." *Sporting Traditions* 6, no. 1 (1989): 25–41.
Evensen, Bruce J. "Boxing Journalism." In *Encyclopedia of American Journalism*, edited by Stephen L. Vaughn, 60–63. New York: Routledge, 2008.
Hall, Donald E. "Muscular Christianity: Reading and Writing the Male Social Body." In *Muscular Christianity: Embodying the Victorian Age*, edited by Donald E. Hall, 3–16. Cambridge: Cambridge UP, 1994.
Hogg, Robert. *Men and Manliness on the Frontier: Queensland and British Columbia in the Mid-Nineteenth Century*. Houndmills: Palgrave Macmillan, 2012.
Howarth, Patrick. *Play Up and Play the Game: The Heroes of Popular Fiction*. London: Eyre Methuen, 1973.
Gorn, Elliott J. *The Manly Art: Bare-Knuckle Prize Fighting in America*. Ithaca: Cornell UP, 1986.
Johnson, David K. *Buying Gay: How Physique Entrepreneurs Sparked a Movement*. New York: Columbia UP, 2019.
Kasson, John F. *Houdini, Tarzan, and the Perfect Man: The White Male Body and the Challenge of Modernity in America*. New York: Hill and Wang, 2001.

Kimmel, Michael S. *The History of Men: Essays on the History of American and British Masculinities*. Albany: State U of New York P, 2005.

Linker, Beth. "Feet for Fighting: Locating Disability and Social Medicine in First World War America." *Social History of Medicine* 20, no. 1 (2007): 91–109.

Martschukat, Jürgen. "'The Necessity for Better Bodies to Perpetuate Our Institutions, Insure a Higher Development of the Individual, and Advance the Conditions of the Race': Physical Culture and the Formation of the Self in the Late Nineteenth and Early Twentieth Century USA." *Journal of Historical Sociology* 24, no. 4 (2011): 472–493.

McKenzie, Shelly. *Getting Physical: The Rise of Fitness Culture in America*. Lawrence: UP of Kansas, 2013.

Moskowitz, Marina, and Marlis Schweitzer. "Introduction: 'The Spirit of Emulation'." In *Testimonial Advertising in the American Marketplace: Emulation, Identity, Community*, edited by Marlis Schweitzer and Marina Moskowitz, 1–22. New York: Palgrave Macmillan, 2009.

Padurano, Dominique. "'Dear Friend': Charles Atlas, American Masculinity, and the Bodybuilding Testimonial, 1894–1944." In *Testimonial Advertising in the American Marketplace: Emulation, Identity, Community*, edited by Marlis Schweitzer and Marina Moskowitz, 173–186. New York: Palgrave Macmillan, 2009.

Painter, Nell Irvin. *The History of White People*. New York: W. W. Norton & Company, 2010.

Patrick, David. *Reporting Genocide: Media, Mass Violence and Human Rights*. London: I. B. Tauris, 2018.

Reich, Jacqueline. "'The World's Most Perfectly Developed Man': Charles Atlas, Physical Culture, and the Inscription of American Masculinity." *Men and Masculinities* 12, no. 4 (2010): 444–461.

Richardson, Niall. "The Queer Activity of Extreme Male Bodybuilding: Gender Dissidence, Auto-Eroticism and Hysteria." *Social Semiotics* 14, no. 1 (2004): 49–65.

Rickard, John. "'The Spectacle of Excess': The Emergence of Modern Professional Wrestling in the United States and Australia." *Journal of Popular Culture* 33, no. 1 (1999): 129–132.

Sammons, Jeffrey T. *Beyond the Ring: The Role of Boxing in American Society*. Chicago: U of Illinois P, 1990.

Sedgwick, Eve Kosofsky. "Paranoid Reading and Reparative Reading, or, You're So Paranoid, You Probably Think This Introduction Is About You." In *Novel Gazing: Queer Readings in Fiction*, edited by Eve Kosofsky Sedgwick, 1–37. Durham: Duke UP, 1997.

Shurley, Jason, and Jan Todd. "Joe Weider, All American Athlete, and the Promotion of Strength Training for Sport: 1940–1969." *Iron Game History* 12, no. 1 (2012): 4–26.

Silbey, David. "Bodies and Cultures Collide: Enlistment, the Medical Exam, and the British Working Class, 1914–1916." *Social History of Medicine* 17, no. 1 (2004): 61–76.

Spierenburg, Pieter, ed. *Men and Violence: Gender, Honor, and Rituals in Modern Europe and America.* Columbus: Ohio State UP, 1998.

The Ring. Edited by Nat Fleischer, vol. 31–47 (1952–1968).

Tomczik, Adam. "'He-Men Could Talk to He-Men in He-Man Language': Lumberjack Work Culture in Maine and Minnesota, 1840–1940." *The Historian* 70, no. 4 (2008): 697–715.

Winter, Jay Murray. "Military Fitness and Civilian Health in Britain during the First World War." *Journal of Contemporary History* 15, no. 2 (1980): 211–244.

CHAPTER 4

Basil Dearden's *Violent Playground* (1958): Masculinity, Class, and Sentimental Politics

Christian Krug

SOCIAL PROBLEM FILMS OF THE 1950S, QUESTIONS OF CLASS, AND THE 'PROBLEM' OF JUVENILE DELINQUENCY

British 'Social Problem films' of the 1950s were the predecessors to the better-known New Wave films of the early 1960s. These issue-based films provided social commentary, often in a didactic fashion, on British post-war readjustment, and while their task to 'inform' and 'educate' tied them to the documentary film tradition of the 1930s and '40s, their specific social realism was firmly welded to popular modes and genres such as melodrama or the crime film. Social Problem films addressed a variety of social developments in post-war Britain that appeared to threaten the ideological fiction of an affluent and consensual society. The 'problems'

C. Krug (✉)
Friedrich-Alexander-Universität Erlangen-Nürnberg, Erlangen, Germany
e-mail: christian.krug@fau.de

© The Author(s), under exclusive license to Springer Nature Switzerland AG 2022
C. Dexl and S. Gerlsbeck (eds.), *The Male Body in Representation*, Palgrave Studies in (Re)Presenting Gender, https://doi.org/10.1007/978-3-030-88604-2_4

these films discussed (and attempted to solve) were mainly those of class, ethnicity (due to migration to the UK from Southern Europe and the Caribbean), and, above all, gender and sexuality. This article focuses on *Violent Playground*, filmed in 1957 and released in British cinemas in mid-January 1958. *Violent Playground* is part of a string of successful Social Problem films director Basil Dearden and producer Michael Relph collaborated on throughout the 1950s. They dealt with racial conflicts amongst dockworkers (*Pool of London*, 1951), racism faced by immigrants from the Caribbean (*Sapphire*, 1959), and the laws governing homosexuality (*Victim*, 1961). The topic they returned to most often, however, was class-inflected discussions of juvenile delinquency (*The Blue Lamp*, 1950, *I Believe in You*, 1952, and *Violent Playground*).

The specific focus of the film is on juvenile delinquency amongst male, working-class Liverpudlians. The film locates its social 'problem' at the intersection of gender, age, region, and class—and in the process offers competing models of masculinity. This makes Dearden's film an interesting object of analysis—both in terms of its own foregrounding of intersectionality, and because popular film in the 1950s was a prominent site where masculinities could be expected to be interrogated (Kirkham and Thumim 1997). In fact, *Violent Playground* arguably provides a paradigmatic example of a 'masculinity in crisis'—the notion that in socially volatile situations, 'dominant' (i.e., widely disseminated and normative) or 'hegemonic' (i.e., socially or politically influential) masculinities come under pressure and need to be reconfigured.[1]

'Masculinity in crisis' has become a popular academic narrative. Scholars have credited various crises with producing a unique body of film in every decade after the war, including the British Social Problem and New Wave films of the 1950s and early 1960s.[2] In these films, the

---

[1] Cf. Messerschmidt (2018) for current terminological distinctions between 'dominant' and 'hegemonic' masculinities.

[2] For the 1930s and 1940s, cf. footnote 4; for the 1950s and early 1960s, cf. Clay (1999). The 1990s provide another prominent example of (white) working-class men 'in crisis', with British films such as *Brassed Off* (1996) or *The Full Monty* (1997), e.g., Monk (1999). As early as 1991, Tania Modleski argued that it is precisely this perpetuity—cycles of crisis and resolution—which serve to consolidate male power (7). The phrase becomes problematic when it is instrumentalized for populist purposes (Kappert 2008), but also if 'crisis' is taken to imply a normalcy where 'masculinity' remains largely unchallenged from within (e.g., alternative, competing masculinities) or without (other genders, but also seemingly unaffected by social structures and intersecting categories of difference).

crisis is usually explained by the transition from an older to a newer working class, which—in conjunction with an encroaching (feminized) mass culture—severs the social and emotional bonds afforded by homosocial communities (represented by brass bands and working-men's clubs) and fundamentally questions traditional patriarchal masculinities. This narrative is at the very heart of British Cultural Studies (in fact, it is set out in one of its formative texts, Richard Hoggart's *Uses of Literacy*, published the same year *Violent Playground* was produced). *Violent Playground* can thus serve as a methodological case study as well—about the productivity of academic narratives that link social change (in this case, reconfigurations of class) with a 'crisis' of masculinity; about the very category of masculinity and to what extent it can be tied to notions of individual identity and to performances of individual bodies in popular film; finally, on what level categories such as 'dominant' or 'hegemonic masculinity' can be applied when dealing with popular media.

This article will argue that *Violent Playground* highlights two competing models of masculinity and promotes the one that better fits Dearden and Relph's social-democratic vision for a new post-World-War-II Britain. Both models are connected to bodies—the first, a physical, and the second, a collective one, in the metonymical sense of a social 'body' which 'incorporates' a specific concept of masculinity. In the next section, I will first locate them in a dynamic field that specifically includes labor, class, and commerce, and then discuss how the film fashions its masculinities in the context of two interrelated symbolic blockages—one sexual and generational, the other commercial. The third section focuses more specifically on an ideological strategy used to promote the film's privileged vision of masculinity. *Violent Playground* affectively ties masculinity (and sociability) to feelings and emotions, which it represents as both, shared and corporeal. Such 'sentimental politics' work at the intersection of ideology and affective corporeality, and I will consider how they impact the representations of characters in the film—and, also, how they are employed to fashion audience responses. Other, contingent, bodies complicate the efficacy of this ideological project, however, and in a final section, I will briefly place them into contemporary scholarship on masculinity.

Symbolic Blockages
and the Heroics of Masculinity

Violent Playground revolves around former CID-Detective Jack Truman (played by Stanley Baker), who has been reassigned as a 'Juvenile Liaison Officer' and charged with reforming young delinquents—a job he only reluctantly takes on. 16-year-old Johnnie Murphy (David McCallum), on the other hand, is the leader of a youth gang controlling the playgrounds of a large housing estate for working-class families in Liverpool. He and his gang are responsible for petty crimes which quickly escalate. Johnnie has two younger siblings who are also involved in petty crime. This focus on adolescents and children allows the movie to examine what will happen to the "next lot"—the next generation of a working-class growing up on the streets of Liverpool (*Violent Playground* 01:08:05–20). At the time, this seemed a pressing question as the working classes were believed to be in a state of transition, affected by the material wealth of a more affluent society (most conspicuously symbolized in New Wave films by the newly acquired television set in working-class living rooms). In 1957, while *Violent Playground* was being filmed, Prime Minister Harold Macmillan famously declared that "most of our people have never had it so good" (Perkin 2002, 418). *Violent Playground* is very much concerned with the role working-class youths could and would play if a professionalized welfare state (associated with Sergeant Truman) were to realize a vision of a more integrated, homogenous, and affluent society. Who would play along? Would the juveniles be true to the lyrics of the title song and "play rough", "get tough" (Luck 1958)—or could they be persuaded to join Dearden and Relph's liberal, social-democratic vision for Britain?

Put another way, in Marxist terms the film enquires into the 'reproduction of the relations of production'—a suggestive phrase since this movie is both obliquely and centrally concerned with (blocked) generational and sexual reproduction. Critics have frequently noticed that Dearden deliberately eschews ascribing any sort of sexual desire to Johnnie (e.g., Chibnall 1997, 150) and have argued more generally that one ideological strategy of Dearden and Relph's films is to create new, post-war communities by means of rational assimilation and a reduction of sensation—that is, they invite a repression of sexual energy which they represent as a necessary price to pay for social community (e.g., Hill 1986, 69–70). In this movie, however, Johnnie's marked lack of heterosexual desire is more specifically placed in a larger context of severed family bonds, blocked reproduction, and threats to hetero-familial norms. The Murphys' father works as a stoker on a ship and is absent for months at a time, their mother has eloped to London, a conventional place of temptation and sin in Victorian domestic melodrama (with which *Violent Playground* shares some affinity). Actual fathers—and with them, parental authorities and traditional working-class breadwinners—are conspicuously absent in the film, which instead features three prominent pairs of siblings. They include Johnnie's younger brother and sister (twins), who are being raised by his older sister Mary, a nurse (played by Anne Heywood). The movie can be seen as an exercise at generational reconfiguration, proposing and testing a series of readily available *ersatz*-fathers for them (a headmaster, a priest, and finally a policeman-turned-social-worker). Structurally speaking, the film focuses more or less on one generation and tackles its problem of a reproductive blockage paradigmatically. It employs a reparative politics that seeks to 'heal' the existing social body by rearranging already-existing elements in new social configurations (which is another feature that aligns it with Victorian melodrama).[3]

Violent Playground locates the social problems it addresses at the intersection of age, class, gender, and ethnicity—but with a twist. Unlike some of the New Wave films released just a couple of years later, *Violent Playground* does not focus on male disempowerment amongst the working classes. It conceives of the relationship between 'work' and 'masculinity' in a wholly different way: An unruly juvenile male energy threatens to disrupt work, and with it, the social fabric. This is a far cry from the representations of fetishized male bodies of laborers featured in some of the celebrated documentary films of the 1930s, "'heroic figures' representative of 'the ardour and bravery of common labour'" (Dodd and

---

[3] Consider how in contrast, New Wave films (and Hoggart's *Uses of Literacy*) often showcase generational conflicts between an older and younger working class and frequently feature sexuality, pregnancy, and abortion. *Violent Playground*, on the other hand, poses *problems* that concern both former and future generations—the absence of both Murphy parents, Johnnie's 'a(hetero)sexual' body threating the reproduction of relations of production, the petty crime of his younger siblings as representatives of the "next lot" (01:08:07) of the working class—but the ideological solutions it offers firmly focus on the here and now—and they embrace the logic of melodrama. The fact that Truman, the chosen *ersatz*-father, turns out to descend from a line of shepherds (i.e., has been a shepherd all along) is significant in this respect. The solution the film offers revolves around (self-)recognition, forging emotional bonds, and realigning social positions accordingly.

Dodd 1996, 43–45),[4] but it also differs from the New Wave films which often shy away from representations of actual bodies at work, focusing on leisure rather than labor (famously, Karel Reisz's *Saturday Night and Sunday Morning* [1960] opens with workers *leaving* the factory at the end of the day). New Wave films also explore an unruly male energy, and there is arguably a link between Johnnie and the more adult, and more clearly misogynist and self-destructive masculinity Jimmy (Richard Burton) exemplifies one year later in Tony Richardson's *Look Back in Anger* (1959). However, both Grierson's documentaries and New Wave films retain manual labor as an implicit norm, and masculinity frequently functions as a corollary of such labor. In *Violent Playground*, on the other hand, manual laborers (e.g., Johnnie's father) are conspicuously absent, physical exertion is relegated to the area of sports (and, as I will argue later on, dancing to rock'n' roll music), and Johnnie's brand of masculinity threatens to *undermine* work by blocking its integration into the social fabric (and this is arguably a more oblique, but nevertheless fundamental 'social problem' the film seeks to address).

The movie represents 'work' in a distinctly limited sense—one that does not comprise manufacture or production (industrial labor is wholly absent), nor one that seems to contain institutional services such as the police or the welfare state (their occupation is represented in terms of a calling or a duty instead). Representations of work almost exclusively cover logistics and retail—in *Violent Playground*'s industrial north, England features as a nation of shopkeepers. Set-pieces involve an overworked female shopkeeper, an irate male market vendor, and specifically, two Asian siblings who deliver laundry—they are all affected by the juvenile delinquent, working-class masculinity represented by Johnnie and his gang. Quite appropriately, once his crimes progress to arson, Johnnie burns down an empty warehouse (rather than a factory).

These representational strategies (and the inclusiveness Dearden and Relph aim for in their films) are most clearly illustrated by Alexander and his sister Primrose (played by Michael Chow and his sister Ts'ai Chin), the hard-working Asian siblings who deliver laundry. In a scene set in the

---

[4] Kathryn and Philip Dodd (and many others) have argued that John Grierson's celebrated documentary films of the 1930s, such as *Industrial Britain* (1933) or *Coalface* (1935), (homoerotically) depict such fetishized male bodies as heroic figures—a strategy which they partly attribute to a perceived 'masculinity in crisis' after World War I (1996, 45; cf. my second footnote).

'violent playground' in the middle of the housing estate, Johnnie's gang accosts them; they empty their van, and throw around the parcels they have to deliver, mocking the process of commercial distribution. Their company truck (a symbol of Alexander and Primrose's social mobility) is misused by Johnnie as a cover for illicit activities, and Alexander is killed by it when Johnnie, pursued by the police, steals the van and runs him over with it. Symbolically speaking, Johnnie and his gang threaten the circulation of commodities—another 'blockage' the film is concerned with. The vital clue that eventually leads the police to Johnnie is the string that holds these parcels (and in extension, commodity culture) together.[5]

As already indicated, *Violent Playground* attempts to deal with this delinquency of unruly young males by showcasing several models of masculinity and playing them off against each other. This accounts for the symbolic pairing of Alexander and Johnnie, but most recognizably for the interplay between the film's two male protagonists, Sergeant Truman and Johnnie Murphy. Both characters are relationally constructed so as to present alternative models of masculinity, with one clearly, even didactically, favored. With Johnnie, masculinity is more performative, tied to the material body, and at least potentially transgressive; with Truman, it is conformist, more aligned with the requirements of a larger social body, and both object and subject of social discipline. This corresponds with different figurations of the male body: While David McCallum plays Johnnie as a body-to-be-looked-at, with limber movements, Stanley Baker (as Truman) uses his massive physique for slow, stiff, methodical movements to project a body image that is about mechanical execution. His low-energy performance seems to be a deliberate attempt to offset the youthful energy of Johnnie and his gang. Both characters, however, serve as male 'heroes'—affective figures offered for identification that allow communities to symbolically incorporate otherwise irreconcilable values, norms, or subjectivities.

When he was younger, Johnnie was considered a 'hero' by the community: Other characters speak fondly about how as a little child, he rescued his brother from a fire. Now he has become a 'firefly', setting fire to buildings. The film carefully places his propensity for arson in a psychological paradigm, pathologizing his actions merely as those of an individual, but

---

[5] The overt symbolism of this construction is easily decipherable. In the broadest of strokes, the film admonishes that if the next-generation working classes fail to labor along, logistics and retail will be affected—and the whole social body will suffer accordingly.

they remain incendiary in a social sense as well: As the representative of the next generation of the working class, the former hero now threatens the social order—and the fiction of a conformist working class which mark Dearden and Relph's films in the 1950s (Chibnall 1997, 148). However, given that the buildings he sets fire to seem to be derelict or industrial ruins, Johnnie indirectly serves as a motor for post-war urban development in Liverpool as well, and his psychopathology is a good example of how the film displays subversive behavior while containing it at the same time.

While Johnnie is meant to represent a fallen hero (a distinct 'male type' in films after the war; Spicer 2001a, b), the film promotes Jack Truman as a prospective new 'hero' for the audience—a hero defined not by the legend of a single deed but by virtue of his social functionality. In a social sense, heroic figurations manage to incorporate the ambivalences and contradictions experienced by a community, focus them in a single figure which can serve as a point of identification, thus imaginarily effecting a coherence of what in real-life terms must remain heterogeneous (von den Hoff et al. 2013). At the end of the movie, this is precisely what Truman is credited with—he comprises the policeman and the social worker, strictness and compassion, combines virility with emotional control—and much more. His character helps absorb the tensions implicit in Dearden and Relph's vision of a consensual post-war society.

Truman's particular brand of masculinity, however, turns out to be neither 'new' (it is heavily influenced by Victorian concepts of masculinity and 'manliness', as I will argue in the next section) nor 'hegemonic'. After all, setting up Truman as the sanctioned hero only works if the film strategically forgets its unresolved social problems and ideological tensions (Hill 1986, 82)—and only if the sheer emotive potential of Johnnie does not disrupt it. The film goes to great lengths to carefully fashion Johnnie's emotions, and the audience's emotional reactions towards him: A fallen hero who was once admired, he is now meant to evoke fear. For an increasingly younger cinema audience, however, the character continues to offer affective points of identification that may not be ideologically sanctioned, including pity and reverence. Johnnie continues to provide a screen onto which an audience can project their feelings, and he arguably remains an alternative emotive hero—albeit a tragic one.

Likewise, Truman's particular brand of ('Neo-Victorian') 1950s masculinity is promoted, but its hegemony remains an ideological vanishing point. It is consistently challenged in the movie (as when his former colleagues at the police station make fun of him) and ultimately fails to make an impact on Johnnie. In this sense, the movie showcases the usefulness of current theoretical distinctions between 'dominant' and 'hegemonic' masculinities—for an increasingly younger cinema audience, Johnnie's brand of masculinity may have already become dominant (it was widely disseminated in US-American melodramas such as *Blackboard Jungle* [1955], an obvious inspiration for *Violent Playground*), and while it may lack any hegemonic impact, it consistently undercuts Truman's masculinity.

The film acknowledges the ascent of this representational form at the very end—at least symptomatically, by the sheer force by which it seeks to regulate and then discard Johnnie's body. In the last ten minutes of the movie, Johnnie first shuts down both emotionally and physically; we mainly find him slumped over a table and barely moving anymore. This contrasts with his former, limber movements and brings him more in line with Stanley Baker's low-energy performance as Sergeant Truman. It seems Johnnie's unruly body needs to be taken care of, and the film next discusses how to best 'dispose' of it—there is a lengthy discussion where he is put, an ambulance or a police van. While this allows the film to evaluate the nature of the 'social problem' it has addressed (medical or a criminal?), it does so in specifically corporeal terms. In fact, the film consistently places emphasis on the body as the nexus of the personal and the social, as I will discuss next with regard to the sentimental politics of the film.

THE SENTIMENTAL POLITICS OF FEELING (JUST) RIGHT

The relational construction of the two male protagonists is most noticeable on the level of feelings (associated more with personal experience) and emotions (which I take to be more obviously socially coded).[6]

---

[6] Both 'feelings' and 'emotions' are thus eminently social, with 'emotions' more overtly conventionalized (as in 'emotional regimes'), and 'feelings' purportedly more 'personal'—even though, as the phrase 'feeling right' already indicates, they both retain normative elements. They are distinguished from 'affect', which I take to denote, in Brian Massumi's words, a pre-personal intensity, an "ability to affect and be affected" (outlined in his "Notes" to Gilles Deleuze and Félix Guattari's *A Thousand Plateaus*, 2019, xv). This notion of affect, which is not limited to individual bodies, allows "moving and being moved" (Chandler 2013, 177)—and, as James Chandler argues, is central to the language of sentimentality.

Dearden and Relph's films frequently conceptualize their 'social problems' in terms of the emotions of individuals and communities, and like in
many other Social Problem films of the 1950s, *Violent Playground*'s overt
didacticism turns out to be emotional and affective rather than cognitive and rational. A trade publication, *Kine Weekly*, referred to *Violent
Playground* as a "sociological melodrama" (January 9, 1958; qtd. in
Burton and O'Sullivan 2009, 222), and the phrase is quite fitting. For all
their ostensible social realism, Social Problem films frequently rely on the
conventional patterns, such as heroism and victimization, and affective
configurations of melodrama. They also operate with 'non-naturalistic'
realisms; for example, they employ an 'emotional realism'[7] in order to
position bourgeois members of the audience within the world of the
working classes they represent—for example, by measuring working-class
characters against bourgeois emotional regimes.

More specifically, *Violent Playground* and other Social Problem films
employ a distinct *sentimental style*—i.e., they invite affective responses
by representing excessive emotions—pity, compassion, empathy, most
conspicuously evoked through displays of suffering and somatically
encoded as tears. These emotions in turn are tied to specific moral values
and ideological norms, and what is supposedly intimate and personal
('feelings') turns out to be public and social. 'Shared' or 'public feelings' and 'feeling right' (the latter phrase evokes one of the sentimental
ur-texts of US-American literature, Harriet Beecher Stowe's *Uncle Tom's
Cabin*, 1852) are all of central importance in the film, and masculinities, too, are consistently tied to them. And as long as they are shared by
the audience as well, such ideologically coded emotions-as-feelings then
also circulate beyond the bounds of the film. Film scholars have argued
that Social Problem films often aim to suppress sexuality and violence,
and more generally, to reduce sensation (Hill 1986, 70). In contrast,
I would suggest that by focusing on the film's "sentimental politics"
(to adopt a phrase from Lauren Berlant, e.g., Berlant 2008), one can
observe how sensation and affect also function as part of a film's ideological project. Sentimental politics works by producing affective intensities

---

[7] The term 'emotional realism' is now associated with Ien Ang's seminal analysis of
soap operas (1985, 41), but it was already used in the 1960s by British film critics,
cf. Lowenstein (2005). Lindsay Anderson, a prominent director within the Free Cinema
movement and the New Wave films, in 1957 similarly called for an "emotional socialism"
in theater and film production, cf. Lacey (1995, 34).

in order to forge affiliations between film characters and between the film and the audience; it is thus predicated on an ethic of 'human connectedness' and frequently intertwined with domestic ideology (Howard 1999). By producing and promoting shared feelings, it can be employed as a strategy of interpellation, but it potentially also permits the fashioning of alternative subject positions by subordinate groups.[8] Focusing on the sentimental politics also allows us to analyze the interplay between the corporeal and the discursive and the ideological uses of the affective in the film. In *Violent Playground*, emotions and feelings are displayed as distinctly corporeal and represented in acts of violence, ludic forms of dancing, and emotional outbursts into tears.

Truman's and Johnnie's relational construction crucially involves their emotional capacities and they are evaluated in terms of the appropriateness of their feelings. At the beginning of the movie, Johnnie *feels too much*, and while he cannot channel those feelings in any socially legitimate sense, he clearly emotes a lot (actor David McCallum was lauded as the "British James Dean" for his portrayal; Burton and O'Sullivan 2009, 220). Johnnie is clearly intended as a point of identification for a new British cinema audience which got progressively younger throughout the 1950s (*Violent Playground* has been called one of Britain's earliest teenpics; Chibnall 1997, 148) and which by 1960 consisted predominantly of what was then considered the working classes (Laing 1986, 109–110; Feldmann and Krug, forthcoming).[9] Former CID-Detective Jack Truman, on the other hand, starts off feeling *too little*—and decidedly 'wrong'. At the beginning of the film, Truman describes himself as

---

[8] While Dearden's films have very occasionally been discussed in terms of an underlying sentimentality (most notably in Wells [1997], who equates sentimentality with nostalgia in order to place Dearden's films in a comic tradition), my use of the term is markedly different and stresses its political dimension.

[9] According to Andrew Spicer, the young, upper-working-class men that came to dominate cinema audiences towards the end of the 1950s preferred American male heroes offering "fantasies of empowerment and success for male cinema-goers estranged by the middle-aged, middle-class orientation of British film producers" by presenting what a preference survey of British audiences undertaken in 1955 called "'models of mobility aspiration': an 'attractive, virile and ambitious hero, pursuing a combination of personal and social aspirations against a hostile environment'" (1999, 85–86). In *Violent Playground*, middle-aged British film producers Dearden and Relph offer these elements in Johnnie's futile attempts at upward mobility (symbolized by being refused entry to the Grand Hotel) and the dangers emanating from his Americanized friend "Slick", who carries a machine gun in his guitar case.

"clumsy", "tactless", "brutal", and recommends keeping women and children in line through domestic violence (*Violent Playground* 00:04:40). Not only is he unable to emotionally connect to children or women—emotions are simply not legible to him: Early on, a seven-year-old girl uses tears to manipulate him after she was caught defrauding a shopkeeper, and Truman needs to be taught, by means of a didactic demonstration, that she can shed tears effortlessly and at will (00:26:15). In the course of the movie, however, Jack Truman, who according to one of his colleagues starts off as the "most insensitive" "*Jack* in the city" (00:03:40; my emphasis), will turn into what the film promotes as a 'true man': His gradual symbolic transition from first to last name is conceptualized as attaining emotional maturity (Chibnall 1997, 148), and by the end of the movie, he combines the compassion demanded by a social worker with an emotionally controlled virility. In its fashioning of a 'true man', the movie evokes a specific concept of patriarchal masculinity which (like many other aspects of this movie) nostalgically evokes Victorian norms and values—in this case, the early-Victorian masculine ideal of bourgeois respectability achieved by discipline and a regulation of 'maleness', an innate male energy (Sussman 1995, 16–72). *Uncontrolled* virility and lack of emotional restraint are traits stereotypically associated with working-class men, including Johnnie and his gang. In this movie, they are represented through another, corporeal trope: Johnnie is a talented athlete who refuses to train. The film promotes running and boxing, which would both allow him to channel his unruly male energy ('maleness' in Victorian terminology), and discus-throwing also serves as an obvious metaphor for 'reaching far'—achieving social objectives (*Violent Playground* 00:34:00). In one sequence of the film, Johnnie runs a handicap race against younger children and fails to catch up to the fastest of them. The former child hero is visibly left behind by younger children who follow the headmaster's training program. As Johnnie's physically exerted body collapses on the ground, Sergeant Truman enters into a discussion about subject positions with him—whether these are malleable or whether you are stuck with 'who you are'.[10]

---

[10] This trope is explored in more detail in New Wave films, most famously in Tony Richardson's *The Loneliness of the Long Distance Runner* (1962), where juvenile delinquent Colin Smith (Tom Courtenay) also has a talent for running which grants him a privileged position at the borstal he is sent to, and in Lindsay Anderson's *This Sporting Life* (1963), where miner Frank Machin (Richard Harris) seeks social advancement by joining

In line with Truman's patriarchal masculinity, the film ends with a bourgeois-familial solution to the problem of working-class delinquency: According to the reformed, true man Jack Truman, society simply misses "[a] lot of Mum and a little bit of Dad" (01:08:05–20). Truman takes on the role of "a little bit of Dad". In an effortless ideological sleight-of-hand, the policeman-turned-social-worker now becomes the father of Johnnie's younger siblings. The confirmed bachelor Truman (who, it turns out, descends from a parental line of shepherds) is (re)confirmed as the chosen *ersatz*-father. Having learned how to feel (and feel right), the true man is then inscribed into a sentimental myth that generalizes 'family' and ties patriarchy to the (industrial) nation: In the last scene of the film, Jack Truman takes a black or mixed-race child (aptly referred to as "Sonny") by the hand—a bodily gesture meant to convey the emotional maturity he has attained. It also incorporates Sonny, symbolically and literally (*incorporare*, "to embody, include", OED), into the national family—the extended patriarchy of a 'multi-ethnic Britain'. In the final shot, he guides him through the industrial wastelands of Liverpool, mere sentimental props in Dearden and Relph's vision for what lies beyond the closing credits: a socially inclusive, post-industrial Britain.

This final scene clearly shows that the film's sentimental politics is not limited to its diegesis (where its 'problems' are only superficially resolved) but also includes the audience, inviting it to join its liberal vision of post-war Britain. The whole final act of the movie can be viewed as an attempt to affectively interpellate the audience as well, teaching them to 'feel right' about the unruly male at the center of the film. Since *Violent Playground* insists that 'feeling' and 'feeling right' have to be learned, and since the film promotes socially acceptable emotional regimes in an almost didactic fashion, it seems only fitting that this final act is set in a school. School functions as an ideological 'apparatus' which offers and promotes specific subject positions (Althusser 1971), and it does so by endorsing specific emotional regimes and privileged feelings.

In this extended sequence, which runs for nearly thirty minutes, juvenile delinquency has escalated dramatically. A small-time criminal at first, Johnnie has become an arsonist, was then involved in a fatal hit and run,

---

a rugby team, channelling his aggressiveness in a socially legitimate form. However, in both films such athletic activities by working-class men are mere pet projects of more powerful, patronising middle-class men—the borstal's governor and a Wakefield captain of industry.

and has now acquired a sub-machine gun and holds a classroom of children hostage. The film adopts a conventional discourse whereby criminal acts invariably follow a logic of escalation that cannot be controlled by criminals themselves; unless they are stopped, their behavior will eventually spiral out of control. School, it turns out, is not the safe, heterotopic space its headmaster (called 'Heaven' by his pupils) claims it to be. Instead, the film consistently stresses that the boundaries between classroom and society are permeable and the events in the classroom are literally and symbolically 'public'. The film continually places Johnnie and his young hostages in front of huge glass windows overlooking a schoolyard full of parents, police, and mass media. He is repeatedly pictured leaning out the classroom window, in a series of shots in tight framings, filmed from just inside or just outside the classroom window. Such shots mark the fact that the windows function as interfaces, rather than boundaries. As interfaces, they allow for negotiations (including those in a literal sense, between Johnnie and the police), and they serve as picture frames for the affective staging of intense, physically displayed emotions. In short: They accommodate the film's sentimental politics. These politics encompass the audience as well, as a few interspersed establishing shots clearly indicate. In them, the large windows serve as obvious metaphors for the cinema screen (at that time, a potent trope in Hollywood films),[11] with the public assembled in the playground doubling as the cinema audience. The film thus self-reflexively visualizes its ideological project—to affectively interpellate both the film's characters *and* its audience through feelings and emotions. The classroom windows are the interface where these levels intersect.

[11] Hitchcock's *Rear Window* (1954) is the best-known example of a sustained, almost allegorical use of windows doubling for the cinema screen. Partly because the introduction of widescreen formats (such as CinemaScope) changed its aspect ratio (i.e., its geometry), the screen had become an object of meta-reflexive attention by the mid- to late 1950s. Changes in the aspect ratio affected a film's potential for intimacy (a point producer Michael Relph was keenly aware of in 1957; cf. Burton and O'Sullivan 2009, 129), and any discussion about a film's sentimental politics, specifically if those involve the audience, also needs to consider cinema as a dispositif—something I can only sketch here: Whereas widescreen formats allowed for more peripheral vision—which arguably complicates Neo-Marxist concepts of subjects being interpellated by the cinematic apparatus, cf. Belton (1992, 185)—, *Violent Playground* was projected in a more narrow format (1.75:1), which, while 'wide', kept focusing the audience's gaze more firmly, thus benefitting the didactic impetus of their Social Problem films.

Feeling right is being taught on both levels. The first, diegetic level involves the pupils in the actual classroom. Amongst them is Mary, the young girl who used her tears to manipulate Truman after she was caught defrauding a shopkeeper. Being threatened by Johnnie now teaches her forcefully under what conditions tears are socially acceptable— when confronted with a German submachine gun. In 1958, Johnnie's MP 40 was easily identifiable as a standard weapon used by the Wehrmacht during the war (it had found its way to Britain as a war-time souvenir and was subsequently employed in criminal activities in the 1950s). The movie thus reminds the post-war generation of (delinquent) youths about the traumatic experiences their parents' generation suffered during the war. In addition, Johnnie was handed the sub-machine gun by "Slick", a young man fashionably dressed according to the style popularized by US-American films, who keeps it, appropriately, in a guitar case. The signifiers of World War II and of a contemporary US-American mass culture—the perceived threats to a British consensual society past and present—are thus conflated or folded into one.

A second level involves the cinema audience. It is also part of this ideological project and addressed, in a very sentimental fashion, by close-ups of crying mothers.[12] These shots are clearly designed to structure the audience's affective responses. Johnnie holds up individual children to the windowpane, one by one, presenting them to the public below and threatening to kill them. The procession of bodies in distress is intercut with a series of individual faces from the masses of suffering mothers, depicted in close-up and full of anguish and despair. At one point, Johnnie reads out a whole list of the names of pupils he holds hostage, while the camera pans across the women's faces (*Violent Playground* 01:16:36). The film takes great care to establish their social inclusiveness; they comprise the traditional English working classes, Italian migrant workers, and black immigrants. The schoolyard—another 'violent playground' of the title— thus becomes a model for a national community united through shared suffering. Fifteen years earlier, representations of war would have facilitated such community building; now, the movie employs a working-class

---

[12] The sentimental responses of cinema audiences in the late 1950s are difficult to gauge in historical hindsight (and there is an obvious danger that current affective responses are projected onto the film), even though the decade saw the first empirical attempts to study audience reports about the tears shed in cinemas (cf. Harper and Porter 1996)—including Dearden and Relph's *The Blue Lamp* (1950).

juvenile delinquent, Johnnie, to do the job. The whole sequence is as didactic as it is cynical: Similar to the salvoes of bullets Johnnie fires from his sub-machine gun, it is designed to inscribe supposedly authentic, ideologically privileged feelings into the characters on- and the audience off-screen.

MASCULINITIES AND MASCULINITY

There are other moments in the film when the relational construction of Johnnie and Truman threatens to collapse—at least as a contrasting pair. In one of the film's most conspicuous scenes, they both return to the Murphys' flat to find Johnnie's (exclusively male) gang dancing to rock'n' roll music. Johnnie first watches, then joins in the group, abandoning himself to the music.

John Hill has observed that in Dearden's films, "music and dancing is inextricably bound up with the primal and dionysiac, consistently upsetting rational order and control" (1986, 74). It signifies danger (the lyrics repeat the phrases "play rough", "play tough") and in another scene, set at the Grand Hotel, the movie offsets rock'n' roll with classical music as a marker of middle- and upper-class gentility. As a part of a globalized mass culture, rock music threatens to undermine a specific British working-class culture. In the Murphys' flat, the music and dancing disrupt families (Johnnie's scared younger siblings are virtually imprisoned in the same room behind a table and a chair) and challenges authority—the dancing stops and the group confronts a stoic Sergeant Truman, demanding that he join in or else receive a beating. For David Buckingham, this moment, with the group "still twitching along to the music like a group of hypnotized zombies[, ...] dramatizes contemporary anxieties about the harmful influence of pop culture to a level of almost comic absurdity" (n.d., n.pag.). However, the music and dancing also render the portrayed bodies as processual rather than static and allow for alternative forms of (fleeting) associations: Even before they verbally invite Truman to join in, an intricate exchange of gazes with him presents more than just a challenge. For Buckingham, they "reflect a kind of homoerotic exhibitionism" on Johnnie's part (n.d., n.pag.). In any case, they serve to forge homosocial bonds between the young men, who become a tight group that subsumes Johnnie. In addition, the music not only features in this scene in the film, it also constitutes the soundtrack and is played over the opening and closing credits—it thus provides an invitation to the audience to join in as well. In terms of the film's gender politics, the gazes exchanged in the scene in conjunction with the music point towards a communal, shared masculinity which does not end at individual bodies. This is a notion worth exploring in more detail.

Academic concepts of masculinity which center on the materiality or performativity of the body and those that emphasize the subjectivizing functions of discourses often share a common focus: They typically consider clearly-delineated, single entities and identities—whether these are conceived as 'individuals' (with a degree of autonomy and agency), 'subjects' (with a constructivist focus on subjection), or otherwise. Some current scholarship, however, seeks to divest masculinity from notions of individual identity and consider it in a more contextual manner. This perspective is already implicit in notions of performativity based on Judith Butler and of masculinity based on Raewyn Connell (as Messerschmidt and Messner [2018] and others have pointed out). However, more recently such contextualizing has been extended by concepts that more fundamentally question clear subject-object distinctions, such as Gilles Deleuze's 'assemblage' (Hickey-Moody 2019) or Bruno Latour's 'associations' and actor-network-theory (2005; Späte 2019). In studies of classical antiquity and specifically the Renaissance (when modern notions of 'individual identity' were being fashioned in the first place), historians have identified understandings of 'masculinity' as something that can be spread across families and larger social units (rather than individual bodies and identities), or something attached to places or social units (such as households).[13] Most film studies, however, habitually focus on individual characters and actors in their analysis of masculinity, and many films (including, as we have seen, *Violent Playground*) foreground such readings themselves. Discussions of 'masculinity in crisis' in British films of the 1950s and 1960s also mostly focus on individuals—single (white) workers affected by social change. This is partly an effect of the films themselves: As Andrew Higson has argued, they recast the urban working-class 'mass' as a single "individual feeling subject, sincere and meaningful, defined in

---

[13] Cf. the special number on "History of Early Modern Masculinities" of the *European Review of History* (2015), specifically Joseph Campana's programmatic essay on "Distribution, Assemblage, Capacity: New Keywords for Masculinity?".

terms of personal (not economic) relations and 'universal' human values, and with a familiar psychic investment" (1996, 147).

But there is also a sense in which *Violent Playground* is transcending individual 'identities' in its negotiations of masculinity and foregrounds their implications for the larger social body. The relational construction of Truman and Johnnie (and, to a lesser extent, Johnnie and Alexander) already undermines notions of individual identity, and with it, simple models of character identification on the part of the audience (Greven [2009] makes a similar point about contemporary Hollywood masculinity in 'double-protagonist' films). The setting of the film in Liverpool, with its long shots of drab, industrial spaces, also evokes conventional tropes of a Northern, i.e., region-bound, "virile working-class masculinity" employed in a number of films in the 1950s and 1960s (Spicer 1999, 86)—a virile masculinity shared between the working-class youths in Johnnie's gang (by way of performance) and, to a lesser extent, even by Truman (by way of the star image of actor Stanley Baker). The notion of a 'male energy' circulating through the film (with its undertones of early-Victorian concepts of 'maleness'), discussed above, may point in a similar direction. Finally, in *Violent Playground*, masculinity is consistently conceptualized in terms of larger social units, ranging from the nuclear to the extended national family, and tied to the audience by means of the film's sentimental politics. And it also always involves the level of film *in consumption*. This is by no means a current insight: in 1958, juvenile delinquents on probation were bussed to cinemas to see *Violent Playground* as "a lesson on the futility of delinquency" (*The Sunday Express*, April 6, 1958, qtd. in Chibnall 1997, 150). Since it was considered a 'quality film' with a social objective, it was used as a didactic tool to interpellate a juvenile audience. What the audience saw, however, was arguably also the failure to establish a 'hegemonic masculinity' tied to a single character (Truman) and offset against competing masculinities. And while the movie excises Johnnie at the end (after some debate about whether his delinquency should be viewed as criminal or pathological, he is finally taken away in the police van rather than the ambulance), it cannot put him to rest—his brand of emotive, machine-gun wielding juvenile male hero will return in Lindsay Anderson's *If* (1968). Fundamentally, Johnnie and his gang represent a potential energy—an energy whose force depends on its relative position in a social field. Like an electric (stimulating, thrilling, dangerous) charge, it runs through British cinema of the 1950s and 1960s, producing specifically bright sparks when it comes into contact with ideological apparatuses such as schools. While Johnnie has been 'switched off' at the end of *Violent Playground*—almost literally, with his inert body slumped over a chair in the last several minutes of the film—this charge, as Mick (Malcolm McDowell) and his friends in *If* attest, remains very much alive and continues to animate the social body.

References

Althusser, Louis. "Ideology and Ideological State Apparatuses: Notes Towards an Investigation." *Lenin and Philosophy and Other Essays*. Translated by Ben Brewster, 121–173. London and New York: Monthly Review Press, 1971.

Ang, Ien. *Watching Dallas: Soap Opera and the Melodramatic Imagination*. London and New York: Methuen, 1985.

Belton, John. *Widescreen Cinema*. Cambridge, MA and London: Harvard UP, 1992.

Berlant, Lauren. *The Female Complaint: The Unfinished Business of Sentimentality in American Culture*. Durham and London: Duke UP, 2008.

Buckingham, David. "Troubling Teenagers: How Movies Constructed the Juvenile Delinquent in the 1950s." In *Growing Up Modern: Childhood, Youth and Popular Culture Since 1945*. https://davidbuckingham.net/growing-up-modern/. Accessed December 28, 2019.

Burton, Alan, and Tim O'Sullivan. *The Cinema of Basil Dearden and Michael Relph*. Edinburgh: Edinburgh UP, 2009.

Campana, Joseph. "Distribution, Assemblage, Capacity: New Keywords for Masculinity?" *European Review of History* 22, no. 4 (2015): 691–697.

Chandler, James. *An Archaeology of Sympathy: The Sentimental Mode in Literature and Cinema*. London and Chicago: U of Chicago P, 2013.

Chibnall, Steve. "The Teenage Trilogy: *The Blue Lamp*, *I Believe in You* and *Violent Playground*." In *Liberal Directions, Basil Dearden and Postwar British Film Culture*, edited by Alan Burton, Tim O'Sullivan, and Paul Wells, 137–153. Trowbridge, Wiltshire: Flicks Books, 1997.

Clay, Andrew. "Men, Women and Money: Masculinity in Crisis in the British Professional Crime Film 1946–1965." In *British Crime Cinema*, edited by Steve Chibnall and Robert Murphy, 51–65. London and New York: Routledge, 1999.

Deleuze, Gilles, and Félix Guattari. *A Thousand Plateaus: Capitalism and Schizophrenia*. Translated and foreword by Brian Massumi. London and New York: Bloomsbury Academic, 2019 [1987].

Dodd, Kathryn, and Philip Dodd. "Engendering the Nation: British Documentary Film, 1930–1939." In *Dissolving Views: Key Writings on British Cinema*, edited by Andrew Higson, 38–50. London: Cassell, 1996.

Feldmann, Doris, and Christian Krug. "Sentimentales, Heroisches und Männliches in filmischen Repräsentationen der britischen Arbeiterklassen, ca. 1960–2000." In *Interdisziplinäre Perspektiven auf soziale Ungleichheit*, edited by Victoria Gutsche, Ronja Holzinger, Larissa Pfaller, and Melissa Sarikaya. Erlangen: FAU Press, forthcoming.

Greven, David. "Contemporary Hollywood Masculinity and the Double-Protagonist Film." In *Cinema Journal* 48, no. 4 (2009): 22–43.

Harper, Sue, and Vincent Porter. "Moved to Tears: Weeping in the Cinema of Postwar Britain." *Screen* 37, no. 2 (1996): 152–173.

Hickey-Moody, Anna. *Deleuze and Masculinity*. Cham: Palgrave Macmillan/Springer, 2019.

Higson, Andrew. "Space, Place, Spectacle: Landscape and Townscape in the 'Kitchen Sink' Film." In *Dissolving Views: Key Writings on British Cinema*, 133–156. London: Cassell, 1996.

Hill, John. *Sex, Class and Realism: British Cinema 1956–1963*. London: British Film Institute, 1986.

Hoggart, Richard. *The Uses of Literacy: Aspects of Working-Class Life*. London: Chatto & Windus, 1957.

Howard, June. "What Is Sentimentality?" *American Literary History* 11, no. 1 (1999): 63–81.

Kappert, Ines. *Der Mann in der Krise: oder: Eine konservative Kapitalismuskritik in der Mainstreamkultur*. Bielefeld: transcript, 2008.

Kirkham, Pat, and Janet Thumim. "Men at Work: Dearden and Gender." In *Liberal Directions, Basil Dearden and Postwar British Film Culture*, edited by Alan Burton, Tim O'Sullivan, and Paul Wells, 89–107. Trowbridge, Wiltshire: Flicks Books, 1997.

Lacey, Stephen. *British Realist Theatre: The New Wave in Its Context 1956–1965*. London: Routledge, 1995.

Laing, Stuart. *Representations of Working-Class Life 1957–1964*. Houndmills: Macmillan, 1986.

Latour, Bruno. *Reassembling the Social: An Introduction to Actor-Network-Theory*. Oxford: Oxford UP, 2005.

Lowenstein, Adam. "'Direct Emotional Realism': The People's War, Classlessness, and Michael Powell's *Peeping Tom*." In *Shocking Representation: Historical Trauma, National Cinema, and the Modern Horror Film*, 55–82. New York: Columbia UP, 2005.

Luck, Johnny, with Ken Jones and His Orchestra. "Play Rough." Written by P. Roberts. Shellac Single. Fontana, 1958.

Messerschmidt, James W. *Hegemonic Masculinity: Formulation, Reformulation, and Amplification*. Lanham: Rowman & Littlefield, 2018.

Messerschmidt, James W., and Michael A. Messner. "Hegemonic, Nonhegemonic, and 'New' Masculinities." In *Gender Reckonings: New Social Theory and Research*, edited by James W. Messerschmidt, P. Y. Martin, M. A. Messner, and Raewyn Connell. New York: New York UP, 2018.

Modleski, Tania. *Feminism Without Women: Culture and Criticism in a "Postfeminist" Age*. New York and London: Routledge, 1991.

Monk, Claire. "Men in the 90s." In *British Cinema of the 90s*, edited by Robert Murphy, 156–166. London: British Film Institute, 1999.

Perkin, Harold. *The Rise of Professional Society: England Since 1880*. 2nd ed. London and New York: Routledge, 2002.

Späte, Katrin. "Akteur-Netzwerk-Theorie (ANT): Potenziale für die Geschlechterforschung." In *Handbuch Interdisziplinäre Geschlechterforschung*, edited by Beate Kortendiek, Birgit Riegraf, and Katja Sabisch, 379–388. Wiesbaden: Springer, 2019.

Spicer, Andrew. "The Emergence of the British Tough Guy: Stanley Baker, Masculinity and the Crime Thriller." In *British Crime Cinema*, edited by Steve Chibnall and Robert Murphy, 83–95. London: Routledge, 1999.

———. "Male Stars, Masculinity and British Cinema, 1945–60." In *The British Cinema Book*, edited by Robert Murphy, 93–100. 2nd ed. London: British Film Institute, 2001a.

———. *Typical Men: The Representation of Masculinity in Popular British Cinema*. London, New York: I.B. Tauris, 2001b.

Sussman, Herbert. *Victorian Masculinities: Manhood and Masculine Poetics in Early Victorian Literature and Art*. Cambridge: Cambridge UP, 1995.

Violent Playground. Dir. Basil Dearden, prod. Michael Relph, screenplay James Kennaway, photography Reginald Wyer, music Philip Green. 35mm, black and white, 106 mins. Rank Organisation, distributed by Carlton Film, 1958. DVD: ITV Studios Ltd, distributed by Strawberry Media, 2011.

von den Hoff, Ralf, et al. "Helden – Heroisierungen – Heroismen: Transformationen und Konjunkturen von der Antike bis zur Moderne. Konzeptionelle Ausgangspunkte des Sonderforschungsbereichs 948." *helden. heroes. héros* 1 (2013): 7–14.

Wells, Paul. "Sociability, Sentimentality and Sensibility: Basil Dearden and the English Comic Tradition." In *Liberal Directions, Basil Dearden and Postwar British Film Culture*, edited by Alan Burton, Tim O'Sullivan, and Paul Wells, 36–58. Trowbridge, Wiltshire: Flicks Books, 1997.

PART II

Fashionable Bodies

Refashioning the Male Body: Contemporary Media Representations of the Spornosexual and the Waif

Jay McCauley Bowstead

INTRODUCTION

In contemporary Western media discourse, men—whether models, celebrities, sportsmen, actors, or influencers—are subject to the desiring and emulating gaze of their audience both on- and offline. This article investigates the pleasures and possibilities that this corporeal turn has permitted men and the extent to which it has subjected the male body to an objectifying economy of looking. The following is an attempt to make sense of the increasing centrality of men's bodies to contemporary fashion, style, and (social) media. I shall argue that two sharply contrasting modes of fashionable physicality, namely the 'spornosexual' physique and

J. McCauley Bowstead (✉)
Cultural and Historical Studies, London College of Fashion, University of the Arts London, London, UK
e-mail: j.mccauleybowstead@fashion.arts.ac.uk

C. Dexl and S. Gerlsbeck (eds.), *The Male Body in Representation*, Palgrave Studies in (Re)Presenting Gender, https://doi.org/10.1007/978-3-030-88604-2_5

the slenderness of the high-fashion model, have predominated in recent years. By investigating the links between these two aesthetically divergent body styles I shall connect them to shifting practices of masculinity, changing patterns of work, and the impact of digital media.

From the idealized proportions of classical statuary to the verisimilitude of the renaissance crucifixion, and from the sinewy musculature of fascist propaganda to the 1980s underwear advert—throughout history, shifting notions of gender, class, race, and sexuality have inscribed themselves onto the male form. In tracing the cultural and ideological shifts that are shaping contemporary masculinities, it is essential to consider how male bodies are fashioned in dialogue with dominant sociocultural, economic, and technological discourses. Today, men's style, fitness, fashion, and grooming, and the advertising and imagery surrounding them, represent particularly important sites for the dissemination of new corporeal ideals. Over the past two decades, those image industries clustered around fashion have increasingly drawn attention to the male form. And as representations of men's bodies have proliferated, issues of identity, aesthetic labor (Warhurst and Nickson 2001), sexuality, and competing ideologies of gender have come to the fore.

For Spring/Summer 2020, the designer menswear catwalks at Loewe, Dior, Prada, and Wooyoungmi presented diverse collections encompassing disparate aesthetic cues, but the male models were remarkably homogenous. With few exceptions they were tall, very slender—often with pronounced cheekbones and clavicles, and narrow thighs—a corporeal aesthetic that is sometimes referred to as waifish or waif-like.[1]

At the same time that these adolescent waifs have come to dominate the menswear runway, a strikingly divergent form of fashionable masculine presentation has emerged in the context of social media, reality television, and in an expanding fitness culture. Characterized by a muscular, gym-honed, smooth, tanned, and often tattooed body, the spornosexual look is disseminated by vloggers, Instagram-users, celebrity sportsmen, and reality TV contestants. Its popularity points to the body as an increasingly crucial site for identity formation amongst aspirational young men while demonstrating the growing role of aesthetic labor in an economy of eroticized masculinities.

---

[1] In this way, the slender body is connected to (romanticised) notions of dispossession, displacement, and poverty, as in the phrase 'waif and stray'.

In this contribution I argue that these two approaches to styling the body act as sites of identity construction, agency, and pride, and, furthermore, that waif and spornosexual aesthetics enable some men to resist the values of orthodox masculinity while carving a space for themselves in the contemporary economy. At the same time, however, the pressure to commodify, brand, and aggressively reshape the self which is implicit in both body styles has the potential to profoundly alienate men from their bodies with psychologically and physically damaging consequences.

Spornosexual Masculinities

Away from the catwalk and high-end magazines, the fashions transmitted via celebrity culture, reality television, sport, and social media have played a significant role in popularizing a new body aesthetic. In a *Telegraph* article from 2014, the journalist Mark Simpson coined the portmanteau term 'spornosexual' to allude to the aspirational, artfully honed male bodies popular in sport and pornography and widely emulated by aspirational working-class young men in particular (though, of course, members of other socioeconomic groups also participate in spornosexual style while the designation 'working-class' is also not as straightforward as it might at first seem).

Drawing upon images of sportsmen, pornographic actors, and reality television contestants, spornosexual self-presentation coheres around a muscular gym-honed body, bleached teeth, a tanned, waxed torso, and, frequently, an abundance of tattoos (Fig. 5.1). Sports media has been particularly significant in disseminating shifting notions of the ideal male form since sports have long represented a privileged space of homosocial bonding, a space in which men are invited to gaze upon one another's bodies, in short, a site of idealized masculinities.[2] For these reasons, the very noticeable changes to the ways in which the sportsman's body is trained, nourished, and styled—particularly in football—has exerted a particular cultural impact. Figures such as Cristiano Ronaldo, Neymar da Silva Santos Júnior, and Toni Kroos with their rippling musculatures, tanned, waxed, and tattooed bodies, and artfully styled hair, demonstrate how new 'technologies of the self' that were once peripheral or taboo have gained a mass audience.

---

[2] In this regard, see also the article on idealized male bodies in boxing and wrestling magazines by Ana Stevenson and David Patrick in this volume.

Fig. 5.1 A muscular gymgoer sports a dragon tattoo (© Alamy Stock Photo, n.d.)

Michel Foucault has described how the body is formed by social and cultural processes that are simultaneously an expression of external influences and a mechanism through which subjectivities are created (1995; Foucault et al. 1988). In this way, the body is understood as deeply cultural not only at the level of representation, but also in its gestures, styling, and formation through various disciplinary regimes including exercise, dieting, and grooming. In his later work, however, Foucault becomes increasingly interested in how individuals care for, create, and 'improve' themselves through what he terms 'technologies of the self' (Foucault et al. 1988). By creatively and self-reflexively shaping their identities, individuals are able to assert some measure of control over their lives (not to escape existing power relations but to intervene in them) (Mitcheson 2012, 59–75). Using Foucault's terms of reference, one can consider the artfully honed spornosexual body as a means through which a, perhaps resistant, identity is articulated.

Contemporary fashion has also been significant in the development of a spornosexual aesthetic. The popular UK-based online fashion business Boohoo has, for instance, championed the spornosexual male body in much of its advertising and social media content. Targeting a youthful demographic, Boohoo Man offers inexpensive own-brand garments marketed using glossy imagery. The Boohoo Man look comprises a mixture of sporty references, unusual fabrications, including metallic and iridescent cloth, foil-blocking, tight muscle-fit t-shirts, fitted tracksuits, and tailored separates, often in a bold plaid. The label's aesthetic references contemporary streetwear, the recent 1990s revival, some of the more exuberant designer menswear labels such as Versace, Balmain, and Riccardo Tisci era Givenchy, as well as cult sportswear brands like Stone Island, Off-White, BAPE, and Palace.

As well as the items of apparel, the models who sport them are also noteworthy. On the Boohoo Man website and Instagram feed, an ethnically diverse cast of muscular, tattooed, and carefully coiffed young men pose against the background of glacial landscapes, on the bonnet of sports cars, in various gritty cityscapes, or by miscellaneous azure coastlines. In a promotional photograph from September 2019, a tanned, peroxide blond, white model with mirrored sunglasses stands in a multistory car park: he wears a utilitarian style waistcoat in an iridescent, shot fabric of petrol green and violet teamed with matching drawstring trousers. The model's shirtlessness, along with the low camera angle, draws the eye to his naked torso, inscribed from the neck down with complex interweaving tattoos, winged skulls, and tessellating geometries outlining his washboard stomach and defined pectorals. In a post from a month earlier, a very muscular black model wearing a durag is pictured against the backdrop of an US-American style garage—the windows of a convertible sports car are just visible within the tightly cropped composition. The model wears a pair of jogging bottoms with a repeat print featuring a gothic M. But at the center of the image, both literally and figuratively, is his smooth torso, highly developed trapezius, and deltoid muscles; the contours of his ample chest and flexing biceps, festooned in a tattooed fantasia—eagles' eyes and feathers peeping out amongst radiating patterns, curlicued lettering, foliage, and various abstract motifs.

The physical ideal celebrated in the marketing imagery of Boohoo Man and other online brands such as ASOS has emerged both in dialogue with contemporary social practice (including the mainstreaming of gym culture and increasing popularity of various forms of grooming) and in relation to mass-media representation. Indeed, the centrality of user-generated content to apps like Tumblr, YouTube, and Instagram has collapsed this distinction between representation and cultural practice, because generating images of the male body, for example gym selfies, has become an integral part of the contemporary social world. The fashion theorist Rosie Findlay has drawn attention to the ways in which a performance of intimacy has become a hallmark of social media and branded content online, as audiences and consumers are invited to form relationships of trust with labels and tastemakers. This dialectical relationship between proximity and aspiration, between the attainable and the out-of-reach is also part of the dynamic of self-branding that underpins the influencer economy, in which the body and the self are seen as infinitely perfectible and marketable commodities (Findlay 2019, 1–17).

Another key site of spornosexual imagery, as I have suggested, is the 'structured reality' television genre. Amongst these programs, ITV's *Love Island*—with its sunny location and scantily clad contestants—is particularly notable in the way that it foregrounds the muscular male body. The program invites male and female contestants to form couples and subjects them to a series of tests and tasks while the audience votes for its favorite pair. In this way, the show exposes its participants to an extraordinary level of scrutiny: not only are their artfully honed bodies almost permanently on display, but their ability to perform intimacy and emotion are also key elements of success or failure. In the first episode of the 2018 series, the female contestants were asked to select from a number of potential male matches based on their appearances—the men appearing dressed only in their swimming trunks. In this episode, many of the issues of spectatorship, sexuality, corporeality, and aesthetic labor, which seem to me to be central to understanding the spornosexual phenomenon, came to the fore as young people, who have worked hard to achieve a particular corporeal aesthetic, engage in a titillating performance as a form of self-branding.

In this sense, perhaps part of the fascination commanded by *Love Island* lies in the way that it schematizes a set of broader cultural and economic shifts. In the contemporary world of work, in intimate relationships, and in media representation, the male body is commodified as never before—through visually oriented, smart-phone enabled dating applications like Tinder and Grindr; in the influencer economy of Instagram, YouTube, and TikTok; and in sport, music, and fashion media. At the same time, the rise of the service and knowledge sectors, of freelance, portfolio careers, and the digital economy has further increased the premium on beauty for both men and women: indeed, the fast-growing fitness sector is entirely predicated on aesthetic and corporeal labor. Whether in retail, gym, or hospitality work, or in the more prestigious fields of consultancy, PR, and marketing, the management of appearance has become increasingly crucial. Not only are bodies publicly exhibited, surveyed, and judged in the context of *Love Island*, but the ability to be likable, relatable, and emotionally accessible is also highly prized. Perhaps then, the collective fascination that *Love Island* so palpably commands is due to the heightened but nevertheless familiar affective landscape it evokes. The need to be desired and liked and the necessity of performing one's identity in a way that seems both emotionally plausible and aspirational is an integral aspect of contemporary social media and the world of work. The aesthetic labor underpinning the participants' spectacular bodies—though not actually pictured—is all too obvious in their carefully crafted appearances, while the contestants' affective labor is the principal content of the show. Raymond Williams describes as 'structures of feeling' the ways in which inchoate social processes express themselves in lived experience, in the texture of everyday language, and crucially in art and culture (2015, 20–28): *Love Island* in its expression of these 'structures of feeling' captures and reflects back to us a set of tensions, social and economic shifts, and cultural preoccupations.

The spornosexual physique, I argue, arises out of a particular set of processes—the rise of 'flexible' precarious work; the integration of digital media and mobile technology into both labor and leisure, as well as the use of self-branding, the body, and the performance of sexuality to manage these impersonal forces. As labor in late capitalism has become less secure for many, freelancers and workers in the gig economy are required to constantly 'hustle' for work. Creating a 'brand' for oneself—a strong, recognizable, and aspirational image—is therefore crucial. Social media feed into this phenomenon because they are engines for generating informal networks of influence and patronage—what Pierre Bourdieu (1986) calls 'social capital'—that rely to an increasing extent on projecting an image of success. Indeed, Bourdieu's theories posit that 'capital' is simultaneously a cultural, economic, and *social* phenomenon in which cultural competencies (cultural capital) as well as social networks operate as mechanisms through which economic hierarchies are both maintained and potentially challenged. Those who adopt elements of the spornosexual look may not be doing so directly or consciously for reasons of economic self-interest (and in some traditionally bourgeois and petit-bourgeois fields of work such aesthetics would place individuals at a distinct disadvantage). But these looks and the techniques underpinning them with their focus on a certain kind of mastery of the body relate to a rhetoric of self-improvement, success, and control of one's destiny that are a direct response to the insecure conditions of our current economic system.

To this extent, the fitness coach, influencer, and author of best-selling diet books Joe Wicks represents an instructive example of the ways in which the 'aesthetic capital' of a handsome face and muscular body, combined with the 'emotional labor' involved in motivational social media posts, can facilitate the promise of social mobility. As he described in a BBC interview (Dillon 2019), despite his economically deprived background, his love of exercise led Wicks to study Sports Science at university—part of the expansion of higher education and vocational subjects instituted during the Blair years—and to join Instagram in 2014, where his distinctive mixture of recipes, selfies, motivational patter, and work-out videos garners him a large following.

With his lean, muscular physique, chestnut curls, high-energy estuary-accented delivery, and supportive advice, Wicks makes for a compelling rags-to-riches story. And while not everyone can replicate his immense success, for many men, a carefully honed body can act not only as a symbolic site of agency and control, but also as a marketable commodity. Traditionally bourgeois professions employ a variety of formal and informal mechanisms of exclusion, such as attending the 'right' kind of university, possessing the 'correct' vocabulary and accent—in other words—the assimilation of an upper-middle class habitus. Despite their precarity, the porous nature of social media and the service economy represent spaces of opportunity not yet colonized by the well-heeled: these emerging sectors are precisely those fields in which corporeal and aesthetic capital are most prized.

The dynamic and shifting nature of working-class masculinities in recent years has been addressed by a number of scholars who have argued that more inclusive and hybrid forms of gender expression are emerging.[3] Steven Roberts in his ethnographic study of working-class men in retail found that the experiences and attitudes of the participants he observed

---

[3] See, for instance, Roberts (2012), Ward (2017), or Stahl (2020).

diverged starkly from a set of (often stereotypical) assumptions about proletarian masculinity (2012, 671–686). Not only was retail work a source of identity and meaning in the lives of the men he interviewed, but the emotional labor of customer service, and, for some, aesthetic expertise, were key to respondents' job satisfaction. It is perhaps unsurprising that these shifts in attitudes and in the structure of the economy often manifest themselves at the level of the body.

As I have argued, spornosexual modes of embodiment are particularly, though not exclusively, associated with aspirational working-class young men: a manifestation of an increasingly aesthetically oriented service economy. In light of these contemporary shifts, however, the designation 'working class' needs to be further interrogated. Social class is a complex and fluid phenomenon and, as a result, deductive schemata for making sense of class are always methodologically fraught affairs. Nevertheless, work by Mike Savage et al. (2013) has emphasized how economic, job market, and cultural developments in recent decades have affected the class structures of the UK in particular. The second decade of the twenty-first century has seen the continued contraction of manufacturing, the further shrinking of the welfare state, and the rise of entrepreneurial, service oriented, and precarious employment in many Western economies. These developments have resulted both in the shrinking of the traditional working class as a segment of the population and in the emergence of new class groupings. Of course, these changes to the structures of social class have a much longer history. Nevertheless, the acceleration of recent shifts in class identity and the specific ways in which they manifest themselves socially and culturally bear further scrutiny. In their 2013 article "A New Model of Social Class?" Savage et al. identify three new demographics sitting outside conventional classificatory schemata:

(a) The group of new affluent workers—"whose members have not benefitted from conventional routes through education to middle-class positions, but have nonetheless achieved relatively secure economic positions and are also relatively socially and culturally engaged" (237–239);

(b) The emergent service workers—who possess "a modest household income of £21k [but have] a high degree of cultural engagement in youthful musical, sporting and internet activities" (240). This is a youthful class segment comprising a high proportion of ethnic minorities, they are marginal in terms of economic capital, but with high levels of cultural capital (240);

(c) The precariat—who are "economically the poorest class, with a household income of only £8k [...]. The scores for both high-brow and emerging cultural capital are the lowest and second lowest, respectively [...]. This is clearly the most deprived of the classes that we have identified, on all measures" (243).

Spornosexuality, in this way, can be understood as an expression of corporeal and aesthetic capital—a strategy for securing a position within the ranks of the 'emergent service workers' or 'new affluent workers' and avoiding the precariat.[4]

Despite these shifts, the classed nature of spornosexuality has not until recently received significant academic attention (Hakim 2021, 57–79). In 2014, the British journalist Clive Martin wrote a piece for the online magazine *Vice*—a sort of irreverent ethnography resulting out of his visits to nightclubs up and down the UK—explaining, in his words "How Sad Young Douchebags Took Over Modern Britain". The article focuses, in particular, on the bodies and appearances of the 'emergent service worker' young men Martin encountered. And while his tone was intended to be humorous, the 'inauthenticity' of spornosexual modes of self-presentation (waxed chests, Maori tattoos, and inflated biceps) were clearly a source of anxiety for the journalist. Although Martin attempts to address issues of class, he does so in a manner that reproduces a set of problematic stereotypes: accusations of 'excess' and 'tastelessness' represent familiar critiques of demotic cultural expression:

> You can't help but get the impression that there's very little weight, bravery or even violence lying below those nutritionally enlarged 'ceps. Really tough guys have sinew on their bodies, scabs on their face and hate in their hearts; the modern British douchebag just has balloon animal muscles and a waxed chest. They're pampered, meek behemoths who look good on the beach but can't fight for shit. (2014, n. pag.)

---

[4] In this sense, the terms 'working class' and 'middle class' are increasingly problematic simplifications: the élite and super-élite have pulled away from other segments of the population becoming ever more wealthy, while, on the other hand, younger members of the professional classes are increasingly insecure (unable to benefit from the expansion of professional jobs enjoyed by the baby-boomer generation).

At the same time, Martin reifies an imagined 'authentic' working-class masculinity of yore—a yore located in the industrial communities of the late nineteenth and early twentieth century and in the military. This fetishization of a misremembered past is one that celebrates the instrumentalization and brutalization of the soldier body, and thankless, repetitive, backbreaking labor—it is one that sees violence perpetrated by and against men as the ultimate metric of masculinity.

In some senses, the spornosexual male body relates to the semantics of strength and dominance that were described by Raewyn Connell and others during the 1980s as key components of the idealized and culturally sanctioned 'hegemonic' form of masculinity (1987). But in other ways, as Clive Martin's trenchant critique suggests, spornosexuals diverge from the dominant norms of twentieth-century Western masculinity. The male bodies disseminated via Boohoo's marketing machine, reality television, and the gym selfies of Instagram are notable for their muscularity, but rather than seeking to 'naturalize' this muscularity, to wrap it in a sporting or laboring alibi, representations of the male body today prioritize the aesthetics of muscularity while detaching them (almost totally) from their prior semiotic connection to manual work.[5]

Rather than aiming for a look that is 'natural', artless, or unassuming, spornosexual style revels in its explicit constructedness: critiques of this corporeal aesthetic in journalism and popular discourse often center upon its lack of 'authenticity'. There is a sense that by drawing attention to the constructed nature of orthodox[6] masculinity, spornosexuals threaten its apparent naturalness and disrupt the economy of gendered looking (in which the male body is the unmarked category rather than the object of the desiring gaze).[7] While the body remains a site of labor, for the

---

[5] This process of delinking may have begun in the 1980s with the increasing eroticisation of the athletic male physique in popular culture (Triggs 1992); nevertheless, the representations produced by the likes of Herb Ritts and Bruce Webber drew upon the iconography of sportsmen, laborers, and (neo-)classical statuary. This use of an established canon of masculine iconography perhaps neutralized some of the subversiveness implicit to the commodification of the male form.

[6] Eric Anderson uses the term "orthodox" rather than hegemonic masculinity: in doing so, he suggests that formerly dominant expressions of masculinity are no longer unambiguously hegemonic and that, amongst certain demographics, other more inclusive and diverse forms of gender expression have become acceptable for men (2009, 30–31).

[7] Of course, there is a long history of eroticized representations of masculinity from antiquity to the present day, and images of the male body have been much discussed

spornosexual this is primarily aesthetic labor. Not only is the physique re-formed through the lifting of weights and the repetition of strenuous exercises, but also through teeth whitening, veneers, spray tans, tattooing, and waxing (Fig. 5.1). This dismissal of a sporting or proletarian alibi for muscularity represents a significant shift away from the symbols of twentieth-century orthodox masculinity—and an embrace of a more explicitly 'performative' model of gender (Butler 1990).[8] And while these forms of self-fashioning point to economic and social shifts, they also enable a reading of the spornosexual body, via Eve Kosofsky Sedgwick, as a potential intervention in social norms, a promotion of semantic innovation, and a step, in Sedgwick's understanding, towards an ameliorative perspective (2003, 147). In this sense, these mediatized, perfected male bodies point to significant changes in gender practice in the late twentieth and early twenty-first centuries.

THE HIGH-FASHION WAIF

As I have suggested, high fashion media representations of the male body have popularized a corporeal ideal very different from the spornosexual physique. But in this context too, shifting discourses around masculinity as well as aesthetic and embodied labor come to the fore. For example, for the Spring/Summer 2020 Céline menswear collection, designer Hedi Slimane sent extremely thin models down the runway. With their pale white skin and protruding Adam's apples, the boys on the Céline catwalk represented the antithesis of the gym-honed pneumatic look favored by Boohoo Men.

While Slimane is noteworthy for the extreme (and sometimes problematic) thinness of the young men who walk for him, designer Ludovic de Saint Sernin has instead garnered attention because of the way that his

---

in relation to 1980s advertising (Triggs 1992; Mort 1996, 109–111; Nixon 1996, 117–120). However, there is something qualitatively different from these 1980s representations of the male body in the mass nature of contemporary spornosexual style. Here, I would argue, the gaze has been internalized on a much grander scale.

[8] For the seminal queer theorist Judith Butler categories of sex and gender—male and female, men and women—are created through discourses, representations, and behavior. In this way, gender is something that you *do* rather than something you *are* intrinsically: Butler describes gender as 'performative' to allude to the ways in which it is produced through habitual, naturalized actions, modes of dress, ways of moving the body, speaking, and so on (1990).

designs expose the slim physique of his models (Fig. 5.2a and b). The casting for the designer's Spring/Summer 2020 catwalk favored youths with slim waists, attenuated limbs, slightly hollow thighs, and smooth, hairless, pale or dark brown skin. In an opening look, a model progressed down the runway clad in a coat and trousers of sheer white voile—his transparent garments barely veiling his slender body. Subsequent outfits featured see-through panels and cut-outs; and then a skin-tight off-the-shoulder top appeared drawing attention to the pronounced collar-bones, shoulder blades, and slender arms of the young man who wore it. As the collection progressed, abbreviated satin shorts were paired with open shirts, and leather coats worn over underpants (Prigent 2019). Saint Sern-in's queered, eroticized, and fetishistic vision for contemporary menswear certainly possessed an audacious elegance, but the runway presentation

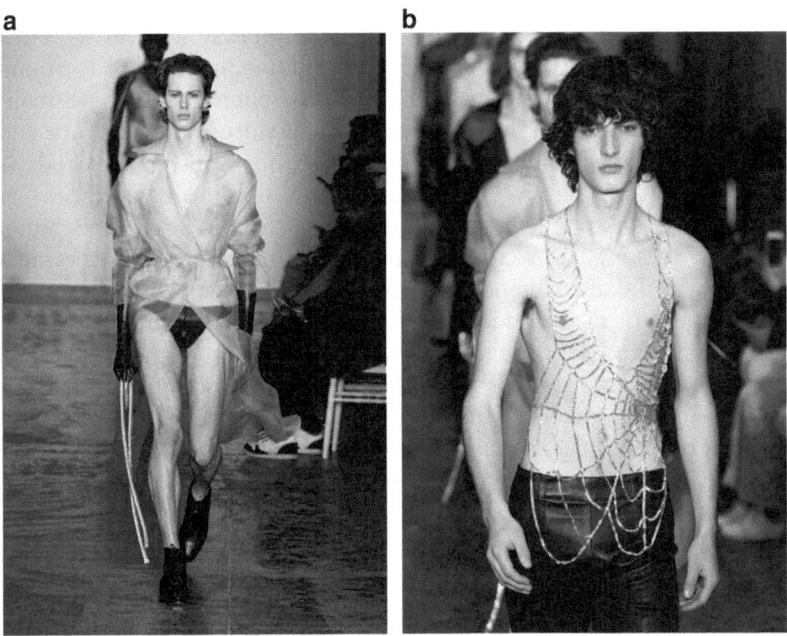

Fig. 5.2 a and b; A model walks for Ludovic de Saint Sernin Fall 2020 Runway (© Alamy Stock Photo 2020)

might have been more successful if his models had been more comfortable and confident in their skimpy garments (some were visibly attempting to cover their slim bodies).

Saint Sernin's models, despite looking very different to the participants in *Love Island*, nevertheless perform a similarly sexualized form of corporeal labor—one that caters to the spectacular nature of the contemporary digital context. The media practices which have developed over the past two decades—online video content, image-based search functions, as well as image sharing applications like Instagram, Pinterest, and Tumblr—have created the conditions for a proliferation of representations of the male body. As I have suggested, the spornosexual ideal is disseminated both through 'traditional' mass-media channels like television and men's magazines and through content sharing applications. Despite catering to a very different demographic, the high-fashion waif aesthetic has similarly reproduced itself through a mixture of digital and analogue channels. Indeed, the contemporary runway show exists much more as a mediatized digital artefact than as a unique temporally bound event. Catwalk images and 'behind the scenes' photographs are disseminated via Instagram, full shows are uploaded as videos onto YouTube and are poured over by commentators in video reviews. In this way, today's catwalk shows are conceived of first and foremost as media spectacles—as demonstrated by the increasing attention paid to *mise-en-scène*, lighting, and stage dressing. As sociologist and fashion theorist Agnès Rocamora has claimed, the digital context has contributed to the hybridization and 'remediation' of media and commercial forms with websites borrowing the visual language of magazines, while catwalk shows use filmic and theatrical conventions (2019, 99–122). In terms of shifting attitudes to the fashionable male body, the significance of these new forms of digital media lies in the wide dissemination of a corporeal ideal that might otherwise have been confined to consumers of and specialists in men's designer *prêt-à-porter*.[9]

---

[9] Another significant vehicle for the dissemination of both the svelte male ideal and designer fashions are Korean K-Pop bands such as EXO and BTS as well as Korean solo-artists like G-Dragon. These musicians are notable not only for the music they produce, but also for their distinctive, fashionable appearances characterized by sumptuous garments, slender frames, clear 'glass skin' complexions, and bleached or brightly colored hairdos.

The centrality of a slim body to contemporary high fashion is reflected not only on the runway and in the music video, but also, of course, in fashion photography.[10] For example, in a spring 2020 special issue of *Hero* magazine, a curiously collaged photo-shoot entitled "Lost Romance" by Toyin Ibidapo and Davey Sutton appears. The cool-toned, smokey, faded photographs feature two young models, Peter Dupont and Lukas Gomann, often in states of undress. These montaged images—taped down, splattered with paint, and layered one atop the other—form a kind of wistful palimpsest. In one set of photographs, Dupont is pictured seated on a bed of crumpled foliage in the hall of an institutional building. Dressed only in his underpants and socks, he tucks his knees to his chest, gazing pensively at the viewer, or smiling while holding a camera—his slender, lightly-muscled body, tousled hair, and impish features are captured over a series of images. In another sequence of photographs Gomann's slender torso, slim waist, faintly outlined abdominal muscles, and long limbs are pictured as he wears a Dior messenger bag strapped diagonally across his bare chest. Today, fashion photographs like these not only exist between the glossy pages of the magazine but are also circulated online, especially via the models' own Instagram accounts.

I have argued that the somewhat forlorn, skinny male models of contemporary fashion photography (often placed in scenarios suggesting desolation, such as abandoned buildings, deserted backwoods, and grimy bedsits, and photographed in prone or unguarded poses) symbolize precisely those aspects of human experience, particularly vulnerability and passivity, that are most taboo within orthodox masculinity (McCauley Bowstead 2018, 102). In this way, these melancholic, slender figures reflect Julia Kristeva's notion of abjection (1982, 61), where that which is abased, cast off, or rejected—particularly qualities coded feminine or maternal—also hold the greatest transgressive potential. While a lithe physique is clearly an important aspect of the representations I have analyzed, the emotional content of the scenarios discussed is also intriguing: a sense of inchoate yearning and melancholia common to the genre. By emphasizing the emotional and physical vulnerability of their male subjects, these representations contest the dominant symbolic order by creating liminal spaces in which the normative codes of masculinity and femininity are blurred; beneath their taut, artfully composed surfaces the

---

[10] For example in such magazines as *Hero, Vogues Hommes, Arena Homme+, Varón,* and *Another Man.*

power of these images lies in the threat of chaos and abjection that they conjure up. In this sense both the physical fragility evoked within this new fashionable ideal and its ambiguous affective register relate to the contestation of the stoicism, the emotional and physical invulnerability that characterized the ideal of hegemonic masculinity.

The prominence of these waifish male bodies in contemporary visual culture and fashion seems to point to an appetite for a greater plurality of masculine archetypes, and, in particular, for male vulnerability to be acknowledged. In this way, from a reparative perspective, such representations can be understood to make space for a greater variety of masculine subjectivities. At the same time, however, the objectifying and fetishistic gaze that these representations potentially invite must also be acknowledged. One has to ask how ethical it is to present adolescent-looking models in suggestive garments and poses; while some models— for example those walking Slimane's catwalks in recent years—appear thin in a manner very few people are able to sustain healthily.[11]

The popularity of the slender male model emerges out of a longer history and set of discourses. In the late 1990s and early 2000s, designers such as Raf Simons and Hedi Slimane employed svelte and youthful models to conjure up an ambiguous, liminal aesthetic that seemed to speak of a renegotiation of gender identities in the twenty-first century. As I have argued elsewhere (McCauley Bowstead 2012, 2015, 2018), by rejecting the built, muscular physique that had dominated the 1980s and 1990s, designers like Simons and Slimane (and photographers such as David Simms, Collier Shore, and Willy Vanderperre) were attempting to advance a vision of masculinity outside of hegemonic norms—one that made space for vulnerability and that appeared less 'artificial' and constructed. The unusual casting of Slimane's and Simons's shows was understood both by commentators and by the designers themselves as an intervention in the language of masculinity (Spindler 1997, 14; Porter 2001, 62). As Slimane himself stated "[t]here is a psychology to the masculine: we're told don't touch it; it's ritual, sacred, taboo. It's difficult but I'm making headway, I'm trying to find a new approach" (qtd. in Cabasset 2001, 70).

---

[11] Moreover, research into the working conditions of male models (Fowler et al. 2016) has underlined the real as well as the symbolic vulnerability of models who are subject to arbitrary demands to remold their bodies, lose weight, or gain muscle, who lack agency within the creative process, and whose employment is extremely insecure.

At the moment in which this intervention was first made, in the late 1990s and early 2000s, it did indeed herald a pluralization of masculine archetypes that spoke to broader attitudinal shifts surrounding gender and sexuality. The body-conscious, close-fitting, and gently draping garments proposed by designers like Slimane at the turn of the millennium alluded to an alternative conception of gender: supple soft leathers, jerseys, satins, and the lithe physiques of the models signified an expanded notion of masculinity sitting outside of hegemonic norms characterized by strength, invulnerability, and muscularity. This renunciation of hegemonic masculinity in the world of men's fashion connected to a broader cultural shift in the early years of the new millennium. Sociologist Eric Anderson (2009)—conducting ethnographic fieldwork amongst British and US men between 1999 and 2004—found striking, unexpected changes taking place, as young men increasingly embraced identities that were more affectionate, more diverse, less delimited by sexism and homophobia, and in which behaviors historically categorized as feminine were given license.

Over the past two decades, this slender, boyish physique has become dominant on the men's designer ready-to-wear catwalk and in much fashion photography, and I have been critical of the sometimes objectifying gaze that men's fashion media trains upon its young models (McCauley Bowstead 2018, 107–110). In some of the representations I have reviewed, the active/passive binary described by Laura Mulvey in her famous essay "Visual Pleasure and Narrative Cinema" (1985) is reproduced, but with a male (rather than female) figure as the object of the voyeuristic, scopophilic gaze. In this way the unequal distribution of power between the bearer and recipient of the gaze remains—as does the fungibility, inertness, and denial of subjectivity implicit in these depictions (Nussbaum 1995, 257)—though the precise nature of the gender dynamics has shifted. Of course, men's fashion has as much right to explore notions of sexuality and the body as any other creative form (indeed, corporeal and sensual concerns are central to fashion practice) but it is incumbent upon designers, casting agents, stylists, and photographers to think more critically about the implications of the representations they produce.

In their explorations of fabrication, cut, silhouette, and gesture menswear practitioners propose new ways of inhabiting a male body and alternative notions of masculinity, sexuality, and desirability less reliant on dominance, strength, and invulnerability. And while, for much of the past decade, designer men's fashion has tended to celebrate one fairly tightly defined body type, new developments in fashion media are beginning to challenge this single prevailing corporeal ideal.

As I have shown, the popularity of the slender male model in high fashion relates to an existing set of symbols associated with edgy youth culture and an unorthodox model of masculinity: over the past two decades, this physique has become central to the aesthetics of luxury men's fashion. In this way, the svelte ideal not only connects to shifting and contested attitudes to gender, but also to cultural and socioeconomic status. Contemporary malnutrition and poverty, especially in industrialized economies, often manifest themselves in both a deficit of nutrients and in a surfeit of calories—calorie dense, industrially produced foodstuffs being the cheapest, most heavily marketed, and most immediately available to those who are poor in time and money. These tendencies have coincided with increasing levels of income inequality (as well as spatial and transport inequalities), all of which have contributed to escalating rates of 'obesity'.[12] In contrast, the slender figure has become aspirational as slimness, vegetable-based diets, and an engagement in—often expensive—'wellness' practices have become associated with high socioeconomic status. In this way, the thin body has become part of a nexus of conspicuous consumption, 'leisure class'[13] signifiers, and a site of middle-class aspiration (Veblen 1994, 108–111). Like the spornosexual physique, proliferating representations of the waif body in fashion and popular culture relate to the increasing significance of aesthetic labor to men's lives, as menswear and grooming markets have grown rapidly over the course of the last two decades.[14] This expansion in images of the male form in popular culture has provided spaces in which competing notions of masculinity could be played out: sites of meaning and aspiration that have enabled young men in particular to construct forms of identity at

---

[12] Campaigners for 'fat equality' might question the use of the word 'obesity' with its tendency to pathologize fat bodies and shame 'fat' people (though the term remains widespread in medical and popular discourse).

[13] In *The Theory of the Leisure Class*, Thorstein Veblen describes how wealth is expressed through engagement in conspicuously non-productive 'leisure' activities. Rituals of sport and leisure are important to the moneyed classes, argues Veblen, because they act to exclude those without the time and capital to participate, and those who are ignorant of the 'correct' forms of dress and etiquette (knowledge which again takes time to accrue).

[14] See for instance Russell (2016), Apparel Online (2017), and Technavio (2020).

odds with orthodox systems of gender. While this expansion in men's fashion imagery has opened up discourses of masculinity, its imbrication in the logic of late capitalism (with its rhetoric of self-branding, self-improvement, flexibility, and agility) has simultaneously reinforced the conditions of exploitation and precarity.

New Tendencies in Fashioning the Male Body

This article has focused on the way in which two aesthetically differentiated body styles have become fashionable in recent decades. As I have suggested, the proliferation of images of the male body in popular culture, and (social) media forms part of a broader set of processes: changes to the economy and work, along with new media technologies and shifting attitudes to gender, have contributed to the popularity of both sportnosexual and high-fashion waif representations. Angela McRobbie has argued that in the arts sector, notions of creativity, identity, and agency have tended to erode the boundaries between work and leisure: creative industries, she suggests, have anticipated many of the broader changes which we now see in the economy as a whole (2014, 19). In this way, fashion and social media exemplify a set of socioeconomic processes characteristic of twenty-first century capitalism in which ideas of self-branding and self-fulfillment are frequently allied to precarious working conditions, low pay, and informal networks of influence (McRobbie 2014; Mensitieri 2018). The necessity of communicating a strong visual brand and of demonstrating cultural capital—which have long been central to creative and artistic *milieux*—are now seen much more broadly across a variety of sectors. These wider economic tendencies have brought about an increasing emphasis on the visual. And, as I have argued, both the svelte silhouette of the high-fashion model and the belabored appearance of the sportnosexual represent crucial sites of corporeal capital. The work involved in maintaining these physiques—dieting, exercise, skin regimes, hair-removal, and other techniques of the body—produces symbolic value. But more than this, for models, fitness coaches, beauty and lifestyle vloggers, celebrities, and influencers, the body is a major site of economic capital—it is their livelihood. This 'body work' can be conceptualized as manual labor for the post-industrial age: labor that, despite its drawbacks, is sometimes more attractive than its alternatives (like the unglamorous exploitation of the Amazon warehouse). At the same time, changing attitudes to gender—and the tolerance of a greater plurality of masculinities—have rendered corporeal practices that would once have been taboo, peripheral, or subcultural much more mainstream, while new ideas about the ideal male body have proliferated in the highly visual, hyper-networked new media context.

The fashionable body styles discussed in this article are by no means entirely unproblematic: they encourage some adherents to adopt unhealthy and psychologically damaging regimens (including stimulant use, obsessive exercise, restrictive or unbalanced diets, and the abuse of anabolic steroids). More generally, seeing oneself as a 'brand' or a 'product' to be sold represents an instrumentalized form of self-esteem in which one's value as a person is at the mercy of the market. It would be too simple, however, to perceive participation in mediatized body styles either as a form of false consciousness or as an uncritical internalization of 'neoliberal' values. The cultural discourses producing both spornosexual and waif-like representations are much more diverse, complex, and polysemic than this reading would allow. As Judith Butler has claimed, "to operate within the matrix of power is not the same as to replicate uncritically relations of domination" (1990, 40). This is to say that, while contemporary regimes of representation, attention, and symbolic capital may reproduce unrealistic self-commodifying ideals, individuals and groups are nevertheless able to use the tools and vocabularies of fashion and the media to find spaces of agency and even resistance to orthodox systems of gender. Pointing out the pleasures and strategies of resistance that individuals and groups find in culture implies subscribing to what Eve Kosofsky Sedgwick has termed a 'reparative reading' of the world. And while looking at the fashionable male body through a reparative lens in these terms runs the risk of seeming naïve, it also makes space for hope. Moreover, the permission to attend to, to care for, and to value one's own body which can be found within these male corporeal styles (albeit in rather circumscribed ways) should not be underestimated.

Beyond that, the spornosexual look discussed in the earlier part of this article not only contests aspects of normative masculinity but also acts to resist negative stereotypes projected onto the bodies of working-class young men in a defiantly showy display of corporeal pride and self-confidence. Spornosexual and waif-like body styles have emerged out of the processes of late capitalism and contemporary discourses of masculinity, but they also contain within them the potential for symbolic resistance to dominant norms and ideologies.

In recent years, there have been signs that the two stylistically bifurcated corporeal fashions I have explored may be beginning to lose their
dominance as a greater diversity of male bodies appear in social media
and in the fashion and lifestyle press. Consumers, designers, stylists,
photographers, and especially influencers have increasingly questioned the
exclusion of older people, fat people, disabled people, trans people, and
those identifying outside of the gender binary from fashionable representation: in this way discourses surrounding inclusivity have come to the
fore (Ripley 2019; Sadkowska 2020, 67–88).

The space in which alternative representations of the male body
have exerted the greatest impact recently has undoubtedly been in the
digital context in which self-authored user-generated content can reach
the widest audience. Through the figure of the influencer—the cultural
intermediary par excellence of this present historical moment—issues of
authenticity and thus of relatability have become increasingly crucial. The
bearded 'plus-size' influencer Marcus Neil aka #Marquimode—whose
colorful, body-conscious, exuberant outfits have garnered attention on
Instagram—is indicative of the contemporary shift towards body diversity in fashion and social media. His jaunty, smiling self-portraits show
a variety of fashionable looks (sheer fabrics, dungarees, and pastel-hues)
while also celebrating a chubby, ample physique hitherto excluded from
fashionable representation. Similarly, the one-armed actor, dancer, and
model Luc Bruyère with his edgy, erotic Instagram selfies demonstrates
a hunger for more diverse and relatable images of male fashionability.[15]
The fact that both of these influencers have been featured in magazine
editorials and catwalk shows underlines the ways in which the fashion
industry and fashion media proper are beginning to change. Ostensibly,
these new, more inclusive fashionable representations may appear the
antithesis of the spornosexual and waif-like body styles I have so far
reviewed, but, on the contrary, I would argue that they have emerged out
of a similar set of sociocultural, economic, and technological processes.
While the slender figure of the high-fashion model may resist some of the

---

[15] These shifts were discussed in a co-authored paper presented in 2019: McCauley
Bowstead, Jay, and Ben Barry. "Influential Images: Diversifying the Male Body in Fashionable Representation." *Fashion Costume & Visual Cultures Conference*. Roubaix: Université
de Lille (Roubaix), July 9–11, 2019.

norms of normative, orthodox masculinity, and while the spornosexual body may challenge bourgeois taste, achieving a more inclusive model of masculinity (Anderson 2009) requires rethinking and rejecting narrow and prescriptive corporeal ideals by embracing variety and diversity.

References

Anderson Eric (2009) Inclusive Masculinity. Routledge, New York

Apparel Resources. *Global Menswear Market Continues to Grow; Brands Launch Standalone Stores*. Apparel Online Report, 2017 edition.

Bourdieu Pierre (1986) The Forms of Capital. In: Richardson JG (ed) Handbook of Theory and Research for the Sociology of Education. Greenwood Press, New York, pp 241–258

Butler Judith (1990) Gender Trouble. Routledge, New York

Cabasset, Patrick. "Portrait: Hedi Slimane: Le Petit Prince New-Look De Dior Homme." *L'Officiel de la Couture et de la Mode de Paris* (2001): 66–71.

Connell, R. W. *Gender and Power: Society, the Person and Sexual Politics*. Palo Alto: U of California P, 1987.

Dillon, Sheila. "Joe Wicks: A Life Through Food." Radio programme. *The Food Programme*. BBC Radio 4. October 13, 2019. https://www.bbc.co.uk/pro grammes/m00099wz. Accessed May 25, 2021.

Findlay Rosie (2019) 'Trust Us, We're You': Aspirational Realness in the Digital Communication of Contemporary Fashion and Beauty Brands. Communication, Culture and Critique 12(4):553–569

Foucault, Michel. *Discipline and Punish*. New York: Vintage Books, 1995 [1975].

Foucault, Michel, Luther H. Martin, Huck Gutman, and Patrick H. Hutton. *Technologies of the Self*. Amherst: U of Massachusetts P, 1988.

Fowler, Jie G., Rongwei Chu, James W. Gentry, and Himadri Roy Chaudhuri. "Vulnerability or Masculinity: Examining 'Aesthetic Labor' from Male Fashion Models' Perspective." *Journal of Global Fashion Marketing* 7, no. 4 (2016): 252–265.

Hakim Jamie (2021) Work That Body: Male Bodies in Digital Culture. Rowman & Littlefield, London and New York

Kristeva, Julia. *Powers of Horror: An Essay on Abjection*. Translated by Leon S. Roudiez. New York: Columbia UP, 1982.

Martin, Clive. "How Sad Young Douchebags Took Over Modern Britain." *VICE* (2014): n. pag. http://www.vice.com/en_uk/read/anatomy-of-a-new-mod ern-douchebag. Accessed March 18, 2014.

McCauley Bowstead, Jay. "Raf Simons: From Genk to Dior." Master's thesis. London: Royal College of Art, 2012.

———. "Hedi Slimane and the Reinvention of Menswear." *Critical Studies in Men's Fashion* 2, no. 1 (2015): 23–42.

———. *Menswear Revolution: The Transformation of Contemporary Men's Fashion.* London: Bloomsbury, 2018.

McRobbie Angela (2014) Be Creative: Making a Living in the New Culture Industries. Polity Press, Cambridge

Mensitieri Giulia (2018) 'Le Plus Beau Métier du Monde': Dans les Coulisses de l'Industrie de la Mode. Éditions La Découverte, Paris

Mitcheson Katrina (2012) Foucault's Technologies of the Self: Between Control and Creativity. J Br Soc Phenomenol 43(1):59–75

Mort Frank (1996) Cultures of Consumption: Masculinities and Social Space in Late Twentieth-Century Britain, 1st edn. Routledge, London

Mulvey, Laura. "Visual Pleasure and Narrative Cinema." In *Film Theory and Criticism: Introductory Readings*, edited by Gerald Mast and Marshall Cohen, 803–816. 2nd ed. New York: Oxford UP, 1985 [1975].

Nixon Sean (1996) Hard Looks: Masculinities, Spectatorship and Contemporary Consumption. St. Martin's Press, New York

Nussbaum Martha C (1995) Objectification. Philosophy and Public Affairs 24(4):249–291

Porter, Charlie. "Body Politic." *The Guardian*, June 1, 2001. https://www.the guardian.com/lifeandstyle/2001/jun/30/fashion1. Accessed May 25, 2021.

Prigent, Loic. "Ludovic de Saint Sernin's First Show." *YouTube*. Video File. July 21, 2019. https://www.youtube.com/watch?v=KN-Ny7MjRXg. Accessed May 25, 2021.

Ripley, Georgina. *Body Beautiful: Diversity on the Catwalk*. Edinburgh: National Museum of Scotland, 2019.

Roberts Steven (2012) Boys will be Boys … Won't they? Change and Continuities in Contemporary Young Working-Class Masculinities. Sociology 47(4):671–686

Rocamora Agnès (2019) Mediatization and Digital Retail. In: Geczy Adam, Karaminas Vicki (eds) The End of Fashion: Clothing and Dress in the Age of Globalization. Bloomsbury Visual Arts, London, pp 99–122

Russell, Michelle. "UK Menswear Market Grows Faster Than Women's in 2016." *Just-Style Global News* (2016): n. pag. https://www.just-style.com/news/uk-menswear-market-grows-faster-than-womens-in-2016. Accessed April 5, 2020.

Sadkowska, Ania. "Pioneering, Nonconforming, and Rematerializing: Crafting an Understanding of Older Men's Experiences of Fashion Through Their Personal Archives." In *Crafting Anatomies*, edited by Amanda Briggs-Goode, Katherine Townsend, and Rhian Solomon, 67–88. London: Bloomsbury, 2020.

Savage, Mike, Fiona Devine, Niall Cunningham, Mark Taylor, Yaojun Li, Johs Hjellbrekke, Brigitte Le Roux, Sam Friedman, and Andrew Miles. "A New Model of Social Class? Findings from the BBC's Great British Class Survey Experiment." *Sociology* 47, no. 2 (2013): 219–250.

Sedgwick, Eve Kosofsky. "Paranoid Reading and Reparative Reading; or, You're so Paranoid, You Probably Think This Introduction Is about You." In *Touching Feeling: Affect, Pedagogy, Performativity*, edited by Michèle Aina Barale, Jonathan Goldberg, Michael Moon, and Eve Kosofsky Sedgwick, 123–151. Durham: Duke UP, 2003.

Simpson, Mark. "The Metrosexual Is Dead. Long Live the 'Spornosexual'." *Telegraph*, June 10, 2014. http://www.telegraph.co.uk/men/fashion-and-style/10881682/The-metrosexual-is-dead.-Long-live-the-spornosexual.html. Accessed February 22, 2017.

Spindler, Amy M. "Strength in Diversity at Men's Shows." *The New York Times (Late Edition)*, July 8, 1997. https://www.nytimes.com/1997/07/08/style/strength-in-diversity-at-men-s-shows.html. Accessed May 25, 2021.

Stahl Garth (2020) 'My Little Beautiful Mess': A Longitudinal Study of Working-Class Masculinity in Transition. NORMA 15(2):1–17

Technavio. *Evolving Menswear Fashion to Boost Growth: Menswear Market 2020–2024.* Report, 2020 edition.

Triggs, Teal. "Framing Masculinity: Herb Ritts, Bruce Weber and the Body Perfect." In *Chic Thrills*, edited by Juliet Ash and Elizabeth Wilson, 25–29. 1st ed. London: Pandora, 1992.

Veblen, Thorstein. *The Theory of the Leisure Class*. New York: Modern Library, 1994 [1899].

Ward, Michael R. M. "Acceptable Masculinities: Working-Class Young Men and Vocational Education and Training Courses." *British Journal of Educational Studies* 66, no. 2 (2017): 225–242.

Warhurst Christopher, Nickson Dennis (2001) Looking Good, Sounding Right: Style Counselling in the New Economy. The Industrial Society, London

Williams, Raymond. "Structures of Feeling." In *Structures of Feeling: Affectivity and the Study of Culture*, edited by Devika Sharma and Frederik Tygstrup, 20–28. Berlin: de Gruyter, 2015 [1954].

CHAPTER 6

English Dandies and French *Lions*: Policing the Male Body in Popular Print and Visual Culture Between 1815 and 1848

John Finkelberg

INTRODUCTION: DANDIACAL PARANOIA AND POPULAR CULTURE

In the first half of the nineteenth century, cultural ephemera like single sheet prints and satirical magazines marketed towards an expanding consumer society often featured fashionably dressed dandies that prompted audiences to wonder about the relationship between manliness

J. Finkelberg (✉)
University of Michigan, MI Ann Arbor, USA
e-mail: johnrf@umich.edu

© The Author(s), under exclusive license to Springer Nature
Switzerland AG 2022
C. Dexl and S. Gerlsbeck (eds.), *The Male Body in Representation*,
Palgrave Studies in (Re)Presenting Gender,
https://doi.org/10.1007/978-3-030-88604-2_6

and sartorial consumption.[1] These works strived to capture and record the actions and motives of the men who demonstrated a keen interest in clothing and fashionable goods. Between 1750 and 1850, several 'dandyesque figures' emerged in both France and England (Chenoune 1993, 32; McNeil 2000, 374–375).[2] The phenomenon was outlined in the debut issue of *Le Lion* (1842–1868), a Parisian men's fashion magazine, published in April 1842. In an introductory message to the readers, the editorial board explained their reasons behind the title:

> The title *Le Lion*, which we adopted, was not chosen as lightly as one might think. Across time, it has been said, that our young generation, our golden youth, has had a monopoly on fashion, but the name of our *merveilleux* has changed following the different political phases: under the Consulate [1799–1804], *the Incroyable* replaced the *Muscadin*, which the Republic [1792–1799] had adopted: soon the Empire [1804–1815] saw the succession of the *Beaux*, the *Élégants*, the *Miriflors*, these last ones were soon dethroned by the Fashionables and the Dandies, the two reigned during the Restoration [1815–1830]: then the *Gants jaune* arrived, and in our day, the *Lion* is the ultimate expression of the man of the world, our fashionable man. We do not have to go back to the original denomination, we limit ourselves to noticing it, and we write it eagerly (we hope it will be successful) on our banner. (20; my translation)

The fashionable men in question were, according to the article, an identifiable category whose needs the magazine intended to serve. However, during the first half of the nineteenth century, another cohort of cultural commentators also latched on to the figure of the dandy, but they rather criticized and lampooned him. This contribution examines the British and French iconography of dandies to show how artists and authors mobilized discourses about manliness and the male body in order to articulate

[1] I wish to acknowledge the assistance of several people including Dr. Jim Ravin, who invited me to work with his collection of rare French and British prints, Juli McLoone for her assistance with reproductions, and Meg Showalter for her photo editing skills. This contribution also benefitted from the insightful comments of Susan L. Siegfried and Dena Goodman as well as my colleagues David, Hayley, Matthew, Molly, Severina, and Taylor. Finally, the images included were obtained with funding from the Institute for the Humanities at the University of Michigan.

[2] In *Dandyism in the Age of Revolution*, Elizabeth Amann has most recently explored the transnational politics of dress and dandyism in France, England, and Spain during the Revolutionary Era (2015).

critical concerns about nineteenth-century consumer culture and its political and social consequences. The period between the restoration of the
Bourbon Monarchy in 1815 and the eventual rise and fall of the July
Monarchy (1830–1848) in France and the final years of King George
IV's regency as the Prince of Wales (known as the Regency Era) and the
early years of the Victorian period (1837–1901) coincides with the parallel
expansions of the clothing industry and a thriving market for print. In
both counties, the first half of the nineteenth century saw the spread of
liberalized commercial practices and the expansion of railway technologies
and growing empires, which together encouraged the spread of a modern
consumer culture entrenched with a gendered hierarchy.

Like the fashions that crisscrossed between the metropolitan centers
of Paris and London, places of thriving, modern consumer cultures, a
shared imagery of and commentary on dandyism informed popular media
and the ways in which they presented contemporary forms of material
consumption to the middle and upper classes in both national contexts
(Hahn 2009, 3; Davidson 2019, 19–20). The dandy, as Rhonda Garelick has previously argued, was also a "hybrid of both cultures" (1998,
6). Dandyism, she explains, is a "performance, the performance of a
highly stylized, painstakingly constructed self, a solipsistic social icon" (3)
that developed in France and England simultaneously. In the first half
of the nineteenth century, men like Beau Brummell in England and the
Comte d'Orsay in France were notorious for how they used clothing,
speech, and leisurely pursuits to cultivate their identity (15–16). The
figure of the dandy also featured prominently in popular literary works
including Thomas Carlyle's *Sartor Resartus*, first serialized in 1833, and
Jules Barbey d'Aurevilly's *Du Dandysme et de George Brummell* from
1845.

Between 1820 and 1850, artists utilized a recognizable visual and
textual discourse about dandyism that encouraged material consumption
while also warning about the dangers of over-styling the masculine self
and the male body. The exact warnings the figure of the dandy referred
to took on different forms, shapes, and shades depending on the specific
historical and national contexts. What is important, however, is that
encouragement and restriction, two opposing forces, both defined how
contemporaries expected men to engage with sartorial goods. This was
an ambivalent strategy, which rendered the dandy's body a liminal and
inherently contradictory one. Moreover, these artists' texts and illustrations recognized that the figure of the dandy and his body have a material

impact on nineteenth-century French and English culture, as men did in fact purchase the clothing represented on these figures, which made the figure of the dandy such a tangible target for criticism.

This contribution presents, following Eve Kosofsky Sedgwick's terminology, a "paranoid" (1997, 6) reading of representations of the dandy. The men who created the popular works discussed in this article were no doubt led by their own 'paranoid' observations about the dandy, and in particular his supposed compromising of the male body. The dandy as construed in these sources played a fundamental role in advancing and upholding masculine norms by demarcating what was and what was not appropriate behavior for middle-class consumers. Men were encouraged to consume as an expression of a productive and virile masculinity, but to over-consume and over-adorn the male body like a dandy was an indication of one's compromised manliness. Moreover, because of the dandy's ambivalence as a figure, he could be used to represent the excesses of elite culture and limited political access for the middle and lower classes as well as anxieties about social mobility and nationalism in nineteenth-century consumer culture. In addition, my conclusion will offer a reparative outlook on the dandy and unveil the implications this figure had for reconceptualizing men's bodies in favor of more pluralistic notions of masculinity, men's fashion, and discourses of male sexuality.

On the one hand, the dandy's body was a visual manifestation of a new masculine silhouette, and on the other, he was a visual reminder that the body and, by extension, the individual, could be manipulated and contorted beyond recognition. Over the course of the first half of the nineteenth century, the portrayal of male bodies in visual and textual culture changed: bloated 'aristocratic' bellies and pushed back shoulders gave way to waists that became smaller, torsos that became wider, and legs that became more muscular. Military practices that had developed during the Napoleonic Wars emphasized stiff, rigid, and disciplined bodies, while medical texts described the benefits of physical activity and promoted more athletic body ideals (Vigarello 2018, 133–141; Davidson 2019, 11–12). The outcome was a new, more sinuous and virile silhouette that appeared in fashion plates and popular lithographs. At the same time, etiquette books and fashion journals increasingly recommended men to purchase form fitting clothing that accentuated the waist, legs, and shoulders (Raisson 1829, 111–114). Images that feature dandies trying to shape their bodies into this new silhouette show the viewer how some men could display the visual qualities of fashionable masculinity and yet how they could lack the perceived masculine virtues of honesty, athleticism, and virility.

The thriving market for cheap printed ephemera in France and Britain at the beginning of the nineteenth century provided audiences with the means to interpret the changes around them and fashion themselves and their bodies through the new possibilities of sartorial consumption. For example, readers of fashion journals had the chance to use fashion plates in order to incorporate the fashions discussed in the magazine into their own lives (Best 2017, 37).[3] Illustrators and editors, moreover, took up the new techniques of lithography and wood engraving to publish prints that "became a prominent form of instruction and entertainment: at once novel consumer products circulating within the urban environment, and artistic forms that offered critical commentary on the environment" (Lerner 2018, 1–2). Images that promised to capture a snippet of 'modern life' were especially popular among middle-class and urban consumers in France and Britain and texts about fashionable men, in particular, were "considered a fitting subject for the entertainment of the masses, a guarantee for healthy sales" (Breward 2000, 222). The audience for these works was neither aristocratic nor working-class, but rather a "broad, mixed, middle-tier public" (Lerner 2018, 13). These works contributed significantly to the social imaginary of the French and British middle class beyond the historical context in which they emerged (Cuno 1983, 347–354; Ten-Doesschate and Weisberg 1994, 4–8). These same sources, especially the more overtly comical and critical ones, also set a restrictive tone: one that delineated proper forms of consumption and thus limited the possibilities of fashioning the male body. This article seeks to continue this line of inquiry by centering on representations of fashionable men in order to show how new ideals of masculinity were formed and challenged through sartorial consumption. The objects in focus include prints and satirical works by the French illustrators Charles Philipon and Cham (Charles Amédée de Noé) and the British illustrators Isaac Robert Cruikshank and John Leech as well as the British author Percival Leigh.

These illustrators and authors used the dandy in works created between 1820 and 1850, whether Regency Era Dandies or Restoration *élegants*, as a means to criticize the consumer market, its effects on individuals, and the political implications of a 'fashionable' masculinity. Like the concept

---

[3] Kate Nelson Best's argument builds on Roland Barthes's understanding of the semiotics of fashion imagery presented in *The Fashion System* (1983).

of masculinity itself, the language of dandyism was malleable and evolved in specific historical contexts (Pascoe and Bridges 2016, 2–6). The dandy was used by his critics to warn of an aberrant form of masculinity premised on the physical manipulation of the male body with clothing goods, false pretenses, compromising national identity, and a devaluation of masculine qualities including sportsmanship, athleticism, and sexual virility. In the British context, the dandy—though originally an English phenomenon— was decidedly 'un-British' because he represented a dishonest, foreign, and effeminate form of masculinity. In France, the figure of the dandy would also be lampooned as a homegrown, but still pernicious figure that was a political liability. The following section traces the origins of the shared imagery of dandyism in France and England during the Bourbon Restoration and the Regency Era. The subsequent sections focus on a concrete example from Victorian England and July Monarchy France, respectively.

English Dandies and French Ridicules

In a lithograph published in *La Silhouette* in 1829 titled "Longchamps / Des Poupées sur des Chaises" ("Longchamps / Dolls on Chairs"), Charles Philipon presents his viewers with an interpretation of a day at the horseraces, a popular and fashionable pastime for both elites and middle-tier Parisians (Roche 2008, 141–143) (see Fig. 6.1). Philipon replaces the human spectators with inanimate objects showing off the latest Parisian fashions. They include mannequins dressed in fashionable menswear and elaborately coiffed busts draped in sumptuous silk gowns. Several splendidly dressed mannequins also populate the background as others arrive in coaches. The horse races are nowhere in sight, rather, these figures seem to socialize and appear enthralled with the spectacle the fashions offer. A caption explaining the details of the image is placed below Philipon's illustration. The text reinforces the artificiality of the supposed attendees and the event itself: "Puppets on chairs, mannequins in fake collars, fake hair, and fake charms" and continues "ridiculous frock coats spread out in coaches, on horses, or trailing in the mud... *voilà* Longchamps!" (1827–1830; my translation). As inanimate objects, the attendees are no longer presented as active subjects but turned into dolls that could be dressed, adorned, and transformed with collars, wigs, and the latest fashions in dress. For the viewer, the fashionable world of horse racing is drained of any actual life or activity, it is merely artifice. Philipon here draws on

Fig. 6.1 Charles Philipon's "Longchamps / Des Poupées sur des Chaises" (© The Trustees of the British Museum)

a longstanding trope about fashion and its association with the dandy: sartorial goods provided an elegant, yet artificial mask that obscured one's real social position as well as potentially distasteful personal habits and characteristics.

Philipon's critical work on the fashions of Longchamps and those who attended the races is paradigmatic of a common assumption about early nineteenth-century fashion culture, namely that clothing and access to new wealth were steadily obfuscating social distinctions. The social upheaval of the French Revolution of 1789 had blurred the categories of differentiation crucial to the formation and identification of social hierarchies in eighteenth-century France. Thus, in attempts to make society legible, individuals turned to physical markers such as dress. People-watching in the public spaces of Parisian boulevards, parks, and the racecourses took on a new importance in the first half of the nineteenth century, as men and women explored how individuals decorated them-selves to judge their social position (Davidson 2005, 265–268). Stylizing the self and engaging in the pleasures of seeing and being seen was a way for individuals to separate themselves and others into social categories based on wealth and access to political rights. However, the increased availability of affordable fashions and the expansion of a consumer market-place meant that even more people had the ability to participate in the latest trends, which made social identification through clothing fungible (Vanier 1960, 125–129). In Britain, a similar anxiety developed as the line that distinguished the aristocracy from the middle class was increasingly blurred during the Regency Era (Burns and Innes 2007, 14–15).

Almost a decade before Philipon, between 1818 and 1819, Isaac Robert Cruikshank illustrates a collection of hand-colored engravings of dandies that identified their dressing habits and the manipulation of male bodies with a disgraceful, pernicious, and dishonest form of masculinity. "Dandies at Tea", published by T. Tegg in 1818, is exem-plary of his collection of images in emphasizing a visual language of dandyism premised on artificiality and the potentially pernicious quali-ties fashionable clothing could hide. In this particular image, two dandies in fashionable clothing drink expensive tea from broken cups in a dusty attic apartment. Exposed in their private dwelling, the fashionable dandies are revealed to be frauds masking their economic straits. There is a clear disjuncture for the viewer between the two dandies' class and their clothing.

Cruikshank's "The Dandy Pickpockets Diving", also published in December 1818 by T. Tegg, invites the viewer to observe a scene occur-ring "near St. James Palace", one of the main centers of consumption in London during the Regency Era where clothing dealers, print shops, tea houses, and coffee shops populated the busy streets between St. James Palace and the West End of London (Breward 2003, 61–64). In the busy and popular district where one would expect to find couples strolling and taking in what the city had to offer, a somberly dressed gentleman and his extravagantly dressed wife are shown enjoying the illustrated prints on display in the window of a print dealer, while being pickpocketed by two dandies. Racecourses, fairs, the bustling London streets, and the modern arcade were "the natural habitat of pickpockets, con men and rogues of every calling" (Murray 1998, 16–17). The criminal activities Cruikshank points to were not new, but rather an everyday occurrence the audience would have been familiar with. What would have been potentially troubling about Cruikshank's image for viewers, however, was the combination of fashionable masculinity and criminal activity. The audience would expect the thief to resemble a rouge or a ruffian, but not the dandy. The historian Tammy Whitlock has suggested that as a new robust consumer culture developed in nineteenth-century England, there was also a new anxiety amongst critics that unchecked consumerism could induce individuals to participate in illicit and criminal behaviors (2005, 3–4). A tendency to privilege consumer and sartorial goods was directly correlated with attempts to live above one's station and even interpreted as a precursor for criminal activity. Cruikshank's dandies are indeed those types of men who, seduced by material goods, were enticed by theft or, at the very least, by dishonesty and false pretenses (Ross 1996, 103–112). By visually connecting the figure of the dandy to illicit and criminal behavior, Cruikshank invites the viewer to think of the dandy as a physical representation of the moral decay wrought by the rise of an urban consumer culture.

Cruikshank's dandies are perhaps also particularly distressing and comical due to how obviously they distort the male body through the use of garments. During the first half of the nineteenth century, the ideal male body went through a period of transformation. The 'aristocratic' puffed up belly and haughty shoulders that evoked a sense of 'nobility' broke down in medical, military, and fashion discourses, especially during and after the Napoleonic era. The changes in representations were subtle at first but became more prominent in the 1830s and 1840s before falling out of fashion in the 1860s. Health manuals and etiquette books emphasized the tightening of belts and encouraged physical activity as a means of attaining the idealized physique (Vigarello 2004, 145–146). The fashion press, furthermore, inundated readers with descriptions of clothing and fashion plates that highlighted a thin waist, broad shoulders, and strong legs throughout the first half of the nineteenth century. However, in "Dandies Dressing", Cruikshank directs the viewers' gaze at a group of men amid their 'toilette' who use corsets and padding to create the illusion of muscular and sinuous bodies, which for well-informed viewers served as indicators of their dishonesty and guile. One of the central figures even admits, while another pulls his stays, that he "shall look more the thing when I get my other calf on".

When caricaturists such as Cruikshank include artificial calves, shoulder-padding, corsets, and toupees as crucial parts of the dandy's wardrobe, they are, in fact, drawing on sartorial practices of reshaping the male body their contemporaries practiced since the end of the eighteenth and beginning of the nineteenth century. As early as the 1770s, some men who wanted to create the illusion of muscular calves, hoping to increase their sexual attractiveness, had already begun wearing artificial ones (Willett Cunnington and Cunnington 1992, 80–81). Hilary Davidson, moreover, has recently shown that both the Prince Regent and his brother, the Duke of Cumberland (the namesake of the Cumberland corset), frequently wore stays (2019, 64). Men could purchase a boned corset from their tailors, corset makers, and hosiers in London and Paris, who also frequently advertised the devices to potential consumers. Corsets also appear in popular media, including novels (Willett Cunnington and Cunnington 1992, 106–107).[4] Though upper-class men were participating in the trends as well, the representations of dandies demonstrate that many British people were uncomfortable with how sartorial goods were being used to misrepresent individuals. George IV began using stays when he had lost control of his figure and wanted—like Tom in "Dandies Dressing"—"to look more the thing" (Cruikshank 1818). Cruikshank's mockery of the artificial calves and corsets, moreover, indicated how attempts to forge ideal bodies with artificial muscles were indeed criticized and derided. By focusing on how dandies used clothing to misrepresent their rank and their intentions via their bodies, these caricatures participated in a restrictive discourse that delineated a proper way for middle-class and upper-class men to consume goods. Consumption was part of the daily life of the nineteenth century, but consuming to misrepresent their identity or distort their body was decidedly 'un-masculine' in the sense that it detracted from other masculine virtues such as honesty, athleticism, and virility.

In France, like in England, men in the professional classes as well as the aristocracy also turned to garments to artificially manipulate their bodies. French caricaturists, such as Philipon, used the practices as a way of criticizing attempts to appear virile and masculine, which in turn

---

[4] One example is Honoré de Balzac's *Ferragus, Chef des Dévorants* (1833).

doubled as salient criticism of the men in power and those with political access during the Bourbon Restoration and, later, the July Monarchy. The French soldier and memoirist Jean-Roch Coignet described his experience with false calves during his time serving in Napoleon's army. He wore artificial calves in his youth to attain a particularly fashionable silhouette when out in Paris. He remembered how on one spring evening in 1810, during a *rendezvous* with his newest mistress, Coignet was using artificial calves underneath his pants, but the idea of taking them off in front of his mistress was rather humiliating. Coignet happily recalled that he had the time to remove his artificial calves while she escaped to her own dressing room to remove her dress, but the following morning, he had to scramble to attach them before she awoke. He soon abandoned them and swore to "have never worn them since" (1883, 264). Though he found them uncomfortable, Coignet described how as a young man he, too, was susceptible to the pressure to show off muscular legs. He was responding to a visual and textual discourse that emphasized muscularity as a facet of sexual attractiveness, but he at once noticed that the artificial calves would not suit him. There was a tension between men wanting to appear athletic, virile, and attractive—like a soldier—and using garments to create this appearance.

Though for Coignet it was a matter of choice, popular lithographs from the 1820s made abandoning artificial calves and corsets a matter of utter necessity, because caricaturists represented men who used them as evidence of a degeneration of French honor and military prowess, especially after the breakdown of the Napoleonic Empire. During the Bourbon Restoration, illustrators cast the men who wore corsets as individuals who only *imitated* the heroic physique of the Napoleonic soldier whose body was shaped by the physical demands of military campaigns at the height of French military prowess. In a series of lithographs of "Ridicules" released between 1824 and 1825, Philipon, for example, depicts an image of a balding man with a powdered face in the midst of applying rouge standing in front of a vanity mirror while his black servant pulls at his stays contorting the 'ridicule's' body (see Fig. 6.2). The protagonist asks his servant, "[h]ave you curled my toupee?" (my translation). By the time he has completed his toilette, his entire upper body is altered to produce an image of fashionable masculinity that obfuscates the central figure's actual appearance. The composition of the image, furthermore, draws attention away from the cropped portrait of a man in military dress, suggesting the replacement of one form of masculinity

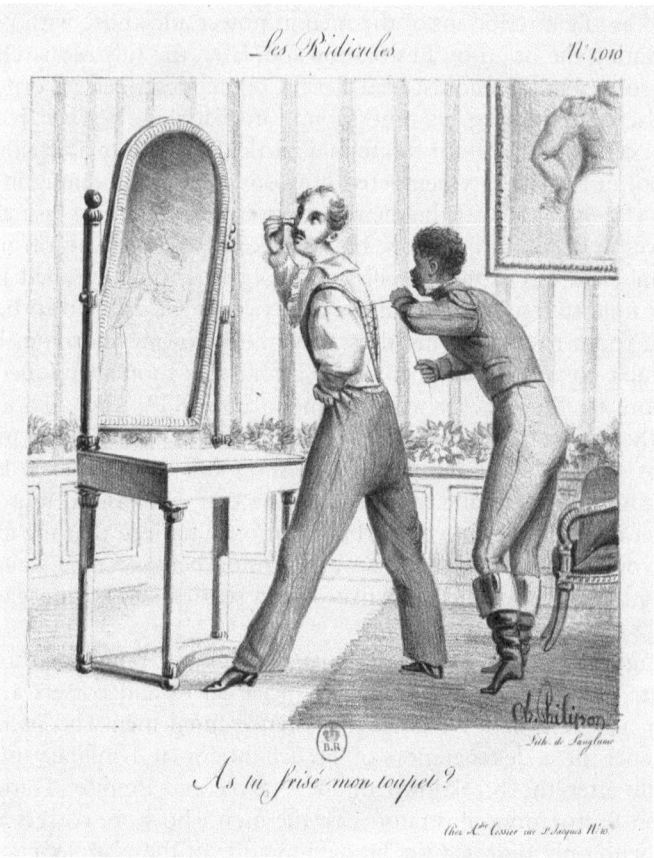

Fig. 6.2 Charles Philipon's "As Tu Frisé mon Toupet?" (© Bibliothèque Nationale de France)

for another. The virile and masculine officer that is figuratively decapitated in the image reinforced a popular criticism of the political culture of the Bourbon Restoration, in particular that French honor, military prowess, and strength had been compromised by a return to a new form of Bourbon influence. While Philipon does not reference the Bourbon Restoration directly, he initially supported the July Revolution in 1830 because it promised an end to the conservativism of the Restoration. This image of the ridicule's attempts at shaping the male body foreshadows

Charles X's disastrous campaigns in Algeria in 1830 that eventually precipitated the July Revolution of 1830 (Sessions 2011, 3, 19–30). The Bourbons' claims to legitimacy, like the ridicule's makeup and stays, are exposed when confronted with in one case a military campaign, and in the other a mirror.

In the following decades, the next generation of British and French illustrators and authors mobilized the same language of dandyism for slightly different purposes. In early-Victorian England, the dandy took on particularly 'un-British' character traits: he was effeminate, and he dressed too French. In July Monarchy France, following the establishment of the constitutional monarchy of Louis Philippe I in July 1830, the figure of the dandy now served to criticize the new monarchy and the men that it benefitted. In both contexts, the foundations of the discourse remained the same: the dandy used sartorial goods to mask his identity and in doing so, he contorted and deformed his body, which was tangible evidence of his moral decay.

THE VICTORIAN 'LADY-LIKE' GENTLEMAN

In early-Victorian England, the dandy was satirized in popular print and visual culture in order to demarcate the boundaries of a distinctly 'English' masculinity. In 1840, the English writer Percival Leigh and illustrator John Leech released their collaborative work *The Fiddle-Faddle Fashion Book and Beau Monde à la Française, Enriched with Highly Coloured Figures of Lady-Like Gentlemen*, a satirical fashion magazine that used the figure of the dandy to criticize fashionable masculinity as both foreign and effeminate. The work is modeled on popular fashion journals that proliferated during this period in the United States and Europe (Best 2017, 16–30). Their texts and images present a stringent criticism of fashionable masculinity: in the early-Victorian period, the contorted and undignified dandies of the Regency became a new breed of un-British and un-manly 'lady-like gentlemen'. Leigh and Leech conceive the figure of the dandy as a French and effeminate foreign invader, at a moment when the British state was making concerted efforts to entice shoppers to spend on British-made goods.

The satirical journal includes an article entitled "Remarks" in which Leigh describes the new 'French' fashions Leech has illustrated. Much like traditional fashion reporting that offered suggestions for how to incorporate new fashions into one's wardrobe, "Remarks" follows the pedagogical standard set in French and British fashion journals. Leigh promises the readers that using the *Fiddle-Faddle Fashion Book* as a guide, they too can be renewed as 'lady-like' gentlemen *à la française*, yet unlike the serious advertisements in fashion journals, they convert the industry standard into a work of comedy: these are not fashions one should replicate. Rather, audiences should laugh at those they see engaging in sartorial consumption to this extreme. The plates are divided in two registers: the top for half-length portraits and the bottom for full-length figures. Leigh explains that the illustrations correspond to French "improvements which are daily taking place in male costume" (1840, 8). The full-length figures model a form-fitting coat "à la demoiselle", redingotes with full skirts, elaborately embroidered and designed dressing gowns, skin-tight trousers, and waistcoats in flamboyant fabrics. Credited explicitly to the French, the new fashions, according to Leigh, have the effect of "softening and redefining male attire, by rendering it, in fact, more *lady-like*" (8; emphasis in original). The remainder of the article provides its readers with explanatory remarks about the illustrations which reinforce how through the manipulation of sartorial goods, English men could become decidedly un-British and 'lady-like'. Unlike Cruikshank's dandies with oversized heads and comically skinny limbs, Leech's figures correspond to his more subdued style of illustration, which was popular with early-Victorian audiences (Miller 2009, 268). Instead of presenting the dandies as monstrous figures, Leech's dandies are characterizations of recognizable members of the Victorian public that chose to embrace the effeminate French style.

The satirical journal reflects a growing tension in early-Victorian England between the nature of cosmopolitanism, Britain's place in the increasingly global consumer market, and the very nature of British nationalism. As Linda Colley has argued, rallying against the French and resisting French influence was a crucial part of British nationalism in the late eighteenth century and continued to influence what it meant to be British well into the twentieth century (1992, 316, 327–329). As France and Britain began competing on an industrial scale in the early nineteenth century, the body of the dandy became the symbol of national contestation. This disdain for Frenchness becomes problematic for the dandy because menswear in England after 1830 was increasingly influenced by changing styles in France, in particular the French-inspired redingote with a wide skirt. In the case of Leigh and Leech's dandies, for example, femininity is directly tied to the 'lady-like' French fashions they wear.

As John Tosh has explained, rejecting femininity was at the center of early-Victorian formulations of middle-class and upper-class masculinity (2007, 102–114). For middle-class professionals such as lawyers, businessmen, and clerks, the 'lady-like' figures are legible and comical figures that represented the men around them who have potentially given into their desired temptations and who have sacrificed both their nation and their masculinity for fashion.

Works such as *The Fiddle-Faddle Fashion Book* illustrate how masculine British subjects were caught in-between a drive to consume and participate in the growing global consumer economy epitomized by the Great Exhibition of 1851 and a desire to remain a 'masculine' British subject. The Exhibition of 1851, as the historian Paul Greenhalgh has argued, represented a concerted effort on behalf of the government and manufacturers to increase the prestige and success of British industry (1991, 21–24). Moreover, in the *Reports by the Juries*, which summarized the various items and products displayed at the Great Exhibition, the catalog shows how menswear items were submitted, displayed, and given the highest honors at the Great Exhibition (1852, 477–484). British men in this period, therefore, were encouraged to consume and participate in the expanding market for sartorial goods, while figures such as Leigh and Leech highlighted both the foreignness and femininity of the dandy and thus defined restrictive contours for proper forms of consumption. Consumption was welcomed when it benefitted British industry.

'Gentlemen of Taste' and the July Monarchy

Meanwhile in France, the dandy's hyper-fashionable body was satirized to criticize the unfulfilled promises of the July Revolution of 1830 and the illegitimacy of the current regime. In *Nos Gentiles Hommes à Goût: Tournure, Élégance, Moeurs et Plaisiers de la Jeunesse Dorée* (*Our Gentleman of Taste: Evolution, Elegance, Morals, and Pleasures of the Golden Youth*; my translation), a series of twenty lithographs published by the Maison Aubert in 1846, Cham (Amédée de Noé) captures fashionable men in embarrassing or compromising scenes of everyday modern life. The protagonists, however, somehow always manage to fall short of what is expected of them. Like many of his contemporaries, the French illustrator built a successful career illustrating individual prints and contributing to popular illustrated dailies. However, unlike his contemporaries who came from common or working-class backgrounds, Cham's father was part of the French aristocracy (Lerner 2018, 30, 189). Versed in the social customs of the Parisian aristocracy and urban middle-class and attracted by the modern forms of urban sociability, Cham was a well-placed observer who documented in satire the fashionable life of the modern 'gentleman of taste', i.e., the dandy: riding, hunting as well as everyday drudgery, including dealing with servants and appeasing rich aunts. Cham's observations of the 'gentleman of taste' offer a critical view of the current political regime, the July Monarchy. Between 1830 and 1848, the male body was frequently targeted in July Monarchy political imagery as a powerful symbol of the political illegitimacy of the regime (Surkis 2011, 60–61). Cham's *Nos Gentiles Hommes à Gout* mobilizes a visual discourse that emphasizes the fashionable dandy and his body as politically illegitimate.

Louis Philippe's constitutional monarchy, established in 1830, encouraged the expansion of the French consumer industry, manufacturing, trade, and especially the banking and the financial sector. This way, Louis Philippe and his government ensured that a combination of the old nobility and new, wealthy elites remained in firm control of France, while excluding working-class men and all women from political participation (Collingham 1988). The 'gentlemen of taste' Cham identifies are the very men who gained wealth, access, and elevated social positions in the economic and political context of the July Monarchy. They shopped in Parisian commercial centers that grew and thrived, and they engaged in modern forms of sociability and leisure, such as attending horseraces, promenades on the boulevards, as well as riding and shooting (Martin-Fugier 1990, 330; Harrison 1999, 100–103). Cham's 'gentlemen of taste' shown in compromising situations criticize the political culture of the July Monarchy, in particular its failures vis-à-vis the working class.

Plate 2, titled "Un objet de prix pour ne rien prendre" ("A Prize Item to Do Nothing"; my translation), immediately draws the viewers' attention to a theme that appears through this work: the men with means and access in the July Monarchy are too concerned with appearing fashionable and in doing so, they are compromised physically and morally, as exemplified in their fashions. In this image, two men are out for an afternoon of shooting. One man, dressed for an afternoon of sport, turns to his companion, whose outfit is better suited for a dining room or a salon, and asks, "[f]or over a month we have hunted together, and I have never seen you fire a single shot?", and his companion responds, "[b]y Jove it is a four-thousand-franc weapon, it would be wrong to use it" (Cham 1846, plate 2; my translation). The dandy's open disregard for the sport suggests an abuse of his privilege as a man with access to economic means. At the turn of the nineteenth century, and especially during the July Monarchy, hunting for sport became increasingly popular amongst middle-class and elite men in France, as well as in England and North America, who associated hunting and sportsmanship with a type of masculinity that emphasized a combination of patience, restraint, and self-awareness with a violent, virile, primitive strength (Sramek 2006, 664–666; Cropper 2008, 85–118). And yet, hunting for sport was out of reach for a significant portion of the working-class population in France and abroad, the same group of individuals excluded from political life (Estève 2004, 74–76). In *Nos Gentiles Hommes à Goût*, the very men with the economic means to engage in the sport are presented as equipped with the right clothing and tools, but unable and unwilling to partici-pate in the hunt. Through figures such as these, who appear oblivious to the political significance of this economic privilege, Cham implicates the July Monarchy itself: the regime has elevated wanting men to positions of power and prestige. They know how to dress and own all the right acces-sories, but they fall short of performing their roles as masculine subjects and as stewards of the nation.

In Plate 17, "Oh hé! Ce Cavalier! Ohè!" ("Oh hey! This Rider! Woo-hoo!"), Cham identifies another 'gentleman of taste' whose sartorial choices and lack of physical ability visually translate into a criticism of the current regime and the men in power (see Fig. 6.3). A fashionable dandy in un-scuffed riding boots appears unable to take control of the horse because, instead of gripping onto its reigns, he is more concerned with holding on to his material possessions: his spectacles in one hand and a cane in the other. To his left, a man dressed in the colors of the repub-lican Tricolor (an unbuttoned white shirt that reveals a muscular chest, blue pants, and red Phrygian cap) offers to exchange the man's horse for a carriage. The fashionable man of taste is no match for his horse, and the ruffian republican has taken notice. This picture invites the viewer to question what these fashionable young men contribute to their commu-nity. Though dressed to cut a certain figure, the fashionable gentleman cannot ride his horse, while the man visually coded as republican offers a solution. *Nos Gentiles Hommes à Goût* is an example of how Cham, and the collaborators at the Maison Aubert, often relied on a middle-class appetite for high-quality and humorous publications that satirize observ-able scenes of everyday life that, unlike caricatures of political figures,

Fig. 6.3 Cham's "Oh hé! Ce Cavalier! Ohè!" (© Bibliothèque Nationale de France)

were not explicitly political in content and therefore could avoid government censorship (Cuno 1983, 51–52). In fashioning the figure of the working-class man in the colors of the revolutionary Tricolor (which the

July Monarchy adopted) and a Phrygian cap, Cham depicts the disjuncture between the 'common' people of France and those with political access. While Louis Philippe claimed to represent the French as the 'King of the French', Cham's illustration suggests that there were indeed two groups of French people: one with access to fashion and political power, and one with physical skills and virtues, but denied political access.

Throughout the series, men who could claim both wealth and political access are presented as debauched, unathletic, lazy, and cunning. Their bodies are slender and physically incapable—a representation which aimed to delegitimize the current regime. The ruffian republican who cannot claim the title of 'gentleman of taste', however, has a broad chest, muscular arms, and powerful legs. Physically, the 'gentleman of taste' is compromised, while the republican's body is not; rather, he is fit to lead. Visibly no match for the strength of the working class excluded from both fashionable and political life, the 'gentleman of taste' continues to enjoy the privileges of his class. Understood in the context of the July Monarchy, Cham's *Nos Gentiles Hommes à Gout* demonstrates how the figure of the dandy, his body, and how he dressed it, served as a discursive tool to undermine the political legitimacy of the current regime, in much the same way that Philipon used the body of the ridicule to express his views on the Bourbons. While in the French example the emphasis is focused on the current regime and not the foreign other, it operates in the same way as in the British example. The dandy's use of clothing to fabricate the social person, manipulate his body, and express general disdain for self-awareness, provided French and British caricaturists and authors with a stable and easy target. By focusing on the dandy, moreover, in both contexts, the critics could make politically charged arguments without drawing the ire of the political establishment precisely because the figure of the dandy was so recognizable to both French and British audiences. The visibility of the dandy, therefore, was also his downfall.

Epilogue: Reading the Dandy as an Emancipatory Figure

Men in the first half of the nineteenth century were eager to participate in the new consumer culture that developed in France and Britain during this period (Breward 1995). The desire to possess new goods was encouraged in fashion periodicals such as *Le Lion* that opened this contribution, but the desire to consume was tempered through cultural representations of dandies who appeared to viewers as overtly comical figures that were to be laughed at, ridiculed, and decried. They were not, however, to be imitated. How illustrators and authors used the figure of the dandy varied according to each national and historical context, but English and French critics mobilized a shared rhetoric and imagery to describe fashionable masculinity as dishonest, potentially criminal, effeminate, and compromising to national identity as well as masculine virtues like athleticism and sportsmanship. Individuals like Jean-Roch Coignet participated in the changing fashions but could also acknowledge how in modifying their bodies artificially, they were exposing themselves to the type of ridicule emblemized in the prints. It was this inherently contradictory understanding of the dandy and his participation in modern consumer culture that explains why his body became a sight for waging debates about social identity, political legitimacy, and the nature of national identity. This contradiction in how men should approach consumption has continued to inform how fashion is overtly gendered in terms of the feminine. When the psychologist J. C. Flügel claimed in his 1930 study that men "gave up" (111) their right to adornment and decoration in the nineteenth century, he was, I argue, working within the discourse established by men like Philipon and Cruikshank almost a century before. For many in the twentieth century, it was impossible to think about middle-class men being interested in fashion precisely because figures like the dandy had been pilloried in popular culture and academic texts since the second half of the eighteenth century.

And yet, the figure of the dandy has also been a site that encourages and invites individuals to imagine a range of potential masculinities beyond the restrictive limits characterizing representation in the sources discussed above. In the early twentieth century, indigenous Indonesians refashioned Dutch clothing to create a distinctly Indonesian dandy. This suggests that within the colonial context, fashion could be employed to articulate a national identity that challenged colonial hegemony (Mrázek 2002, 131–132, 157–160). In twenty-first-century popular culture, moreover, the dandy is no longer a symbol or marker of moral decay as Cruikshank imagined him, but rather an example of a type of masculinity that has discarded the tropes of white, cis-gender, and heterosexual masculinity. The cultural phenomenon of the Congolese *Sapeurs*, or Congolese dandies, who are known to dress in extravagantly colorful and elegant suits and impeccable shoes on the streets of Brazzaville, speaks to the emancipatory ability of masculine sartorial adornment and display. While some have argued that the Congolese dandy is merely perpetuating cultural imperialism, the *Sapeur* can provide a different prospective and reparative perspective. When asked about the relationship between dandyism and colonialism, the infamous *Sapeur* Papa Wembe was quoted stating that "[w]hite people invented the clothes, but we make an art of it" (Evancie 2013, n. pag.). Therefore, while the dandy was perhaps an original site for erecting a strict gender binary, he is also an inspirational figure that can demonstrate the emancipatory possibilities of sartorial consumption and adornment.

References

Amann, Elizabeth. *Dandyism in the Age of Revolution: The Art of the Cut.* Chicago: U of Chicago P, 2015.

Balzac, Honoré de. *Ferragus, Chef des Dévorants.* Paris: Gallimard, 1833.

Barbey d'Aurevilly, Jules. *Du Dandysme et de George Brummell.* Paris: Emile-Paule frères, 1918 [1845].

Barthes, Roland. *The Fashion System.* Translated by Matthew Ward and Richard Howard. Los Angeles: U of California P, 1983.

Best, Kate Nelson. *The History of Fashion Journalism.* London: Bloomsbury, 2017.

Breward, Christopher. *The Hidden Consumer: Masculinities, Fashion, and City Life 1860–1914.* Manchester: Manchester UP, 1995.

———. "The Dandy Laid Bare: Embodying Practices and Fashions for Men." In *Fashion Cultures: Theories, Explorations and Analysis*, edited by Stella Bruzzi and Pamela Church Gibson, 221–238. London: Routledge, 2000.

———. "Masculine Pleasures: Metropolitan Identities and the Commercial Sites of Dandyism, 1790–1840." *The London Journal* 28, no. 1 (2003): 60–72.

Burns, Arthur, and Joanna Innes. *Rethinking the Age of Reform: Britain 1780–1850.* Cambridge: Cambridge UP, 2007.

Carlyle, Thomas. *Sartor Resartus.* Philadelphia: The Rogers Co., 1890 [1833].

Cham (Charles Amédée de Noé), illustrator. *Nos Gentils Hommes à Goût, Tournure, Élégance, Moeurs et Plaisirs de la Jeunesse Dorée.* Paris: Maison Aubert, 1846.

———. "Oh hé! Ce Cavalier! Ohè!" In *Nos Gentiles Hommes à Goût*, Plate 17, 1846. Lithograph, hand-colored, 33.6 × 25.0 cm. Private collection, Toledo, Ohio.

Chenoune, Farid. *A History of Men's Fashion.* Translated by Deke Dusinberre. Paris: Flammarion, 1993.

Coignet, Jean-Roch. *Les Cahiers du Capitaine Coignet.* Paris: Hachette et Cie, 1883.

Colley, Linda. "Britishness and Otherness: An Argument." *Journal of British Studies* 31, no. 4 (1992): 309–329.

Collingham, H. A. C. *The July Monarchy: A Political History of France, 1830–1848.* London: Longman, 1988.

Cropper, Corry. *Playing at Monarchy: Sport as Metaphor in Nineteenth-Century France.* Omaha: U of Nebraska P, 2008.

Cruikshank, Isaac Robert, draftsman. "Dandies Dressing." Woodcut, hand-colored, 23.3 × 32 cm. London: T. Tegg, 1818. Private collection, Toledo, Ohio.

———. "The Dandy Pickpockets Diving." Woodcut, hand-colored, 23.3 × 32 cm. London: T. Tegg, 1818. Private collection, Toledo, Ohio.

Cuno, James. "Charles Philipon, La Maison Aubert, and the Business of Caricature in Paris, 1829–1841." *Art Journal* 43, no. 4 (1983): 347–354.

Davidson, Denise Z. "Making Society 'Legible': People-Watching in Paris After the Revolution." *French Historical Studies* 28, no. 2 (2005): 265–296.

Davidson, Hilary. *Dress in the Age of Jane Austen: Regency Fashion.* New Haven: Yale UP, 2019.

Estève, Christian. "Le Droit de Chasse en France de 1789 à 1914. Conflits d'Usage et Impasses Juridiques." *Histoire & Sociétés Rurales* 21 (2004): 73–114.

Evancie, Angela. "The Surprising Sartorial Culture of Congolese 'Sapeurs'." *The Daily Picture Show*, National Public Radio, May 7, 2013. https://www.npr.org/section/pictureshow/2013/05/07/181704510/the-surprising-sartorial-culture-of-congoloes-sapeaurs. Accessed October 1, 2020.

Flügel, J. C. *The Psychology of Clothes.* New York: International UP, 1971 [1930].

Garelick, Rhonda. *Rising Star: Dandyism, Gender, and Performance in the Fin de Siècle.* Princeton: Princeton UP, 1998.

Greenhalgh, Paul. *Ephemeral Vistas: The Expositions Universelles, Great Exhibitions and World's Fairs, 1851–1939.* Manchester: Manchester UP, 1991.

Hahn, Hazel. *Scenes of Parisian Modernity: Culture and Consumption in the Nineteenth Century.* New York: Palgrave Macmillan, 2009.

Harrison, Carol E. *The Bourgeois Citizen in Nineteenth-Century France: Gender, Sociability, and the Uses of Emulation.* London: Oxford UP, 1999.

Leigh, Percival. "Remarks." In *The Fiddle-Faddle Fashion Book and Beau Monde à la Française, Enriched with Highly-Coloured Figures of Lady-Like Gentlemen,* written by Percival Leigh and illustrated by John Leech, 8–9. London: Chapman and Hall, 1840.

Leigh, Percival, and John Leech, illustrator. *The Fiddle-Faddle Fashion Book and Beau Monde à la Française, Enriched with Highly-Coloured Figures of Lady-Like Gentlemen.* London: Chapman and Hall, 1840.

Lerner, Jillian. *Graphic Culture: Illustration and Artistic Enterprise in Paris, 1830–1848.* London: McGill-Queen's UP, 2018.

Martin-Fugier, Anne. *La Vie Élégante, Ou, La Formation Du Tout-Paris, 1815–1848*. Paris: Fayard, 1990.

McNeil, Peter. "Macaroni Masculinities." *Fashion Theory* 4, no. 4 (2000): 373–403.

Miller, Henry J. "John Leech and the Shaping of the Victorian Cartoon: The Context of Respectability." *Victorian Periodicals Review* 42, no. 3 (2009): 267–291.

Mrázek, Rudolf. *Engineers of Happy Land: Technology and Nationalism in a Colony*. Princeton: Princeton UP, 2002.

Murray, Venetia. *High Society: A Social History of the Regency Period, 1788–1830*. London: Viking, 1998.

N. N. "Avant-Propos." *Le Lion, Journal des Nouveautés et des Modes d'Hommes* 20 (1842): 3–4.

Pascoe, C. J., and Tristan Bridges. "Introduction." In *Exploring Masculinities: Identity, Inequality, Continuity, and Change*, edited by C. J. Pascoe and Tristan Bridges, 1–37. Oxford: Oxford UP, 2016.

Philipon, Charles, draftsman. "As Tu Frisé mon Toupet?" *Les Ridicules*, Plate 1,010, c.1824–1825. Lithograph, 34.4 × 26 cm. Bibliothèque Nationale de France, Paris, France.

Philipon, Charles, draftsman, and Victor Ratier, printer. "Longchamps / Des Poupées sur des Chaises." *LaSilhouette* 1–21 (1829–1830): 29. Lithograph, hand-colored, 20.9 × 21.1 cm. The British Museum, London.

Raisson, Horace. *Code de la Toilette, Manuel Complet d'Elégance et d'Hygiène. Contenant les Lois, Règles, Applications et Exemples de l'Art de Soigner sa Personne, et de s'Habiller avec Gout et Méthode*. Vol. 4. Paris: J.P. Roret, 1829.

Reports by the Juries on the Subjects in the Thirty Classes into Which the Exhibition Was Divided: Reports, Classes XVII to XXVIII. London: Spricer Brothers, 1852.

Roche, Daniel. "Equestrian Culture in France from the Sixteenth to the Nineteenth Century." *Past & Present* 199 (2008): 113–145.

Ross, Marlon B. "Scandalous Reading: The Political Use of Scandal in and Around Regency Britain." *The Wordsworth Circle* 27, no. 2 (1996): 103–112.

Sedgwick, Eve Kosofsky. "Paranoid Reading and Reparative Reading; or, You're So Paranoid, You Probably Think This Introduction Is About You." In *Novel Gazing: Queer Readings in Fiction*, edited by Eve Kosofsky Sedgwick, 1–37. Durham and London: Duke UP, 1997.

Sessions, Jennifer E. *By Sword and the Plow: France and the Conquest of Algeria*. Ithaca: Cornell UP, 2011.

Sramek, Joseph. "'Face Him Like a Briton': Tiger Hunting, Imperialism, and British Masculinity in Colonial India, 1800–1875." *Victorian Studies* 48, no. 4 (2006): 659–680.

Surkis, Judith. "Carnival Balls and Penal Codes: Body Politics in July Monarchy France." *History of the Present* 1, no. 1 (2011): 59–83.

Ten-Doesschate, Chu, and Gabriel P. Weisberg. "Introduction." In *The Popularization of Images: Visual Culture Under the July Monarchy*, 1–9. Princeton: Princeton UP, 1994.

Tosh, John. *A Man's Place: Masculinity and the Middle-Class Home in Victorian England*. New Haven: Yale UP, 2007 [1999].

Vanier, Henriette. *La Mode et ses Métiers, Frivolités et Luttes des Classes, 1830–1870*. Paris: Armand Colin, 1960.

Vigarello, Georges. *Historie de la Beauté: Le Corps et l'Art d'Embellir de la Renaissance à nos Jours*. Paris: Seuil, 2004.

———. *Le Corps Redressé: Histoire d'un Pouvoir Pédagogique*. Paris: Édition du Félin, 2018 [1978].

Whitlock, Tammy C. *Crime, Gender, and Consumer Culture in Nineteenth-Century England*. London: Routledge, 2005.

Willet Cunnington, Cecil, and Phillis Cunnington. *The History of Underclothes*. New York: Dover Publications, 1992.

CHAPTER 7

Stiliagi Masculinity and the Re-Fashioning of the Male Body in the Soviet Union (1948–1958)

Alla Myzelev

INTRODUCTION

In the streets of early 1950s Moscow, a young man wearing a grey *Komsomol* uniform approaches a group of flamboyantly dressed youth. A beautiful woman comes close to him, says hello, and gives him a sensual kiss suggestively right next to his mouth, thereby leaving a bright trace of her lipstick on his face, before she returns to her friends. The uniformed youth appears a bit dazed but is very impressed. Then, another young man, who belongs to the same group of friends and stands right next to the protagonist, turns towards him, obviously jokingly, and kisses him on the exact same spot, thus smudging the trace of the woman's lipstick. The young man in the uniform, Mels, reacts aggressively, firmly pulling

A. Myzelev (✉)
State Univeristy of New York at Geneseo, Geneseo, NY, USA
e-mail: myzelev@geneseo.edu

© The Author(s), under exclusive license to Springer Nature Switzerland AG 2022
C. Dexl and S. Gerlsbeck (eds.), *The Male Body in Representation*, Palgrave Studies in (Re)Presenting Gender,
https://doi.org/10.1007/978-3-030-88604-2_7

147

the other man's lapel. The kisser responds in kind, pulling Mels' collar. The camera zooms in on the intense gaze between the two men—a gaze that is filled with the tension between the men's aggression and their homoerotic longing, thus suggesting that from this moment on anything is possible: violent fight or sincere embrace (*Stiliagi* 00:19:09–00:20:12). This snippet from Valerii Todorovsky's 2008 film *Stiliagi* demonstrates not only different reactions towards the same scenario, a kiss from a man and a woman, in order to suggest what is and what is not considered appropriate sexual conduct within its specific setting. By conveying the tense atmosphere that the men's erotic encounter engenders, the film also points to the social taboo of homosexual desire—i.e., a desire that may not be, as the contrasting representation of and reaction to the kisses—namely, the one framed in terms of heterosexual normativity, the other framed in terms of homoerotic play—suggests (Fig. 7.1).

While the film could well feature a kiss between a man and a woman only to construct the male character as straight, it makes a point in foregrounding the idea of homoeroticism and homosociality. This allusion and Mels' response that points out his struggle between conforming to heteronormative imperatives on the one hand and his lust for embracing the homoerotic encounter on the other, reminds the viewer that any form of romantic attraction and sexual desire among men was considered a

Fig. 7.1 Violent fight or romantic attraction? Film still from Valerii Todorovsky's *Stiliagi* (00:19:26)

taboo in the Post-WW II Soviet Union and is—to this day, it seems—a controversial issue among the *Stiliagi* and non-*Stiliagi*.

This contribution is concerned with representations of the *Stiliagi*[1] in a variety of media, including satirical magazines, interviews,[2] films, and literary and life writing accounts, and explores how different, conflicting concepts of masculinity, as they prevailed in the Post-WW II Soviet Union, played out on the *Stiliagi* body.[3] It inquires into the challenge that the *Stiliagi* presented to Soviet notions of hegemonic masculinity and how they furthered an interest in men's fashion that was later developed by star designers such as Slava Zaitsev and Alexander Igmand. In the Soviet Union of the late 1940s and 1950s, the bodies of the *Stiliagi* were cast as a battleground onto which different social conceptions of masculinity were projected. I argue that the figure of the *Stiliaga* can be read as an embodied negotiation of the Soviet regime, with the *Stiliagi* movement challenging the regime and its etiquette in terms of behavior and actions, musical tastes, and fashion choices. The *Stiliagi* body's signification varies according to the actors involved: they are represented as masculine, urban, homosocial, cultured, and stylish by the members of

---

[1] In line with the usage of these terms in Russian, I use *Stiliaga* in the singular to refer to one member of the *Stiliagi* movement and *Stiliagi* to describe both the plural of *Stiliaga* and the movement itself.

[2] The interviews used in this article were conducted between 2017 and 2019 as part of a research project on politics and fashion in the Soviet Union. I interviewed 35 people, predominantly men, in person and on Skype, mostly in form of discussions that followed the snowball principle: every informant had the chance to recommend someone considered suitable for my research. In relation to the *Stiliagi* movement, the questions discussed revolved around memories of who the *Stiliagi* were, how they differed from non-*Stiliagi*, and whether the informant was considered to be one. The interviewees recalled what they knew about *Stiliagi* of the earlier generation. Some were children of *Stiliagi* and shared memories of their fathers' experiences and knowledge that had been passed on to them. Most interviews were conducted in Toronto with Soviet expats or online with people living in Kiev, Moscow, Ufa, St. Petersburg, Odessa, and Novosibirsk. Naturally, the interviewees' memories are not always reliable and tainted by their later understanding of events. All interviews in this article have been translated by me.

[3] According to my interviewees, women were part of the movement but not dominant in it. The fact that women played only secondary roles did not mean that they were considered less important or 'secondary participants' in the movement; rather, they seemed to have different sets of interests. It is, however, important to remember that the *Stiliagi* existed in a patriarchal Soviet context; thus, gender relations among them seem to have functioned within this framework.

the movement themselves, while the same bodies are portrayed as subversive, effeminate, weak, and often animal-like by conservative critics of the style.

This article also explores how friendship between men was understood in the *Stiliagi* movement. I argue that these friendships and their narrative mediation emerged within the protective discourse of private homes and materialized in the form of alternative embodiments of masculinity. While the *Stiliagi* were merely spending their leisure time differently than their *Komsomol* counterparts,[4] public discourse construed them as the *Komsomol*'s 'Other': intellectually inferior, drunk, unable to make decisions as well as perpetually unemployed and thus a threat to the Soviet national body. Against this background, the article suggests that the movement's initially apolitical stance gave way to an increasing political investment due to severe criticism, and at times punishment, from state authorities and media representatives.

THE *STILIAGI*: MORE THAN A FASHION MOVEMENT

The *Stiliagi* movement, for the first time since the Tsarist period, brought forward the idea that male clothing has aesthetic and not just functional qualities, and could be used to express some form of personal freedom. The ideal notion of masculinity that prevailed from the Bolshevik revolution to the late 1940s dictated that masculinity and fashion were antithetical. However, after the Great Patriotic War (1941–1945), Stalin's purges temporarily eased, which gave respite to the masses celebrating the end of the war and awaiting the returning soldiers. These soldiers brought back cultural material from the West and orally shared their tales of what they had experienced while moving through European countries towards Berlin. This short-lived yet essential cultural openness, along with the few movies from capitalist countries that were shown in the Soviet

---

[4] *Komsomol* was the Soviet youth organization. Most young people in the Soviet Union were members, *Stiliagi* included. Due to their lifestyle, many *Stiliagi* faced expulsion from *Komsomol*, which had serious consequences for them, such as a lower chance of finding employment, an exclusion from the communist party, and a potential expulsion from post-secondary studies.

Union at the time, for instance H. Bruce Humberstone's *Sun-Valley Sere-nade* (1941),[5] influenced the younger generation of Soviet citizens. Too young to fight in the war, this generation looked for male role models different from their parents in the late 1940s and early 1950s. The hegemonic concept of masculinity dominating the time was represented by war veterans that were considered strong, experienced, and loyal to their Soviet motherland and therefore hailed as ideal citizens. Visual culture of the period depicts the ideal Soviet body as strong and muscular, and while many soldiers were seriously wounded or mutilated in the war—many had lost limbs and were severely traumatized—the official media representation concentrated on the physical strength and moral virtue of these individuals.[6] Partly a reaction to the 'military masculinity' of the previous generations, partly due to the rapidly closing window to the West, there were, however, many young men and women who attempted to recreate and uphold what they perceived as a Western style of clothing and living in the post-war Soviet Union (Edele 2002; Fürst 2015).

The *Stiliagi* movement originated in the late 1940s and had largely dissipated by the early 1960s. It was the first example of a youth subculture in the Soviet Union. The term stems from the Russian word '*stil*', which means 'style'. The word '*Stiliagi*' was first used in an essay written to satirize young men who seemed to pay too much attention to their self-stylization by wearing fashionable clothes and endorsing their typical subcultural lifestyle. The *Stiliagi*'s emergence roughly coincided with the rise of Western countercultural movements, such as the *Zazous* in France, the Teddy Boys in England, and the Swing Kids in Germany (Peiss 2012; Lebina 2015; Vainshtein 2018). There is no indication that the *Stiliagi* consciously modelled themselves after these Western countercultures, and

---

[5] The film was released in the Soviet Union as late as 1961, although music from the film was available in larger urban centers as early as 1945. Other films included the MGM *Tarzan* series produced by Sol Lesser, the German trophy film *The Woman of My Dreams* (1944), and the US-American films *His Butler's Sister* (1943), *The Thief of Bagdad* (1940), and *Waterloo Bridge* (1940). For more information, see, for example, White (2015, 66–69).

[6] The historical situation was different. The musician and *Stiliaga* Alexei Kozlov, for example, recalls that during the post-war years, Moscow was full of mutilated bodies of soldiers; they could not work due to PTSD and/or injuries they suffered from and often became alcoholics (1998, 52–53). As Martina Kübler's article in this collection shows, even the wounded veteran's body was idealized and represented in morally superior terms in cultural productions.

it is hard to imagine that they had any extensive or comprehensive knowledge of them (Litvinov 2009; Vainshtein 2018). It is more productive to think of their culture as a bricolage that was influenced by disparate pieces of information about life in the United States and Western Europe and merged them into a new countercultural movement. The movement itself involved young people, mainly students living in larger urban centers, who dressed and behaved differently from the norm. They assembled on central places and strolled the streets, thus showcasing their colorful clothing while talking loudly to each other. They also often met in the apartments of individual members of the movement to listen to jazz music and dance. Initially, the *Stiliagi* as a movement had no coherent political or social vision; their main goal was to escape the rigid confines of regular Soviet life which they perceived as bland, boring, and prescriptive (Edele 2002; Fürst 2012, 2015).

The politicization of the movement was a response to Soviet authorities and media coverage (Gorski 2018, 98–101) that constructed and degraded the *Stiliagi*'s bodies as different. Most scholars agree that the *Stiliagi*'s style of self-fashioning was an eclectic, yet unique combination of Western influences, with jazz musicians and foreign movies serving as initial sources of inspiration. Later, the *Stiliagi* borrowed from the style of Elvis Presley, especially the cocked hairstyle and semolina platform shoes along with colorful shirts and ties typically associated with the rock 'n' roll star. The bright clothing and unusual hairstyles visibly accentuated young men's bodies and contrasted starkly with the badly dressed, aged, and often disabled bodies of the older generation. The *Stiliagi*'s style was not limited to clothing but comprised a range of embodied practices: they developed their own repertoire of gestures, movements, and behavior, including forms of greeting and saying goodbye as well as ways of walking, dancing, and interacting with each other. They created neologisms or russified English terms to form their own vocabulary; some of these words were even incorporated into informal Russian and exist to this day.[7] Most of the (published) memoirs and personal interviews

---

[7] An example is the word *zhlob* which means 'square' or 'redneck' in English. The word has Polish origins and acquired its meaning in Odessa criminal circles in the early twentieth century. The *Stiliagi* popularized it by using it in relation to people of the working classes (Smirnov 2003).

with representatives of the group indicate that the movement revolved around a love of jazz and swing music, which was frowned upon by Soviet officials.[8] As some scholars argue, the *Stiliagi* movement was the first fashion-conscious countercultural movement since the October Revolution of 1917.[9] Its contribution to the cultural history of the Soviet Union lies in the fact that it alerted state authorities and public masses to the notion that Soviet men could, and perhaps should, be fashion-conscious at a time when any kind of fashion for men was disparaged (Lebina 2015, 65–80), and any interest in it was considered effeminate, excessive, and a sign of depravity.[10]

The fashioning of the *Stiliaga* body also contradicted the hitherto prevailing norm of the youthful body: in line with Soviet conventions of the *Komsomol* youth, it was supposed to be sporty and healthy while at the same time covered by oftentimes poorly fitting dark-colored clothing. The colors and styles embraced by *Stiliagi* and the deliberate break with Soviet conventions that their self-fashioning entailed called those limiting rules into question and, by implication, posed a threat to the regime's values. As already mentioned above, the *Stiliagi* also embraced new ways of dancing and walking. Their dance moves were quick and liberated from the more rigid steps of foxtrots and waltzes. When walking the streets, they often acted as if on a runway. Their styles of moving emphasized the pleasures of inhabiting and exhibiting a body that was otherwise discouraged: the *Stiliagi* brought the idea of experiencing pleasure through music, clothing, friendships, and relationships (both homoerotic and heterosexual) to the lexicon of conventional Soviet masculinity, while simultaneously presenting a challenge to the same.

[8] In general, there was no official Soviet position towards jazz, blues, swing, and rock'n' roll. Glenn Miller and other jazz musicians the *Stiliagi* admired were intermittently allowed and forbidden at different times and in different locales. For further information on music and entertainment during the Soviet Union of the 1950s and 1960s, see Tsipursky (2016).

[9] See, for instance, Bartlett (2010, 2013), Fürst (2012), and Vainshtein (2018).

[10] The deliberate lack of interest in fashion was connected to the communist ideology that proliferated after the Bolshevik revolution. In addition, economic and social distinction also played a role. Interest in fashion was considered a bourgeois endeavor and condemned as a form of disloyalty to socialist doctrines.

Fashioning Post-War Soviet Masculinities

As discussed by Raewyn Connell, hegemonic masculinity should be understood as the "configuration of gender practice which embodies the currently accepted answer to the problem of the legitimacy of patriarchy, which guarantees (or is taken to guarantee) the dominant position of men and the subordination of women" (1995, 77). That is, patriarchal hegemony builds on the myth of 'strong' men in opposition to both 'weak' women and non-hegemonic types of masculinity. If hegemony is understood—in Gramscian terms—as a phenomenon that dominates not only through physical force but also through the creation of a consensus of what is considered masculine and thus successful (Germino 1990, 38; Gramsci 2000, 56–62), then, as Hooper argues, "[h]egemonic masculinity gets transformed through constant challenges and struggles, to resemble whatever traits happen to be most strategically useful for the getting and keeping of power" (2001, 61). In this sense, the most strategically useful type of masculinity after the Great Patriotic War was embodied by men who had survived the horrors of the war but retained their belief in a communist future. As Lilya Kaganovsky discusses, the traditional socio-cultural construction of men in the 1930s as hardworking and utterly dedicated to serving their country and Stalin changed—with the beginning of the war—into a notion of 'sacrificial masculinity' that in essence equated itself with the destiny of the Soviet Union (2008, 12–18). In this sense, Stalin was celebrated as the leader and father figure of the nation. The tall, upright, stiff, and rarely smiling Stalin, who mainly wore variations of the military tunic, served as a role model for the form of masculinity that was represented by the body of the veteran, thus solidifying its hegemonic status.[11]

The notion of masculinity in this disembodied character, however, corresponds with prevailing norms of representation: For once, Stalin's portraits and photographs often show only his face and a part of the torso. Such representations follow specific conventions of depicting leaders of the communist party, e.g., Lenin (Gill 2020, 120–125). Moreover, Stalin's body remained mainly covered and hidden from the public eye due to his dress choices. While fighting in the war was an intensely physical experience, representations and recollections of the war, especially in the

---

[11] I see the figure of Stalin as a veteran of the October Revolution (1917) and the Russian Civil War (1918).

Soviet Union, mostly omitted the corporeality of soldiers. The portraits sent home from the front by soldiers or shown in the newspapers and later on television were intensively idealized and focused solely on the fighters' faces. This form of disembodied representation continued after the war. The physical impact of the war as represented by mutilated, hurt, and disfigured bodies never entered the media or official discourses and was obliterated and removed from urban centers, which suggests the potential threat it posed to the narrative of Soviet military glory. By contrast, the *Stiliagi*'s presence and the glamour they embodied served to create an alternative type of masculinity, one that was not rooted in Soviet or military ideology but that represented an indulgence in the pleasures post-war life in larger cities had to offer. The *Stiliagi* embodied non-hegemonic notions of masculinities and negotiated what James Messerschmidt has identified as 'dominant' and 'dominating' types of masculinity (2015, 4).

The contrast between two generations and two types of masculinities—older, experienced, and military versus younger, educated, and more fashion-conscious—was an omnipresent issue in public discourse in the Soviet Union during the late 1940s and 1950s. In these comparisons, the *Stiliagi*'s bodies and, as a consequence, their morals were always criticized. A more favorable representation of the *Stiliagi* can be found in the 1962 novel *Kollegi* (*Colleagues*) by the Soviet dissident writer Vasily Aksenov. In the novel, two young men befriend a war veteran and come to understand his critical position towards the *Stiliagi*. Aksenov demonstrates that the generation that fought in the war preserved the values associated with heroism and hegemonic masculinity, such as keeping emotions at bay, turning to violence as a last resort, the consumption of alcohol as a form of escapism from traumatic memories about the war, and, finally, loyalty to Stalin and the Soviet Union. As I have argued elsewhere, these examples offer insights into the generational conflict as well as the mutual understanding of each generation's historical situatedness (Myzelev forthcoming). Such a representation of the *Stiliagi* in particular, and the younger generation of urban men in general is unusual for the period.

The *Stiliagi* represented, to some extent, an identity crisis of a group of youth that could not—and were not willing to—fulfill the masculine ideals of the previous generation. The students who mainly constituted the movement did not have the chance to become war heroes, because there was no war for them to fight, and they also could not compete with the working-class bodies, often depicted in an idealized way in Soviet monuments. For instance, one of the most prominent sculptures of the time, *Worker and Kolkhoz Woman* (1937) by sculptor Vera Mukhina, which became the logo of Mosfilm (Moscow Film Studios), represents a muscular, upright, and trained half-nude body that projects not only health and strength, but also the values of physical work and insistent dedication to socialist ideas. This type of masculinity was foreclosed for the educated, non-working-class *Stiliagi*. The younger generation thus used different ways of asserting itself. Significantly, as Graham H. Roberts notes, they became the first generation of self-conscious consumers (2013, 192–195). Their interest in change was mainly predicated on fashioning themselves as individuals who were not part of the masses, a distinction achieved in part through consumption. Due to the limited availability of consumer objects in the Soviet Union, the *Stiliagi* cultivated their difference through an interest in jazz, dance styles, insider language, and jokes.

While differentiating themselves from others was indeed part of the movement's motivation, it is equally important to acknowledge its political impact, that is, a push for renewal, specifically expressed in the *Stiliagi*'s interest in contemporary Western music, which resonated with the modernization processes of this period. Implicitly, their interest in Western clothing and dancing constituted an embodied desire to escape the oppressive ideological climate of the Soviet Union and perhaps, to some extent, to feel free. The *Stiliagi* aimed at creating an alternative version of masculinity, one less rigid than that of the previous generation. These men were interested in reformulating notions of manhood. Countering disembodied and idealized notions of masculinity, the *Stiliagi* created a more playful image of the contemporary urbanite, corresponding better to post-war realities and reflecting optimism for social change through an affirmation of (Western) fashion, music, and technology, such as music recorded on discarded X-ray plates as well as the newer radio and vinyl players. In this way, the *Stiliagi* body is emblematic of the ideological tensions, generational conflicts, and gender anxieties within the post-war Soviet Union, but can at the same time also be read as a 'future'-oriented body, enabling young urbanites to envision new forms of masculinity, albeit within a limited framework.

THE *STILIAGI* IN THE SOVIET MEDIA

My research on the *Stiliagi* movement reveals that there are no positive representations of the *Stiliagi* in the Soviet media. The international press was not interested in or aware of the movement, and contemporary Soviet media portrayed the *Stiliagi* exclusively in a negative light, thereby employing mainly two strategies of depiction. The first retained a critical stance, yet involved aspects of ambivalence. Since all the representations were carried out under the auspices of the regime, the authors were expected to criticize the *Stiliagi*. Thus, despite their bias, these representations provided insights into what it was like to be a *Stiliaga* and arguably helped to shape the *Stiliagi* movement and its legacy. While satirizing and criticizing the *Stiliagi* and representing them in a stereotypical way, some magazines, such as *Krokodil*, simultaneously portrayed their fashion choices and bodies as funny, humorous, and as attractive as possible, which lent their works an ambiguous quality and ambivalent position towards the *Stiliagi*. Responding to such representations, younger readers of the magazines learned about the *Stiliagi* fashion style and started to copy it. One example of a writer working under and to some extent circumventing official censorship is Nikolai Nosov who published the children's book series *Neznaika*, which was very popular in the 1950s and the following decades. *Neznaika* (*Dunno's Adventures*) was first published in 1954, and the description of the male main character Neznaika's clothing includes aspects such as a large wide-brimmed hat, yellow trousers, an orange shirt, and a pea-green tie, which corresponds with the style of the *Stiliagi* of the early 1950s. Neznaika further represents many characteristics that were attributed to the *Stiliagi* in the critical press: he does not like to work hard, is obsessed with his appearance, and often gets into trouble. He is ignorant in many ways and must be enlightened by his friends. At the same time, he is charismatic, precocious, and popular. According to Nosov, the censors did not realize that he was seeking inspiration from the *Stiliagi* movement for his books and thus allowed him to not only model his main character after the *Stiliagi*, but also portray him as a likable figure (Zagidulina 2010, n.p., fn 18).

The second type of representation was more adverse and centered on the *Stiliagi*'s alleged lack of masculinity and taste. For example, the satirical magazine *Krokodil*, the only national magazine of its kind available

Fig. 7.2 Caricature comparing a *Stiliaga* to a parrot (Dukhovichnyi and Slobodskii 1960, 9)

throughout the Soviet Union, published "Pochti po Bremu: Popugai"[12] in 1960 (Fig. 7.2). Comparing the colorful and flamboyant style of a *Stiliaga* to a parrot, it proposed that a *Stiliaga* was never an original but always mimicked others, especially Westerners. The accompanying short poem also stresses the imitation that was presumably at the core of the *Stiliaga* character. The first verse says that "unlike a parrot, a *Stiliaga* is known not for his beautiful feathers but for his imitation of the colors" (Dukhovichnyi and Slobodskii 1960, 9; my translation). The illustration

[12] The title "Almost According to Brehm: Parrot" (my translation) refers to Alfred Edmund Brehm (1829–1884), a German zoologist who wrote *Brehm's Life of Animals*, a work that became highly popular in Russia.

shows the *Stiliaga* with a small body and large head decorated by the famous *kok* (a cocked hairstyle consisting of slick sides and a teased wave styled high above the forehead), which in this case is compared to that of the parrot. The feet are covered in sandals and very colorful socks, one of the main attributes of the *Stiliagi*, and reminiscent of the parrot's inverted claws. The illustration also alludes to the fact that a *Stiliaga* would do anything to showcase his socks, even if this means wearing sandals with a winter coat. Moreover, the numerous details, including pockets, decorative stitching, and large buttons on the sandals and coat mark these items as foreign. Contemporary clothing produced in the Soviet Union did not feature many decorations and tended to be simple to streamline its mass production.[13] Particularly noteworthy is the colorful flamboyant tie that ends with a beer opener, suggesting that the *Stiliagi* enjoyed drinking. The illustration's accentuation of short, small legs implies that *Stiliagi* men do not have what was considered a masculine physique and that their bodies—similar to their minds—are weak.

Another notable example, also from *Krokodil* (1958), shows a *Stiliaga*'s lack of expertise as a camp counselor (Fig. 7.3). The young man with glasses and the characteristic *kok* appears unsuited for life outdoors: he sports a sizable belly and narrow shoulders, cannot swim, do pull-ups, or even catch butterflies—all of which are highly popular activities in a Soviet summer camp. He lacks the conventional attributes associated with Soviet manhood such as muscles, a short haircut, and the necessary skills that are considered indispensable for a camp counselor whose task it is to propagate masculine values of survival and skills in exploring nature. Here, the skit is not primarily aimed at the *Stiliagi* only, as the man in the pictures does not wear colorful clothes, but at any urban and intellectual male who desires fashionability.

An even more telling representation of the *Stiliagi* is found in a film reel from *Leningradskaia Khronika* (1956). Here, in addition to criticizing the group of the *Stiliagi* for being interested in Western culture,

---

[13] The clothes the *Stiliagi* wore were either altered or newly tailored clothes. In addition, their eclectic style comprised items they found on illegal clothing markets in different Russian cities; some were occasionally available in stores. See, for instance, Edele (2002), Bartlett (2010), and Vainshtein (2018) for further research on this topic.

Fig. 7.3 A *Stiliaga* as long-haired and inept camp counselor (Fedorov 1958, 6)

listening to and trading illegal jazz recordings, and being unemployed,[14] the short documentary puts their concept of masculinity into question. In one of the shots, the camera zooms in on a *Stiliaga* who has just been arrested while the narrator is recounting why he and other young *Stiliagi* men ended up in the police station and, in particular, points out that this person is "neither a man nor a woman" (00:01:28; my translation). After a short close-up, the narrator considers it necessary to clarify that this is a man but that his haircut looks feminine. The *Stiliaga* whose look causes this controversy has longer dark curly hair and a bit of a *kok*.

These examples show that in Soviet mainstream media, the body of a *Stiliaga* is represented—in Judith Butler's terms—as the "materialization" of a subversive and abnormal lifestyle. Butler argues that matter has to be conceived of as a *"process of materialization that stabilizes over time to produce the effect of boundary, fixity, and surface we call matter"* (1993, 9; emphasis in original). Consequently, the bodily distinctive characteristic of *Stiliagi* identity, such as a more slender and feminine physique, the members' hairstyle, and their clothes, were not just considered a result of bad taste but also a manifestation of their personal shortcomings. These visible characteristics were seen as symptoms of an inner weakness—a malaise of the soul. Numerous illustrations in *Krokodil* and other satirical journals ridicule the *Stiliagi*'s style, especially their wide trousers, wide-shouldered and loose blazers, colorful ties and shirts, and shoes with high platforms, but they also show mainly men who look smug and idle (Fig. 7.4).

These representations of idleness marked the *Stiliagi*'s body as criminal. Having no real occupation or profession had also been associated with being apolitical, decadent, and superfluous at the time and beyond (Polotskaya 1992; Diment 1998). Curiously, all representations of the *Stiliagi* in *Krokodil* feature only one individual *Stiliaga*; a male *Stiliaga* is never shown in a group, and only at times are these men depicted dancing with women. As life writing and interviews reveal, however, *Stiliagi* often danced together, not as pairs but in groups in which women were a minority or not represented at all (Aksenov 1962; Kozlov 1998, 60–70). The singular depiction of the *Stiliagi* in *Krokodil* as well as other

---

[14] Unemployment was a punishable crime in the Soviet Union. Between 1952 and 1954, around 150,000 people were arrested for unemployment and 1339 found guilty (Łoś 1988).

Fig. 7.4   Caricature of a flamboyantly dressed male *Stiliaga* (Zmoiro 1958, 15)

magazines might serve to ward off even the slightest allusion to homo-eroticism, and depicting *Stiliagi* dancing with women can be considered an attempt to avoid debates about potential homoerotic relations.

Importantly, all critical responses to the *Stiliagi* served at least one of two functions. First, by discussing predominantly *Stiliagi* men, maga-zines and journals emphasized that the movement was male-centered. The focus on *male* members here also reveals masculinity as a more fragile concept than femininity, more fraught with anxiety and in need of constantly being proven. Second, they foregrounded notions of effem-inacy, due to the fact that men displayed what was conventionally considered feminine behavior, such as an excessive preoccupation with their appearance, a passion for fashion, expansive dance movements, and an urge to be seen. The examples that I have discussed deploy a carni-valesque exaggeration of this supposed effeminacy to make that point.

Paradoxically, this strategy helped to promulgate and normalize images of the very gender-ambiguous body that Soviet ideology wanted to eradicate.

Representations of the *Stiliagi*'s Body in Life Writing and Interviews

Life writing of *Stiliagi* and conversations with those who were part of it consist of narratives that diverge starkly from those the media attempted to instill. One of the interviewees recalled that he was friends with several other young men who studied in the same institute in Kyiv. They enjoyed jazz and liked playing music. They dressed up to be recognized by those with similar interests, and "attracted young women who liked the same music and liked to dance. For us, it was a way of finding and keeping like-minded friends".[15] Another interviewee noted that "[w]e wanted to be different, especially from those who also studied in my institute but just came from villages. I do not know why, but it was very important for us to be seen as urban, sophisticated. We dressed up and strolled to demonstrate our difference from others".[16] These two parts of interviews are exemplary of many of the *Stiliagi*'s memories[17] which underscore their wish for belonging to a community and building friendships with like-minded peers. With regard to the accusation of effeminacy, my informants usually shrugged it off or noted that it was an idea imposed from the outside. Yuli Ganetz summarizes it as follows:

> I never felt less because I thought of myself as a *Stiliaga*. I always felt that I was more of a man because of that. I attracted the attention of young women, and my friends always approved of my clothing. Yes, sometimes older people, especially older women, would say something like "shame on you, we did not fight for this in the war". But honestly, I took it as a compliment. That meant that my appearance worked.[18]

[15] Dvorinskii, Zhora. Interview by Alla Myzelev. Personal Interview. Toronto, December 2018.

[16] Rappoport, Evgenii. Interview by Alla Myzelev. Personal Interview. San Diego, July 2012.

[17] See, for instance, Guk (1997), Bek (2004), Mamedova (2005), and Skorikov (2015).

[18] Ganetz, Yuli. Interview by Alla Myzelev. Personal Interview. Toronto, November 2017.

Two aspects that need to be extrapolated here are the notion of homosociality and the idea of eliciting social and political criticism as a sign of positive self-fashioning. The phenomenon of the *Stiliagi* has often been construed as a homosocial movement by critics at the time, by members of the movement as well as by scholars and memoirists in the past twenty years. As Eve Kosofsky Sedgwick demonstrates, "there is an asymmetry in our present society between, on the one hand, the relatively continuous relations of female homosocial and homosexual bonds, and on the other hand the radically discontinuous relations of male homosocial and homosexual bonds" (2015, 2–3). Additionally, she argues that there is a radically disrupted continuum in our society between "sexual and nonsexual male bonds" (3–4), while female homosocial desire is palpable and seen as acceptable.

In discussing "our society", Sedgwick refers to Western societies in the 1980s; however, homosocial relationships in the post-war Soviet Union were treated similarly. Friendships between women were socially accepted, while friendships between men were perceived differently. Male friendships in the Soviet Union were considered acceptable only if those friendships subscribed to rituals that Connell characterizes as traditional male bonding (1995). The idea of a brotherhood of soldiers during the war transformed into a discourse of friendship, held together by a nostalgic longing for the past as well as a shared idea of male heroism: most representations in the media revolved around reminiscences of participating in sporting events and conquering nature. Friendships were relegated to either the private sphere of apartments, the countryside, or nature. The less virile or trained body of a *Stiliaga* already posed a threat to discourses of heteronormativity and hegemonic masculinity. Friendships among men and especially the *Stiliagi*'s breaking of norms added to this threat and evoked what might be called the 'specter of homosexuality' (Sedgwick 2015).

As has been suggested before, this was reflected in how the *Stiliagi* engaged in the cultural practice of dance. *Stiliagi* often danced next to or opposite each other. At times, two men danced together and, occasionally, even held hands. Igor Berukshtis, a Russian *émigré* and jazz musician based in New York City, recalls the following episode:

> In 1949, I was about 16 and vacationed in Adler. There I saw two people dressed in khaki. Two happy, successful, refined lovers of culture. [...] There was a piano player who played in the style of popular-at-the-time

pianist Alexander Tsfasman. When he played, those two "brother acrobats" danced holding hands and then separated, in the style that the *Stiliagi* would later dance on Moscow dance stages. After, the authorities posted signs: "It is forbidden to dance in vulgar *Lindu*[19] style".[20]

The idea of men holding hands not only made the Soviet cadres uncomfortable but even Berukshtis himself, who recalled this episode during a conversation with other former *Stiliagi* men. Their condescending tone indicated their unease. Berukshtis's word choice, for instance the term "brother acrobats", signals that the two men's bodies were flexible and artistic—decidedly not masculine. Also, the word "brothers" suggests a sense of intimacy or rather closeness and connectedness different from that of Berukshtis and his peers, making clear that he wants to distance himself from notions of homoeroticism. In the conservative climate of the late Stalinist and early Thaw Soviet Union, even a slight change in the understanding of masculinity seemed radical. It is therefore important to note that it is possible that some of my informants or memoirists did not mention homoeroticism or homosexuality out of (a latent) fear of inviting the label 'homosexual'.[21]

In terms of the two types of male friendships, "vertical/hierarchical and horizontal homosociality", that function within patriarchal societies, as described by Nils Hammarén and Thomas Johansson (2014, 5), hierarchical homosociality aims to maintain hegemony and thus the 'masculine status quo'. The conventional friendships in the Soviet Union of the 1940s and 1950s that were portrayed in films and the media fit this description. Horizontal homosociality, as described by Sedgwick in reference to women, "points towards relations that are based on emotional closeness, intimacy, and a non-profitable form of friendship" (2015, 708). The relationships between the *Stiliagi*, as described in life writing and interviews, point towards the horizontal model. Such unconstrained and

---

[19] *Lindu* is one of the dance styles popular among the *Stiliagi*. It is similar to swing.

[20] Berukshtis, Igor. Radio Interview on Four Past *Stiliagi*. 2001. https://stiliagi.svo boda.org/a/1966933.html. This interview was featured on the Internet radio channel Svoboda. I last accessed it in December 2019, yet when I tried to follow the link in the course of working on this article, it appeared broken. My email inquiries about restoring the website were not answered. I find the fact that only this part disappeared from the extensive Svoboda website curious. It raises the question in what respect the 'specter of homoeroticism' haunts Soviet memories until today.

[21] I would like to thank Silvia Gerlsbeck for noting this point.

casual relationships between men and women were discouraged. Especially threatening to the prevailing ideal of masculinity was the alleged serial monogamy or even polygamy of the *Stiliagi*. *Krokodil* and other magazines almost exclusively portrayed philanderers as *Stiliagi*. However, according to the interviews that I conducted, the relationships among *Stiliagi* men were based on mutual support, curiosity, discovery, pleasure in music and dance, and a newly acquired sense of freedom.

The memoirs, along with literary sources and personal interviews, point towards a discursive shift with regard to constructions of masculinity and cultural identity: the *Stiliagi* wanted to feel 'less Soviet' and more cosmopolitan, US-American, or Western European, depending on the group one talks to. Some were fascinated by US-American culture and music, others liked the British or the French one. The movement's heterogeneity reflects the youth's desire for more cultural openness towards Western influences and, more importantly, for social change within the Soviet Union.

CRITICAL REFLECTIONS: THE *Stiliagi* BODY BETWEEN POLITICS AND PLEASURE

With the *Stiliagi* movement, the male body became the center of an ideological conflict for the first time since the October Revolution: The non-Soviet way of life of the *Stiliagi* threatened dominant ideologies and ideals of manhood in the Soviet Union. Urban, educated young men introduced and, to some extent, popularized a new taste in clothing and music. Gradually, the movement's initial hedonism and apoliticism gained political importance, as they signified opposition to the Soviet regime. Thus, the movement became political even though it never actively opposed the regime. The presence of such difference made Soviet cadres uncomfortable to such an extent that *Stiliagi* were sometimes hunted and attacked by members of the Soviet youth organization *Komsomol*: their *koks* were trimmed or their narrow trousers cut. Moreover, the regime and the media ascribed negative qualities such as laziness, alcoholism, an inability to work physically, and a refusal to think originally to members of the movement. The *Stiliagi* responded to such accusations in various ways: some appreciated the attention, even if negative; others struggled with the obstacles they encountered in finding work after graduating, if prospective employers sensed that they belonged to the *Stiliagi* movement.

Members of the movement realized the pleasures associated with the *Stiliagi* lifestyle in mostly private apartment rooms that served as safe havens. In this contribution, I tried to suggest that the relationships between male *Stiliagi* were in many cases homosocial. Yet, the Soviet media and even the *Stiliagi* themselves avoided mentioning any kind of romantic relationship that might be labelled 'homoerotic'. While the *Stiliagi* were allowed to flaunt their different lifestyle in public spaces, such as busy streets of large cities, restaurants, and bars, most of the movement's social life was relegated to private spaces. Precisely due to the fact that the *Stiliagi* mostly gathered away from the gaze of the public eye, the notion of homoeroticism remains a 'specter' that haunts discussions of the movement. It is closely tied to the *Stiliagi*'s interest in aspects of social life that in the Soviet Union were associated with women and thus seen as effeminate, such as consumption, fashionability, *flâneuring*, and socializing. The fear of 'inappropriate' gender and sexual behavior that was considered a threat to the national body determined the negative reaction of the Soviet media and their critical treatment of these homosocial bonds. Against this background, it is tempting to ponder the role of un-, under-, and somewhat realized homoerotic desires played among members of the group. Yet potential homoerotic relations among the *Stiliagi* were and still remain a taboo subject. In many discussions, the topic seems to be the proverbial 'elephant in the room'.

References

Aksenov, Vasily. *Colleagues*. Translated by Margaret Wettlin. London: Putnam, 1962 [1960].

Bartlett, Djurdja. *FashionEast: The Spectre That Haunted Socialism*. Cambridge, MA: MIT Press, 2010.

———. "Socialist Dandies International: East Europe, 1946–1959." *Fashion Theory: The Journal of Dress, Body and Culture* 17, no. 3 (2013): 249–289.

Bek, Tatiana. "Ia i est' mladshii brat nastoiashchikh Stiliag" («Я и есть младший брат настоящих Стиляг»). *Stiliagi. Vospominaniia* (*Стиляги. Воспоминания*), 2004. http://www.beliy.ru/work/stilyagifilm/id=38-1.htm. Accessed June 10, 2021.

Butler, Judith. *Bodies That Matter: On the Discursive Limits of Sex*. New York: Routledge, 1993.

Connell, Raewyn. *Masculinities*. Berkeley: U of California P, 1995.

Diment, Galya. *Goncharov's Oblomov: A Critical Companion*. Evanston: Northwestern UP, 1998.

Dukhovichnyi, Vladimir, and Mikhail Slobodskii. "Pochti po Bremu: Popugai" («Почти по Брему: Попугай»). *Krokodil* (*Крокодил*), no. 1 (1960): 9.

Edele, Mark. "Strange Young Men in Stalin's Moscow: The Birth and Life of the *Stiliagi*, 1945–1953." *Jahrbücher für Geschichte Osteuropas* 50, no. 1 (2002): 37–61.

Fedorov, Yuryi. "My s nashim vozhatym provodim vse vremia" («Мы с нашим вожатым проводим всё время»). *Krokodil* (*Крокодил*), no. 14 (1958): 6.

Fürst, Juliane. *Stalin's Last Generation: Soviet Post-War Youth and the Emergence of Mature Socialism*. Oxford: Oxford UP, 2012.

———. "Swinging Across the Iron Curtain and Moscow's Summer of Love: How Western Youth Culture Went East." In *Transnational Histories of Youth in the Twentieth Century*, edited by Richard Ivan Jobs and David M. Pomfret, 236–259. London: Palgrave Macmillan, 2015.

Germino, Dante L. *Antonio Gramsci: Architect of a New Politics*. Baton Rouge: Louisiana State UP, 1990.

Gill, Graeme. "The Face of the Regime: Political Portraiture in the Soviet Union and Russia." In *The Political Portrait: Leadership, Image and Power*, edited by Luciano Cheles and Alessandro Giacone, 130–149. New York and London: Routledge, 2020.

Gorski, Bradley. "Manufacturing Dissent: Vassily Aksyonov, *Stiliagi*, and the Dilemma of Self-Interpretation." *Russian Literature* 96–98 (2018): 77–104.

Gramsci, Antonio. "Socialism and Culture." In *The Gramsci Reader: Selected Writings 1916–1935*, edited by David Forgacs, 56–62. New York: New York UP, 2000.

Guk, Olesia. "Tarzan v svoem otechestve" («Тарзан в своем отечестве»). *Pchela* (*Пчела*) 11 (1997). http://www.beliy.ru/work/stilyagifilm/-id=43. htm. Accessed August 17, 2020.

Hammarén, Nils, and Thomas Johansson. "Homosociality: In Between Power and Intimacy." *SAGE Open* 4, no. 1 (2014): 1–11. https://doi.org/10. 1177/2158244013518057. Accessed August 18, 2020.

Hooper, Charlotte. *Manly States: Masculinities, International Relations, and Gender Politics*. New York: Columbia UP, 2001.

Kaganovsky, Lilya. *How the Soviet Man Was Unmade: Cultural Fantasy and Male Subjectivity Under Stalin*. Pittsburgh: U of Pittsburgh P, 2008.

Kozlov, Aleksei. *Kozel na sakse: I tak vsiu zhizn* (*Козёл на саксе: И так всю жизнь*). Moskva: Vagrius, 1998.

Lebina, Natalia. *Muzhchina i zhenshchina: Telo, moda, kultura. SSSR-ottepel* (*Мужчина и женщина: Тело, Мода, Культура. СССР-оттепель*). Moskva: Novoe Literaturnoe Obozrenie, 2015.

Leningradskaia Khronika (*Ленинградская Хроника*). Dir. Mikhail Dobrovoi. Vol. 6. Rossiiskii Gosudarstvennyi Arkhiv. Leningrad: Lenfilm, 1956. https:// youtu.be/md-fFYdWW_0. Accessed June 15, 2020.

Litvinov, Georgi. *Stiliagi: Kak eto bylo* (*Стиляги: Как это было*). Sankt-Peterburg: Amfora, 2009.

Łoś, Maria. "Law, Ideology and Economy: The Case of Anti-Parasite Laws." In *Communist Ideology, Law and Crime: A Comparative View of the USSR and Poland*, edited by Maria Łoś, 78–104. London: Palgrave Macmillan, 1988.

Mamedova, Maia. "Nina Dorda: Menia perevospityvala ministr kultury" («Нина Дорда: Меня перевоспитывала министр культуры»). *Trud* (*Труд*) 79 (2005). https://www.trud.ru/article/05-2005/87272_nina_dorda_menja_p erevospityvala_ministr_kultury.html. Accessed June 15, 2021.

Messerschmidt, James. *Hegemonic Masculinities and Camouflaged Politics: Unmasking the Bush Dynasty and Its War Against Iraq*. New York and Oxford: Routledge, 2015.

Myzelev, Alla. "Guys in a Strange Style: Urban and Soviet Social Class of Soviet *Stiliagi*." *Critical Studies in Fashion and Beauty* 12, no. 2 (2021), forthcoming.

Nosov, Nikolai. *Prikliucheniia Neznaiki i ego druzei* (*Приключения Незнайки и его друзей*). Leningrad: Lenizdat, 1988 [1954].

Peiss, Kathy. "Excerpt from Zoot Suit: The Enigmatic Career of an Extreme Style." *Journal of Transnational American Studies* 4, no. 2 (2012): 157–182.

Polotskaya, Anna. "Ilya Oblomov and the Superfluous Men of the 1880s and 1890s." *Scottish Slavonic Review* 19 (1992): 27–37.

Roberts, Graham H. "Revolt into Style: Consumption and Its (Dis)Contents in Valery Todorovsky's Film *Stilyagi*." *Film, Fashion & Consumption* 2, no. 2 (2013): 187–200.

Sedgwick, Eve Kosofsky. *Between Men: English Literature and Male Homosocial Desire*. 30th Anniversary ed. New York: Columbia UP, 2015 [1985].

Skorikov, Gennadyi. "Rasskazhu ia vam istoriiu takuiu: zakhiliali raz na khatu neplokhuiu…" («Расскажу я вам историю такую: захиляли раз на хату неплохую…»). *Stiliagi. Vospominaniia* (*Стиляги. Воспоминания*) (2015). http://www.beliy.ru/work/stilyagifilm/-id=355-1.htm. Accessed June 15, 2021.

Smirnov, Valeryi P. *Polutolkovyi slovar odesskogo iazyka* (*Полутолковый словарь одесского языка*). Moskva: Poligraf, 2003.

Stiliagi (Hipsters). Dir. Valery Todorovsky. Distributed by Central Partnership, 2008. https://www.youtube.com/watch?v=4QfZb0Ve_bw. Accessed June 30, 2021.

Tsipursky, Gleb. *Socialist Fun: Youth, Consumption, and State-Sponsored Popular Culture in the Soviet Union, 1945–1970*. Pittsburgh, PA: U of Pittsburgh P, 2016.

Vainshtein, Olga. "Orange Jackets and Pea Green Pants: The Fashion of Stilyagi in Soviet Postwar Culture." *Fashion Theory* 22, no. 2 (2018): 167–185.

White, Frederick. "Tarzan in the Soviet Union: British Lord, American Movie Idol and Soviet Counterculture Figure." *The Soviet and Post-Soviet Review* 42, no. 1 (2015): 64–85.

Zagidulina, Marina. "Obraz Neznaiki i ego vospriatie (literaturnyi geroi v informatsionnom prostranstve)" («Образ Незнайки и его восприятие [Литературный герой в информационном пространстве]») *Zenon* 74 (2010). http://zenon74.ru/krug-obsheniya/obraz-neznaiki-i-ego-vospri yatie-literaturnyi-geroi-v-informatsionnom-prostranstve. Accessed June 6, 2020.

Zmoiro, Eduard P. "No Title." *Krokodil* (*Крокодил*), no. 15 (1958): 15.

PART III

Passing Bodies

Claiming the *Flâneur*'s Body: Cross-Dressing Women, Autobiographical Self-Fashioning, and the Pleasures of Passing and Not Passing as a Man on the Street

Sandra Dinter

INTRODUCTION

The French sociologist Marcel Mauss claims that techniques of the body, the ways in which individuals habitually use their bodies, are as much physiological movements as they are expressions of conditioning. Mauss proposes that techniques of the body "vary [...] between societies, educations, proprieties and fashions, prestiges" (1973, 73). Using walking as his primary example, Mauss argues that although all able bodies are capable of bipedal movement, the exact ways in which people walk and how others perceive their walking are cultural matters. According to Mauss, gaits

S. Dinter (✉)
Friedrich-Alexander-Universität Erlangen-Nürnberg, Erlangen, Germany
e-mail: sandra.dinter@fau.de

© The Author(s), under exclusive license to Springer Nature
Switzerland AG 2022
C. Dexl and S. Gerlsbeck (eds.), *The Male Body in Representation*,
Palgrave Studies in (Re)Presenting Gender,
https://doi.org/10.1007/978-3-030-88604-2_8

173

do not only differ across cultures but "are divided and vary by sex *and* by age" (76; emphasis in original), suspecting that differences in men's and women's walking can be traced back to their distinct physiques as well as their socialization (77). Mauss suggests that the walking body—in this case, a walking male body—is "a material entity that is itself subject to interpellations into discourses and systems" (11), as Carmen Dexl and Silvia Gerlsbeck note in the introduction to this volume. The body's movement on foot is neither purely physical, nor is it only discursive. In this sense, walking is always performative. Tim Edensor argues with reference to anthropologist Jane C. Desmond that "walking bodies communicate meaning through rhythms and gestures, constituting racial, ethnic, class and subcultural allegiances which are 'signalled, formed and negotiated through bodily movement'" (2000, 82). Masculinity, which can be added to this list, thus also comes into existence because legs and feet move in manners and spheres which are coded as masculine. Recognizing the diversity and plurality of social constructions of masculinity, this article examines pedestrian performances of masculinity that are not tied to the male body. It focuses on three self-representations of women in the nineteenth and early twentieth centuries who set foot on urban streets as men, whereby they claimed for themselves privileges that hinge on the male body.

For this purpose, it is necessary to recapitulate how walking was gendered in this period. I would like to commence with a rare literary scenario: when Lucy Snowe, the protagonist of Charlotte Brontë's *Villette* (1853), arrives in London, she decides to go out for a walk. Exploring St Paul's Cathedral, the Strand, and Cornhill on foot, she feels "[e]lation and pleasure [...] in my heart: to walk alone in London seemed of itself an adventure. [...] I went wandering whither chance might lead, in still ecstasy of freedom and enjoyment [...]. To do this, and to do it utterly alone, gave me, perhaps, an irrational, but real pleasure" (Brontë 2000, 49). Lucy's experience is remarkable since the gender ideology of nineteenth-century England discouraged women of higher social status to leave their homes without chaperones, let alone travel on their own. As Mica Nava explains, independent female mobility was condemned: "Disreputable women were associated with the immorality of public life in the city [...] [while] [r]espectable and virtuous women were connected to the home" (1996, 42). According to Rebecca Sundharam, women's solitary walking aroused suspicion because of the figure of the streetwalker – the fallen sister of the asexual 'angel in the house', whose itinerancy on the Victorian streets signaled her sexual availability [...]. [T]he streetwalker's physical mobility came to stand as a powerful symbol of her sexually tarnished and morally questionable status that cast a shadow over all acts of women's walking. (2011, 11)

Lone walks raised doubts on women's sexual and moral integrity and were therefore to be avoided.

At the same time, medical authorities promoted the idea of the frail female body, proposing that women were unable to cover long distances or to even walk 'properly' at all. In 1836, physician Donald Walker claimed that "[o]wing to the excessive shocks which both of these exercises communicate, neither [...] [running nor leaping] are very congenial to woman" (109). An article in the satirical periodical *Punch* in 1854 joked that "[t]he softness of the softer sex is sometimes excessive, not only in respect of heart and head, but also of general bodily constitution. [...] Women do not in general walk; only amble along or pace to and fro, with the sort of crawl called 'promenade'" (Anonymous 134). Women were expected to walk moderately, which illustrates that discourse, the lens through which societies interpret bodies, regulates scopes and modes of pedestrian mobility.

Lucy Snowe's stroll therefore bears transgressive potential. Walking on her own, potentially exposed to other passers-by, she undermines the gendered topography of London and the assumptions commonly made about women's bodies in the Victorian era. No third-person narrator finds fault with Lucy's pleasure, neither does she face any consequences on the plot level. Presenting solitary walking as a suitable leisure activity for middle-class women, *Villette* counters the writings of Charles Baudelaire, Thomas de Quincey, Edgar Allan Poe, Charles Dickens, and Walter Benjamin that primarily tied urban wandering to the male body.

A uniform definition of the *flâneur* does not exist—sometimes he is presented as a waif, at other times as an aristocrat. While some scholars read him as a metaphorical character, others conceive of him as a historical reality. He epitomizes hegemonic heterosexual masculinity as well as more fluid concepts of gender and sexuality.[1] Nevertheless, most critics would probably agree that the *flâneur* "captures a sense of idly walking in the city, with no specific destination, taking pleasure in the act of walking

---

[1] For an overview of the *flâneur*'s different facets and appearances, see Wilson (2001).

while making observations on urban life" (Coates 2017, 28). David Frisby characterizes the *flâneur* as "someone clearly at home in the metropolis and capable of combining observation, watchfulness and preserving his incognito" (1994, 92). Remaining a fleeting glimpse himself, the *flâneur* can take pleasure in observing others.

David Serlin points out that the *flâneur*'s invisibility relies on a normative, 'unmarked' body (2006, 198). Following the publication of Janet Wolff's article "The Invisible *Flâneuse*" in 1985, feminist critics have asserted that the *flâneur* can remain unseen because he is male.[2] Since gender ideology had naturalized men's presence in the public sphere, the *flâneur* did not stand out. In contrast, women frequently experienced street harassment.[3] Recent voices have drawn attention to race, arguing that it is not least the *flâneur*'s implicit whiteness that allows him to be overlooked, while people of color are more visible and vulnerable.[4] Serlin suggests that the concept of *flânerie* similarly perpetuates "narratives of normative able-bodiedness" (199) because it excludes bodies that require wheelchairs, crutches, or other forms of assistance to move along. From an intersectional point of view, the *flâneur*'s body therefore combines a set of privileges relating to class, gender, race, ability, and age.[5]

The supposedly unique potential of the white male body to be overlooked deserves more scrutiny. In what follows, I analyze autobiographical works by three European women authors about their attempts to claim the *flâneur*'s male body and its privileges. These writers and works are Flora Tristan's *London Journal* (1840/1842), George Sand's *Story of My Life* (1854–1855), and Vita Sackville-West's memoir *Portrait of a Marriage* (written 1920–1921; published by her son Nigel Nicolson in 1973). The three women were known for their unconventional lifestyles.

---

[2] Many critics have challenged Wolff's claim that *flâneuses* did not exist. Elizabeth Wilson, for example, argues that Wolff accepts at face value the nineteenth-century ideology of separate spheres and thus underestimates women's roles outside the home (2001, 79). While critics like Nava (1996), Parsons (2000), and Wilson (2001) acknowledge that male pedestrians enjoyed exclusive privileges, they point to ways in which women have moved in public space beyond the narrow paradigm of *flânerie*.

[3] For studies of debates about street harassment in the Victorian press, see Walkowitz (1998) and Nead (2000, 62–73).

[4] For two contemporary accounts of the experiences of black pedestrians, see Cadogan (2016) and Forna (2018).

[5] There is little research on *flânerie* and age. For an article on the *flâneur* as an adult that considers the possibility of a child *flâneur*, see Tribunella (2010).

Having to support herself and her children after leaving her husband, Tristan became an outspoken feminist and socialist. Sand, who also separated from her husband, was a popular novelist known for having many lovers and posing as a man. Yet, as Lauren Elkin remarks, despite similarities to Tristan, "Sand [...] was not exactly a feminist" (2016, 104). Aristocratic writer and gardener Sackville-West stayed married to her husband Harold Nicolson despite their many affairs, often with partners of the same sex.

Tristan, Sand, and Sackville-West all chose to walk the streets of London and Paris in cross-dress. As far as is known today, they identified as cisgender women, so that living out or claiming an idealized notion of male identity was not the primary aim of their cross-dressing.[6] Instead, they were frustrated with the constraints they faced in urban space and discovered cross-dressing as an opportunity for 'conquering' spaces and practices that demanded male bodies. In this article, I examine how Tristan, Sand, and Sackville-West represent their motives for and experiences of walking as men. My focus will lie on the issue of passing, i.e., the question of whether their cross-dressed bodies are read as male or not. Whereas Sand and Sackville-West describe themselves as passing for male *flâneurs*, Tristan does not. My aim is to illustrate that both moments—passing and not passing—function as occasions for autobiographical self-fashioning. While Tristan's depiction of her failed passing allows her to stage herself as a woman who spectacularly disrupts patriarchal norms, Sand portrays herself as a writer who cunningly subverts but ultimately leaves intact such norms. Sackville-West's approach is reminiscent of Sand's, but because she frames her cross-dressing as an abnormal act, her memoir reinstates patriarchal norms more resolutely than Sand's. I aim to show that these representations of cross-dressing lend themselves to what Eve Kosofsky Sedgwick (1997) has called 'paranoid' and 'reparative' readings insofar as they not only expose how female mobility is oppressed in urban spaces but, as exciting adventures, they equally generate pleasure. The appropriation of the *flâneur*'s body thus serves a versatile vehicle for Tristan, Sand, and Sackville-West to construct their own personas and life stories.

---

[6] Sackville-West's gender identity was more ambiguous and fluid than Tristan's and Sand's, as I show further on in this article. Yet Sackville-West is usually not referred to as transgender.

ON CROSS-DRESSING AND PASSING

Cross-dressing was by no means a mainstream activity for cisgender women in nineteenth-century Europe, neither was it unheard of. Several cases of women dressing up as men have been documented. Swiss writer Isabelle Eberhardt, for example, travelled North Africa in male attire to move without any constraints and French archeologist Jane Dieulafoy wore men's clothes on scientific expeditions (Chouiten 2015, 95–140; Segrave 2018, 7).[7] This is remarkable since dress codes were strictly segregated in terms of gender, especially in France. As Elkin explains, in 1800, a new law criminalized women's wearing of trousers in public. Exemptions could be obtained, but the applicant had to present medical evidence of a deformity that would make it 'unsightly' for her to wear skirts. Even when such a permit was granted, it was still prohibited for women in trousers to attend public events (Elkin 2016, 111–112).

According to Kerry Segrave, the reasons why some women cross-dressed were manifold, ranging from deliberate acts of resistance to practical motives:

> The major reason for women to wear male apparel was an economic one – more jobs were available to men and jobs held by men paid more than those held by women. Other reasons were convenience and mobility – that is, traveling and moving about. The simple act of walking the streets was easier and safer for men than it was for women. Some […] women […] hardly got a few blocks from their homes, disguised as men, before they were stopped. Others went out and about on the streets on a bet, while some did it just for a lark. Then there were females who undertook more extensive travel […]. Such activity would have been impossible for any woman wearing the standard and conventional female apparel of the day […]. (2018, 130)

A desire for physical and socio-economic mobility was thus a key motivation for cisgender women to cross-dress, which substantiates the feminist stance that an 'unmarked' male body lay at the core of *flânerie*. As my subsequent readings will demonstrate, however, cross-dressings were not

---

[7] Lynda Chouiten also mentions Willa Cather, Dorothy Richardson, Sidonie-Gabrielle Claudine Colette, Rosa Bonheur, and Sarah Bernhardt as female artists who regularly cross-dressed in Britain and France (2015, 99). For a survey of modernist female cross-dressers, see Gubar (1981).

always deliberate political or (proto-)feminist acts. Indulging in private pleasure and thrill was another important motivation.

Cross-dressing can result in passing. Passing happens when an individual performs as a member of another gender, ethnicity, class, or age and is accepted in this role. In other words, passing entails cross-dressing that is not recognized as such. Passing is relevant to the study of masculinities because it challenges biologistic concepts of the body. As Elaine K. Ginsberg puts it,

> the possibility of passing challenges a number of problematic and even antithetical assumptions about identities, the first of which is that some identity categories are inherent and unalterable essences: presumably one cannot pass for something one *is not* unless there is some other, pre-passing, identity that one *is*. Further, passing forces reconsideration of the cultural logic that the physical body is the site of identic intelligibility [...]. Finally, allowing the possibility that 'maleness' or 'whiteness' or ethnicity can be performed or enacted, donned or discarded, exposes the anxieties about status and hierarchy created by the potential of boundary trespassing. For both the process and the discourse of passing challenge the essentialism that is often the foundation of identity politics, a challenge that may be seen as either threatening or liberating but in either instance discloses the truth that identities are not singularly true or false but multiple and contingent. (1996, 4; emphases in original)

Ginsberg asserts that passing requires certain physical features, body languages, and performative behaviors, as well as accessories. Physique, hair, stride, and clothing determine whether a passer-by is accepted as male *flâneur* or not. Some features are more easily performable than others—whereas a coat, shoes, and a hat can be bought, height is usually fixed. Ginsberg proposes that passing unsettles essentialisms because it involves corporeality. Bodies are commonly naturalized; they are seen as direct outcomes and foundations of binary gender identities. According to this logic, gender and sex collapse, i.e., a man is considered masculine because of his biological sex. Conversely, passing infers that masculinity does not require a male body. Robin Maltz argues that

> [p]assing is a question of public (and sometimes private) legibility and requires a spectator in order to legitimate the pass. Passing is performative in the sense that it relies on a spectator for validity and requires the

construction of a visible, intelligible appropriation inscribed on the body counter to the predetermined racialized body or the biologically sexed body of the subject. (1998, 277–278)

Passing implies that perception constitutes the male body, not its sex. In this way, it highlights the constructed character of identities.

As Christine Mayerhofer points out, passing relies on a discrepancy of awareness between the person who assumes an identity and the validating spectator who remains unaware of this transgression (2014, 26). This imperceptibility, Mayerhofer argues, distinguishes passing from other forms of cross-dressing and mimicry that are subversive because they highlight the discrepancy of an 'actual' and an 'adopted' identity (25). The pleasure of passing can lie in 'getting away' with a violation of norms without being sanctioned, in being accepted in a desired identity, or a combination of both. With its capacity to challenge existing gender ideologies on the one hand and to facilitate experimentations, explorations, and appropriations of gender identities on the other hand, passing is as much a paranoid as a reparative endeavor.

Flora Tristan: Failed Passing as a Spectacle of Female Disobedience

Flora Tristan visited London several times between 1826 and 1839. In 1842, she published her impressions of the English capital in her *London Journal*. Her opening chapter presents London as the ideal city for *flânerie*. Tristan notes that

> in the magic light of millions of gas-lamps, London is superb! Its broad streets stretch to infinity; its shops are resplendent with every masterpiece that human ingenuity can devise; its multitudes of men and women pass ceaselessly to and fro. To see all this for the first time is an intoxicating experience. (1982, 17)

However, Tristan only evokes this image of a glamourous city with endless opportunities for consumption to dismantle it. She clarifies that "the foreigner soon recovers his senses and opens his eyes to the arid egotism and gross materialism which lurk behind that ideal world" (17). What follows is, in the words of Yäel Schlick, the depiction of "an anti-touristic (i.e., activist) form of travel" (2012, 110). Rather than presenting walks along major sights, Tristan explores on foot the marginalized areas of the city where prostitutes, Irish immigrants, and factory workers reside in miserable conditions; she ventures where respectable middle-class women are not supposed to go. Tristan's pedestrian movement is political labor. Her walks expose the social inequality that defines the topography of London. Tristan's socio-critical spectatorship is a bold move, as Deborah Epstein Nord explains:

> Only a woman with Tristan's sense of personal and political mission would have taken on the project of urban observation in the 1820s and 1830s, when respectable women had no place as spectators on the city streets; and only the experience of *flânerie* – or of its attempt – could have crystallized for Tristan in quite so dramatic a way the pangs of economic and sexual marginality. (1995, 116)

In addition to providing a form of political activism, Tristan's walks allow her to fashion herself as a spokesperson for women and the lower classes. In this role, she disassociates herself from the passivity that is, in her view, the fate of English women. Tristan satirically notes that "English women lead the most arid, monotonous and unhappy existences imaginable. Time has no meaning for them: days, months and years bring no change to the deadening uniformity of their lives" (1982, 245). Married women, she proposes, "cannot stir from the house without *the permission of their husband*" (249; emphasis in original). Carrying nationalist undertones, these statements assert France's superiority as the more progressive country.

In Chapter 6, Tristan assumes the male body to take her political agenda even further. Dressing up as a man allows her to go beyond a mere documentation of social injustices; she physically disrupts the institutional apparatus that she sees as the backbone of England's patriarchy and class structure. In that way, she presents herself not only as a critical observer but as an activist who takes matters into her own hands. Tristan's key motivation is the exclusion of women from the House of Commons (57). She wants to enter the Houses of Parliament as a man.[8] Tristan not

---

[8] Sarah Richardson clarifies that although women had been excluded from the House of Commons from 1778 onwards, this did not mean that no women were ever present in the building. In the early nineteenth century, "[a] limited number of women were permitted to attend the House and listen to debates in what became known as the ventilator or lantern – a small attic space high above the chamber" (2019, 122). Tristan does not

only has to pass as a man on the street but relies on official ushers to admit her to an institution. She imposes upon herself the gravest challenge of passing for a man that exists in nineteenth-century London.

Staging her appropriation of the male body as a quest, Tristan stresses the effort she puts into her preparations. Paradoxically, she relies on men to undermine the patriarchal system. First, she asks one of her acquaintances, a Tory member of the House of Commons, to lend her clothes. Ridiculing how he "turned white with fear, red with indignation" (58) and denies her assistance, Tristan depicts this representative of the patriarchal order as a coward, whilst simultaneously foregrounding her own courage. She becomes only more determined. Suggesting that "[t]he will of woman is the will of God" (58), she fashions herself as an omnipotent figure. Finally, "an eminent Turkish gentleman" lends her his clothes, "an elaborate Turkish costume" (59) with a turban, as well as "his admission card, his carriage, and his own amiable company as escort" (59). It is telling that Tristan collaborates with another foreigner and decides to wear an 'exotic' male outfit; all this underlines her anti-English sentiments. Furthermore, in contrast to Sand and Sackville-West, Tristan aims to pass not just as male, but appropriates the body and identity of a man who differs from white upper-class English masculinity.[9] In her performance of the male body Tristan also appropriates another culture, ethnicity, and religion.

Interestingly, Tristan's chapter never implies that her performance of masculinity is ever taken seriously. She recounts this episode in a way that gives the impression that she never passes as a Turkish man. Waiting to enter the building, for example, the usher asks not her but her male escort for the admission card. Tristan describes how she can immediately hear the people around her saying "There's a woman in Turkish clothes!'" (59), which distresses her. She merely maintains that her "appearance inspired respect. I overcame my agitation and preserved a calm demeanor

mention this in her *Journal*. However, Richardson asserts that it is unclear when this practice was introduced (122). It may not yet have been common practice when Tristan visited London. Moreover, it is possible that Tristan was not aware of this option or chose not to mention it. In 1852, a new House of Commons was opened that included a ladies' gallery (127).

[9] Epstein Nord proposes that "[t]hrough a kind of mystification of the Oriental, Tristan welcomes the robes' accentuation of her otherness and senses that they lend her a kind of serenity and control. [...] [S]he is now more foreign, more exotic, more mysterious than before, and her feelings of virtuous indignation increase accordingly" (1995, 120).

for such is the influence of costume that, in donning the Turkish turban, I had acquired the serious gravity habitual to the Moslem" (59–60). Tristan excludes the usher's reaction. In her narrative, her passing remains an ambiguous, if not sketchy, issue. The fact that Tristan neither goes into detail with respect to her disguise—readers do not find out how she styles her hair, moves her legs, or whether she uses any make-up—enforces this ambivalence.

And this is where Tristan's pleasure in not passing comes into the picture. Her pleasure is not concerned with attaining freedom but celebrating her protest. In fact, she even surpasses her initial goals. Because her appropriation of the male body never appears to be convincing, she can pride herself in having entered the House of Commons as a person suspected of being a woman. She does not need the body designated for entering parliament. By accessing her desired territory nonetheless, she can disrupt and openly reject this patriarchal foundation.[10] While passing would have rendered her invisible and left the gendered topography of the House of Commons in order, she becomes a center of attention once she is on the gallery. As a woman in male clothes, she can make tangible for her readers the suppression of women in English society. Instead of only observing how badly women are treated as she does in other chapters, she can elaborate on the aggression she experiences herself. In a melodramatic and moralistic manner, she describes how men "passed in front of me, staring at me boldly through their lorgnettes and exchanging remarks about me in loud voices", "breach[ing] [...] good manners and hospitality" (60). Tristan focuses on negative bodily sensations like her violent heartbeat, how she blushes, and feels embarrassed (59–60). By the end of her visit, she "feel[s] extremely fatigued" (62). Tristan's appropriation of the male body causes more stress than anything else.

Tristan presents herself as a *flâneuse* who is willing to take risks and set back her personal wellbeing for a greater political good, which makes her an ideal heroine. She orchestrates her cross-dressing as a sacrifice that she undertakes as a socialist and feminist; at no point in the journal does she ever feel the elation of classic *flânerie*. The failure of her passing becomes her political tool as it allows her to destabilize the corporeal and discursive order of gender. Without it, Tristan could not lay bare to her readers the

---

[10] Perhaps her failed passing is even a calculated act. Tristan mentions, for example, that her costume "was much too big and I felt uncomfortable in it" (1982, 59), which suggests that she suspects that passing for a man is rather unlikely.

patriarchal restrictions on women's mobility, spectatorship, and political participation. For her audience in France, the cross-dressing episode of the *London Journal* serves as a climax, a spectacle that elevates a French author and her nation above the English. By setting her appropriation of the male body in a foreign country, Tristan—consciously or not— displaces her feminist criticism and distracts from the social and gendered inequalities of her own country. George Sand's autobiography, my next case study, can be read as a testimony to the fact that moving around freely was perhaps not as readily available for women in Paris as Tristan may have wished.

George Sand: Claiming the Male Body for Artistic Freedom

The four parts of George Sand's *Story of My Life* (published in install-ments between 1854 and 1855 in the newspaper *La Presse*) extend over 1100 pages. At the time of publication, Sand had been a literary celebrity for over two decades. With a far wider readership than Tristan, Sand knew that her commissioned autobiography would be a unique opportunity to create an authoritative account of herself and her *oeuvre*. In *Story of My Life*, Sand repeatedly showcases how she consciously edits and presents her own life story. As Benita Eisler suggests, retrospective self-fashioning pervades Sand's autobiography:

> The memoir's French title, *Histoire de ma vie*, sets an agenda of ambi-guity. The word *histoire* means either 'story' or 'history,' and Sand the novelist took full advantage of the space between the two meanings to arrange, improve, embroider, invent, and omit in her self-portrait. Then, too, the edited life conspires with the blurring effects of time and memory. Chronology gets chancy. Invention steps in to fill in the blanks. (1991, 51)

The carefully arranged *Story of My Life* is surprisingly conventional for an author who is known for her unconventionality. According to Janet Hiddleston, Sand follows a "chronological and teleological, purposeful and determined" (1999, 52) structure that produces

> a traditional *Bildungsroman*, insisting retrospectively on its logic, offering various keys to her development at different points. [...] She frequently

identifies turning points and moments of choice, making the reader increasingly aware of her dreaminess as a child, her unusual upbringing, her alienation from local society and her difference from other young women of her class. (51)

One of these turning points appears in the section "From Mysticism to Independence" about the years between 1819 and 1832. Here, Sand describes how, in 1831, she leaves rural Nohant to live in Paris, just a year before her first novel *Indiana* becomes an instant success. For several months, Sand resides on Quai Saint-Michel on her own before her daughter joins her. Envying her friends who enjoy "[l]iterary and political events, the excitement of the theatres and the museums, the clubs and the streets" (1991, 892), Sand states that "for a woman without money to fulfill these fantasies was impossible" (892). In contrast to Tristan's activism, Sand assumes the male body to find inspiration and to acquire cultural and social capital for a literary career. For Sand, being perceived as a man is the only chance to "be morally and artistically free, in a world where I asked only to go unnoticed and to be allowed, unenslaved, to earn my daily bread" (904).

Just like Tristan, Sand voices her frustration with the limits imposed upon her mobility. However, while Tristan dramatizes her decision to cross-dress as an act of courage, Sand fashions herself as a woman who has no choice but to act within the patriarchal order. Whereas for Tristan the city is a place of oppression and hypocrisy, in Sand's writing, it emerges as a place of personal opportunity in which she competently maneuvers herself. In this way, Sand can distinguish herself from 'ordinary' women and simultaneously adhere to her narrative logic of the *Bildungsroman*. For Sand, cross-dressing is a necessary step so that she can advance. She describes her performance of the male body in a way that inevitably accepts the separation of spheres. She pragmatically concludes that only "dressed in [...] men's clothing [...] allowed me to be enough of a man to see a milieu that otherwise would have remained forever closed" (903). Despite her preoccupation with her own progress and pleasure, this does not mean that the cross-dressing episode in Sand's autobiography does not allow any subversive readings. Precisely because she presents her passing as such an easy, playful, and casual act, as I will illustrate shortly, it can be read as dismantling of an essentialist concept of the male body.

Sand insists from the start that she considers it "not [...] at all shocking" (893) to dress up as a man. In fact, she maintains that her mother suggests cross-dressing as a convenient way of freely moving about Paris, having done so herself as a young woman (892–893). This reference to her mother normalizes Sand's appropriation of the male body, as it presents it as a common practice among upper-class women of all generations. In this way, Sand also affirms her status as a cisgender woman, clarifying that she does not assume the male body to 'live out' a masculine identity. Unlike Tristan, Sand depoliticizes her cross-dressing. She represents it as discrete option of subversion potentially available to all women.

In contrast to Tristan who borrows her male clothes from a friend, Sand has hers custom-made, which contributes to her passing on the streets and in theaters:

> So, I had a 'sentry box redingote' made for myself, out of thick gray cloth, with matching trousers and vest. With a gray hat and a wide wool tie, I was the perfect little first-year student. I cannot tell you the pleasure I derived from my boots – I would gladly have slept in them, as my brother did in his youth, when he put on his first pair. With those little iron heels, I felt secure on the sidewalks, I flew from one end of Paris to the other. It seemed to me that I would have made a trip around the world. Also, my clothing made me fearless. I was on the go in all kinds of weather, I came in at all hours, I sat in the pit in every theatre. No one paid attention to me, no one suspected my disguise. Aside from the fact that I wore it with ease, the absence of coquettishness in costume and facial expression warded off any suspicion. I was too poorly dressed and looked too simple – my usual vacant, verging on dumb, look – to attract or compel attention. (893)

This passage abounds with tropes associated with the *flâneur*: losing track of time, Sand merges with the crowd, observes the urban spectacle around her, and remains invisible throughout. To be in this position as a woman is empowering; it gives her confidence and levity. Sand's cross-dressing is a thoroughly pleasant experience. She even claims to feel more 'natural' in male clothes.[11] As spectators of different sexes accept her as a man, Sand undercuts essentialist conceptions of masculinity, suggesting that with the

---

[11] This passage contrasts with her description of walking along in Paris in women's clothing, which makes her feel insecure and impractical: "But on the pavements of Paris I was like a boat on ice. Delicate footwear cracked in two days; overshoes made me clumsy; I wasn't used to lifting my skirts. I was muddy, tired, runny-nosed, and I saw my shoes

right planning she can indeed perform a male body. Sand emphasizes her success by chronicling encounters with men who do not recognize her disguise. For many years, her friend Monsieur Rollinat, for example, allegedly believes her to be a man (896). When Sand visits the theater again ten years later with her son, she claims that "my as-yet beardless son was often taken for me" (896).

Yet in the longer passage above, Sand implies that she only remains invisible because she passes as a young man of the lower class, not as a man of the cultural elite. The upper-class theatergoers likely overlook and thereby accept her as a man because her appearance evokes poverty and inexperience. Sand can take up the marginal position of the *flâneur* because her cross-dressed body does not signal any economic or social capital to others. Even as an exceptionally educated woman, Sand can only get ahead by posing as a less educated man. Significantly, Sand does not use this moment for social criticism, as feminist Tristan likely would have done. On the contrary, she prides herself in having perfected her role of a lower-class man. Her comment that her look "verges on dumb" is indicative of her own prejudices and her privileged speaking position as an aristocratic heiress. Here, Sand's complicity with the patriarchy is evident.

Sand concludes that in her world, she can only free herself from the restraints of gender ideology in male disguise, a step that she considers necessary for becoming an artist. After having spent many weeks in male attire, Sand writes, "I was no longer a lady, nor was I a 'gentleman.' I was jostled on the sidewalk like a thing that got in the way of busy passers-by. I didn't care; I wasn't busy. No one knew me, no one looked at me, no one gave me a second thought; I was an atom lost in the immense crowd" (904–905). Here, Sand affirms the notion that only masculinity, as the unmarked gender in a patriarchal order, can provide her desired invisibility. The position of this passage in *Story of My Life* is crucial because it precedes Sand's description of how she attains her masculine pseudonym 'George Sand', a name that she still identifies with when she writes her autobiography. Her pedestrian excursions as a man rehearse her adoption of a male model of authorship. Rather than creating a possibility for a female authorship, Sand finally emulates masculine norms.

---

and clothing – not to mention the little velvet hat – spattered in the gutters, falling into ruin with frightening rapidity" (Sand 1991, 892).

Vita Sackville-West: The Self-Condemning *Flâneuse*

In her memoir *Portrait of a Marriage*, Vita Sackville-West chronicles her childhood and youth in an aristocratic family, before she delineates her marriage and affairs, particularly her relationship with author Violet Keppel (later Trefusis) in 1918.[12] In contrast to Tristan's and Sand's self-confident narratives, Sackville-West apprehensively calls her memoir, which she never intended to publish, a "confession" and refers to her life as "a morass [...] a bog, a swamp, a deceitful country, with one bright patch in the middle, the patch that is unalterably his" (Nicolson 1973, 10). The masculine possessive pronoun here refers to her husband, Harold Nicolson, whom she installs as a morally upright anchor in her memoir, while she calls herself into question.

Sackville-West's self-deprecating tone also pervades the depiction of her cross-dressing. Although she celebrates her initial experience of *flânerie* as a liberating moment facilitated by her androgynous physique, she embeds this account into an episode of her life in which she cross-dressed extensively to spend time in public with Trefusis. This contextualisation has the effect that Sackville-West's attempt at male *flânerie* can be read as an affirmation of stereotypes about lesbianism/bisexuality of her own time.[13] She frames her homosexual actions as guilty confessions, rather than claiming the privileges of mobility associated with the male body for herself irrespectively of her sexual identity. In accordance with the ideologies of gender and sexuality of her time, Sackville-West pathologizes her walks in disguise. She implies that they liberate an identity that was regarded as 'unnatural' in the early twentieth century. In other words, Sackville-West suggests that she cannot help but pose as a male *flâneur* because this is the only self-representation that allows her to realize her lesbian or bisexual desires without any punitive consequences.

---

[12] As Georgia Johnston clarifies, the publication of the memoir is problematic, for Sackville-West's son, Nigel Nicolson, edited his mother's writing, and added to the book three sections of his own to assess his parents' marriage. According to Johnston, Nicolson not only "buries the lesbian question" (2007, 60) and blames his mother for the turbulent marriage (61), but also omits crucial information, for instance, "that the affair with Violet begins five months after Nicolson may have contracted venereal disease [...] and that Nicolson continued to have affairs, which Sackville-West countenanced" (61).

[13] For a nuanced discussion of Sackville-West's sexual identity, see Kaivola (1999). Since it is beyond the scope of this contribution to explore this issue in greater detail, I refer to Sackville-West as 'lesbian or bisexual', suggesting that both options are possible.

Sackville-West describes her first experience of walking in cross-dress as

> one of the boldest things I ever did. I will tell you about it: I changed
> in my own house in London late one evening (the darkened streets made
> me bold), and drove with Violet in a taxi as far as Hyde Park Corner.
> There I got out. I never felt so free as when I stepped off the kerb, down
> Piccadilly, alone, and knowing that if I met my own mother face to face she
> would take no notice of me. I walked along, smoking a cigarette, buying a
> newspaper off a little boy who called me 'sir', and being accosted now and
> then by women. In this way I strolled from Hyde Park Corner to Bond
> Street, where I met Violet and took her in a taxi to Charing Cross. (The
> extraordinary thing was, how natural it all was for me.) Nobody, even in
> the glare of the station, glanced at me twice. I had wondered about my
> voice, but found it could sink sufficiently. (111–112)

Sackville-West here portrays herself in the spirit of the prototypical *flâneur*
who embarks on a nightly adventure. Crossing the threshold of the
contained, semi-private space of the taxi, she walks the most iconic and
frequented streets of central London on her own, absorbing the fleeting
urban atmosphere around her. Just like Sand, Sackville-West depicts
a moment of pleasure far removed from Tristan's pedestrian activism.
Passers-by of all genders and ages, Sackville-West proposes, address her in
her masculine role, suggesting that she passes for a man. Buying cigarettes
on her way, she risks being discovered. Her conviction that not even her
mother would be able to recognize her underlines her certainty. Like the
male *flâneur*, Sackville-West attracts no attention; even when the lights
of Charing Cross station threaten to expose her and she uses her voice,
she claims to remain invisible.

Her description suggests, in tandem with Sand, that masculinity can
indeed be performed without a male body. Sackville-West also proclaims
that her invisibility constitutes a new experience of freedom in her life,
which—compared to most other women of her social standing in the early
twentieth century—was already autonomous. This freedom, one can infer,
would not have been available to her had she left the taxi as a woman.
The fact that Sackville-West, who is just as old at this point as Sand was
when she moved to Paris, is addressed as 'sir' suggests that she can inhabit
a higher social status as a man than Sand could almost ninety years earlier.
Yet this may simply be the effect of Sackville-West's physique. She specifically notes that "[m]y height was of course my great advantage" (111).

Sackville-West's body encourages passers-by to inscribe a masculine identity upon her. Moreover, Sackville-West's remark that her experience as a
man in central London feels "natural" to her could be read as an additional anti-essentialist impulse to defy the notion of gender as a binary
biological category.

Sackville-West goes on to describe how she meets up with Violet after
her solitary walk, and that they check into a lodging house where "[t]he
landlady was very benevolent and I said Violet was my wife" (112),
followed by a trip to Knole, the estate where Sackville-West grew up. No
one ever suspects Sackville-West to be a woman. She then writes about
her time with Trefusis in Paris:

> [I]n Paris I basically lived in that role. Violet used to call me Julian. We
> dined together every evening in cafés and restaurants, and went to all the
> theatres. I shall never forget the evenings when we walked back slowly to
> our flat through the streets of Paris. I, personally, had never been so happy
> since. (112)

It becomes clear that Sackville-West's initial solitary walk in male clothes
serves as a test to find out whether she can safely enter the public
sphere with her female partner. While her months in cross-dress certainly
allow her to live out her sexuality and to attain mobility, Sackville-West
still frames this episode as a confession ("I have never told a soul of
what I did. I hesitate to write it here, but I must" 111), not as an
achievement or act of resistance, as do Sand and Tristan. Sackville-West
presents her successful performance of the male body as a compulsive
act that is—despite its thrills—ultimately wrong. One might argue that
precisely because walking as a man feels so natural to Sackville-West,
it serves as a symptom of her supposedly 'unnatural' sexual desires. As
Johnston observes, Sackville-West affirms the notion of the lesbian as
an invert, i.e., the conviction that "the lesbian is a man caught within
a woman's body" (2007, 66). According to Johnston, Sackville-West
narratively splits herself into two halves, "so that she is able to absolve
the straight, feminine, married side of wrongdoing, while agreeing with
everyone surrounding her that the side desiring Violet is abhorrent" (59).
In the end, Sackville-West's representation of her cross-dressing is indicative of the hegemonic discourses of gender and sexuality of her time. She
affirms rather than subverts the hegemonic status quo. Sand accepts the

patriarchy as a fixed reality, but she is determined to undermine it secretly with its own weapons. In turn, Sackville-West's framing of her pleasures in cross-dress as 'abnormal' appears to be an even more overt product of patriarchal norms than Sand's. Sackville-West's memoir attests to Jeff Hearn's claim that "materiality can be understood as reproduction in a fuller sense, as both reproduction of the social relations of production, *and* the reproduction of society through ideas, ideology and discourse" (2011, 200; emphasis in original). She understands and represents her body in cross-dress according to the social and discursive orders of her own time.

Conclusion: Reparative Walking and Writing

This article proceeded from the premise that even the most mundane techniques of the body such as walking are gendered. The case of *flânerie* demonstrates that gender regimes shape topographies and mobilities that foster privileges for a few male bodies, whilst marginalizing or excluding other corporealities. Read from a paranoid perspective, the autobiographical writings of Tristan, Sand, and Sackville-West urge their readers to acknowledge the 'real-life' limitations this order imposed upon women in the nineteenth and early twentieth centuries. Yet *London Journal*, *Story of My Life*, and *Portrait of a Marriage* should not be reduced to such a reading. The three works imply just as much that with creativity and courage these boundaries could be overcome, be it as a personal experiment or as a calculated political act. Even if the three women had no choice but to appropriate a normative male body to achieve their individual goals, this body emerges as one that can be replicated or ridiculed and is therefore not exclusive to the male sex. In this sense, the three memoirs also invite reparative readings. Finally, the authors' decision to write about their walking adventures in cross-dress and—at least in Tristan's and Sand's cases—to make these accounts available to the public bears even more reparative potential. Although passing may remain hidden in the moment it is achieved, as a textual representation and mode of autobiographical self-fashioning it becomes perceptible in cultural history.

References

Anonymous. "Progress of Woman." *Punch, or the London Charivari* 27 (1854): 134.

Brontë, Charlotte. *Villette.* Oxford: Oxford UP, 2000 [1853].

Cadogan, Garnette. "Walking While Black." *Literary Hub* (2016): n.p. https://lithub.com/walking-while-black/. Accessed December 20, 2019.

Chouiten, Lynda. *Isabelle Eberhardt: A Carnivalesque Mirage.* London: Lexington Books, 2015.

Coates, Jamie. "The Key Figure of Modernity: The Flâneur." *Social Anthropology* 25, no. 1 (2017): 28–41.

Edensor, Tim. "Walking the British Countryside: Reflexivity, Embodied Practices and Ways to Escape." *Body and Society* 6, no. 3–4 (2000): 81–106.

Eisler, Benita. *Naked in the Marketplace: The Lives of George Sand.* New York: Counterpoint P, 2006.

Elkin, Lauren. *Flâneuse: Women Walk the City in Paris, New York, Tokyo, Venice and London.* London: Vintage, 2016.

Epstein Nord, Deborah. *Walking the Victorian Streets: Women, Representation, and the City.* Ithaca and London: Cornell UP, 1995.

Forna, Aminatta. "Power Walking." *Literary Hub* (2018): n.p. https://lithub.com/power-walking/. Accessed December 20, 2019.

Frisby, David. "The *Flâneur* in Social Theory." In *The Flâneur*, edited by Keith Tester, 81–110. London and New York: Routledge, 1994.

Ginsberg, Elaine K. "Introduction: The Politics of Passing." In *Passing and the Fictions of Identity*, edited by Elaine K. Ginsberg, 1–18. Durham, NC, and London: Duke UP, 1996.

Gubar, Susan. "Blessings in Disguise: Cross-Dressing as Re-Dressing for Female Modernists." *The Massachusetts Review* 22, no. 3 (1981): 477–508.

Hearn, Jeff. "The Materiality of Men, Bodies, *and* Towards the Abolition of 'Men.'" In *Männlichkeiten denken: Aktuelle Perspektiven der kulturwissenschaftlichen Masculinity Studies*, edited by Martina Läubli and Sabrina Sahli, 195–215. Bielefeld: transcript, 2011.

Hiddleston, Janet. *George Sand and Autobiography.* Oxford: Legenda, 1999.

Johnston, Georgia. *The Formation of 20th-Century Queer Autobiography: Reading Vita Sackville-West, Virginia Woolf, Hilda Doolittle, and Gertrude Stein.* Basingstoke: Palgrave Macmillan, 2007.

Kaivola, Karen. "Virginia Woolf, Vita Sackville-West, and the Question of Sexual Identity." *Woolf Studies Annual* 4 (1999): 18–40.

Maltz, Robin. "Real Butch: The Performance/Performativity of Male Imperson-ation, Drag Kings, Passing as Male, and Stone Butch Realness." *Journal of Gender Studies* 7, no. 3 (1998): 273–286.

Mauss, Marcel. "Techniques of the Body." *Economy and Society* 2, no. 1 (1973): 70–88.

Mayerhofer, Christine. *Living a Lie? Passing and Concepts of Identity in Contemporary Novels and Life Narratives.* Trier: wvt, 2014.

Nava, Mica. "Modernity's Disavowal: Women, the City and the Department Store." In *Modern Times: Reflections on a Century of English Modernity*, edited by Mica Nava and Alan O'Shea, 38–76. London and New York: Routledge, 1996.

Nead, Lynda. *Victorian Babylon: People, Streets, and Images in Nineteenth-Century London.* New Haven and London: Yale UP, 2000.

Nicolson, Nigel. *Portrait of a Marriage.* London: Weidenfeld and Nicolson, 1973.

Parsons, Deborah. *Streetwalking the Metropolis: Women, the City, and Modernity.* Oxford: Oxford UP, 2000.

Richardson, Sarah. "Parliament as Viewed Through a Woman's Eyes: Gender and Space in the 19th-Century Commons." *Parliamentary History* 38, no. 1 (2019): 119–134.

Sand, George. *Story of My Life*, edited by Thelma Jurgrau. Albany: SUNY P, 1991 [1854].

Schlick, Yaël. *Feminism and the Politics of Travel.* Lewisburg: Bucknell UP, 2012.

Sedgwick, Eve Kosofsky. "Paranoid Reading and Reparative Reading, or, You're So Paranoid, You Probably Think This Introduction Is about You." In *Novel Gazing: Queer Readings in Fiction*, edited by Eve Kosofsky Sedgwick, 1–37. Durham and London: Duke UP, 1997.

Segrave, Kerry. *'Masquerading in Male Attire': Women Passing as Men in America, 1844–1920.* Jefferson, NC: McFarland, 2018.

Serlin, David. "Disabling the Flâneur." *Journal of Visual Culture* 5, no. 2 (2006): 193–208.

Sundharam, Rebecca. *Choosing to Walk at all Risks: Female Pedestrianism in Victorian Literature.* Doctoral dissertation. Reading: University of Reading, 2011.

Tribunella, Eric L. "Children's Literature and the Child Flâneur." *Children's Literature* 38 (2010): 64–91.

Tristan, Flora. *The London Journal of Flora Tristan 1842, or The Aristocracy and the Working Class of England.* Translated by Jean Hawkes. London: Virago, 1982 [1848].

Walker, Donald. *Exercises for Ladies; Calculated to Preserve and Improve Beauty, and to Prevent and Correct Personal Defects, Inseparable from Constrained or Careless Habits: Founded on Physiological Principles.* London: Thomas Hurst, 1836.

Walkowitz, Judith K. "Going Public: Shopping, Street Harassment, and Street-walking in Late Victorian London." *Representations* 62 (1998): 1–30.

Wilson, Elizabeth. *The Contradictions of Culture: Cities, Culture, Women*. London: Sage, 2001.

Wolff, Janet. "The Invisible *Flâneuse*. Women and the Literature of Modernity." *Theory, Culture & Society* 2, no. 3 (1985): 37–46.

CHAPTER 9

Jake and Ellen in Transition: On Clarissa Sligh's Mutable Bodies

rl goldberg

Wrongly Bodied: Two Forms of Transition

Clarissa Sligh's book *Wrongly Bodied: Documenting Transition from Female to Male* (2009) is concerned with two different forms of transition from female to male: the first is that of Sligh's photographic subject, Jake McBee, a trans man who transitioned in Texas. Secondly, but no less importantly, the book chronicles Ellen and William Craft's escape to freedom. Both were formerly enslaved in Georgia, and their narrative details how Ellen 'transitioned' by passing as a disabled white man. Specifically, the representation of the Crafts' narrative in Sligh's book, which is drawn from their 1860 account *Running a Thousand Miles for Freedom*, tells how light-skinned Ellen passed as a white, male slaveowner, while her husband William posed as 'his' slave accompanying him for medical treatment in the North.

RL. Goldberg (✉)
Society of Fellows, Dartmouth College, Somerville, MA, USA

C. Dexl and S. Gerlsbeck (eds.), *The Male Body in Representation*,
Palgrave Studies in (Re)Presenting Gender,
https://doi.org/10.1007/978-3-030-88604-2_9

Wrongly Bodied tracks Jake before he begins medical transition and follows him through hormone therapy, surgery, surgical complications, the dissolution of romantic relationships, loss of friends, and finding new communities. Though the narrative is chronological, the book does not present Jake's narrative as linear. Rather, it is punctuated by a similarly fragmented re-telling of William and Ellen Craft's narrative, suggesting that in order to understand the trans body, we must, as Sligh does, turn to the archive of slavery.[1] The book's formal doubling—Ellen's story on one page, Jake's opposite it—might also be read as a translation project in which the nineteenth-century story of passing is transferred into a contemporary context. Jake's and Ellen's stories, braided together, work to undermine independent concepts of archives on transness and race as ostensibly singular, unrelated markers of identity. At the same time, however, they also compare and contrast two different dramas: in one, passing as male is a performative strategy, deployed only temporarily, and is not a question of identification. As Sligh writes, William Craft "assures the reader that his wife would never have taken on the disguise of a man had it been possible to do so as a woman, that since in the South white women were not allowed to travel alone with their black male slaves, she had no choice" (2009, 32). In Jake's narrative, on the page directly opposite, readers see Jake attempt to manage a drama of choicelessness, expressing his desire to just "look like what I feel like...[and] be true to who I thought I was" (33). The implication: Jake, like Ellen, had no other way to achieve 'freedom', yet for Jake transition was of a permanent, rather than temporary, nature. The two narratives do converge again, as Sligh's juxtaposition shows us that passing for both Ellen and Jake is a matter of life or death—where 'juxtaposition' means speaking 'with' and 'against' each other and evidences notions of both contrast and relation.

---

[1] This is a point compellingly made by C. Riley Snorton in *Black on Both Sides: A Racial History of Trans Identity* (2017). For Sligh, turning to the archive of slavery allows for an amplified understanding of crossing, and thereby of transness. Snorton's intervention is different: like Hortense Spillers, Snorton conceives of slavery as the foundational rupture in gendered syntax, whereby gender becomes enclosed as the property of whiteness, and the enslaved become, in Spillers's term, "ungendered" (68). Snorton offers the case narrative of J. Marion Sims, the 'father of modern gynecology', and his brutal experiments to cure vesicovaginal fistula on enslaved women. For Snorton, Sims is emblematic of the ways in which the enslaved body was used to shore up modern ideas on gender/sex through the abuse of enslaved, ungendered 'flesh' (19–20).

Though it is obvious that Sligh refracts Jake's experience through that of the Crafts' to understand the structures of 'passing', what needs to be extrapolated from this juxtaposition are crucial differences between these two narratives. To name a few: (a) the differences between trans gender transition and racial passing; (b) how Ellen Craft's strategic passing for white is qualitatively different from Jake's identification with whiteness; (c) how Jake's narrative focuses on his claim of gendered identity, while Ellen's deals with her strategic passing as a white man; and (d) the kinds of looking and seeing these two 'transitions' structurally demanded. This last difference is particularly suggestive for the severity of their contrast: indeed, what affirms Jake in his materiality—being photographed, being seen, being visually tracked and captured across his journey—defines the conditions under which the Crafts' transition would have been structurally impossible, and, indeed, fatal. This pairing thus raises the question of how Sligh's relationship with the materiality of the trans male body deepens when mediated by the archive of enslavement. Ultimately, I aim to show that by critically engaging with these two archives, it becomes obvious that the materiality of both the trans masculine body and the racialized body can throw rigid categories into crisis, as underlined by these narratives of passing.

ARCHIVE AND REPERTOIRE: ON RACIAL AND GENDERED PASSING

While there is a vast amount of scholarship theorizing racial or gendered passing,[2] the juxtaposition of trans *and* racial passing and their theorization is far thornier insofar as comparison invites compartmentalizing aspects of racial and gendered identity in order to attempt a discrete analysis. In his 2016 book *Trans: Gender and Race in an Age of Unsettled Identities*, Rogers Brubaker describes how the imbrication of trans and racial passing—often stylized as *transracialism*—emerged only after a

---

[2] On racial and gendered passing, see also Werner Sollors's *Neither Black nor White Yet Both: Thematic Explorations of Interracial Literature* (1997) and Marjorie Garber's *Vested Interests* (1992) respectively. The messiness of the discourse of 'transracialism' can be seen at its worst in Rebecca Tuvel's 2017 article "In Defense of Transracialism" and in the academic community's beleaguered response to it. The publication of the article immediately resulted in an open letter of opposition, with nearly 900 signatories and a string of resignations on the editorial board.

public debate that conflated a white woman's self-identification as black with a trans woman's public transition. That is, Brubaker points out, public discourse around Rachel Dolezal and Caitlyn Jenner joined questions of racial and gendered passing in ways in which they had rarely been joined previously. Brubaker cites a few examples—most notably, work by Cressida Heyes, which explores the factual demand for medical intervention on racially marked bodies—but, as he points out, 'racial passing' and 'trans passing' are rarely considered together. As he notes, a "common reaction to the pairing of the terms in the Dolezal affair was that transracial, unlike transgender, was 'not a thing'; the word was a treated as a pointless or pernicious neologism" (2016, 18). Thus, there is good reason for the limited theorization of trans and racial passing: the kinds of loss these forms of 'passing' describe are structurally different; when compared, they are forced into a syllogistic logic, undercutting the legitimacy of identity claims.

Jake's trans male body, in its becoming, offers Sligh an occasion to explore the body as a site of interrogation on three registers: in terms of what trans masculinity might look like, how narrativization constructs race and gender, and finally, how viewers engage with and against the representation of the trans body. In the book's afterword Sligh writes:

> The project placed us both in unfamiliar territory. How did my own perception of being in the world influence the framing of a photograph? Without realizing it, I lost my objective observer status as I became more and more entangled in [Jake's] emotional reactions to the responses of his friends and lovers. Encouraging and supporting him in his process, made me realize that I had a stake in its success. I was torn, at war with myself because Jake seemed to want me to be loyal to his view of a world in which who I was as a black woman did not have equal value to who he was to become as a straight white man. (152–153)

The materiality of Jake's white trans male body is a chiasmatic starting point—of prejudice, of disagreement, of misunderstanding, of documentation, of frisson—by which Sligh accesses what can only be immaterial to Jake: questions of history, structural racism, and narratives of the enslaved. This is not to say that Sligh has had no access to these questions before meeting Jake. Quite the opposite is the case. Sligh notes that it is *because* of her identification as a black woman and her emotional bonds to her family and their history that she is able to relate to Jake. I therefore suggest that through approaching Jake's material body as both an archive and repertoire, and pairing this with the archive of Black American history in which the memory of her family is imbricated, she reckons with what is immaterial to *him*. In addition to that, through Sligh's photography which traces and collects Jake's transition from female to male, his body becomes an 'archive' in itself. Here, I understand the archive to be, in Ann Cvetkovich's words, a "repository" (2003, 7) that collects not simply texts or ephemera, but also affect. She describes her 'archive of feelings' as including not only the content of the texts themselves, but also "the practices that surround their production and reception" (7). Accumulating images, moments, and vestiges of Jake's transition, Sligh's photographic practice is committed to creating such an 'archive of feelings'. It thereby bridges the overlapping sites that performance studies scholar Diana Taylor calls 'the archive', that is, "supposedly enduring materials (i.e., texts, documents, buildings, bones)", and 'the repertoire', as "embodied practice/knowledge (i.e., spoken language, dance, sports, ritual" (2003, 19), in affective ways. Taylor argues that part of what performance studies can do is to "take seriously the repertoire of embodied practice as an important system of knowing and transmitting knowledge. The repertoire, on a very practical level, expands the traditional archive used by academic departments in the humanities" (26). Sligh's project is keenly aware of the ways in which her work with Jake and the Crafts bridges this divide between archive and repertoire: relying on Jake's physical presence, through photography, she turns the trans masculine body into an archive. Similarly, drawing on the archive of slavery, she attempts to make sense of Jake's physical presence and what kinds of embodied knowledge the trans masculine body allows access to. Saidiya Hartman's practice of 'critical fabulation' as a mode of engaging in the archive is crucial: here, scholars might fill in the gaps in those archives—particularly archives of slavery—where often people are listed just by name, or, more commonly, unnamed but listed only by type. Thus, critical fabulation for Hartman allows to "fashion[...] a narrative, which is based upon archival research" and helps to "paint as full a picture of the lives of the captives as possible" while "enacting the impossibility of representing the lives of the captives precisely through the process of narration" (2008, 11). Critical fabulation is a methodological practice that Sligh uses as well to frame Jake's narrative in an affective way and turn the physically present body into an archive that can provide knowledge about trans masculinity. Where Hartman begins from a place of type and extrapolates individuals, Sligh uses Jake's singularity as an archive for engaging with the concept of trans masculinity, and the affects that Jake's transition evoke for her. At the same time, Jake's subjectivity is opaque to Sligh. Thus, by turning to Ellen Craft's narrative of passing, she is able to paint a fuller "picture of the lives of captives" (11) and, through the process of that narration, consider the trans archive more broadly.

The trans male body enables Sligh to ask what the idea of 'crossing'—racial or gendered, or both—conveys. Sligh lets Jake describe how he understands his manhood in terms of corporeality and corporeal ability, rather than as an essential gender identity: walking the dog, lifting weights, returning to the US Army as an officer. While 'trans' remains an elusive term in the book, the term 'sex change', which is today considered inappropriate, is used rather liberally and is meant to describe a transsexual, or a person who medically and/or hormonally changes their sex. For the purposes of this article, however, I consider trans more expansively in terms of trans gender, to account for trans-identifying people who might choose not to undergo medical intervention to 'cross' genders and recognize their genders to be subjectively constituted.[3] The indeterminacies of race, gender, and transness in Sligh's work can be traced in the lineage of theories that underline the ontological uncertainty of these categories. Theories of race and gender have long insisted on the discursive constructedness and performativity of these categories— as the work of Judith Butler, Roderick Ferguson, and Sara Ahmed shows. Butler's foundational *Gender Trouble* (1990) argues, for instance, that "if gender is the cultural meanings that the sexed body assumes, then a gender cannot be said to follow from a sex in any one way. Taken to its logical limit, the sex/gender distinction suggests a radical discontinuity between sexed bodies and culturally constructed genders" (9); in Butler's terms, "gender itself becomes a free-floating artifice" (9). For Ferguson, the promise of a queer of color critique lies in the attunement to the contradictions emerging from this artifice: Understanding the most marginalized, he argues, entails locating them precisely "within a national culture that disavows the configuration of [...] racial, gender, class, and

---

[3] This understanding of trans corresponds with current scholarship in trans studies, like Eliza Steinbock's use of the term as a cluster "under the holey umbrella of transgender (it doesn't catch all the possibilities) in order to better stress the gendered elements of subjective identity formation" (2019, viii), or Patrick Califia's sense that the term transgender registers how gendered 'boundaries' are permeable (2003, xiv).

sexual particularity" (2004, 11). And as Ahmed points out, one way to consider the constructedness of these categories is to study the concept of orientation, which "allows us to expose how life gets directed in some ways rather than others, through the very requirement that we follow what is already given to us" (2006, 21). Gender then is "an effect of the kinds of work bodies do, which in turn 'directs' those bodies, affecting what they 'can do'" (60). Collectively, their work underscores how the categories of gender and race are grounded in mimetic reiteration, but are no less powerful for the material and lived realities these performances solicit. Along those lines, Sligh's project underlines how both blackness and whiteness are socially constructed categories while for Jake, his *white* male materiality precludes the expansive understanding Sligh is able to work through.

Due to the fact that the text is co-produced by Sligh and McBee, the archive presented and created is rarely consistent, as it is continually mediated by the camera, by at least two sets of fluctuate desires, at least two sets of historical and propulsive memories. The chiasmatic confluences of their bodies and subjective mediation raise questions about the nature of the archive itself, especially as it pertains to the trans male body. At base, these are questions about the politics of the archive and about the ethics of recognition. Jacques Derrida writes of the political significance of the archive: "[T]here is no political power without control of the archive, if not of memory. Effective democratization can always be measured by this essential criterion: the participation in and the access to the archive, its constitution, and its interpretation" (1995, 4). This political import is doubly compelling in Sligh's book for the ways in which 'democratization' happens unevenly between the different, non-isomorphic subject positions of Sligh and her subjects—black, white, non-trans, trans, gay, straight, female, male.

Exploring these archives brings into focus the nexus of transness, blackness, archival practice, and loss, and troubles the line between what Eve Kosofsky Sedgwick theorized as 'paranoid' and 'reparative' readings. A paranoid reading of Jake's transition is structurally impossible without amounting to a critical interrogation of transphobia and the relevance of its rejection; a reparative reading of the Crafts' narrative suggests there might be something salvageable from within the context of slavery. Conversely, a reparative reading of Jake's transition interpellates Sligh, as a black woman, into a project of recovery or a kind of care work that she explicitly refuses. And a paranoid reading of the Crafts' narrative is self-evident for how it challenges and criticizes then prevailing ideologies of race and gender by exposing them as constructed and disciplined categories. Sligh's juxtaposition, then, complicates what might be a reparative archival project, and how this repair comes into visibility, in an unwieldy archive. It is thus helpful to follow Jacques Derrida's call in *Archive Fever* (1995) to study the archive starting with the etymological roots of the term: as *Arkē*, signifying both *commandment* and *commencement*. In so doing, I attend to the ways in which *Wrongly Bodied* offers compelling insights into both the beginning of an archival project and the intervention of the law undergirding both narratives Sligh documents. Her work undermines the conventional trans narrative that assumes an atomized and self-conscious subject who has 'always' known they were trans. Rendered as an archival project that exceeds the individual—indeed, that necessarily depends on histories older and different from the conventional trans narrative which draws on the language of imprisonment as "the dominant metaphor to summarize a 'life-plot' of cross-gender identification" (Meyerowitz 2002, 139)—*Wrongly Bodied* articulates a compelling, if complicated, narrative of trans identity. Part of what makes this history uniquely complicated is the intervention of the law, and the legal fictions of personhood that derive from it, from US legal justifications for slavery to twenty-first century bureaucratic control of gender. The scale and material differences of these legal injustices also produce a productive frisson in Sligh's project, whereby she draws attention to the ways authority not only intercedes in the archive, but also in narratives about personhood.

COMMENCEMENT: THE ARCHIVE AS BODY

Though it is generally sensible to begin at the beginning, *Wrongly Bodied* troubles what, precisely, constitutes a beginning in the trans archive. In part, the concept of 'beginning' is complicated by terminology: the word 'transgender' was not in popular use until the mid-century. Yet cross-sex identification has existed for far longer than the term 'transgender' allows if we simply begin the archive with the use of the term. If, as Jules Gill-Peterson has argued in *Histories of the Transgender Child* (2018), trans archives privilege Western sexological accounts of medical treatment and sex change in line with conventional trans narratives of medicalization and institutional intervention as the originary point for any trans narrative (11), Sligh offers an invitation to consider trans archives that do not derive from a specifically medicalized perspective. In part, Sligh's intervention is one of historiographical revision—that is, she suggests that we might embrace a narrative as 'trans', even if it does not follow from an explicitly sexological viewpoint. From the perspective of Jake's narrative, beginning simply means the commencement of his transition; it demands us to consider an earlier time, for instance, when he first began to recognize himself as trans. But Sligh problematizes any idea of a coherent, discrete beginning, suggesting that the beginning of Jake's narrative far predates him; she locates it in the story of two formerly enslaved people, Ellen and William Craft, who have no direct relation—familial or narrative—to Jake. In what follows I consider the stakes of 'beginning' to illustrate how history, and the histories of identity, do not operate in necessarily linear, ordered ways: where and how Sligh begins, how beginning structures the trans archive, and finally, what such accounts of commencement reveal about the materiality of the trans body.

"It is often said that the camera doesn't lie, but the picture first reveals itself in your mind" (148–149), Sligh writes in the afterword of *Wrongly Bodied*, proposing a genesis of the photograph before it becomes the photograph—material, tangible, discernible. She continues, "[i]n the beginning I focused on recording Jake's physical body. Bodily changes were not always apparent but as his behavior fluctuated, my perception of what I was to photograph became less clear. The way I saw him shifted in and out of focus" (149). If the photograph is first imagined before the material object, before the staging, before the camera clicks—if its genesis is first imagined in the photographer's mind, there is a similarly recursive timeline discernible in Sligh and McBee's project. It began with a false start, an act of misrecognition: Sligh thought she was photographing a masculine woman, not a man in transition. No surprise, then, that the image first revealed in her mind was *not* one of a man. When Jake announces to her, however, his upcoming transition, Sligh is given over to the project's commencement: how one engages with Jake's physical body depends on her focus shifting behind the camera. Perhaps, then, the most complicated question is how Sligh sees Jake as a man. We might consider this from the vantage point of how she stages the photographs, beginning with a photo of Jake in bed, looking in the mirror, before his double mastectomy. On first glance, this photograph might be read as undercutting Jake's claim to maleness by the archival reminder of the presence of his breasts, but this scene might also be read affirmatively, as admitting to the fact that Jake's maleness does not begin only after his mastectomy but rather predates it.

This question of commencement is compelling not only in the project's development, but also in its narration: if one beginning of the project is Sligh learning to revise her perception of Jake, another version of this project begins more properly in the archive, when she takes recourse in the Crafts' narrative, dwelling with it as a kind of anterior posterior, in order to understand Jake's transition. As Gayle Salamon writes,

> Sligh discovers that her disbelief in Jake's avowed gender has at its root a referendum about her own gender, as her anxiety about her own femininity and relation to masculinity emerges. She says, when initially meeting Jake: 'Trying to avert my eyes so as not to stare, I thought, if this chick is a man, then what in the hell am I?' Her photographic series, then, is a portrait of Jake's transition, but also of Sligh's: she documents her own transition on the question of transsexuality itself, a transition in which she turns from disbelief to uncertainty to a measure of respect and an acknowledgment of the difficulties of Jake's process. (2016, 314)

If the text depicts two transitions from female to male, it also depicts Sligh witnessing these transitions, over the course of which, she, too, experiences a transition of sorts. Yet where Salamon describes the project as ambivalently beholden to Sligh's "feminizing hermeneutic through which she invites the viewer to read [Jake's] transmale body" (314), I depart from her highlighting and criticizing this hermeneutic as a fault intrinsic to Sligh's perspective on the project. While moments in *Wrongly Bodied* do certainly read as feminizing, I read this less as a question of Sligh's own referendum about transsexuality itself and more as symptomatic of an archival project rooted in an asymmetrical juxtaposition. Trying to understand Jake's transness through Ellen Craft's passing might help Sligh to recognize what she calls an identity change of a certain 'magnitude' (2009, 11), but the difference in transition is not one of magnitude, but one of kind. Said differently, while certainly there is a feminization that happens in the structure of the project—in the way the book's cover consciously submits itself to be one of a binary transition from "Female to Male"—the turn to Ellen Craft's passing as male does instantiate a feminizing hermeneutic within Sligh's project. It reminds us of the imbrication of gender and race for *every* concept of identity and shows, as Snorton puts it, how "blackness finds articulation within transness" (2017, 8) and vice versa. What Snorton means here, and what Sligh's project bears out, is that trans and race cannot be considered separate categories, but can only be strengthened by reading them in dialogue for the moments in which they speak both with and against each other. While beginning with Craft offers Sligh the opportunity to think identity change in the abstract—and gives her access to a materiality closer to her own experience—it simultaneously posits Ellen's transition to be isomorphic with Jake's, which it clearly is not. In so doing, Jake's materiality—the reality of his trans body—is undermined, if not lost, in the balance.

In Sligh's descriptions of the project, she both glosses its structural conceit as well as her perception of Jake's desires for it:

> Jake and I did not know each other when I began photographing him. In hindsight, I think there was a reality that he wanted me to create through the photographs, due to his perception that what he was before was a fiction. In his view of 'straight photography,' if the pictures said he was a man, he was a man. (2009, 153–155)

This last statement is worth unspooling. As Sligh understands it, the photographs have a validifying function for Jake: if the pictures depict him as a man, the evidence confirms that he is a man. Through the photographs Jake might thus reverse-engineer masculinity, confirming it not from the validation of lived experience but instead from within the stylization of the still image. There is a way in which to be male is to be captured as male, to hold open the possibility of being archived as male. But to be archived is also to be dispossessed of one's capacity to narrate. And because this is an archive of transition from female to male, the fact of the archive cannot but overlay a 'feminizing hermeneutic': the archive is haunted by it, by the body Jake had before his transition, confirming not what the pictures suggest about Jake being a man, but, as part of an archive, a narrative of change. To have this archived undermines the perception that "what he was before was a fiction" (155). As the photographs evoke and perhaps confirm his maleness, the archive reminds us of the history of that image, the 'fiction' it holds, like a kernel, inside it. And this is deeper than a 'feminizing hermeneutic': it is a hermeneutic of loss. Certainly, in this sense, the hermeneutic of loss can be read, as Salamon reads Sligh's project, as the loss of the 'female' body, though this is not at all how Jake interprets his transition. More accurately, the male body form becomes visualizable in and through loss, from the material— the loss of Jake's breasts—to the social—the loss of Jake's community. That is to say, it is through witnessing the difficulties and losses of Jake's transition that Sligh comes to recognize his materiality as male.

On the one hand, loss is, perhaps, inextricable from what an archive is and does: more than a site of storage, it is a bulwark against total forfeiture. The archive is the attempt to retain whatever it is that remains from the site of loss. But, as David Eng and David Kazanjian claim, "loss is inseparable from what remains, for what is lost is known only by what remains of it, by how those remains are produced, read, and sustained" (2002, 2). Whether or not it is appropriate, or justified, for Sligh to approach Jake with a hermeneutic of loss—and here I agree with Salamon, the loss of the 'female' subject seems to be what Sligh initially most proximately mourns—is beside the point. By juxtaposing the Crafts' story with Jake's narrative of transition, *Wrongly Bodied* cannot but be suffused with this loss, even as it attempts to visualize what remains.

But there is a way of reading Jake's body-archive, when related to the Crafts' narrative, so that what is mourned here is not the loss of the 'female', but the very possibility of claiming a body. This sense of loss can be read as a reference to Sligh's own family history, particularly as it relates to Hortense Spillers's theorization of the loss of black bodily integrity under slavery. In her 1987 "Mama's Baby, Papa's Maybe: An American Grammar Book", Spillers describes the conditions under which gender was made impossible to Black Americans under slavery and urges for its restoration, not in terms of a rigid binary, but in terms of potentiality. Under the conditions of slavery, the symbolic integrity of gender distinction breaks down. To be property is not to have access to gendered self-determination—it is to be reduced to flesh. Spillers calls this an 'American grammar', which marks another point of origin, or commencement, of the archive. Thus, Spillers urges the reclamation of the possibility of gender differentiation to restore to captive flesh not only the prospect of gender, but also much of what travels along with it—ownership of a gendered body and related identity, ethics, and power:

> At a time when current critical discourses appear to compel us more and more decidedly toward gender 'undecidability,' it would appear reactionary, if not dumb, to insist on the integrity of female/male gender. But undressing these conflations of meaning, as they appear under the rule of dominance, would restore, as figurative possibility, not only Power to the

Female (for Maternity), but also Power to the Male (for Paternity). We would gain, in short, the potential for gender differentiation as it might express itself along a range of stress points, including human biology in its intersection with the project of culture. (67)

Sligh's mourning of this greater cultural and human loss becomes more complicated in the context of photographing Jake McBee, a white trans man. Indeed, much of the work Jake does to live comfortably as a man shows how whiteness permits, if not demands, the integrity of gender difference. In this regard, his experience could not be more opposed to Ellen Craft's.

Her experience of 'transition' is figured as a loss of the identity she would conventionally claim and temporarily abandoned, rooted in the passing she had to perform to escape enslavement. Jake's, however, is not—for him, transition is his "whole world opening up" (Sligh 2009, 105). Again, Ellen's story reveals another crucial difference. Perhaps, in the long term, passing does open up her world—she and William escape the US-South to safety in England. But at no point does the world offer Ellen the same open seam it does for Jake. For her, there is no security in white masculinity. In order to pass, Ellen affects various disabilities. In the image provided above, Ellen Craft is depicted with glasses (described in the text as having a dark tint so as to signify blindness) and she wears a sling and poultice around her neck. When she finds herself in a railcar with Mr. Cray, a friend of her master's, she feigns deafness, so she does not have to reply to him and reveal herself through her voice (Craft 1999, 29). The narrative *Running a Thousand Miles for Freedom* cobbles together numerous instances in which she was saved only by some prosthesis that suggested disability and allowed her to hide—her voice, her face, her inability to write. These prostheses indicate that Craft passes not as a white man, but specifically as a disabled white man. The distinction is critical: she uses prostheses to cover up her body's materiality that would reveal her identity. This evokes Christina Crosby's striking formulation about the reductive social perception of her identity in terms of disability: "I no longer have a gender. I have a wheelchair" (qtd. in Jochem 2016, n. pag.). Passing as a *disabled* man reveals a similar—though lifesaving—trajectory for Craft.

Maintaining gendered integrity is, conversely, important to Jake. In an interview with Sligh, he explains:

> If I had been born a genetic male, I would have been a big pig. I don't think I hated women; I hated the fact that I was a woman. I loathed myself, but I knew I was different. I was the youngest of three girls and my father raised me as a male. In his own way he is culturally a misogynist. He believed that the wife was the wife and she had her place and he read *Playboy* magazine and that was OK. I feel the same way. (2009, 42)

Opposite this, Sligh provides the first image of Jake's chest after masculinizing surgery. The image is striking in its clinical symmetry. Jake stands, shirtless. The photo captures only his shoulders, chest, and hips, fully anonymizing him. Two medically taped scars laterally bisect his chest. His nipples, re-grafted in surgery, are beginning to darken, fenced in by new scab. The photo, though visually arresting, is unremarkable in the context of the book, save its placement: on the next page, just after our encountering Jake's newly masculinized body, is the account of Ellen Craft feigning deaf, attempting to avoid the gaze of Mr. Cray. This placement in proximity to the narrative of Craft's feigned disability might, on first glance, undercut Jake's sense of his maleness, emphasizing the prosthetic aspect of his embodiment. Instead, however, the juxtaposition reveals, as Susan Stryker has called it, how the "same anarchic womb has birthed" those trans and nontrans alike (1994, 241). By comparing the passing disabled body and the trans body, Sligh's project reveals that the claims of identity and narratives of becoming as represented by Jake and Ellen are—just as narratives of selfhood in general are—constructed.

Commandment: The Body as Archive

If the status of 'beginning' is troubled in the archives *Wrongly Bodied* offers, so too is the status of the law, the other etymological root of 'archive'. Certainly, this is vexed for multiple reasons, not least of which is that in Ellen Craft's narrative, racial and gender passing were both federally proclaimed 'illegal' to prevent black people from escaping to freedom. Though medical transition has been happening in the United States since the mid-twentieth century, equal federal rights and protections are still not extended to trans people. Thus, the heavy hand of the law orders the archive. One reason Sligh compares Ellen and Jake is that they both are forced, given the constraints of the laws that structure their lives, to pass. While Ellen's passing for white, upper class, disabled, and male is limited to her escaping slavery, Jake's 'passing' is, for Sligh, an ongoing legal conundrum. As she writes of the Crafts:

> At that time and place, the law was on the side of those who opposed their desire to be free from the oppression of slavery. Today, you can have the surgical procedures to change your gender, but because many states do not have laws that allow for a legal gender transition, transgender people must continue to 'pass.' It is law that governs western societies, but can it embrace the complex nuances of who we are as human beings? It takes a lot of courage to be oneself; this is my issue. (2009, 12)

Sligh is not the first to suggest that the law is too blunt and dumb an instrument to "embrace the complex nuances of who we are as human beings". That her comparison between transness and enslavement hinges, in part, on a different kind of materiality—the body of law and its material effects—raises thorny questions about Jake's white male body. These questions are especially compelling in moments when Jake is not legible as trans, and thus when his body is read as 'the law', or as 'the neutral' which masquerades as universal.[4] Said differently: Jake's white trans body puts stress on the internal contradictions of the archive, especially when he is not perceived as trans but, instead, as 'authority', either in his capacity in the US Army or simply as a white man.

Once again, Ellen's and Jake's pleated narratives are insightful here. Both accounts seem to suggest that though the archive is structured by the law, the law misses a lot. William Craft expresses it this way: "From having been myself a slave for nearly twenty-three years, I am quite prepared to say, that the practical working of slavery is worse than the odious laws by which it is governed" (1999, 11). What he refers to as the "practical working of slavery" is where he begins his narrative: with both brutal and sentimental accounts of white youth sold into slavery, then with his own experience being sold and separated from his family. Only after detailing these inhumane scenes does Craft shift registers to discuss the law. Citing the Louisiana Civil Code, the Constitution of Georgia,

---

[4] Jake says as much when he comments about meeting a trans man for the first time: "I went down there expecting the worse [sic]. But he looked like a guy. He didn't look like he had five eyes or three noses. You wouldn't notice him in the street. I was so impressed. I thought, 'My God that is what I want to be – normal.' Whatever the hell that is, but I knew I had not been that. I just wanted to go to work and live my life and have my relationships and just be normal" (Sligh 2009, 31).

and Brevard's Digest, he shows the distance between the law and the practical workings of slavery. This reveals what the law cannot contain: after William's sister is sold, he remains on the auction stand. He begs the auctioneer to let him say farewell to his sister but is denied this request. Instead, as he writes, "he grasped me by the neck, and in a commanding tone of voice, and with a violent oath, exclaimed, 'Get up! You can do the wench no good; therefore there is no use in your seeing her'" (8). The syntax of the law contains no space for William Craft's feelings; instead, it suggests that social order must be preserved, white male authority must be respected. That the law stands in the way of the Crafts' freedom is obvious. And in a brilliant rhetorical move, William Craft begins to detail their narrative of escape, but first pauses to list the laws that governed slave states, literally putting the law ahead of their narrative.

Jake's relationship to the law is different: the law appears for him predominantly in the form of bureaucratic convolutions—annoying, unhelpful, outdated, time-consuming, and expensive. The law enters only as a bureaucratic system through which Jake must confirm and name his gender; this is a process he must indeed seek out. On the other hand, the law is what the Crafts must decidedly avoid in their attempt to escape what the law ensures: their enslavement. The law is not after Jake in the same way that it literally chases after the Crafts, forcing them into fugitivity. Indeed, one might say that the law is not really after Jake at all: *he* is before the law. In becoming a straight white man, Jake desires what straight white masculinity will afford: inconspicuousness, selfhood. He does not call this privilege—it is not easy being a $5'2$ straight man, he claims (2009, 45)—but he does admit to greater confidence, greater peace once he is read publicly as a white man. At the same time, there is something a bit deflating—to use Jake's word, *anticlimactic*—about the law and its symbolic trappings:

> It has been such a big ordeal. Yet, it is kind of anticlimactic because at the end all you are is a normal guy. You go through all this pain, through all this growing, through all this terribly hard growth and when you come out you are just some 'Joe Blow' on the street. That's all I ever wanted to be – some middle class guy [sic] who maybe was going to get married and who had a truck, a dog, a house and a wife. And it is unbelievably gratifying to have those things. (102–103)

Jake now 'passes' as a straight white man, as the subject and guarantor of the law. Despite his gratification at finally having access to this life he has so desired, these possessions he has romanticized, Jake finds himself alienated. There is nothing he names to detail where, and why, precisely, the law leaves him cold; indeed, he can only rely on dry banalities and cliché to articulate this anticlimax: "[Y]ou are just some 'Joe Blow' on the street". But this is precisely where *Wrongly Bodied*, treating Jake's body as an archive, manages to represent what the law cannot fully contain since there is no grammar yet to frame Jake's experience beyond the legal fiction of a distinctive gender marker. If Jake passes in his everyday life, his transness—the big ordeal, the terribly hard growth—is erased. Sligh's photographs, however, capture what Jake describes as those difficult moments of growth, these moments in which he stands both before, but also irrevocably apart from, the law. At times Jake frames this in terms of the relationships between carcerality and feeling 'wrongly bodied':

> I felt like I was in jail and I wasn't aware of it because I had these feelings inside that I had never identified. As I look back in my life I've always felt like a man, always thought like a man, always felt like I should have been a man. [...] Each surgical operation has been like getting a little more freedom. As I go through this I feel like I'm closer and closer to getting out of jail. To be able to walk down the street and not have anyone wonder who I am is going to be 'the freedom.' I want it now. It is so hard to wait. I want it now. (61)

Elsewhere Jake represents this in sculpture. Sligh photographs one piece Jake created in which a black and white image of him is loosely wrapped in a tented wreath of barbed wire. Jake explains that this piece represents his feeling imprisoned in his body, alienated from it and from the world. Another point of pressure the juxtaposition of the Crafts' and Jake's story permits is about the legal archive: in the above lines Jake is able to imagine himself into 'freedom' and to effect that change. Though it is clear he has support—from friends, from partners—through his transition, the process is framed as fairly atomistic. In nearly every photograph he is depicted alone; in some he is doubled, holding a mirror in front of himself. These images reflect back the vast expanse of his white male body, invoking a kind of redundancy, but also a kind of power, the filling up of space, the ability to say and enact—felicitously, if haltingly: "I want it now".

Redundancy, in these images of Jake, stands in contrast to the facts of the archive: transitioning in 1996, there were few models for Jake to follow. Aside from a brief mention of the photographer Loren Cameron and the few trans men Jake meets in support groups, there is no archive for him to draw upon as he aspires toward freedom. The same is, in some ways, true for the Crafts. With few models to emulate in their escape to freedom—certainly with no direct guidance from formerly enslaved people who escaped—the archive they are left with is limited, incomplete, closed off. The published accounts of formerly enslaved people who managed to escape—William Grimes's, Moses Roper's, Mary Prince's, Henry Box Brown's—formed an archive impenetrable to the Crafts. They could not read.

The most compelling reason to juxtapose the Crafts' narrative with Jake's, then, is that both stem from and enter the archives for those who otherwise would not have access to these impossible narratives. This is what is at stake in these archives: the future. Nothing would need archiving if there was no possibility of loss. But, as Derrida explains, "[t]he archive has always been a pledge, and like every pledge, a token of the future" (1995, 18). And in this way, the commandment that sutures both narratives together, is only the imperative to remember that other worlds are possible. While loss may structure the archive and provide, as Eng and Kazanjian suggest, a hermeneutic to discuss what is no longer, loss also is future-oriented, and can act as an animating power to read and theorize what remains and what perdures (2002, 2). Tracking Jake's transition is just one mode, whereby Sligh is able to attend to questions of the material body. Just as the logging of Jake's transition underlines a transient period in his life, it also maintains a record of this time, preserving it for those who come after Jake. The conclusion of this project, of Jake's archive, becomes the beginning of hermeneutic exploration for others. That is, Jake's material body functions as a starting point for interrogating claims about embodiment and materiality (for posterity) and the workings of the archive. Readers, trans or not, might thus glean new understandings of embodiment and of the self's relationship to the body. Reading his body in the archive is an invitation to consider the trans masculine body from a beginning other than the sexology of the 1950s; instead, readers begin with his lived experience as mediated by Sligh's development of archival—and racial and gender—constructedness. This tell us two things: first it reaffirms the cruciality of the archive in documenting what is otherwise historically elusive and, at the same time, it reinforces the fluidity of the archive. If, as Sligh wagers, Jake's trans narrative might not begin with him at all, but with the Crafts, there is no telling just where, or whom, his archive might one day reach. Its material life extends, then, in directions unknown.

REFERENCES

Ahmed, Sara. *Queer Phenomenology: Orientations, Objects, Others*. Durham: Duke UP, 2006.

Brubaker, Rogers. *Trans: Gender and Race in an Age of Unsettled Identities*. Princeton: Princeton UP, 2016.

Butler, Judith. *Gender Trouble: Feminism and the Subversion of Identity*. New York: Routledge, 1990.

Califia, Patrick. *Sex Changes: Transgender Politics*. San Francisco: Cleis Press, 2003.

Craft, William, and Ellen Craft. *Running a Thousand Miles for Freedom*. Athens: The U of Georgia P, 1999 [1860].

Cvetkovich, Ann. *An Archive of Feelings: Trauma, Sexuality, and Lesbian Public Cultures*. London: Duke UP, 2003.

Derrida, Jacques. *Archive Fever: A Freudian Impression*. Chicago: The U of Chicago P, 1995.

Eng, David, and David Kazanjian. *Loss: The Politics of Mourning*. Berkeley: U of California P, 2002.

Ferguson, Roderick. *Aberrations in Black: Toward A Queer of Color Critique*. Minneapolis: U of Minnesota P, 2004.

Garber, Marjorie. *Vested Interests: Cross-Dressing and Cultural Anxiety*. New York: Routledge, 1992.

Gill-Peterson, Jules. *Histories of the Transgender Child*. Minneapolis: U of Minnesota P, 2018.

Hartman, Saidiya. "Venus in Two Acts." *Small Axe* 26 (2008): 1–14.

Jochem, Greta. "Q&A with Author Christina Crosby." *Boston Magazine*, March 28, 2016. https://www.bostonmagazine.com/arts-entertainment/2016/03/28/christina-crosby-a-body-undone/. Accessed July 16, 2021.

Meyerowitz, Joanne. *How Sex Changed: A History of Transsexuality in the United States*. Cambridge: Harvard UP, 2002.

Salamon, Gayle. "The Meontology of Masculinity: Notes on Castration Elation." *Parallax* 22, no. 3 (2016): 312–322.

Sligh, Clarissa T. *Wrongly Bodied: Documenting Transition from Female to Male*. Asherville: Blue Ridge Printing, 2009.

Snorton, C. Riley. *Black on Both Sides: A Racial History of Trans Identity*. Minneapolis: U of Minnesota P, 2017.

Sollors, Werner. *Neither Black nor White Yet Both: Thematic Explorations of Interracial Literature*. New York: Oxford UP, 1997.

Spillers, Hortense J. "Mama's Baby, Papa's Maybe: An American Grammar Book." *Diacritics* 17, no. 2 (1987): 65–81.

Steinbock, Eliza. *Shimmering Images: Trans Cinema, Embodiment, and the Aesthetics of Change*. Durham: Duke UP, 2019.

Stryker, Susan. "My Words to Victor Frankenstein Above the Village of Chamounix: Performing Transgender Rage." *GLQ* 1, no. 3 (1994): 237–254.

Taylor, Diana. *The Archive and the Repertoire: Performing Cultural Memory in the Americas*. Durham: Duke UP, 2003.

Tuvel, Rebecca. "In Defense of Transracialism." *Hypatia* 32, no. 2 (2017): 263–278.

CHAPTER 10

"A Most Unlikely Hero": Disability, Masculinity, and Sexuality in Harlequin Superromance Novels

Jonathan A. Allan

INTRODUCTION: THE POPULAR ROMANCE AND DISCOURSES OF DISABILITY

This article focuses on representations of masculinity and the male body, particularly the disabled male body, in the genre of the popular romance novel by studying two US-American name-brand popular romance novels published in the first two decades of the new millennium: *A Man Like Mac* (2000) by Fay Robinson and *A Hero in the Making* (2012) by Kay Stockham. A popular romance novel is characterized by two key elements, namely "a central love story and an emotionally satisfying and optimistic ending", as the Romance Writers of America have defined the genre (n. pag.). There are, of course, more complex definitions, for instance,

J. A. Allan (✉)
Brandon University, Brandon, MB, Canada
e-mail: AllanJ@BrandonU.CA

Pamela Regis (2003) outlines eight, Catherine Roach (2016) presents nine, and Janice Radway (1991) identifies fourteen essential elements, but all definitions agree on the two central elements that are identified by the Romance Writers of America: a love story and a satisfying and optimistic ending, colloquially known as 'happily ever after' or the recent innovation of the 'happy for now'. Beyond these, there is one additional element that is worthy of consideration: In the popular romance novel, heroes and heroines have "not merely 'normal' bodies, but perfect bodies" (Schwab 2012, 126). The protagonists of the romance are represented as having ideal bodies; bodies that are conventionally eroticized and desired. How then do romance novels think about bodies that are different from these normative representations?

Emily M. Baldys writes that disability has recently become a "hot trend" in popular romance fiction, so much so that scholars now speak of "the romance genre's growing obsession with disability" (2012, 126). Given the reality that romance novels are increasingly exploring disability, so too should scholars. To date, however, as Ria Cheyne notes, "the critical conversation about disability in romance novels has only just begun" (2017, 201). Cheyne's work provides a theoretical overview of Disability Studies and popular romance novels, which helps lay the framework for how these discourses function alongside one another. In particular, she is adamant that critics must recognize that the popular romance novel is a genre that has its own rules and expectations. That is, readers cannot expect that the romance novel will, for instance, necessarily end sadly or tragically once it explores disability; instead, the romance novel depends upon—and readers demand—the aforementioned "emotionally satisfying and optimistic ending" (Romance Writers of America, n. pag.). In writing about the genre conventions of the popular romance, scholars have attended to a range of concerns regarding disability. Baldys, for instance, has explicitly considered how sexuality and disability intersect in the popular romance novel by studying five novels.[1] Each of the novels analyzed explores what one might understand as neurodiversity,[2] for instance, in Peggy Webb's novel, we read: "'She's not Down's syndrome,

---

[1] These are *Tim* (1974) by Colleen McCullough, *A Special Man* (1986) by Billie Green, *A Prince for Jenny* (1993) by Peggy Webb, *Simple Jess* (1996) by Pamela Morsi, and *The Madness of Lord* by Ian MacKenzie (2009).

[2] Katherine Runswick-Cole understands neurodiversity as "a biopolitical category concerned with promoting the rights of, and preventing discrimination against, people

as you know it,' her doctor explains, but 'there is a short circuit some-where'" (qtd. in Baldys 2012, 129). Baldys thus "examines how romance novels, as instruments of heterosexual hegemony, exploit the conjunction between heterosexuality and able-bodiedness to reinscribe and contain the dangerous sexuality of people with disabilities" (2012, 127–128). She moreover argues that "while purporting visibility and inclusion, [these novels] function primarily to bring both compulsory heterosexuality and compulsory able-bodiedness to bear on disabled sexuality" (2012, 128). Simply, it is impossible to treat disability and sexuality separately because they intersect with one another (McRuer, qtd. in Baldys 2012, 127).

In "Happily Ever After for Whom? Blackness and Disability in Romance Narratives", Sami Schalk extends the scope of disability and popular romance studies by paying attention to blackness. Schalk speaks of a "representational double-bind when attempting to depict the sexualities of disabled people", and subsequently asks: "Do we want to emphasize sexuality to resist the desexualization of people with disabilities or down-play sexuality to reject the hypersexualization of black people?" (2016a, 1245). This approach, informed by an intersectional praxis, reminds readers that people—real or fictional—cannot be reduced to a single identity, but rather comprise a number of differential identities that are entwined. The challenge, thus, lies in attesting to this "representational double-bind". In other scholarly studies, there has often been a focus on particular disabilities, for instance, Sandra Schwab has explored blindness in two novels by Teresa Medeiros (2012), while Jayashree Kamblé has considered PTSD and the figure of the hero (2012, 153–163).

In another important turn, Schalk has asked timely questions about the "supercrip", which is an idealized disabled person who overcomes all social obstacles and hence epitomizes not only the typical US-American success story but also reinforces ableist fantasies and social norms. While Schalk's article "Reevaluating the Supercrip" is not explicitly or solely about the popular romance, it has significant implications for the genre. The supercrip has become "an unquestioned and potentially damaging stereotype of disability that must be challenged", Schalk argues (2016b, 71), or, as Eli Clare explains, it is

---

who are neurologically different from the 'neurotypical' (or the non-autistic) population" (2014, 1120).

one of the dominant images of disabled people. [...] A boy without hands bats .486 on his Little League team. A blind man hikes the Appalachian trail from end to end. An adolescent girl with Down's syndrome learns to drive and has a boyfriend. A guy with one leg runs across Canada. The nondisabled world is saturated with these stories. (qtd. in Schalk 2016b, 73)

The figure of the disabled hero in popular romance novels, who embodies what Radway identified as "purity of his maleness" (1991, 128), may be turned into a supercrip. This supercrip narrative speaks to an ableist fantasy, featuring a hero who overcomes all odds and defies all predictions. While it is tempting, perhaps, to read narratives of these figures' heroism as success stories or as "positive interpretations" of disability (Cheyne 2017, 212), it must also be admitted that

[s]everal scholars assert that supercrip narratives not only set unreal expectations for people with disabilities to 'overcome' the effects of their disabilities through sheer force of will, but also, simultaneously, these representations depend upon our ableist culture's low standards for the lives of disabled people. (Schalk 2016b, 74)

In this contribution, the supercrip serves as an important stereotype, perhaps archetype—a recurring image—in the study of masculinities and disabilities in the popular romance novel. While Schwab has noted that "in romance [novels] it is the hero who is often physically impaired" (2012, 276), it must also be admitted that few studies have attended to the specific question of *how* disabled masculinities are construed in the genre. Accordingly, in this article, I draw on critical studies of men and masculinities, but given the many names within this subfield, it is imperative that I clearly outline what I understand to be its contours: Firstly, the critical study of men and masculinities is a subfield in the broader field of Gender Studies. Its historical, epistemological, and methodological origins can be found in Women's Studies. Additionally, the subfield is interdisciplinary or perhaps even beyond discipline. While undoubtedly the subfield has its founders in sociological training, as the editors outline in the introduction, that does not mean that it is a sociological discipline. Critical studies of men and masculinities are resolutely committed to a pro-feminist, anti-homophobic, anti-racist pedagogy, as Jeff Hearn has outlined (2013, 26–38), and work towards an inclusive paradigm that recognizes the complexities of a term like "masculinity", which is why it privileges the plural (Connell 2005).

In many ways, the concept of the body has been central to theoretical work on men and masculinities. In *Masculinities in Theory*, Todd W. Reeser outlines what "might be the most central aspect of masculinity, namely the male body. For the male body might appear to be the most natural element of masculinity: after all, almost all men have a penis, testicles, facial hair, an Adam's apple, a prostate, and the Y chromosome" (2010, 91). In his work, Reeser criticizes this rather monolithic definition which collapses notions of the physical male body and of masculinity. He notes that gender is largely a social construction but suggests that this is how the male body is conventionally seen and understood—it is considered representative of men and masculinities. Admittedly, such an approach is rather traditional, but it seems to me that we cannot negate the relationship between the two. While I undoubtedly agree with Eve Kosofsky Sedgwick who argued that "it is important to drive a wedge in, early and then if possibly conclusively, between the two topics, masculinity and men, who relate to one another it is so difficult not to presume" (1995, 12), I also find myself agreeing with Reeser's perspective, that is, the male body is there, it is real, it is material. How we understand the body is, of course, gendered. That is, the male body becomes masculine because of the cultural frameworks in which we happen to find ourselves. Connell has coined the concept of "hegemonic masculinity", which can be defined "as the configuration of gender practice which embodies the currently accepted answer to the problem of the legitimacy of patriarchy, which guarantees (or is taken to guarantee) the dominant position of men and the subordination of women" (2005, 77).

In this article, I am interested in how the male body is imagined, particularly when it is disabled, and in so doing, how it confounds expectations of the male body. The popular romance novel, as a form and genre, has long celebrated what Radway calls "spectacular masculinity", noting that "every aspect of [the hero's] being, whether his body, his face, or his general demeanor is informed by the purity of his maleness" (1991, 128). Even readers entirely unfamiliar with the popular romance novel are probably familiar with the dominant images of this genre, most prominently, the bare-chested figure of Fabio, bulging biceps, and shirtless hunks. These are representations of normative models of masculinity that prevail in the genre's imagery and the cultural imaginary. So, what happens when the popular romance novel presents readers with a disabled hero? What happens when a wheelchair, for example, is included on the cover of a romance novel?

This article is divided into two parts, the first will provide a close reading of the novels, with a particular focus on how disabled bodies are represented. While some scholars argue that these representatives afford "positive interpretations" of disability (Cheyne 2017, 212), I intend to challenge and complicate this notion. This leads to the second part of the contribution which explores the tensions that arise from these "positive interpretations". I do this by drawing on Sedgwick's work on paranoid and reparative readings. These "positive interpretations" are a kind of "reparative reading", but one might ask, for whom are these readings "reparative"? How are we to think critically about the ways in which these positive interpretations work and do not work? What are the ethical demands of the reparative? This article resembles what Northrop Frye has called a "polemical introduction" (1957) and hopes to join the "critical conversation" (Cheyne 2017, 201) on this topic by studying masculinities in popular romance novels that include and address disability. Additionally, this work expands upon my earlier research on men and masculinities, which has tended to focus on normative bodies. In this article, I am hoping to understand how the genre thinks about "alternative masculine behaviors and practices" by considering "multiple male subjectivities across contexts rather than lumping all men into a single category" (Carabí and Armengol 2014, 4). I thus analyze disability in the popular romance novel as one potential way of how the genre challenges normative assumptions of masculinity.

Representing the Disabled Hero, Engaging the Trope of the Supercrip

My article explores the disabled hero's body by drawing on two exemplary romance novels: *A Man Like Mac* (2000) by Fay Robinson and *A Hero in the Making* (2012) by Kay Stockham. Both novels were published by Harlequin, and both are classified as "Superromance" novels. From Harlequin's marketing perspective, Superromance novels are ideal for readers who "want romance plus a bigger story! Harlequin Superromance stories are filled with powerful relationships that deliver a strong emotional punch and a guaranteed happily ever after" (Harlequin, n. pag.).

Fay Robinson's *A Man Like Mac*, which won the Best First Book RITA award from the Romance Writers of America, features a hero in a wheelchair, who used to be a successful athlete. As the back cover informs readers, Mac has "overcome adversity and met challenges that could have destroyed him. He's not only handsome, determined, and sexy, he knows exactly what matters in life". Fern Michaels, a New York Times bestselling author, opines that Fay Robinson "did the impossible—she made me fall in love with a most unlikely hero". One is tempted to ask: Why is Mac a "most unlikely hero"?

In the novel, Keely Wilson, an Olympic runner, seeks out the help of her former coach Mac after she had been in an accident that has made it seemingly impossible for her to run again. After having had a discussion of the situation at the gym, the following episode occurs:

> [H]e grabbed his towel and slung it around his neck, then reached out and grabbed his wheelchair, pulling it closer. He started to transfer but Keely shrieked, attracting not only Mac's attention but the attention of everyone working out around them.
>
> He froze at her expression of horror.
>
> "My God! What happened to you? Why are you in a *wheelchair?*"
> (Robinson 2000, 20; emphasis in original)

Throughout the novel, Keely works to come to terms with Mac's disability. Her desire to run again is contrasted by his reality. He explains to Keely: "I assumed you knew. There was an accident and I can't use my legs anymore. I'm paralyzed" (20). While Keely is training to recover her ability to run, she is in the presence of a man who had a similar accident, but unlike her, he is paralyzed. It is important to recall that Mac is not a *new* man in her life, in the sense that they have just met serendipitously, but rather that she is returning to a man from her past:

> Next to her late father, she admired Mac McCandless more than any man she'd ever known. At one time she'd even imagined herself a little in love with him, as most of his female students probably had. That rugged face, those eyes the color of expensive chocolate, had driven her to distraction whenever she was close to him. As a coach, he was as gifted as anyone in the business.
>
> Now he was paralyzed. Dear God! (2000, 21)

Leaving aside the Oedipal narrative that is clearly alluded to here, one which is compounded all the more by the 12-year age difference between Keely and her former coach,[3] it becomes clear that Keely already knew Mac before his accident, and thus before he was paralyzed, i.e., she knew the able-bodied Mac. She is haunted by his past and must come to terms with his present.

In Kay Stockham's *A Hero in the Making* (2012), published twelve years after *A Man Like Mac*, we find a similar narrative in which the hero is paralyzed from the waist down. Unlike Robinson's text, this novel confronts readers with the topic of disability early on, as the wheelchair is not 'hidden' away, nor utilized as a narrative surprise, but rather boldly shown on the cover of the novel: It features the hero, Marcus White-feather, in a wheelchair race, seemingly having done quite well in it. This novel, like other Superromances, brings together a number of challenges, for instance, the heroine and hero have previously been lovers, she is now a widow, and she has a child, who, readers will learn, is not her husband's child, but a child of Marcus, the hero of the novel. Accordingly, Marcus, who abandoned both his son Cody and Skylar Matthews after an accident that left him paralyzed, must prove that he is good enough to now be a father and a lover.[4]

In both novels, readers encounter a similar narrative, one in which the protagonist proves to those around him that even though he is disabled,

---

[3] My intention in naming the Oedipal narrative here is to highlight how complex the popular romance novel can be. The genre is oftentimes all too quickly dismissed as a simplistic form of conservative entertainment, but these novels lend themselves to different readings across a range of theoretical perspectives, and in this case, one could offer a rich psychoanalytic reading. The Oedipal narrative becomes all the more pronounced when readers learn that Keely's mother asked her father for a divorce and he then died two months later. Keely's relationship with her mother is presented as fractured and tenuous throughout the novel. Certainly, the narrative I am outlining here is one that follows the Freudian tradition, but one could just as well provide a Jungian reading of *A Man Like Mac*.

[4] I discuss *A Hero in the Making* in "One Sexy Daddy: Desirable Dad Bods, DILFS, and the Popular Romance Novel" (2022). In that article, I analyze how the hero must become 'lovable' to both the child and the heroine. This chapter considers the romance novel in light of recent media discussions of the dad bod. If the romance novel is about desire, for instance, how does the 'dad bod' appear in it? Thus far, after a cursory search, the dad bod is still a relatively rare topic of romance novels. But the genre engages the trope of the father figure in interesting ways, that is, he must be a good, active, involved father so as to be desirable to the heroine. This contribution is part of my ongoing work on alternative masculinities and the popular romance.

he can do just about anything that he sets out to do. For instance, *A Hero in the Making*'s Marcus has become a respected sculptor in the time after his accident, one of his works is even commissioned for the Statehouse. The novels thus create and represent heroes who, despite their disability, are desirable and sexy, for both the heroine and the reader.

In the following, I suggest that *A Hero in the Making* and *A Man Like Mac* lend themselves to not only a critical but also a reparative reading: They interestingly re-write a common narrative in which "disabled people are outside of the system of sexuality altogether", recognizing as Robert McRuer does that "disabled people have often been discursively constructed as incapable of having sexual desires or a sexual identity, due to their supposed 'innocence'" (2015, 168). In both novels, not only are the protagonists represented as having clearly defined sexual desires and identities—after all sexual identity is essential to the genre—, but they also have "great sex" (Roach 2016, 25) in terms of intense sexual intercourse and sexual relationships. In her analysis of the romance novel, Roach outlines nine essential elements of the romance novel, one of which is explicitly about sex:

> *Romance leads to great sex, especially for women.* The romance story is sex-positive. [...] Lovers bloom in sexual joy. Whether the intimacy is cozy or spicy, sex shared lovingly with a partner adds joy to life and depth to a relationship. The romance teaches that sexuality is meant to be a good thing, an important and positive part of being human. Sexuality is not shameful, dirty, or sordid but natural, healthy, and empowering. (2016, 25; emphasis in original)

I share Roach's argument about sex being essential to the romance novel—whether it happens explicitly on the page or not. Even in the sweetest of romances, the happily ever after ending promises the sex that will come. More importantly, sex is also a key topic in romance novels that feature disabled characters. And in many ways, it is sex that reveals the body so intimately, as the characters negotiate a body that is not normative. They express anxieties and uncertainties about these bodies at the same time as they find reassurance in them.

In *A Hero in the Making*, the sex scene begins with the main characters, Marcus and Skylar, addressing their nervousness: "It was ridiculous to feel this nervous. It wasn't as though they hadn't made love before. Many, many times. In many, many ways" (Stockham 2012, 225). Skylar asks, "'Marcus, why are you so nervous?'" and notes that "'I know I'm not the first woman you've been with since your accident'" (226). It becomes clear that Marcus's nervousness results from being with Skylar again, but now, unlike the last time, his body is disabled. She explains to him that "you're not the only one who's changed. Pregnancy and child-birth do a number on a woman's body" (227). Strikingly here, pregnancy is imagined as having as profound an effect upon the body as disability. Such a conflation is polemical, if not problematic, but it enables readers to imagine how much bodies can and do change over time—indeed, all bodies are differently abled bodies, even if momentarily. The line between ability and disability is leaky and the categories are unstable.The scene does what readers expect, it provides "great sex", but it also demon-strates Marcus's strength, for "in an instant, Marcus lifted her up – he was so strong! – and placed her beside him on the bed while he ripped open the condom" (227). Ultimately, the sex scene reaches its climax in the following passage:

> The hotel room was filled with the sounds they made. Marcus kissed her until she clutched his shoulders, her grip urging him on. The friction built the tension inside her to a feverish peak until it spread, expanded. Shattered through her until all she could do was hold Marcus until he buried his head in her neck and groaned.
> "I love you... Ah, sweetheart, I love you." (232)

The further description of this sex scene presents what can be described as a 'normalization' of Marcus, a kind of 'passing' as able-bodied. A similar narrative unfolds in *A Man Like Mac*. The scene begins with Keely "help[ing] him [Mac] out of his clothes. For a moment, when she peeled off his underwear, he felt helpless" (Robinson 2000, 150). Over the course of this scene, readers learn what Keely has learned, for instance, she tells Mac: "Vicki assured me that people with spinal injuries who can't have traditional sex can at least have a satisfying experience if they stop worrying about what they *can't* do and concentrate on what they *can*" (151; emphasis in original). Though he is unable to penetrate her, the text explains,

> [h]e touched her gently at first, wanting to drive her to the edge without going over it too quickly. He held her gaze and watched the emotions play across her face, watched desire turn her eyes to molten blue, as he slid the

pad of his thumb back and forth between the folds and across the sensitive nub hidden in there. (152)

In this scene then, he is seemingly focused on her pleasure, a not entirely uncommon phenomenon in the popular romance novel, where her orgasm may well become a measure of his masculinity (Allan 2020, 40–51). As the scene continues, his climax is depicted as both an intense experience and realization of his love and thus picks up a central feature of the genre of the popular romance:

> She cried his name, and the explosion in her body washed through him like a giant wave, carrying him along. Keely was on the crest of the wave and he was somewhere in the churning water below, but it was still a pleasurable trip – and unexpected. He had heard paras and quads talk about feeling 'something' during sex that was like a climax, but he had never experienced it firsthand.
> He almost cried from sheer joy.
> Keely had collapsed on his shoulder, unaware of the wonderful gift she had given him. He stroked her back, realizing suddenly what had made the difference between tonight and the times before.
> This time, he loved the woman in his arms. (Robinson 2000, 154)

As is expected, especially within the genre, both scenes depict "great sex" and a confirmation of love, or what Roach has called "the money shot of popular romance" (2016, 102). I argue that these scenes are not superfluous or merely sensational, rather they are doing critical work in the novel. Scholars should not treat these scenes dismissively as a kind of 'porn for women' where the pornographic is understood as a rhetorical negative. Instead, sex scenes have narrative functions that enable readers to see the development of a relationship. These scenes prove that the hero and heroine are sexually compatible, in the case of Keely and Mac, she has done "something" (Robinson 2000, 154) to him that he has only heard about. But these scenes also pose a statement about the disability of the hero: even though he is disabled, he is still sexually active, and both sexually satisfied and sexually satisfying. This is important because, as Schalk notes, "in the United States, people with disabilities are often represented as nonsexual, having either no desire or no capacity for sexual interactions", and further that "this stereotype is supported by [...] [in part] the lack of mainstream representation" (2016a, 1241). These popular romance novels then work to rewrite this stereotype and aim to fill a gap by showing sexually active disabled characters.

REASSESSING THE SUPERCRIP: PARANOID AND REPARATIVE PERSPECTIVES

In some ways, scholars are caught between two critical readings of these novels, notably what Sedgwick defined as paranoid and reparative readings. In overly simple terms, paranoid reading is critical reading, the terms have become synonymous with one another. As Sedgwick writes, "not surprisingly, the methodological centrality of suspicion to current critical practice has involved a concomitant privilege of the concept of paranoia" (2003, 125). For those scholars making use of critical theory "paranoia has by now candidly become less a diagnosis than a prescription" (125). This has led to a bifurcation of theoretical and critical practice, "in a world where no one need be delusional to find evidence of systemic oppression, to theorize out of anything *but* a paranoid critical stance has come to seem naïve, pious, or complaisant" (125–126; emphasis in original). As such, scholars are often beginning from a position in which the goal is to account for and expose the systemic oppression contained within a cultural object or literary text. For Sedgwick, there must be something other than, i.e., an alternative or addition to, the paranoid critical stance. Sedgwick calls this other position the reparative. In her schema, she seeks to reclaim the reparative, while recognizing the challenges therein:

> The monopolistic program of paranoid knowing systematically disallows any explicit recourse to reparative motives, no sooner to be articulated than subject to methodical uprooting. Reparative motives, once they become explicit, are inadmissible in paranoid theory both because they are about pleasure ('merely aesthetic') and because they are frankly ameliorative ('merely reformist'). What makes pleasure and amelioration so 'mere'? Only the exclusiveness of paranoia's faith in demystifying exposure: only its cruel and contemptuous assumption that the one thing lacking for global revolution, explosion of gender roles, or whatever, is people's (that is, *other* people's) having the painful effects of their oppression, poverty, or deludedness sufficiently exacerbated to make the pain conscious (as if otherwise it wouldn't have been) and intolerable (as if intolerable situations were famous for generating excellent solutions). (144; emphasis in original)

I cite this passage at length because it outlines quite astutely the seeming difference between the two reading positions. In terms of Popular Romance Studies, it seems that many critics have adopted this paranoid position, that is, there is a desire to expose to the presumed (female) reader, how she is, in the words of Germaine Greer, "cherishing the chains of her bondage" (2003, 202). That is, the reader, who in this context is always conceived as a woman (only 18 percent of readers are male according to statistics from the Romance Writers of America), is interpellated into the act of interpretation and becomes essential to any understanding of the text. In some ways, she becomes synonymous with the heroine. Such a perspective is not without its own critique; after all, not all readers will identify with the heroine, some will side with the hero, and others just enjoy the story. As Sedgwick notes, "the paranoid trust in exposure seemingly depends, in addition, on an infinite reservoir of naïveté in those who make up the audience for these unveilings" (2003, 141). Thus, Sedgwick contends that there has to be another model that is not so explicitly about 'unveiling' the text's oppressive nature to a reader who seemingly is unable to understand or recognize this underlying structure. Accordingly, Sedgwick explains,

> [n]o less acute than a paranoid position, no less realistic, no less attached to a project of survival, and neither less nor more delusional or fantasmatic, the reparative reading position undertakes a different range of affects, ambitions, and risks. What we can best learn from such practices are, perhaps, the many ways selves and communities succeed in extracting sustenance from the objects of a culture – even of a culture whose avowed desire has often been not to sustain them. (150–151)

This reparative model has been used in Popular Romance Studies,[5] including in the study of disability. Cheyne, for instance, in a study of Mary Balogh's novels, writes:

> In claiming Balogh's novels as challenging various negative stereotypes, I am not aiming to fix these novels as 'positive' representations which should be placed on some hypothetical list of 'acceptable' representations of disability (Mitchell and Snyder 42). Rather, I am arguing for a positive *interpretation* of these novels: one which sees them as being potentially

[5] Roach, for instance, has made exceptional use of reparative reading practices in *Happily Ever After: The Romance Story in Popular Culture* (2016).

useful in the struggle to break down social barriers. (2017, 212; emphasis in original)

I understand Cheyne's approach as being akin to Sedgwick's reparative reading, even though Cheyne does not frame it in these terms. Cheyne and Sedgwick share a desire to read anew, freed from a paranoid reading position. To a certain extent, I wholeheartedly agree with them, because too often the negative affects seem so central to literary and cultural analysis. But, even while I admit here that as much as I respect Sedgwick (Allan 2015, 1–16), I am also struck by a new anxiety with respect to reparative reading and wonder for *whom* the reading might be reparative?

Having a closer look at novels like *A Man Like Mac* and *A Hero in the Making*, I argue that they would benefit from what Cheyne calls a "positive" interpretation (2017, 212). If we compare the two novels, we might, for instance, consider the role of the wheelchair. The wheelchair becomes a symbol—a very real one—of the disability that affects the hero. In *A Man Like Mac*, the disabled hero comes as a 'surprise' for the reader, i.e., it is only over the course of the novel that the reader learns about his disability, whereas in the latter novel, disability is showcased from the outset. In both novels, however, it is the reader who benefits from 'positive' interpretations, for both novels present characters who learn to successfully handle their disabilities and thus leave readers behind with a normative ableist perception of the world.

Taking a reparative reading position "encourages us [as readers] to loosen our commitments to any singular program of analysis and ask ourselves instead how our own desires, aspirations, fears, and anxieties might provide a key to new ways to read the culture we make and that, in turn, makes us" (Fawaz 2019, 27). I admit that this reparative impulse has been very important to my work, but as I reflect on this in the space of these romance novels, I cannot help but note how all of this becomes an issue about the reader and the reader's affective relation to the text, and not about the text. We read the texts anew to consider and understand "our own desires, aspirations, fears, and anxieties" (Fawaz 2019, 27). It seems to me that the two romance novels under consideration here, which can be read "positively", as Cheyne would have it, are cutting both ways. On the one hand, these novels explore masculinity, disability, and sexuality, and they do not deny the heroes' sexuality, but, at the same time, these sex scenes normalize in such a way that the disabled hero almost seems to 'pass' as able-bodied. In their work, Jeffrey A. Brune and Daniel

J. Wilson note that disability passing "refers to the way people conceal social markers of impairment to avoid the stigma of disability and pass as 'normal'" (2013, 1). But, in the case of *A Man Like Mac*, the topic of Mac's disability very quickly reappears. Following the post-coital bliss, the two lovers fall asleep. Upon waking up Mac exclaims:

> 'Oh, please!' he prayed out loud. Not now. Not with this woman. But it was already too late for prayers, too late to do anything but wait for the awful reality to destroy the dream. The stupid cripple had done one thing he feared above everything else. The stupid cripple had wet the bed. (Robinson 2000, 159–160)

His disability is presented prominently and is held responsible for "destroy[ing] the dream" (160) by Mac himself. The "awkwardness" of the disability returns, and the narrative becomes one of self-humiliation, as the phrase "stupid cripple" shows. It causes readers to pause, because, on the one hand, a paranoid reading would demand extrapolating the problems associated with the language and its derogatory suggestion of deviation. On the other hand, a reparatively positioned reader might imagine that this is how the character defines himself by attending to nuances of focalization and by reclaiming words. Either way, the uneasiness remains, and my tentativeness is insistent.

As much as I appreciate Cheyne's deployment of "positive" interpretation and Sedgwick's 'reparative reading', it is important to recall that these reading modes or practices do not imply an either/or decision, but rather constitute a both/and practice. In other words, these reading modes or practices interdigitate. This uneasiness might be productive because it forces readers to think about the inherent tensions therein. Lauren Berlant and Lee Edelman have rightly noted that the "and" in the title of Sedgwick's essay, "Paranoid Reading *and* Reparative Reading" fulfills a purpose. They suggest:

> if we read Eve's title (though would this be to read it reparatively or paranoically?) as an instance of hendiadys, then the *and* that binds its terms must also separate them as well, making difference out of sameness by naming as two what amounts to one in order to figure, albeit paradoxically, that underlying unity. In doing so the *and* displaces the digitalizing *or*, which then gets banished into the subtitle, or rather into the undefined space between title and subtitle that indicates their relation: "Paranoid Reading and Reparative Reading; or, You're So Paranoid, You

Probably Think This Introduction Is About You." (2019, 44–45; emphasis in original)

All of this leaves Berlant and Edelman to ponder the relation between the two reading practices. This relation is not one of antagonism but can rather be defined as what Northrop Frye called "the double vision" (1991, 166–238). Drawing on William Blake, Frye explains that the double vision is about how "the conscious subject is not perceiving until it recognizes itself as part of what it perceives. The whole world is humanized when such a perception takes place. There must be something human about the object, alien as it may at first seem, which the perceiver is relating to" (1996–2012, vol. 4, 184). Thus, in the case of the romance novels, the perceivers (or readers) must recognize their role in the text as well. The text takes on this meaning, because readers are consciously and self-reflexively reflecting on the challenges of the text. I suggest that this is necessary to the "positive" interpretation that Cheyne elucidates, it is not a matter of 'passing' away the disability in the novel, but rather the constant push and pull dynamics of a paranoid and reparative reading practice that affects and influences how the text is perceived and understood. It would, in some sense, be quite easy to point out all of the problems in the romance novels, but what is to be gained from such an approach? Sedgwick reminds us that reparative reading is "frankly ameliorative" (2003, 144). However, I do not believe that the approach should discount those paranoid moments. Indeed, as Berlant and Edelman summarize,

[r]eparativity similarly repeats the schizoid practice it claims to depart from paranoia, and thereby erasing the division between paranoia's division and its own repair, it is able, ironically, to enact 'repair': the repair that undoes what we now call reparativity's murderous divisions – and that undoes it by way of its own implication in the negativity it seems to negate. (2019, 45)

Thus, a certain feedback loop is essential to paranoid reading and reparative reading. For Berlant and Edelman, "Eve hopes for something other than drama that feels dramatic and threatening to the possibility of staying attached to life" (47).

While I am trying to be careful in my readings, I am aware of the fact that readers and scholars might fail at some point. I hope that these failures are read reparatively rather than paranoically. In this article, I tried to take a both/and decision, not dismissing or embracing one or the other reading practice. I think, however, that one of the goals of reading should be to avoid the hopelessly naïve. That is, one can be critical of a text without being negative.

While this contribution has focused on 'visible disabilities', I want to underline the diversity of disabilities, including invisible disabilities. Romance novels have also attended to the complexities of neurodiversity and romance. In *Love on the Spectrum*, the hero Hervé explains that "a one-legged man doesn't have to explain that he has only one leg. A white cane or a service dog is usually enough for a blind person to be recognized as such" (Nortan 2020, loc. 58). Hervé, unlike the one-legged man or the blind person, has an invisible disability, namely Asperger syndrome. Throughout the novel, Hervé confronts his own disability alongside the disability of his lover. At the close of the novel, he asks "who could have imagined the best cure for the disability of one would be the disability of the other?" (loc. 1703), thus reflecting on the fact that he and Luc share similar, though different, histories. Even though it is not possible to medically cure their disability as it might be possible with a disease, they are both cured of the anxieties that prevented them from love.[6] And Hervé responds:

> But not really. They are not disabilities. They are part of us, elements that make us who we really are. We may hide our true selves from strangers, but knowing there is someone who accepts us unconditionally is the most wonderful gift possible. It's what makes us feel human. (loc. 1704)

In this novel, readers are presented with the stereotype of the supercrip. At the end of the novel, Hervé has overcome significant obstacles in his personal as well as his professional life, having moved from a reclusive employee to a manager in charge of several employees. This novel allows for what Cheyne calls a "positive interpretation"; however, this does not mean that novels that include "'positive' representations [...] should be placed on some hypothetical list of 'acceptable' representations of disability" (2017, 212). Rather, there is a 'reparative' potential to these novels. *Love on the Spectrum*, as *A Man Like Mac* and *A Hero in*

---

[6] Finding a way to love again after having experienced a particular trauma is another trope in the genre.

the Making, embraces an ableist fantasy in which the disabled character is able to function just as well as an able-bodied character. These 'supercrip narratives' speak to a readerly desire for the characters' cure. Admittedly, this is where the challenge of a reparative reading arises, what if readers are left with an essentialist view of disability that once again works to erase disability? In the case of these novels, no character is 'cured' of his disability, but rather the characters learn about disability and overcome both social problems they have to face and a sense of social exclusion they internalized once they learn about the disability. These novels work to showcase disabled heroes, but we should not assume that these novels offer 'perfect' representations. I therefore argue that a reparative reading must also account for imperfections.

CONCLUSION

This article has focused closely on two romance novels and assessed their negotiation of the disabled male body. In each novel, a heroine encounters a disabled hero in a wheelchair. These novels seek to make disabled heroes desirable to the heroines and the readers. While on the surface, the texts may thus seem to offer something innovative and even positive, as a scholar, I admit my own discomfort with these positive interpretations, which are reparative in nature. Simply, it seems to me that the popular romance novel, when it explores disability, masculinity, and sexuality, is not without challenges, including ableist fantasies of the supercrip, for instance, in which the disabled person has managed to overcome all adversity. In spite of these challenges, there is still room for 'positive interpretations', which, for instance, introduce a reader to a new character, a character who confounds the normative expectations of the genre. The disabled hero, a "most unexpected hero", challenges the ideas of "spectacular masculinity" in which every element of his character testifies to the "purity of his maleness" (Radway 1991, 128). In the novels, the heroine and the readers learn about the hero and his disability, and, of course, his body. These bodies are without doubt disabled bodies, often with references to wheelchairs, for instance. The bodies thus present challenges to the heroine, not just psychically, but also physically. She must learn how to love again, that is, to learn to love anew in light of his disability. In the two novels this contribution considered, *A Man Like Mac* and *A Hero in the Making*, the heroine's anxieties about the hero's body and his disability are elements that must be overcome so that she can love him, and in some ways, he too must overcome his own anxieties. The characters thus, while on the journey towards a happily ever after, also must find acceptance and appreciation for their bodies and the body of their lover. Indeed, the novels are at their most interesting when they explore the bodies of these heroes, when they show the challenges and the new ways of thinking that can emerge through both the hero's and heroine's openness towards alternative models of eroticism and sexuality. The popular romance novel as a genre continues to push the boundaries of what is considered desirable and sexy, whether it be virgin heroes, widower heroes, or disabled heroes. These texts, like all texts, are flawed, but they certainly do imagine a world in which characters are afforded their happily ever afters.

References

Allan, Jonathan A. "Falling in Love with Eve Kosofsky Sedgwick." *Mosaic: A Journal for the Interdisciplinary Study of Literature* 48, no. 1 (2015): 1–16.
———. *Men, Masculinities, and Popular Romance*. London: Routledge, 2020.
———. "One Sexy Daddy: Dad Bods, DILFS, and Popular Romance Fiction." *Fashionable Masculinities: Queers, Pimp Daddies, and Lumbersexuals*, edited by Vicki Karaminas, Adam Geczy, and Pamela Church Gibson. New Brunswick: Rutgers UP, 2022.
Baldys, Emily M. "Disabled Sexuality, Incorporated: The Compulsions of Popular Romance." *Journal of Literary & Cultural Disability Studies* 6, no. 2 (2012): 125–141.
Berlant, Lauren, and Lee Edelman. "What Survives." In *Reading Sedgwick*, edited by Lauren Berlant, 37–62. Durham: Duke UP, 2019.
Brune, Jeffrey A., and Daniel J. Wilson. *Disability and Passing: Blurring the Lines of Identity*. Philadelphia: Temple UP, 2013.
Carabí, Àngels, and Josep M. Armengol. "Introduction." In *Alternative Masculinities for a Changing World*, edited by Àngels Carabí and Josep Armengol, 1–13. New York: Palgrave Macmillan, 2014.
Cheyne, Ria. "Disability Studies Reads the Romance: Sexuality, Prejudice, and the Happily-Ever-After in the Work of Mary Balogh." In *Encounters Between Disability Studies and Cultural Studies*, edited by Anne Waldschmidt, Hanjo Berressem, and Moritz Ingwersen, 201–216. Berlin: Transcript Verlag, 2017.
Connell, R. W. *Masculinities*. 2nd ed. Berkeley: U of California P, 2005.

Fawaz, Ramzi. "'An Open Mesh of Possibilities': The Necessity of Eve Sedgwick in Dark Times." In *Reading Sedgwick*, edited by Lauren Berlant, 6–33. Durham: Duke UP, 2019.

Frye, Northrop. *Anatomy of Criticism*. Princeton: Princeton UP, 1957.

———. *The Double Vision: Language and Meaning in Religion*. Toronto: U of Toronto P, 1991.

Greer, Germaine. *The Female Eunuch*. New York: HarperCollins, 2003.

Harlequin. "Harlequin Superromance." https://www.harlequin.com/shop/brand/harlequin-superromance.html. Accessed June 23, 2021.

Hearn, Jeff. "Methods and Methodologies in Critical Studies on Men and Masculinities." In *Men, Masculinities and Methodologies*, edited by Barbara Pini and Bob Pease, 26–38. New York: Palgrave Macmillan, 2013.

Kamblé, Jayashree. "Patriotism, Passion, and PTSD: The Critique of War in Popular Romance Fiction." In *New Approaches to Popular Romance Fiction*, edited by Sarah S.G. Frantz and Eric Murphy Selinger, 153–163. Jefferson: McFarland, 2012.

McRuer, Robert. "Sexuality." In *Keywords for Disability Studies*, edited by Rachel Adams, Benjamin Reiss, and David Serlin, 167–170. New York: New York UP, 2015.

Nortan, Alec. *Love on the Spectrum*. New Mexico: Nine Star Press, 2020.

Radway, Janice A. *Reading the Romance: Women, Patriarchy, and Popular Literature*. Chapel Hill: U of North Carolina P, 1991.

Reeser, Todd W. *Masculinities in Theory: An Introduction*. London: Wiley-Blackwell, 2010.

Regis, Pamela. *A Natural History of the Romance Novel*. Philadelphia: U of Pennsylvania P, 2003.

Roach, Catherine M. *Happily Ever After: The Romance Story in Popular Culture*. Bloomington: Indiana UP, 2016.

Romance Writers of America. "About the Romance Genre." https://rwa.org/Online/Resources/About_Romance_Fiction/Online/Romance_Genre/About_Romance_Genre.aspx?hkey=dc7b967d-d1eb-4101-bb3f-a6cc936b5219. Accessed June 23, 2021.

Robinson, Fay. *A Man Like Mac*. Toronto: Harlequin, 2000.

Runswick-Cole, Katherine. "'Us' and 'Them': The Limits and Possibilities of a 'Politics of Neurodiversity' in Neoliberal Times." *Disability & Society* 29, no. 7 (2014): 1117–1129.

Schalk, Sami. "Happily Ever After for Whom? Blackness and Disability in Romance Narratives." *Journal of Popular Culture* 49, no. 6 (2016a): 1241–1260.

———. "Reevaluating the Supercrip." *Journal of Literary & Cultural Disability Studies* 10, no. 1 (2016b): 71–86.

Schwab, Sandra. "'It Is Only with One's Heart That One Can See Clearly': The Loss of Sight in Teresa Medeiros's *The Bride and the Beast* and *Yours Until Dawn.*" *Journal of Literary & Cultural Disability Studies* 6, no. 2 (2012): 275–289.

Sedgwick, Eve Kosofsky. "Gosh, Boy George, You Must Be Awfully Secure in Your Masculinity!" In *Constructing Masculinity*, edited by Maurice Berger, Brian Wallis, and Simon Watson, 11–20. New York: Routledge, 1995.

———. *Touching Feeling: Affect, Pedagogy, Performativity.* Durham: Duke UP, 2003.

Stockham, Kay. *A Hero in the Making.* Toronto: Harlequin, 2012.

PART IV

Pioneering Bodies?

CHAPTER 11

Of Cyborgs, Aliens, and Tricksters: Posthumanist Perspectives on the Male Body in Caribbean Speculative Literature

Carmen Dexl and Silvia Gerlsbeck

Introduction: Body Matters in Caribbean Speculative Fiction

Cyborg bodies, aliens, trickster characters, and mythological figures intermingle in the social universes crafted in *Xenowealth* (2015) by Tobias S. Buckell and *Skin Folk* (2001) by Nalo Hopkinson, the two short story collections that are at the center of this critical analysis. Both portray posthuman transitions to raise questions about the consequences

C. Dexl
American Studies, University of Regensburg, Regensburg, Germany
e-mail: carmen.dexl@ur.de

S. Gerlsbeck (✉)
English Studies: Literature and Culture, Friedrich-Alexander-Universität Erlangen-Nürnberg, Erlangen, Germany
e-mail: silvia.gerlsbeck@fau.de

© The Author(s), under exclusive license to Springer Nature Switzerland AG 2022
C. Dexl and S. Gerlsbeck (eds.), *The Male Body in Representation*, Palgrave Studies in (Re)Presenting Gender,
https://doi.org/10.1007/978-3-030-88604-2_11

239

of technological progress and efforts of human enhancements as well as embodied consciousness, which allows us to read them against the backdrop of what has been labelled the 'post-human turn' in the humanities.[1] Critically engaging millennial concerns about the future of humankind, scholars have turned towards literary representations of posthumanism to explore facets of technological innovation in all fields of social existence as well as the consequences this might have for experiencing the world, especially in corporeal terms. Following M. Keith Booker, posthumanist fictions are often set in worlds "in which humans have either been replaced by a new dominant species on earth or have evolved in such dramatic ways as to be effectively a different species than the original human one" (2014, 198). This includes imagining and pondering details of technological advancement that might also enable the formation of new—cyborgian—forms of embodiments. Literary representations of the posthuman then use the cultural power of fiction to envision possible scenarios of transition and transgression that—in line with the philosophy of posthumanism and its critique of humanist thought (Wolfe 2009, xv)—critically negotiate Enlightenment values, most notably the primacy of the mind over the body, the privileging of humankind, the rigid differentiation of species, a nature/culture divide, and Western-centric narratives of and beliefs in progress.

Xenowealth and *Skin Folk*, both published after the millennial turn, offer posthumanist interventions along those lines: The two books feature black male bodies that are cybernetically enhanced and use these formations of the posthuman to negotiate essentialist notions of 'the human' as coherent, uniform, rationally thinking—white male—subject, and confront this Western concept with what it excluded, i.e., non-Western bodies and epistemologies. Instead, they offer figurations of "alternative human embodiments" (Ferrando 2015, 220), specifically attending to the question of how posthuman boundary crossings impact on the sense of embodiment of their male central characters (who are framed as postcolonial subjects) and their conceptions of masculinity.

---

[1] The skepticism towards humanist ideas that transpires in the work of Jacques Lacan, Louis Althusser, or Michel Foucault in the mid-twentieth century and is inherent to posthuman critique here stands in contrast to the emergence of posthuman bodies in popular culture at the same time. The latter were "committed to a defence of humanism" (Badmington 2000, 7) and spoke to a profound anxiety that "[man's] position at the centre of things was at risk" (8).

Xenowealth and *Skin Folk*, while standing out for the insights they offer into male social experience, are but two literary publications in what now constitutes the flourishing field of Caribbean speculative fiction (CSF). The last two decades have witnessed a proliferation of CSF, both in terms of its production and reception.[2] The designation 'speculative fiction' is mostly used as "an umbrella term for science fiction, fantasy, and several other subgenres of improbable what-ifs" (Lord 2016, 7). We conceive of the speculative not as a fixed genre category, but rather more flexibly as a discourse that—according to John Rieder—enables to account for a text's agency and signification upon and relation to other texts, genres, subgenres, or types of narrative (2010, 193).[3] This discourse of the speculative offers the opportunity to explore alternative worlds, imagine different social visions, and probe the boundaries of what might be im/possible. It resonates with the heterogeneity that is characteristic of Caribbean literature, as it draws on multiple literary forms, modes, and genres in figurations of the posthuman. In this vein, the ancient revengeful Gods, demonic creatures, shape shifters, machine-bodies, and animated techno-objects that populate the social universes of *Xenowealth* and *Skin Folk* are framed in a blend of fantastic, gothic, and especially science fiction elements.

Science fiction has traditionally been a white-authored literary form that has, since its origins dating back to the nineteenth century, been complicit with colonial ideologies (Rieder 2008, 1–33). Therefore, the mode of the speculative that informs science fiction in terms of what

---

[2] Significant anthologies that have collected and furthered CSF include, for instance, the *Dark Matter* collections by Sheree R. Thomas (2000 and 2004), the short story collection *New Worlds, Old Ways: Speculative Tales from the Caribbean* (2016) edited by Karen Lord, as well as three volumes of short stories, (co-)collected and (co-)edited by Nalo Hopkinson: *Whispers from the Cotton Tree Root* (2000), *Mojo: Conjure Stories* (2003), and *So Long Been Dreaming* (2004). This proliferation of fictional texts was met with an increase in scholarship since the 2010s: Noteworthy studies that focus on CSF include, for instance, Ingrid Thaler's *Black Atlantic Speculative Fiction* (2010), Jessica Langer's *Postcolonialism and Science Fiction* (2011), or Andrea Shaw Nevins's *Working Juju: Representations of the Caribbean Fantastic* (2019). In 2019, the *Journal for West Indian Literature* has also dedicated a special issue to 'Caribbean Science/Speculative Fiction'.

[3] We embrace Rieder's position, which warns against focusing on genre too narrowly and urges to acknowledge science fiction's inherent diversity (2010, 192–193). In this vein, we are aware that our decision to label and read the selected representations as examples of speculative fiction decisively shapes our interpretive approach towards them.

Darko Suvin describes as 'cognitive estrangement' (2016, 15) seems particularly well suited to approach questions of racial inequalities, neo-colonial enterprises, power asymmetries, and forms of exploitation in the face of global capitalism, as race has—due to the intricate interrelation between racism and capitalist development—constituted "a tool for naturalizing [and rationalizing] the inequalities produced by capitalism" (Jenkins and Leroy 2021, 3). In this context, CSF also negotiates the impact of technoscience on 'othered' bodies and highlights a continuity from colonial ideologies steeped in Enlightenment values to contemporary forms of oppression through capitalism and technology, as Donna Haraway identifies it: "[R]acism and colonialism flourished in the travelling habits of the cosmopolitan Enlightenment and […] the intensified misery of billions of men and women seems organically rooted in the freedoms of transnational capitalism and technoscience" (1997, 3). In appropriating the parameters of the speculative, *Xenowealth* and *Skin Folk* engage with dominant cultural narratives and, more importantly, provide not only revised, but rather more complicated accounts of history, its continuities, and its impact on conceptions of the body and identity against the backdrop of Caribbean histories and cultures. The parameters of Caribbean history and culture that inform *Xenowealth* and *Skin Folk* evoke forms of domination, exploitation, and subordination characteristic of postcolonial experiences.[4]

We situate ourselves within this emerging field of scholarship on CSF, yet shift the focus significantly. Both collections discussed use cyborg figurations as fusions of organisms and cybernetics (Graham 2002, 3) to negotiate the artificial boundaries between the 'technological' and the 'natural', thus echoing anxieties regarding "the ontological purity according to which Western society has defined what is normatively

---

[4] While postcolonial is notoriously difficult to define and cannot be discussed in its entirety in this article, we consider it—similar to our understanding of speculative fiction and the posthuman—as a mode of thinking and approaching texts. This lines up with Bart Moore-Gilbert's well-known definition of postcolonial criticism as a reading practice that is "preoccupied principally with [the] analysis of cultural forms which mediate, challenge or reflect upon the relations of domination and subordination—economic, cultural and political—between (and often within) nations, races or cultures, which characteristically have their roots in the history of modern European colonialism and imperialism and which, equally characteristically, continue to be apparent in the present era of neo-colonialism" (1997, 12). In this respect, the term itself attests to a "widespread, epochal crisis in the idea of linear, historical 'progress'" (McClintock 1992, 85) that occupies Western thinking—and the genre of science fiction.

human" (5).[5] While these bodies have populated science fiction for centuries, their cultural functions and critical purposes have shifted with feminist and postcolonial interventions in the genre. These include, as *Xenowealth* and *Skin Folk* illustrate, foregrounding the increased weight of matter for marginalized bodies, interrogating the discourses that have produced racialized bodies, the racialized body's relation to information technology and general disruption through it (Georgi 2011, 7–8), or inquiring into a possible erasure of embodiment through technology altogether.[6]

Intriguingly, those studies on CSF that do emphasize and negotiate 'body matters' are focused on female authors and/or the portrayal of female characters, and here particularly the potentials posthuman bodies seem to offer for feminist endeavors.[7] While this focus is justified and relevant, as it goes hand in hand with a revaluation of the role of the female subject in CSF and, related to that, a rethinking of the role of technology for feminist aspirations, it evidences a crucial blind spot: It seems to perpetuate notions of the male body as the 'invisible norm'. Our contribution wishes to propose an intervention in the existing scholarship and shifts the focus to male bodies as well as constructions of masculinity to explore how CSF—as represented by our selected texts—negotiates the persistence of humanist, Western-centric ideals that equate technological with social progress and tackles their androcentric foundations by revisiting these themes within a postcolonial setting. The male body in these fictions resembles a 'docile body' and thus becomes, in Foucault's sense, legible as a scene of "power relations [...] [that] invest it, mark it, train it, torture it, force it to carry out tasks" (2012, 25), and simultaneously as a "productive body" (26) that serves to maintain the existing social and political order. In negotiating both historical and contemporary contexts, the representations shed a critical light on biopower

---

[5] The books' simultaneous inquiry into the potentials of technoscience to transcend limiting embodiments as well as their skepticism towards humanist values resonates with what in academic discussions has surfaced as opposing notions of trans- vs. posthumanism.

[6] Francesca Ferrando, for instance, wonders whether "the posthuman body [will] still be shaped in terms of gender, race, age, class, (dis)ability and sexuality among others" (2015, 219).

[7] Confer here, for instance, Erin M. Fehskens's analysis of Nalo Hopkinson's *Midnight Robber* (2010) or Jarrel De Matas's analysis of Karen Lord's edited collection *New Worlds, Old Ways* (2019).

and -politics in the digital age as being implicated in and "ensnared by late capitalism" (Mitchell and Snyder 2015, 213–214).[8] Emerging from Haraway's border-crossing conception of the cyborg (2016), we argue that *Xenowealth* and *Skin Folk* formulate notions of black masculinity that defy racial categorization and stereotypification, but hesitate to applaud posthuman interventions for 'marked' bodies. We suggest this points to the limited gender roles that have historically been available to black men whose bodies were imagined as either 'emasculated' or 'hypersexualized' in contrast to what was construed in normative terms as white hegemonic masculinity. Within this framework, available subject positions for black men are limited. This is vividly shown in *Xenowealth*, which does not move beyond conventional gender norms, in contrast to *Skin Folk*, whose technological interventions at least point to alternative visions of embodiment and gender.

Significantly, postcolonial investments in the speculative, which bend boundaries on the levels of content and form of representation, do not only enable ideological critique, suggesting what Eve K. Sedgwick terms a 'paranoid' reading, but also contain a 'reparative' potential by refining readers' perception of the world through revaluing notions of pleasure and vulnerability. Hence, Hopkinson's claim that postcolonial science fiction must "take the meme of colonizing the natives and [...] pervert it, fuck with it" (2004, 9) does in our understanding of the speculative not merely refer to revisionist endeavors but also hint at its creative power to reorganize possibilities of being. *Xenowealth* and *Skin Folk* then use the speculative for once to expose oft-neglected historical complexities as well as technology's ideological underpinnings and inscription into a Western-centric framework. In addition to this critical focus on social problems, *Skin Folk* in particular also considers not yet realized imaginations of the world and the bodies that might inhabit it. We therefore conclusively suggest that CSF as a mode of storytelling can participate in yielding new epistemologies of bodies and literary texts.

---

[8] Biopower, as a method of biopolitics, is, with Foucault, "a power bent on generating forces, making them grow, and ordering them" (1990, 136) and exercised via the body and its "controlled insertion [...] into the machinery of production and the adjustment of the phenomena of population to economic processes" (141).

MASCULINIZING OUTER SPACE: TOBIAS BUCKELL'S *XENOWEALTH* STORIES

The Grenadian-born author Tobias S. Buckell has become a household name in CSF. Buckell's most notable works are his *Halo* novels (2008 and 2017) and the Xenowealth series, comprising *Crystal Rain* (2006), *Ragamuffin* (2007), *Sly Mongoose* (2008), *The Apocalypse Ocean* (2012), and the short story collection *Xenowealth* (2015). To account for the comparability of representations of posthumanism in one and the same narrative form, we focus our analyses on *Xenowealth* (next to *Skin Folk*), which continues narrative strands of its four predecessors. Set in a planetary universe where humanity has fled to after aliens, the Satrapy, have colonized Earth, it revolves around humans-turned-cyborgs who serve the enigmatic company ShinnCo as indentured laborers. It is via this evocation of neo-slavery and the fact that mentions of the Earth are made only in—nostalgic—reference to the Caribbean that Buckell negotiates both a historical and contemporary Caribbean setting.[9] The allegorical portrayal of the colonial encounter as a conflict between human and alien species has invited postcolonial critical readings,[10] yet, beyond this, *Xenowealth* offers a multitude of entry points for postcolonial critique as it presents various scenarios of oppression—via colonial rule, neo-imperialist claims, and technological control—on a continuum and adds a distinct thematic concern with the body to this.[11]

In its exploration of posthumanism, *Xenowealth* to some extent refracts essentialist conceptions of the racialized body through attributing the cyborg's 'power' to it, but it is precisely also at the site of the body—the male body specifically—where the crossing of categories ends. We argue that the text in an insistence on what we call 'category purism' reinstalls

---

[9] This includes historical references to the Black Atlantic and the Middle Passage or the Great Migration, which are revisited within an outer space setting, as well as negotiations of racial capitalism, imperialism, and new forms of slavery.

[10] As Shaw Nevins observes, the generic description of science fiction as depicting an encounter with the 'strange' evokes the experiences of Africans in the transatlantic slave trade, to whom European colonizers must have resembled 'aliens' (2019, 102).

[11] The (sparse) scholarship on Buckell reads his works predominantly as imagining alternative histories in line with Afrofuturism (Howard 2019) and as putting forward an "alternate, positive model of race consciousness" (DeGraw 2015, 41). Shifting the focus to the text's category purism, particularly pertaining to notions of 'the human' and gender, our analysis complicates such readings.

binary thinking and, in a profound techno-skeptical stance, highlights technology's complicity with and perpetuation of the dominant social order. Contrary to the readings that emphasize the book's embrace of diversity (e.g., DeGraw 2015; Howard 2019), we claim that its portrayal of male techno-bodies leaves the transgressive potential of the cyborg to think beyond strict categorization unfulfilled.

Category Purism in Xenowealth

Xenowealth foregrounds the intersection of the male body and cybernetic implants, yet remains insistent on technology as a "deterministic, monolithic force" (Graham 2002, 228) that alienates 'man' from 'nature'. The collection conceives technology in a pessimistic stance as deterministic, rejecting what posthuman theorists like Katherine Hayles understand as desirable—namely, the dispersal of prevailing concepts of subjectivity based on the erasure of embodiment through cybernetics (1999, 1–24)—, and reinstalls rigid distinctions between 'norm' and 'difference'.

This particularly pertains to the main character Pepper, a Caribbean mercenary (Buckell 2015, 2, 8), whose 'otherness' is emphasized on the levels of form and content. Introduced in the collection's first story by a third person narrator, the Chinese fish seller Li Hao-Chang, Pepper emerges as a liminal, "dark figure" (2), a "ghost"-like specter (3) who has through cybernetics been fashioned into a "killing machine" (175). Interestingly, the text delays details regarding the exact status of his body, initially featuring only speculations among other characters about Pepper's invincibility, such as "[h]ow many back-up blood pups are laced through his torso? How much artificial adrenaline is produced by small chemical factories in his stomach?" (3). The sheer extent of his body's technological alteration is only explicated in "Manumission", the second story, which shares the character's background and presents him in action, electrocuting his corporate overlord's enemies with wires in his wrists (18, 26) or reading encrypted messages through a special membrane in his eyes (18, 21). The text's deferral of specific information on the techno-body is in line with portrayals in *Crystal Rain*, for instance, where it serves to foreground the protagonists' 'humanity' and seeks to stir the readers' empathy with the characters.

While high-tech may enable Pepper to win every battle, it does not liberate but rather discipline him. Pepper, who also questions his own human status (38, 74), has been turned into corporate property and is exploited for his special warrior skills by ShinnCo, a big corporation that produces and abuses cyborgs in order to destroy opponents and gain (economic) influence throughout outer space (23). Accordingly, Pepper's body was enhanced through a fusion of human-made and alien technologies, branded (26), robbed of its memories (20, 33), and furnished with a ticking bomb that prevents him from discarding his implants (23). This framing of technology as a disciplinary tool used as part of ShinnCo's investments into practices of neo-slavery and pursuits of economic power allows the text—in a critical stance on transhumanism—to underscore technology's complicity with neo-imperialist, capitalist endeavors. It here offers critical postcolonial perspectives in twofold ways—in both the rejection of what is presented as a colonial (alien) rule on Earth and of neo-colonial forms of exploitation under corporate capitalism.

Pepper, in an attempt to escape corporate enslavement, is initially driven by a desire to return to his 'natural' body and discard all machinic body parts (23). His sense of split subjectivity—half 'man', half 'machine'—is reflected on the narrative level in the usage of a second-person narrator in some of the short stories that present his perspective. The fragmented narrative parallels Pepper's sense of self and suggests that he is rather a disembodied 'you'. The binary between 'the human' and 'the technological' the text reinstalls through descriptions of Pepper's cyborg status and war body as "more alien machinery than human" (147) and even 'monstrous' (20), is complemented by an insistence on rigid species distinction.[12] Even though Pepper eventually completely turns himself into a machine (184), the text does not embrace the cyborg body's "technological complicity" that "recognizes the plasticity of categories of being" (Graham 2002, 228). It rather climaxes in reinforcing the otherness of Pepper's body when he is being asked in the last short story, "Ratcatcher", "*what* are you being?" (Buckell 2015, 174; our emphasis), thus renouncing the cyborg's hybrid nature and concomitant denial of "organic wholeness" (Haraway 2016, 8) in favor of a belief in the "innocence" of the natural (12).

---

[12] Curiously, Pepper is categorized and identifies himself as "[h]uman" (38) *vis-à-vis* other species, who are then framed as 'alien its' (37–38, 150).

Hypermasculine Warriors in Xenowealth

The primacy of the 'natural' opposite the alienization of technology also extends to gender: In *Xenowealth*'s masculine universe, the representation of male bodies echoes Haraway's seminal figure; yet, while Haraway conceives the cyborg as an anti-androcentric figure (Braidotti 2006, 198) that transgresses boundaries towards the 'other-than-human' and as "a creature in a postgender world" (Haraway 2016, 8), cyborg men in *Xenowealth* are stifled by and complicit with masculine imperatives. The male body is conspicuously and continuously portrayed as being under social pressure, whereas the (few) female bodies must conform to a masculine order, as the cyborg characters of Susan Stamm, Yamaxtli, and Nashara, who are construed in line with the image of masculine warriorhood, show.[13] Their cyborg status enables them to 'cross' gender boundaries to some extent, which is, however, not geared towards gender fluidity but rather serves to affirm essentialist notions of categories.[14] Where *Skin Folk* depicts the post-human as reveling in the 'feminine' or the folkloric, *Xenowealth*, while evoking women's contribution to technology, dismisses these ideas. Susan Stamm in "Manumission", for instance, is revealed to have an insight into Pepper's 'mechanics' and has designed her own weapons that override his systems (Buckell 2015, 28). She manages to cleanse his body from the alien technology to enable him to travel offworld—"I scrubbed clean all your systems. [...] I've set you free from them" (29)—, but the text evidences Pepper's reluctance to accept shedding off his 'war body' through female intervention. As his body 'reboots' and "retool[s] itself" (31), Susan offers her help a second time, only to be refused by Pepper: "Take too long. [...] Your trick probably wouldn't have worked anyway" (32–33). The male body in *Xenowealth* is an enhanced, hyper-technological, super-human war body, fortified against any 'feminine interventions' that suggest an escape from this logic.

---

[13] By contrast, the more conventionally feminine character of Mei is faced with murder in this masculinist universe.

[14] This is amplified with the character of Nashara: While only identified as Pepper's granddaughter in the *Xenowealth* short story "Placa del Fuego", *Ragamuffin* explains that she is in fact Pepper's clone and thus a 'man' in a 'female' body. Further, Nashara had to give up her womb to be "fitted with quantum computers running intrusion devices that can overpower lamina and make it extensions of our minds" (Buckell 2007, 105).

The text's reinforcement of gender binaries is most visible in the story "Ratcatcher", where differing ideals of 'the machinic' *vis-à-vis* 'the natural' are mapped onto male and female bodies, respectively. The character of Yamaxtli, for instance, is construed as a woman in need of salvation by Pepper, her aged and frail body foregrounded. While Pepper eventually rips his natural body to shreds to ensure his survival through high-tech (184), he conversely frees Yamaxtli's body from its machinic parts. With Pepper thus becoming more cyborg and Yamaxtli more 'natural', the female character is reinscribed in discourses that have historically equated the 'female' with the 'natural' and the body. The reinstalment of the gendered order is emphasized in Yamaxtli's now "peaceful" appearance (185). Yet while the text also allows Yamaxtli to return to her position as a hunter, making her a more flexible character that at times can claim a position within a masculine social order, it portrays no category flexibility for its male protagonists, and it further does not allow a blurring of categories: The ultimate machinization of Pepper corresponds with an exaggeration of the male bodies' masculinity towards the image of a hypermasculine 'killing machine', thus conflating the narrative resolution with the reinstalment of a 'natural' gender order.

The restoration of a gendered social order here parallels the nostalgia of recovering a lost origin and returning to the 'natural' body. While warning of an all-too enthusiastic embrace of technoscientific advancements and reflecting an awareness of the ideological underpinnings of transhumanism, which are particularly relevant for the postcolonial subject, the text remains trapped in dominant epistemologies, particularly the categorical separation of the 'human' and 'non-human', 'nature' and 'culture', and—related to that—of masculinity and femininity. Thus, where science fiction has typically constructed cultural difference based on implicit notions of race, Buckell's text retains this framework and displaces it from race onto the 'non-human'. Technological advancement is in this context criticized for 'contaminating' the 'human' but also reinforces gender norms. As a consequence, the cyborg in *Xenowealth*, even though transforming science fiction's inherent 'whiteness', fits in with the majority of pop cultural portrayals as hypermasculine (Rehling 2009, 181), i.e., as an anti-Harawayan figure that reinforces categories rather than enables their crossing.

BREAKING WITH MASCULINE IMPERATIVES: NALO HOPKINSON'S *SKIN FOLK*

Nalo Hopkinson is probably the most well-known author of CSF, with her novels *Brown Girl in the Ring* (1998) and *Midnight Robber* (2000) attracting most academic interest to date. Less researched is her 2001 publication *Skin Folk*, a collection of short stories that interweaves science-fiction scenarios with African and West-Indian folklore as well as European fairy tales. The generic markers of CSF in *Skin Folk* have been predominantly read as offering transformative potential "specifically for women" (Bacchilega 2008, 186), and Hopkinson's focus on the body as "problematiz[ing] the postcolonial condition" (Bessette 2012, 167) for how it gives shape to, i.e., 'embodies', the oppressive history of colonialism (168).

To attend to the hitherto neglected representations of male bodies in her work, we will focus on "Something to Hitch Meat to" and "Ganger". Both short stories feature male protagonists, Artho and Cleve, for whom the collection's larger focus on 'skin' expresses their subjection to processes of othering, as based on the differential categories of race, gender, sexuality, and class that structure the body. Both texts then introduce posthuman corporeal transgressions into this setting to expose the impact of intersecting structures of racism, capitalism, exploitation, and technological discipline on black men's corporeal schema (Fanon 1986, 112)[15] and, related to that, show the characters' difficulties of developing interpersonal relations and relations to the world.

In contrast to Buckell's deterministic view of technology that devaluates its possible disturbance of ontological certainty, Hopkinson's work also acknowledges the potential of posthuman bodies for initiating transformations in corporeal, perceptual, and social terms. This can, however, only be productively realized, as both selected stories suggest, when scientific progress also incorporates what has historically been othered by Western epistemologies: (a) African and Caribbean folklore or (b) notions of feminine pleasure. The two short stories illustrate this by confronting the male body with such categorical crossings that prompt Artho and Cleve to see themselves and their relation to the world anew.

---

[15] In *Black Skin, White Masks*, Frantz Fanon famously recounts how, being subjected to the white gaze, "the corporeal schema crumbled, its place taken by a racial epidermal schema" (1986, 112).

DISCIPLINED BODIES AND CRITICISMS OF TRANSHUMANISM IN *SKIN FOLK*

The two texts retain an ambivalent position towards promises of transhuman developments, as for both Artho and Cleve, the details and effects of realizing the liberatory potential of technological intervention in the racialized body are not spelled out. "Something to Hitch Meat to" construes technology as an instrument that disciplines and commodifies bodies in line with hegemonic norms and capitalist demands and thus as implicated in perpetuating racist structures. The text revolves around the web designer Artho, whose job at Tri-Ex Media is to edit erotic images for the company's websites by manipulating the models' bodies. The text hints at Artho's Caribbean origin, yet leaves his exact cultural heritage open. That his otherness only becomes perceptible through racist comments by white people illustrates that even though race is discursively constructed, its ascription onto bodily matter burdens the protagonist. The social power of skin, particularly prevalent for racialized bodies, is deliberately exploited as part of Artho's professional activities—and here specifically in the interest of marketing purposes and sales numbers, which underscores his implication in the logics of consumer capitalism. Artho has to modify human bodies to such an extent that they assume grotesque forms, as the example of the "autofellatio man['s picture]" (Hopkinson 2001, 25) shows. In this case, Artho manipulates the photograph of an above-average muscular black male body and magnifies his erection, thereby suggesting that the man was able to orally pleasure himself, if he just bent down enough. Further, Artho follows his boss Charlie's instructions "[to] make that guy blacker" (26) and darkens the man's skin, only to find himself again disciplined—and discriminated against—by Charlie, who then remarks "'Jesus! Arth! He's blacker than you. [...] Betcha his dick's no match for yours, though'" (26).

The scene evokes the persistence of hypersexualization as a discourse of framing and selling black bodies under conditions of racial capitalism. Modern technologies—in this case, enabling image manipulation—are complicit with perpetuating racial stereotypes and reinscribing structural inequalities, even demanding black men to comply with these logics. Here, it is Artho who—depending on his job for financial reasons—is exploited for his labor power and simultaneously involved in the production of hypersexual bodies and dissemination of their images. Outlining these intricacies, the text expresses a criticism of racial capitalism and—echoing Foucault's concept of the production of docile bodies—exposes technology's role for disciplining bodies in the interest of maintaining the existing social and political order.

In response to this, Artho keeps up the masquerade of 'coolness'. He only learns to look through the exploitative workings of racial capitalism, when—after a magical encounter with a trickster figure—his body is modified so that he is able to click with his finger and reveal what lies beyond the disciplined body (31). Yet even this skill does not liberate him, as the story's open ending, recalling Fanon's interpellation of the black body as 'other' through the white gaze, suggests. It depicts Artho walking through the streets and realizing how an elderly woman clings to her purse upon 'seeing' him, i.e., seeing the racial prejudice she projects onto his body (33). Artho is faced with stereotypical figurations that equate black masculinity with criminality. The ending of the short story once again emphasizes the inescapability from 'race' and the illusory nature of transhuman promises that equate technological and social progress.

Skin Folk's second-to-last story "Ganger" also draws on techno-bodies and the cyborg as embodiments of disciplinary control and focuses on negotiations of transhuman technologies and their meanings for race, but also gender and sexuality, in the private, even the most intimate sphere: the bedroom. Focusing on (artificial) skin and its receptive quality for getting closer, it casts an ambivalent light on cybernetic enhancements that are instigated by imperatives of self-disciplining the body in line with neo-liberal demands. The story starts *in medias res* in the bedroom of the Jamaican couple Issy and Cleve and shows them having sex while wearing their "Senstim Co-operation's 'wetsuits'" (174), an artificial second skin of an ectoplasmic quality (185) that reacts to human touch (179), adapts to the body's form, and thus intensifies sensory perceptions (175). The suits, promising a "full body aura alignment" (175), it is revealed, were Cleve's idea to 'spice up' the couple's love life and get closer to each other. Cleve, who manages his body through sports and asceticism—*vis-à-vis* Issy, who is portrayed as more sensual, voluptuous, even gluttonous—subscribes to corporate promises of self-improvement and the "marketing lie that the suits were 'consensual aids to full body aura alignment,' not sex toys" (175). Attempting to secure his masculinity, he accepts the corporate infringement on and control over his body.

Because the suits adapt to the wearer's body, the couple decides to change skins to feel the other sex's sensations during sex and to achieve a better understanding of each other. The promise of high-tech products to bring the estranged couple closer to each other culminates in a catastrophe when, after their lovemaking, Issy and Cleve negligently cram their skins into the wardrobe: The 'innie', Issy's suit, and the 'outie', Cleve's suit, named after the forms of male and female genitals respectively and adapted to their owners' bodies, morph into a monstrous cyborg creature—the Ganger—which is now both innie and outie and hermaphroditic:

> [T]he thing [...] was a human-shaped glow, translucent. [...] Eyes, nose, mouth were empty circles. A low crackling noise came from it [...]. A pattern of coloured lights flickered in it, limning where spine, heart, and brain would have been, if it had had those. It did have breasts [...] and a dick. (185)

Resonating with Foucault's notion of subjugated, yet productive bodies, the ectoplasmic and electrically charged Ganger, whose touches almost kill Issy and Cleve, is a monstrous manifestation of disciplinary techniques steeped in neo-liberal and capitalist ideologies that form and enhance the body and infiltrate every realm of being; an optimization of sexual performance that is, moreover, fraught with imperatives of normative masculinity, as Cleve feels the pressure to sexually perform and satisfy Issy. Yet Cleve's reliance on the suits, it is ultimately revealed, is an attempt to "[w]rap it all in fake skin" (181) and to channel his emotions into socially accepted expressions. This is steeped in fears of being interpellated as an 'aggressive' black man, it is a form of 'racial passing': "Look at the size of me, the blackness of me. You know what it is to see people cringe for fear when you shout?" (192). The Ganger is an embodiment, a revenant of transhuman promises of progress that sublimate structural inequalities based on differences in race, class, sex, or gender. In it, the incorporation of the 'other' body into the existing social order structured by late-capitalist values shows itself as monstrous. In "Ganger", the experience of sublimation is extended to readers, who learn only in the final lines that Cleve's behavior was caused by the experience of everyday racism. In this way, "Ganger" continues critical concerns about the subjugation of black masculinity to hegemonic discourses that Artho's story initiated.

Trickster and Cyborg Potentials in *Skin Folk*

Yet Hopkinson's stories do not stop at condemning the disciplinary workings of technology for 'othered' bodies and their implication in perpetuating systemic racism, but allow for a much more differentiated reading. Here, 'skin' as occupying a privileged site also offers another perspective: It always extends beyond a single body and facilitates other affiliations, as Sara Ahmed and Jackie Stacey state in their introduction to *Thinking Through the Skin* (2001):

> [T]he skin as a boundary object [...] and as the site of exposure or connectedness, invite[s] the reader to consider how the borders between bodies are unstable and how such borders are already crossed by differences that refuse to be contained on the 'inside' or the 'outside' of bodies. (2)

Echoing this crossing, technology in *Skin Folk* is also envisioned as a means for the male protagonists to (temporarily) break from their over-determined bodies. In exploring the 'infusion' of the male body with what was historically conceived as 'other' and inquiring into the suspension of fixed categories resulting from it—with Sedgwick, probing the creative energy that helps to reorganize existing possibilities of being (1997, 22–25)—, Hopkinson's stories examine the cyborg's potential.

In "Something to Hitch Meat to", the cyborg's characteristic crossing of boundaries pertains to the distinctions between "animal-human (organism) and machine" (Haraway 2016, 11) that collapse on the central character Artho's body, when it amalgamates with the mouse of his computer. When Artho manipulates the image of the 'autofellatio man' and exaggerates his erection, he also places a tattoo of the Adinkra symbol "nkyin kyin" on his shoulder. This West-African symbol—meaning "changing oneself always" (Hopkinson 2001, 31)—signals a belief in transformation as a constant of human life. As a consequence of this image manipulation, the body of the model here becomes grotesque in Mikhail Bakhtin's sense, where it is always a 'becoming' one, "outgrow[ing] its own self, transgressing its own body [...] [and] conceiv[ing] a new, second body" (1984, 316–317). This is reflected in the magical transfer of the Adinkra symbol from the 'autofellatio man' onto Artho's body. The fact that the symbol then appears on the surface of every object Artho touches with his hand, i.e., clicks on, allows the text to underscore the significance of Artho's reconnection with his Afro-Caribbean heritage for gaining an 'edited', more refined vision of the world.

This finds its climax in his encounter with a young black girl called Nancy, who initiated his cyborgification and turns out to be an embodiment of the tarantula-like trickster figure Anansi, the master of transformation in West-African and Caribbean folklore. According to Henry L. Gates, Jr., the trickster is capable of outsmarting opponents through tricks, which is why this figure has constituted for oppressed groups a source of inspiration for how to 'signify on', i.e., play with dominant discourses and subvert power asymmetries (1989). It is only after a confrontation with Nancy in the space of his office, the emblematic site for Artho's implication into racial capitalist logics, that Artho is able to realize his skills of looking beneath the façade in favor of more in-depth insights into the workings of the world and to eventually recognize the girl for the shape shifting trickster she is:

> He'd figured out who, what she was. Appeared as a skeleton sometimes, in a top hat. Watcher at the boundaries, at the crossroads. Sometimes man, sometimes woman. Always trickster. He couldn't really tell in the dark, but she seemed furrier now, or more bristly, or something. Sometimes spider? (Hopkinson 2001, 33)

Through Artho's own corporeal transformation and the new perception of the world he acquires through it, the mythical as embodied in Nancy-as-Anansi is valorized. By thus infusing the Western metropolis with 'magical' elements, the short story places the city under a 'Caribbean spell'. The ending shows Artho dancing through the streets, excited about the knowledge of his special talent to "peel off the fake skins" (32) and look beneath the façade, as represented, for instance, by skin color. Artho's potential to imagine subjectivity beyond the weight of marked bodies then builds on the fusion of technoscience with folklore on the site of his cyborg body. Picking up central concerns of CSF, the text thus suggests that the transcultural crossing of Western epistemologies with folkloric knowledges (Langer 2011, 9) contains reparative dimensions in promoting a new social vision that acknowledges plural, more diverse forms of embodiments—e.g., as represented by Artho's cyborg body in the text—and the alternative perspectives upon the world they can provide.

While this potential is, however, not yet realized at the end of "Something to Hitch Meat to", "Ganger" more pronouncedly imagines technology's liberatory potential. Contrary to Sharon De Graw's assessment that "black males serve as major antagonists in Nalo Hopkinson's postcolonial fiction" (2015, 50), the story is at its most radical when foregrounding Cleve's vulnerability, his fear that he is unable to (sexually and emotionally) fulfil his wife's needs, and thus his break from dominant scripts of masculinity: "The only time we seem to reach each other now is through our skins. So I bought something to make our skins feel more, and it's still not enough" (Hopkinson 2001, 191), Cleve states. It is also the figure of the Ganger-as-cyborg that not just unearths repressed emotions and internal struggles resulting from systemic (and internalized) racism and thus functions as a figure for ideology critique, but also allows for a reparative perspective on the male bodies, particularly under conditions of postcoloniality, through posthuman interventions: Echoing Haraway's conception of the cyborg as transgressing categories of gender and Maurice Merleau-Ponty's notion of 'intercorporeality', a mutual affecting of bodies that enables intersubjective understanding—"as if the other person's intentions inhabited my body and mine his" (2010, 215)—, the Ganger is a fusion of Issy and Cleve, both formed by technology and the couple's intimate wishes. Representing this notion of intercorporeality, it functions as a mediator between the couple; as such, it can also be understood as a manifestation—and co-mingling—of subconscious desires and hence as a crossing into the other's body and overcoming of gender boundaries and related limited sensations. While Cleve, albeit urging Issy to change suits in the first place (Hopkinson 2001, 173–176) and to occupy Issy's position, is initially still hesitant to "describe the sensation he was seeking" (175) and to yield to the experience of feminine pleasure,[16] the touches of the hermaphroditic cyborg ultimately allow him to—temporarily—move beyond the boundaries of

---

[16] In the scene where the couple changes suits to experience the other gender's bodily sensations, Issy enjoys the new-found power the suit gives her: "God, it's good. [...] Like being fucked, only she had an organ to push back with" (176). Cleve, on the other hand, is initially unable to stand the penetration of the male body by the female: "[I]t started to feel like, I dunno, like my dick had been *peeled* and it was inside out, and you, Jesus, you were fucking my inside-out dick" (177; emphasis in original). His fear of losing sexual prowess correlates with male anxieties of being reduced to an object in the face of female sexual emancipation, and his subscribing to disciplinary body regimes: "If I'm not there, there's always sugar, or food, or booze. I'm just one of her chosen stimulants" (189).

his body to experience what Lacan describes as feminine *jouissance*, a non-phallically structured form of bliss that enables a crossing of the limitations of male pleasure (1999). While the story focuses predominantly on Issy's perceptions and sensations—the Ganger's electrocuting touches cause her an "unspeakable" orgasm (Hopkinson 2001, 187)—Cleve's rather secondary perceptions, mentioned only in passing, are telling: His "groan[ing] like he was coming, but with an edge of terror and pain" when the Ganger touches him and his urging it to "[c]ome to me, not her" (188) in an attempt to save Issy can, in a contrapuntal reading, also be understood as an urge to *also* experience feminine pleasure. In illustrating how social relations at large play out in the most intimate sphere, the Ganger indicates the undermining of strict oppositions and hierarchies on various levels: Like Haraway's cyborg, it moves beyond "the polarity of public and private" and "defines a technological polis based partly on a revolution of social relations in the *oikos*, the household" (2016, 9).

BACK TO THE FUTURE? CONTEMPLATING THE BODY OF THE TEXT

Both Buckell's and Hopkinson's stories evidence a skepticism of transhumanism and instead foreground the continued weight of matter in a high-tech age. Thereby, they are also part of a larger revisionary project unique to CSF that counteracts the invisibility of black bodies in science fiction and its rather exclusive support of "the alignment between white bodies and information technology" (Georgi 2011, 7). That is, in placing black bodies and postcolonial concerns center stage, CSF 'perverts', i.e., challenges or undermines, Western paradigms of authorship and the predominance of white heroic characters in the field of science fiction. Despite their differing assessments of the potentials of cyborgian developments and their varying degrees of skepticism regarding category confusion through posthuman interventions, *Xenowealth* and *Skin Folk* share one thematic point of convergence and a similar vision of CSF's cultural power: Both construe an analogous relationship between the body of 'postcolonial subjects' and the body of the text. In doing so, the two collections reevaluate the status of the body in the digital age, particularly as regards its crucial role for partaking in modes of storytelling. Mediated through metaphors of corporeality, storytelling in both books thus constitutes a cultural practice to be taken forth to preserve memories and produce knowledge in an increasingly digitized future.

Xenowealth, in its last story, foregrounds corporeality as a means of gaining access to and making sense of the world, a rather striking feature for a setting where memorization would only require uploading and storing information and therefore no longer depend on the body. At the end of "Ratcatcher", Pepper's and Yamaxtli's future exploration of the Xenowealth universe and, by implication, the continuation of the story, is imagined as a bodily practice: first, their bodies have to be restored in "healing tanks" before continuing their space travels and then, "a brand new notebook and pen" is presented as the preferred means to manually record "new memories" (Buckell 2015, 187). The memories Pepper and Yamaxtli have lost and which, as is hinted at in different stories in *Xenowealth*, have supposedly been digitized by ShinnCo, remain inaccessible. Gaining and storing new memories is thus shown as depending on a bodily, experience-based approach to the world. From this 'return' to the body, the text suggests, the *text body* is to emerge. These metafictional elements in "Ratcatcher" then also draw attention to the 'body' of the text and its function as 'embodying' the idiosyncratic facets of memories of Caribbean history, which are, however, not subject to nostalgic idealization, but envisioned to be significant for the future due to the insights they will then offer.

In *Skin Folk*, a haptic, affective, sensory access to the world is given preference and mediated through metaphors of the eponymous 'skin', as the concern with bodies touching each other in "Ganger" shows. Yet, despite the prologue's promise—"[w]hen the skin comes off, their [the skin folk's] true selves emerge" (Hopkinson 2001, 1)—, the short story collection rather counters notions of 'shedding one's skin' and of 'true' selfhood. On the contrary, stories like Artho's render 'skin' for racialized and gendered subjects as a palimpsestically inscribed, signifying matter that constantly needs to be returned to and revaluated. The storyteller's skill—like Artho's—is imagined as being able to create new perceptions of skin and thus accord it new social meanings, as Artho's eventual understanding of the Anansi's rhyme to "[t]ake off your skin / And dance around in your bones" (22) suggests. The infusion with trickster knowledge allows Artho, even within the limited frames of racial capitalism, to form new, more adequate, non-stereotypical representations and tell different stories through them.

Other stories in *Skin Folk*, for example "Greedy Choke Puppy", use 'skin' to foreground the tense relation between orality and writing in the Caribbean and relate instances of shedding one's skin to dismantle the primacy of Western, allegedly objective, 'rational' knowledge *vis-à-vis* folk tales and myths.[17] Here, skin also functions as central site to question the binaries of the oral and the textual as well as of 'other' and 'self' and to negotiate a transcultural blend of "Western scientific methods and indigenous methods of knowledge production" that Langer considers characteristic of CSF (2011, 9). In this vein, both *Xenowealth* and *Skin Folk* point beyond themselves by urging to return to the signifying body to continue and remake conventions of storytelling and thus yield new epistemologies. The books here also urge readers to return to the body of the text and reread it—to cite Buckell: There is "[a] whole blank page to explore" (2015, 187).

REFERENCES

Ahmed, Sara, and Jackie Stacey. "Introduction: Dermographies." In *Thinking Through the Skin*, edited by Sarah Ahmed and Jackie Stacey, 1–18. London: Routledge, 2001.

Bacchilega, Cristina. "Extrapolating from Nalo Hopkinson's Skin Folk: Reflections on Transformation and Recent English-Language Fairy-Tale Fiction by Women." In *Contemporary Fiction and the Fairy Tale*, edited by Stephen Benson, 178–203. Detroit: Wayne State UP, 2008.

Badmington, Neil. "Introduction: Approaching Posthumanism." In *Posthumanism*, edited by Neil Badmington, 1–10. Basingstoke: Palgrave Macmillan, 2000.

Bakhtin, Mikhail. *Rabelais and His World*. Translated by Hélène Iswolsky. Bloomington: Indiana UP, 1984 [1965].

Bessette, Lee Skallerup. "'They Can Fly': The Postcolonial Black Body in Nalo Hopkinson's Speculative Short Fiction." In *The Postcolonial Short Story: Contemporary Essays*, edited by Maggie Awadalla and Paul March-Russell, 167–181. Basingstoke: Palgrave Macmillan, 2012.

Booker, M. Keith. *Historical Dictionary of Science Fiction in Literature*. Lanham: Rowman & Littlefield Publishers, 2014.

Braidotti, Rosi. "Posthuman, All Too Human: Towards a New Process Ontology." *Theory, Culture & Society* 23, no. 7–8 (2006): 197–208.

Buckell, Tobias S. *Crystal Rain*. New York: Tor Books, 2006.

———. *Ragamuffin*. New York: Tor Books, 2007.

———. *Xenowealth: A Collection*. Self-published, 2015.

---

[17] The tense relation between orality and writing is also emphasized in stories that draw on European fairytales.

DeGraw, Sharon. "Tobias S. Buckell's Galactic Caribbean Future." *Extrapolation* 56, no. 1 (2015): 41–61.

De Matas, Jarrel. "Of Cyborgs and Immortal Women: Speculative Fictions of Caribbean Posthumanity in Selected Stories of New Worlds, Old Ways: Speculative Tales from the Caribbean." *Journal of West Indian Literature* 27, no. 2 (2019): 39–51.

Fanon, Frantz. *Black Skin, White Masks.* London: Pluto P, 1986 [1952].

Fehskens, Erin M. "The Matter of Bodies: Materiality on Nalo Hopkinson's Cybernetic Planet." *The Global South* 4, no. 2 (2010): 136–156.

Ferrando, Francesca. "The Body." In *Post- and Transhumanism: An Introduction*, edited by Stefan Lorenz Sorgner and Robert Ranisch, 213–226. Frankfurt a. M.: Peter Lang, 2015.

Foucault, Michel. *The History of Sexuality: Volume 1: An Introduction.* Translated by Robert Hurley. New York: Vintage Books, 1990 [1976].

———. *Discipline and Punish: The Birth of the Prison.* New York: Random House, 2012 [1975].

Gates, Henry Louis, Jr. *The Signifying Monkey: A Theory of African-American Literary Criticism.* New York: Oxford UP, 1989.

Georgi, Sonja. *Bodies and/as Technology: Counter-Discourses on Ethnicity and Globalization in the Works of Alexandro Morales, Larissa Lai and Nalo Hopkinson.* Heidelberg: Universitätsverlag Winter, 2011.

Graham, Elaine L. *Representations of the Post/human: Monsters, Aliens and Others in Popular Culture.* Manchester, UK: Manchester UP, 2002.

Haraway, Donna Jeanne. *Modest_Witness@Second_Millennium. Female-Man©_Meets_OncomouseTM.* London and New York: Routledge, 1997.

———. *Manifestly Haraway.* Minneapolis and London: U of Minnesota P, 2016.

Hayles, Nancy Katherine. *How We Became Posthuman: Virtual Bodies in Cybernetics, Literature, and Informatics.* Chicago: U of Chicago P, 1999.

Hopkinson, Nalo. *Skin Folk.* New York, NY: Warner Books, 2001.

———. "Introduction." In *So Long Been Dreaming: Postcolonial Visions of the Future*, edited by Nalo Hopkinson and Uppinder Mehan, 7–9. Vancouver, BC and London: Arsenal Pulp; Turnaround, 2004.

Howard, Jacinth. "Black Technologies: Caribbean Visions and Versions in the Speculative Narratives of Tobias Buckell and Karen Lord." *Journal of West Indian Literature* 27, no. 2 (2019): 1–14.

Jenkins, Destin, and Justin Leroy. "Introduction: The Old History of Capitalism." In *Histories of Racial Capitalism*, edited by Destin Jenkins and Justin Leroy, 1–26. New York: Columbia UP, 2021.

Lacan, Jacques. *On Feminine Sexuality, the Limits of Love and Knowledge—Encore: The Seminar of Jacques Lacan, Book XX.* Edited by Jacques-Alain Miller, translated by Bruce Fink. New York: Norton, 1999 [1972–1973].

Langer, Jessica. *Postcolonialism and Science Fiction*. Basingstoke: Palgrave Macmillan, 2011.

Lord, Karen. "Foreword." In *New Worlds, Old Ways: Speculative Tales from the Caribbean*, edited by Karen Lord, 7–9. Brooklyn, NY: Peekash P, 2016.

McClintock, Anne. "The Angel of Progress: Pitfalls of the Term 'Post-Colonialism'." *Social Text*, no. 31/32 (1992), 84–98.

Merleau-Ponty, Maurice. *Phenomenology of Perception*. Translated by Colin Smith. London and New York: Routledge, 2010 [1945].

Mitchell, David T., and Sharon L. Snyder. *The Biopolitics of Disability: Neoliberalism, Ablenationalism, and Peripheral Embodiment*. Ann Arbor: U of Michigan P, 2015.

Moore-Gilbert, Bart. *Postcolonial Theory: Contexts, Practices, Politics*. London: Verso, 1997.

Rehling, Nicola. "Fleshing Out Virtual Bodies: White Heterosexual Masculinity in Contemporary Cyberfantasy Cinema." In *The Future of Flesh: A Cultural Survey of the Body*, edited by Zoe Detsi-Diamanti, Katerina Kitsi-Mitakou, and Effie Yiannopoulou, 181–198. New York: Palgrave Macmillan, 2009.

Rieder, John. *Colonialism and the Emergence of Science Fiction*. Middletown, CT: Wesleyan UP, 2008.

———. "On Defining SF, or Not: Genre Theory, SF, and History." *Science Fiction Studies* 37, no. 2 (2010): 191–209.

Sedgwick, Eve Kosofsky. "Paranoid Reading and Reparative Reading; or, You're So Paranoid, You Probably Think This Introduction is About You." In *Novel Gazing: Queer Readings in Fiction*, edited by Eve Kosofsky Sedgwick, 1–38. Durham, NC: Duke UP, 1997.

Shaw Nevins, Andrea. *Working Juju: Representations of the Caribbean Fantastic*. Athens, GA: The U of Georgia P, 2019.

Suvin, Darko. *Metamorphoses of Science Fiction: On the Poetics and History of a Literary Genre*. Edited by Gerry Canavan. Oxford: Peter Lang, 2016 [1979].

Wolfe, Cary. *What Is Posthumanism?* Minneapolis, MN: U of Minnesota P, 2009.

CHAPTER 12

Fashionable Men in Skin-Tight Pants: Shifts in Body Images and Concepts of Masculinity in the History of Men's Legwear

Melanie Haller

INTRODUCTION

There is a new word in the contemporary fashion industry, and it always appears with the following explanatory definition: meggings, leggings for men, especially cut for male bodies.[1] Neologisms like these mostly constitute a merchandizing strategy to sell new products; at the same time, however, they point to so much more than mere marketing efforts. Meggings are skin-tight pants made by high-stretch fabrics that emphasize the legs and the lower body and in this way offer new body images of men in the contemporary fashion system. In Western fashion cultures,

---

[1] The website of the US-based fashion company "Kapow" is a case in point as regards advertising the male leggings.

M. Haller (✉)
University of Paderborn, Paderborn, Germany
e-mail: melanie.haller@uni-paderborn.de

C. Dexl and S. Gerlsbeck (eds.), *The Male Body in Representation*, Palgrave Studies in (Re)Presenting Gender, https://doi.org/10.1007/978-3-030-88604-2_12

263

meggings are becoming more and more popular, but they also spark controversy, as the responses by fashion critics in different journals, blogs, social media, and on YouTube indicate. The contemporary Western opinion on meggings is that they do not constitute a 'typically male' or 'masculine' garment. From a critical perspective, this suggests that meggings challenge, destabilize, and deconstruct conventional concepts of masculinity as well as popular notions of what it means to 'be a man'. The cultural controversy surrounding items of dress that made and make men's legs visible is intertwined with a long history of constructions of masculinity in relation to fashion and the body that has emblematically manifested on the male leg. Masculinity is commonly not associated with an emphasis on legs; however, a look into the history of dress—in this special case, the meggings—reveals this striking point: to show legs or not has been an issue of gender debate (Fig. 12.1).

Research into fashion that focuses on specific body parts (Vincent 2009, xv; Merrill and Ben-Horin 2015, 6) emphasizes that bodies are socially constructed and assigned gendered categories. The gendered distinctions that emerge through particular forms of dressing have depended on the historical context. It was only in the last ten years that Fashion Studies, an interdisciplinary and international field of scholarship in Western cultures, discovered men's fashion as a relevant subject of research, which is curious considering the long history of Masculinity Studies as well as the proliferation of Fashion Studies. Jo B. Paoletti's concern about the neglect of men's dress and its social meanings is paradigmatic here: "It's always been a puzzle to me why more dress historians don't study men's clothing" (2015, 61). Since the 2010s, research on men's fashion is increasingly growing, but the subject of male *bodies* is only ever present implicitly and not per se the subject matter of analysis. Fashion Studies conceive of fashion as a symbolic system (Kawamura 2004, 61), in which dress influences the social construction and perception of bodies as well as notions of race and ethnicity, age, class, gender, and sexuality. From this point of view, masculinity emerges as a cultural concept that is embedded in materialized embodiments of clothing and communicated through differentiations between fashions, anti-fashion—which Elizabeth Wilson has termed and discussed as oppositional dress (2007, 254)—and unfashionable dress. For a long time, as stated above, men's clothing has largely been perceived as static and neglected in research. Paoletti explains this neglect in *Sex and Unisex: Fashion, Feminism, and the Sexual Revolution*: "Modern men's dress is a

Fig. 12.1 Image of a model wearing Kapow brand men's leggings © Kapow Meggings

paradox: dull but interesting. For the last 150 years it has been conservative and resistant to change" (2015, 64). The existing scholarship on men's dress tries to counter this myth of men's dressing as dull, as a mode of unfashion. Recent research considers concepts of the male body in fashion and highlights the relations between male bodies, fashion, and different concepts of masculinity. However, it mostly addresses notions of hypermasculinity on the one hand, and the figure of the dandy or constructions of queerness on the other. The majority of these publications is premised on a performative, constructivist idea of masculinity, where masculinity emerges through what Judith Butler has outlined as the repetition and reiteration of performative acts of human bodies (1990, 179); this includes the embrace of gender-specific clothing.

From the perspective of a body-sociologist and fashion-theoretician, this contribution seeks to show how body ideals have materialized in particular clothes like meggings or tight stockings for men, which I trace back to the proliferation of especially African-American, and non-Western, particularly Japanese, influences in the field of cultural performance and fashion. Thus locating contemporary Western forms of menswear in a complex cultural history, this article will show that meggings and tight stockings for men are emblematic of a shift in gender constructions, from being a marker of a more conventional and hegemonic conception of the male body towards more diverse and queerer fashionings that emphasize the inextricable intertwinement of gender and race. As I have elaborated in "Mode Macht Körper" in greater detail (Haller 2015), in dress and fashion, human bodies are constructed over different stages of design processes and decisions. However, these depend on the complex conditions of the fashion system (Kawamura 2004, 61), such as distinct measurement-systems, 'nationally distinct' clothing sizes, pattern-systems, different garments, and materials, which all assign clothing a symbolic meaning and contribute to generating the gendered bodies we recognize and 'know'.[2] I use Joanne Entwistle's "styles of masculinity" (2000, 173) to refer to the embodiment of masculinity through fashion. Her concept also picks up Butler's arguments about the stylizations of the body and their functions: "The effect of gender is produced through the stylization of the body and, hence, must be understood as the mundane way in which bodily gestures, movements, and styles of various kinds constitute the illusion of an abiding gendered self" (1990, 179). My take on the fashionable male body in this article subscribes to that, foregrounding the very interrelation between gender performativity and bodily materiality in the context of fashion.

---

[2] I have published extensively on the topic of design decisions and fashion systems in a number of articles in the past few years, see Haller (2015, 2018, 2019, 2020).

In addition to Fashion Studies and body sociology, my third field of reference are Masculinity Studies. This area of studies, as Elizabeth Stephens and Jørgen Lorentzen stress in a special issue of *Men and Masculinities* on male bodies, seeks to counter "the traditional tendency to universalize and idealize 'the male body'" (2007, 5). Questioning this "enduring understanding of 'the male body' as a singular, unified construct" (5), they highlight the diversity of different concepts of masculinity. This is particularly relevant in a time when street style enjoys immense popularity, fashion blogging and fashion posts on Instagram are increasingly gaining currency, and Valerie Steele, a seminal fashion theoretician, discusses the phenomenon of "stylistic proliferation" (2000, 7). The question arises how men's fashion and monolithic constructions of the male body have been altered by these current trends.

A brief look into the history of fashion shows that emphasizing the male leg is not a recent phenomenon. Constructions of male bodies through fashion are inexorably intertwined with the production of images of masculinity that aim at a critical negotiation of hegemonic masculinity.[3] As Entwistle, who first highlighted the interrelation between fashion and the social construction of the body, explains: "Clothing is one of the most immediate and effective examples of the way in which bodies are gendered, made 'feminine' or 'masculine'" (2000, 141). In this vein, this article also aims to inquire into the extent to which clothing construes and informs gendered identities.

The first part of this article will zoom into fashion history to show that the accentuation of male legs tended to symbolize white hegemonic masculinity. This changed with the emergence of the bourgeoisie and what fashion theoreticians have called the rise of fashion as a modern phenomenon in the West: For it was in this context that the construction of male bodies in male fashion or male dress came to generate and underline different conceptions of masculinity. The second part will focus on a relevant later context to understand discourses surrounding the meggings, namely the countercultures from the 1960s to the 1980s, particularly the Peacock Revolution of the 1960s and the glam rock era of the 1970s and 1980s, which are closely linked to histories of pop cultures and discourses

---

[3] For scholars of Fashion Studies and to a large part also for dress historians, the differentiation between dress and fashion is not a trivial endeavor: Dress is often seen as standing in contrast to fashion, with fashion being an evaluative modern system and a symbolic process that generates socio-cultural meaning.

of ethnicity. These countercultural examples are placed and read within a theoretical framework of 'anti-fashion'. The third and last part will discuss the historical perspective on the emergence of the meggings in relation to contemporary discourses on athleisure and sportswear to explore how the meggings has contributed to generating new images of male bodies and revised notions of masculinity. It is therefore a cultural phenomenon that invites not only, but also a reparative viewpoint.

HISTORICAL PERSPECTIVE I: POWER, HEGEMONY, AND MALE LEGS

Fashion historians[4] point out that the emphasis on and visibility of men's legs correspond to a specific embodied ideal of masculinity which has historically been connected to a—by now criticized—Western concept of fashion that emerged in the second half of the fourteenth century (Laver 1995, 62) and separated dress along gender lines into male and female clothing. As Susan J. Vincent points out: "[S]artorially speaking, only men had legs, the bifurcated clothing that covered them were the defining garments of gender" (2009, 97). The accentuation and display of legs, she shows, was a history of men only and served as a symbol of masculinity and power (97).

For roughly 500 years, in the period between around 1350–1850, tight-fitting stockings and accentuated legs constituted the norm for men's dress and fashion. From medieval times to the Renaissance over the Thirty Years' War and up until the Baroque, tight breeches were fashionable, "leaving the legs uncovered except for tight-fitting stockings" (Lipovetsky 2002, 20–21). This suggests that the emphasis on men's legs has a much longer historical tradition than the fashion ideal of hidden calves and thighs predominant in the twentieth and twenty-first centuries:

> This [eighteenth-century] process was culturally freighted, for the legs of elite men symbolized power and sexuality, highlighted in close fitting white hose and skin-tight breeches, showcased in countless paintings of the era, legs upholding the social order. Their limbs were stylistically deployed through gesture and pose. (Lemire 2016, 6)

---

[4] This includes, for example, Laver (1995), Vincent (2009), and Welters and Lillethun (2018).

Tight stockings transcended mere clothing and signaled a privilege of the upper class, as a "man's stockings were essential for the communication of his masculinity and identity as a gentleman within society" (Gernerd 2015, 20). As Elisabeth Gernerd points out: "In addition to acting as a barometer of an individual masculinity, particularly of the élite, the stocking was a visible articulation of the health of Britain's dominant sex, on whose legs the nation and empire stood" (4).

In the course of the eighteenth century, the sartorial clothing for men in Western societies slowly began to change and embrace the ideal of hidden legs. Christopher Breward describes this process with the concept of a "masculine corporeality" (1999, 55) and explains that in the period between 1870 and 1914, for men, manliness was not dependent on fashion. Being a man entailed being rational, which contrasted with fashion as a concern and marker of what was then considered the frivolity of women (48). In this context, a fashionable male person was considered effeminate and thus construed as the 'other' in gendered terms; a process that, as Alla Myzelev's contribution on the *Stiliagi* in post-Soviet Russia in this volume shows, is not only a Western phenomenon. Fashionable men have historically been attributed different labels, as dress historians outline, including the macaroni (McNeil 2018), the fop, or the dandy (Miller 2009). Importantly, as Andreas Krass points out in his elaboration on the 'metrosexual', gender identity is closely intertwined with concepts of sexuality (2008, 108), and effeminacy as, for instance, embodied in metrosexuality, has been associated with homosexuality. This fashionable 'otherness' has been opposed to the modest and even dull "stiffly tailored business suit that traditionally symbolized masculine rectitude" (Steele 2000, 15). With the transition from feudal to civil society marking the end of the idealization of men's legs as a symbol of power, the (business) suit has become the "icon[ic item] of masculinity" (Paoletti 2015, 62) and is glorified in Anne Hollander's *Sex and Suits: The Evolution of Modern Dress* as "relentlessly modern, in the best classical sense" (1994, 1). The suit's typical "inverted triangular shape" (McNeil & Karaminas 2009, 3) presupposes and accentuates the ideal body image of a narrow waist in contrast to a broad chest and upper body, while completely hiding the leg. Breward problematizes this reduction of masculinity to this idealized shape of male bodies as it offers a clear parallel to the display of the acrobat, the strongman or the male impersonator on the music hall stage. Men's bodies as a site of desire were being reappraised and redrawn. [...] [T]he figure of the athlete presented the ideal formula for twentieth-century notions of masculine fashionability and attractiveness, though the maintenance of a fine distinction between vain excess and sartorial perfection ensured that the logical destination of fashion, a kind of sexual self-love, remained safely in check. (2001, 180)

The black suit for the male bourgeoisie is emblematic here. Notions of exaggerated fashionability became marked as feminine: "Under the patriarchal organization of society, where the social unit was the man (with his dependents), the dress of the women was an exponent of the wealth of the man whose chattels they were" (Veblen 1894, 199). With the new self-conception of the bourgeoisie, centering on the notion of the rational self, fashion was turned into an exclusively female concern and, in John Carl Flügel's words, culminated in the "great male renunciation" (1930, 111). According to this 'modern concept' of fashion, men and fashion are seen as polar opposites.[5] The renunciation promoted a body ideal as represented in the jacket of the suit, whose intricate patterns, different interfacings (like hair canvas), paddings, and shoulder pads require an elaborate workmanship and meticulous construction in order to create the ideal physique. It is thus not surprising that tailors speak in fact of 'building a suit' (Sprenger 2009, 184), because of the difficult layering of different materials (see Fig. 12.2). This workmanship began with the creation of military uniforms, the starting point for the ready-made-clothing industry and the symbol for rational, male subjectivity. Contrarily, legwear became more neglected and was not awarded the same focus on detail and sartorial complexity as the jacket, since the legs, hips, and crotch were now rather hidden under the pattern of the trousers.

[5] Due to the fact that the majority of canonized fashion theoreticians are men, including most prominently Thorstein Veblen, Georg Simmel, John C. Flügel, and Friedrich Theodor Vischer, who all stress that in modern times, fashion was associated with notions of female frivolity, it is important to consider that their position is informed by their bourgeois habitus. That is, their work reflects their own position towards the renunciation of fashion for men, which has been shaped by the bourgeois society they represent.

Fig. 12.2 Complex
interfacing in suits
(Sprenger 2009, 121)

While men's legs remained concealed for a long time due to the rise of the suit, fashion began to accentuate the visibility of women's legs. As Jane Merrill and Keren Ben-Horin show in their study *She Got Legs: A History of Hemlines and Fashion* (2015), the emergence of visible female legs is connected to social and cultural changes in the twentieth century. Only the 'death' of representing male legs in tight stockings gave rise to the visibility of women's legs and to related notions of an objectifying male gaze. The uncovered female leg became a twofold symbol of eroticization and sexual objectification on the one hand, and sexual liberation and emancipation on the other hand; especially during the Roaring Twenties, when the flapper style gained popularity: "It was in the 1920s that well-shaped legs became an asset" (Merrill and Ben-Horin 2015, 82). What is distinct here is the shift in signifiers of masculinity—from the visible male leg to the covered male leg—that offered the female leg the opportunity to become a visible symbol of eroticization. Men in shorts (typically with sandals and socks), ballet dancers in tights, or queer popstars in tight pants have caused public debates, because due to the changing history of menswear that has been outlined here, the exposure of the male leg is not considered congruent with hegemonic ideals of masculinity. To understand the developments that led to the rise of the meggings, it is important to take a closer look at more contemporary contexts, namely the rise of anti-fashion in the pop culture of the 1960s and 1970s, more precisely the Peacock Revolution, glam rock, and African-American fashion cultures.

HISTORICAL PERSPECTIVE II: ACCENTUATED LEGS AND EXPOSED SEXUALITY

In the past few centuries, hegemonic notions of masculinity and underlying sartorial norms—as represented by Hollander's glorification of the suit—have changed: Fashion historiography has shown that in the 1960s and 1970s, the era of the so-called Peacock Revolution and the beginning of the glam rock era, new concepts of masculinity emerged which were directly linked to the development of pop cultures and the sexual revolution of the time. Icons like David Bowie, Marc Bolan, Freddie Mercury, or Mick Jagger were wearing tight pants in the 1970s and 1980s while singing and dancing, thereby questioning normative ideas of masculinity. Thus, it was not only their fashion choice and style—for instance, their long hair—that broke with traditional notions of gender, but also the provocative, sexually charged movements of their accentuated hips, their singing, and their posing as part of their on-stage performance.

At the time, the social and cultural concept of fashion changed dramatically: fashion was no longer a trickle-down phenomenon, a means of social class distinction—fashion in the 1970s "was not in fashion" (1997, 280), as Steele points out. In the 1970s, many diverse anti-fashion cultures arose from social movements against fashion capitalism.[6] It was an era when concepts of style that were interlinked with different anti-fashion movements gained more relevance. Anti-fashion as an aesthetic attitude signals,

---

[6] See König (1973), Steele (1997), Davis (2007), Wilson (2007), Hebdige (2008), Polhemus (2011).

according to German cultural sociologist René König, a structural transition that manifests not only in fashionable clothing but also in visual culture:

> This structural change [anti-fashion] appears to be all the more lasting in that parallel with it runs a change of consciousness; there is a rising awareness of the uniqueness of this new situation, which also develops a new attitude to fashion, new yardsticks of valuation, new guiding ideas, a new outlook on the world, becoming more and more widespread not only politically but also aesthetically and in the realm of fashion. (1973, 202)

The rising glam rock scene at the beginning of the 1970s constitutes such a countercultural movement, and studies on popular music, especially on glam rock,[7] have shown that tight pants were an essential clothing item for male glam rock and glam metal bands in the 1970s up to the 1980s. There is no substantial scholarship on the observation that these male glam artists all wore tight pants while performing, but the style and clothing of glam rock artists as well as the creation of a new music and performance culture plays an important role in breaking with hegemonic notions of masculinity. Furthermore, studies in popular music point out that manliness was articulated through an exposed sexuality and "offered a new, implicitly queer, image of masculinity" (Auslander 2006, 240): The musicians' tight pants, next to the legs, particularly foreground the crotch as well.

Studies on pop cultural phenomena like the Peacock Revolution and glam rock refer to the different concepts of masculinity as successful anti-fashion phenomena, thus responding critically to 'modern' ideals of hegemonic masculinity. They link these anti-fashion movements with new notions of masculinity, mostly in connection with the sexual revolution taking place at that time. The Peacock Revolution, thus named by the journalist George Frazier, is connected to the sexual revolution in the USA, which inspired "young men to explore sexual exhibitionism with body-hugging suits, tight pants, see-through shirts [...] among other sexualized forms of clothing" (Hill 2018, 169). Daniel Delis Hill shows that the Peacock Revolution in US-American menswear was made possible through a number of different sociocultural developments, such

---

[7] See Auslander (2006), Kurennaya (2012), Turner (2013), Krämer (2014), Chapman and Johnson (2016), Reynolds (2016), Buckingham (2019)

as the baby boomer generation, who looked for a purpose beyond the consumerism and the "drudgery of a nine-to-five job" (81) that had marked their parents' generation, as well as the invasion of British rock'n' roll bands and their glam rock styles with new "nontraditional masculine dress" in the 1970s (169). It coincided with social movements, including demands for free speech and students' rights, anti-war activism, Black Power, Red Power, gay liberation, second-wave feminism, and the sexual revolution. What fashion theoreticians later called 'anti-fashion' thus started in the 1950s with the increasing cultural influence of revolting youth cultures that subverted traditional understandings of clothing and promoted new notions of gendered identities as well as new body images, in relation to their social and cultural beliefs.[8]

There is, however, one important link missing in these new concepts of masculinity: the sexualization of black male bodies in the 1960s[9] and the counterculture of the Black Power Movement. Philipp Dorestal has shown how clothing, respectively the style of African Americans in the 1960s, was important for identity politics, which he extends, in reference to Kobena Mercer, to style politics by declaring that the relation of the black body and fashion must be understood in the context of racist discourses and processes of social exclusion (2017, 313).

One radical example of this African-American style politics that aims at claiming phallic and, by implication, patriarchal power through fashion is represented by Eldridge Cleaver, who invented the famous 'penis pants' in 1975 (Fig. 12.3).

These pants visibly mark and foreground the crotch and the penis and re-sexualize the black male body in a highly provocative way, as Art Blake points out: "The pants, in both their design and in the act of being worn, materialize acts of raced and gendered insurrection in a web of historical power relations that privilege whiteness and cisgender masculinity" (2018, 7). With these specific style politics, black men appropriated the ascription of the hyper-sexualized black male body by an inversion of these

---

[8] Often quoted is the Beat Generation, its members later caricatured as Beatniks. They were identified with "the notion of a rebellious youth counterculture" (Hill 2018, 35) and expressed their criticism of "a conformist society, oppressive politics, the police, and [...] life itself" (31) in an explicit rejection of everything that was associated with fashion and in a different counter-fashionable style (Welters 2005).

[9] Matthew Bannister (2006) provides interesting research on the relationship between whiteness and the pop culture of the indie rock scene.

Fig. 12.3 Eldridge Cleaver's 'penis pants' (*Rolling Stone Magazine* [US], October 1975)[10]

[10] For their generous provision of this image, I would like to thank Ulrich Duve and the Klaus-Kuhnke-Archiv in Bremen.

attributions: "Key to the development of this distinct cultural identity was a new visible presentation of self, beginning with a rejection of white standards of beauty and dress" (Hill 2018, 148). This rejection included the male body of the bourgeois standard in dull suits that was denied to black men. Monica Miller framed this considerable history in the context of black male dandies and their self-fashioning. In her cultural history of the black dandy, focusing on cultural performance and representations in literary and visual culture from the eighteenth century until today, she shows how clothing and dress, including a 'stylish' suit, are used to define identity. From her point of view, "the black dandy figure embodies the construction and deconstruction of masculine identity relative to negotiations of race, sexuality, and class" (2009, 5).

In the style politics of the Black Power Movement, especially in the style of the Black Panther Party (BPP), references to other countercultures are recognizable. Referring, for example, to the Beat Generation, the Black Panthers wore a turtleneck and beret as a symbol for "intellect and nonconformity" (Dorestal 2017, 323). These fashion(able) performances of men in the context of the cultural movements in the 1960s contributed to the anti-fashion discourse of the 1970s. Hence, it does not come as a surprise that in the era of the Peacock Revolution, the exposed male leg served as a symbol of virility—not of a feminization of the male body, as Hill states: "The sexual exhibitionism of skintight pants that accentuated youthful narrow hips, flat abdomens, muscular thighs and buttocks, and the crotch were reinforced by the emerging sexual revolution of the 1960s" (2018, 170). Furthermore, it was directly linked to the reframing of a "racialized masculinity" (Blake 2018, 5): This masculinity was imitated in the style cultures of anti-fashion that sexualized male bodies. This supposed 'new' concept of an obviously erotic masculinity was in fact not new at all, as, for instance, the codpiece[11] in the context of Renaissance and Spanish fashion shows, but rather constituted an appropriation of the style promulgated by excluded bodies in Western cultures. More specifically, the countercultures of the 1970s refer to and adopt a clothing style inspired by African Americans and new notions of gender. Carol Tulloch provides an interesting study on African-American style cultures, where she finds that 'coolness' plays a central part in the history of modern style cultures, especially in relation to concepts

---

[11] In the Renaissance, the codpiece was a padded and particularly emphasized part in male trousers that accentuated the crotch.

of masculinity (2016, 4): These counter-cultures show a willingness to stylize the male body in reference to fashionable looks, thus counteracting white hegemonic concepts of dress that reduced fashionability to the feminine.

This refashioning of male bodies changed the relationship between masculinity and femininity, as Paoletti points out: "What was changing during this era was not masculinity in isolation, but masculinity as it related to the feminine, which was also in a state of rapid change" (2015, 61). While fashionable masculinity was premised on the sexualized black body as it proliferated in fashion discourses of the 1970s on the one hand, it also entailed a distinction from the more sexualized body of the woman on the other. A heteronormative discourse is thus reinstated through fashion: In that time, fashion underlined the gender divide because it accentuated bodily differences between men and women. At the same time, these tight clothes also provoked hegemonic masculinity because "for approximately the past one hundred years, the expression of sexuality in men's clothes has been largely taboo, while women's clothes throughout the period remained sexually expressive" (Crane 2000, 194).

Moreover, androgynous concepts of masculinity in pop culture were only possible within the boundaries of a critique of the fashion system: Since, as I have shown, fashion was not in fashion in the 1970s, there were many alternative concepts of dressing. Therefore, Paoletti is right to suggest that "the Peacock Revolution was exaggerated at the time and seems only to have grown in the popular imagination" (2015, 59). Yet even if we consider the Peacock Revolution a short event, in which "suddenly, fashion was for men too" (169), it is noteworthy as a symptom "of the feminization of young men" (Hill 2018, 171) that allowed them to claim new subject positions through fashion. These identities in glam rock, that now would be defined as 'queer', are also influenced by a new view of homosexuality, as Robert Duncan explained: "Being homosexual, or at least seeming homosexual, was the new way to be black in rock'n' roll. To seem homosexual was the new way to be different, cool, special, a romantic outlaw" (1984, 93).

The Peacock Revolution ends in "repudiation and regression" (Paoletti 2015, 59) and is followed by what fashion theorists call 'power dressing' or, following John T. Molloy and his book of the same title, an attempt to "dress for success" (1975) in the 1980s. The hip-hop culture denigrates the tight clothing associated with the Peacock era as 'homosexual' and 'effeminate', as Joel Penney (2012) explains. At the same time, the anti-fashion of the Punk era illustrated that concepts of anti-fashion might question the status quo; however, they do not necessarily also question dominant concepts of masculinity.[12]

Surprisingly, it is the 'dress for success' uniformity of the 1980s that holds potential for alternative concepts of gender, as suits were not considered an exclusively male garment anymore. Furthermore, there were fashion designers like Giorgio Armani, who created jackets for men that were no longer stiff and padded like the tailored suits. At the same time, Armani sexualized the male look as well. The Armani looks also exemplify how the shift to leisure wear has found social acceptance. This shift finds its peak in sports style or athleisure wear originating in the anti-fashion context of youth culture in the pop era of the 1980s, when sportswear came to be appreciated beyond its mere functional aspect. Armani's revolutionary influence, however, did not extend to men's legs, as in high fashion, trousers tend to continue hiding the leg. But the emergence of the contemporary phenomenon of the meggings is directly linked to the popularization of the sports style and the athleisure trend and suggests new concepts of masculinity.

The Meggings—Advancing New Body Images and Reimagining Masculinity?

For fashion-indifferent people, the meggings might at first be an aesthetic shock, but considering the history of the male leg as outlined above, they are an unsurprising and expectable development. Tight pants and the visibility of male legs in menswear have historically undergone a shift in signification—from signaling the privilege of the upper class and, as Gernerd (2015) shows, serving as a marker of gentlemanly status and taste, to symbolizing a new sexualized masculinity in the 1970s, to its contemporary re-signification as an innovative, unusual clothing for men. In my understanding, the meggings emerges from a longer trajectory of fashioning men's legs; it has more specifically derived from intercultural exchanges after the millennium, merging aspects of Western popular streetwear, *haute couture* fashion, and Japanese youth wear.

---

[12] In *Subculture: The Meaning of Style* (2008), Dick Hebdige, for example, never questioned gender concepts in Punk culture.

For once, the meggings has its origins in the skinny jeans for women in streetwear, popularized in the early 2000s and represented by pop icons like Britney Spears, and in the new skinny silhouettes for men, reinvented by Hedi Slimane, as Nick Rees-Roberts (2013) and Jay McCauley Bowstead (2018) have shown. This skinny silhouette became desirable again for both men's and women's fashion, and Slimane refers explicitly to the glam rock era of the 1970s. Dress historians might retrospectively term it the 'skinny leg style'.

At the same time, sportswear is increasingly gaining popularity across all genders in Western cultures. This fashion trend intensifies with 'athleisure wear'—the literal combination of athletic and leisure time—, a clothing concept that accords sportswear a new branchs within the fashion industry. Its growing importance starts at the beginning of the 2000, when famous fashion designers such as Yohji Yamamoto (in 2001) and Stella McCartney (in 2004) started working for Adidas (Y3), or Karl Lagerfeld combined *haute couture* with sneakers for Chanel for the Spring/Summer collection in 2014. This transformation from functional sportswear to an aestheticized sports style shows a shift in meaning of sports clothing in Western societies of the twenty-first century (Haller 2017). A casual, sporty look and well-defined bodies are central factors of the athleisure style, that is based on an athletic body norm.

Interestingly, this kind of 'sporty' style can also be found in Japanese youth street style, and it is here where another origin of the meggings is located. As Masafumi Monden shows in his research on Japanese fashion cultures, young men in Japan diversify their styles to discover new concepts of masculinities, "to reinvent a mode of masculinity that works in contrast to the worn-out, dowdy 'salarymen'" (2015, 151). This expression of anti-fashion follows the same logic as other, earlier countercultures and pursues the same goal: achieving a fashionable form of masculinity. The rise of the athleisure style in Japan goes hand in hand with an emergence of new body types that also constitute a countermovement to the predominantly Western "Greek god-like, 'Adonis-complex-obsessed' body" (153) by favoring a more "boyish, slender" (64) style that serves as "an alternative to the established, 'hegemonic' mode of Japanese masculinity" (15). This street style is thus a form of anti-fashion *vis-à-vis* hegemonic masculinity. In Japanese male youth cultures, the meggings originated from the so-called 'short over long' style and were identified by the famous fashion blog "The Sartorialist" in a street style shot in Tokio in 2010 "as a very popular look". Since, as Ruth Barnes and

Joanne B. Eicher point out, "dress is both an indicator and a producer of gender" (1993, 7), this Japanese street style constitutes not only a form of resistance against traditional concepts of gender, but also a representation of a new concept of masculinity. Here, and analogous to the Peacock Revolution and the glam rock era, masculinity is constructed through a conscious use of fashion and builds especially on the willingness to expose the male body. In this context, fashion for men extends the stereotype "that men dress for utility rather than for aesthetics" (Monden 2015, 150).[13] In times when fashion blogging is a serious and profitable business, more and more fashion blogs run by male influencers become popular. Unsurprisingly, many of them wear meggings.[14]

The concept of a 'fashionable' masculinity, as it was influenced by Japanese street style and is now represented in the meggings, became a global phenomenon, and athletic, muscular bodies wearing meggings are not a rarity anymore. A look at the European runways in the last couple of years shows that there have been some collections that put athleisure style and especially the meggings center stage, for example the Spring/Summer collection of Givenchy in 2009.[15] The majority of representations of the meggings still feature it combined with shorts, following the 'short over long' style. An online search for meggings reveals that they are mostly linked to a sporty, athletic, or at least slim and slender concept of male bodies.[16] On the one hand, this may offer men a new sense of freedom to wear casual clothing, but on the other hand, it is obvious that this kind of garment entails a normative pressure for sporty, slim, muscular, and fit bodies.

A glance into the history of fashion underscores this process of constructions of masculinities and male bodies through clothing and style in terms of 'styles of various kinds': For more than 500 years, the emphasis on visible legs has been associated with hegemonic masculinity

---

[13] In Fashion Theory, there is a seemingly self-evident distinction between functionality and aesthetics that is unquestioned. This opposes theories of architecture, where the distinction of functionality and aesthetics is revealed as a modern myth.

[14] See, for instance, "Meggings" on *Lookbook* or an article on how a jacket could be combined with a meggings on the German lifestyle blog *Kaisers neue Kleider*.

[15] See, for instance, Leisa Barnett's article on the Givenchy Spring/Summer 2009 menswear collection in *Vogue*.

[16] The icons for this style are unsurprisingly David Beckham or the fashion blogger Brian Boy, two men who have been labelled 'metrosexuals'.

and fashionability. Later, the legs and the crotch were hidden; the 'dull' civil suit aimed to stress an ideal of non-fashionability for male bodies, construing men in tights and tight pants as effeminate, as these items were associated with female fashionability. In the 1970s, tight pants again represented virility, appropriated from previously marginalized racialized and sexualized male bodies.

But what about today? The world in the twentieth and twenty-first century is characterized by transnational and intercultural exchange, and this also includes fashion: Japanese street style, on the one hand, has influenced athleisure trends in the West and led to extremely athletic, defined muscular bodily images. On the other hand, meggings are discussed as effeminate since they emphasize the legs and the crotch. The differing connotations are grounded in the combination of particular styles with meggings. Thus, the meggings' contribution to new ideas of masculinities must be analyzed in the context of 'styles of various kinds' that encompass, for instance, special haircuts (like the 'man bun'), beards, or the 'short over long' style. Different gestures and movements also create differences in performances of masculinity. Thus, the meggings promotes a new offensively stylish masculinity grounded in anti-fashion discourses, and challenges traditional notions of a rationalized, bodiless, and hegemonic masculinity. Tight pants for men have signified differently throughout the history of dress, and the different discourses surrounding the meggings show this garment's ambivalence: Visible legs in tight pants can be considered a sign of male power or, conversely, of effeminacy, a sign of a virile, sexualized, potent masculinity or emphasizing an athletic, self-disciplined concept of male bodies—all in all, this item of clothing was and still is emblematic for different concepts of masculinity in relation to hegemonic notions of gender. The history of the meggings illustrates the cultural power inherent to just one piece of clothing for only a single part of the body, thereby highlighting the interrelations between materiality and the discursive production of bodies, fashion, and the social construction of masculinity.

References

Auslander, Philipp. *Performing Glam Rock: Gender and Theatricality in Popular Music*. Ann Arbor: U of Michigan P, 2006.

Bannister, Matthew. *White Boys, White Noise: Masculinities and 1980s Indie Guitar Rock*. Aldershot: Ashgate, 2006.

Barnes, Ruth, and Joanne B. Eicher. *Dress and Gender: Making and Meaning in Cultural Contexts*. Providence: Berg, 1993.

Barnett, Leisa. "Givenchy Spring/Summer 2009 Menswear Collection." *Vogue Britain*, June 27, 2008. https://www.vogue.co.uk/shows/spring-summer-2009-menswear/givenchy/collection. Accessed October 12, 2020.

Blake, Art. "Re-dressing Race and Gender: The Performance and Politics of Eldridge Cleaver's Pants." *Fashion Studies* 1, no. 1 (2018): 1–37.

Breward, Christopher. "Renouncing Consumption: Men, Fashion and Luxury." In *Defining Dress: Dress as Object, Meaning and Identity*, edited by Amy de La Haye, 48–62. Manchester: Manchester UP, 1999.

———. "Manliness, Modernity and the Shaping of Male Clothing." In *Body Dressing*, edited by Joanne Entwistle and Elizabeth Wilson, 165–181. Oxford: Berg, 2001.

Buckingham, David. "Glitter, Glam and Gender Play: Pop and Teenybop in the Early 1970s." *David Buckingham*, 2019. https://davidbuckingham.net/growing-up-modern/glitter-glam-and-gender-play-pop-and-teenybop-in-the-early-1970s/. Accessed October 12, 2019.

Butler, Judith. *Gender Trouble: Feminism and the Subversion of Identity*. New York: Routledge, 1990.

Chapman, Ian, and Henry Mabley Johnson. *Global Glam and Popular Music: Style and Spectacle from the 1970s to the 2000s*. New York and London: Routledge, 2016.

Crane, Diana. *Fashion and Its Social Agendas: Class, Gender, and Identity in Clothing*. Chicago, IL: U of Chicago P, 2000.

Davis, Fred. "Antifashion: The Vicissitudes of Negation." In *Fashion Theory: A Reader*, edited by Malcolm Barnard, 89–102. London: Routledge, 2007.

Dorestal, Philipp. "Dressing the Black Body. Mode, Hairstyle und Schwarzsein in den USA—von den 1970er-Jahren bis zu Barack Obama." *Zeithistorische Forschungen/Studies in Contemporary History* 14, no. 2 (2017): 311–336.

Duncan, Robert. *The Noise: Notes from a Rock'n'Roll Era*. New York: Tickner & Fields, 1984.

Entwistle, Joanne. *The Fashioned Body: Fashion, Dress and Modern Social Theory*. Cambridge: Polity Press, 2000.

Flügel, John Carl. *The Psychology of Clothes*. London: Hogarth, 1930.

Gernerd, Elisabeth. "Pulled Tight and Gleaming: The Stocking's Position Within Eighteenth-Century Masculinity." *Textile History* 46, no. 1 (2015): 3–27.

Haller, Melanie. "Mode Macht Körper – wie sich Mode-Körper-Hybride materialisieren." *Body Politics* 3, no. 6 (2015): 187–211.

———. "Mode – Sport – Körper: Vom zeitgenössischen Phänomen zur historischen Betrachtung." In *nmt 2017*, edited by Netzwerk Mode Textil, 71–77. Augsburg: Wißner Verlag, 2017.

———. "Plus Size Blogs als Diversität von Moden? Zu Praktiken visueller Repräsentationen und der Infragestellung weiblicher Normkörper in der Mode." In *Körperbilder – Körperpraktiken: Visualisierung und Vergeschlechtlichung von Körpern in Medienkulturen*, edited by Elke Grittmann, Katharina Lobinger, Irene Neverla and Monika Pater, 245–260. Köln: Halem, 2018.

———. "Implizites Geschlecht – Kleidergrößen in zeitgenössischer Kindermode." *Gender* 11, no. 1 (2019): 92–107.

———. "Zur Relationalität des Gestischen. Über den Zusammenhang von Körpern, Kleidern und Bewegung." In *Out of Line: Perspektiven gestischer Forschung*, edited by Peer de Smit and Veronika Darian, 253–268. Berlin: Neofelis, 2020.

Hebdige, Dick. *Subculture: The Meaning of Style*. London: Routledge, 2008 [1979].

Hill, Daniel Delis. *Peacock Revolution: American Masculine Identity and Dress in the Sixties and Seventies*. London: Bloomsbury, 2018.

Hollander, Anne. *Sex and Suits: The Evolution of Modern Dress*. New York: Knopf, 1994.

Kapow Meggings. https://kapowmeggings.com/. Accessed August 19, 2020.

Kawamura, Yuniya. *The Japanese Revolution in Paris Fashion*. Oxford: Berg, 2004.

König, René. *The Restless Image: A Sociology of Fashion*. London: Allen & Unwin, 1973.

Krämer, Thomas. *Androgynie, Alterität und Alienität im britischen Glam 1970–74*. Berlin: LIT, 2014.

Krass, Andreas. "Metrosexualität. Oder wie schwul ist der moderne Mann?" *Queer Lectures*, no. 1 (2008): 108–138.

Kurennaya, Anya. "Look What the Cat Dragged In: Gender, Sexuality, and Authenticity in 1980s Glam Metal." Master's Thesis. New York City: Parsons School of Design, 2012.

Laver, James. *Costume and Fashion: A Concise History*. 4th ed. London: Thames & Hudson, 1995.

Lemire, Beverly. "A Question of Trousers: Seafarers, Masculinity and Empire in the Shaping of British Male Dress, c. 1600–1800." *Cultural and Social History* 13, no. 1 (2016): 1–22.

Lipovetsky, Gilles. *The Empire of Fashion: Dressing Modern Democracy*. Princeton: Princeton UP, 2002 [1987].

McCauley Bowstead, Jay. *Menswear Revolution: The Transformation of Contemporary Men's Fashion*. London: Bloomsbury, 2018.

McNeil, Peter. *Pretty Gentlemen: Macaroni Men and the Eighteenth-Century Fashion World*. Yale: Yale UP, 2018.

McNeil, Peter, and Vicki Karaminas. *The Men's Fashion Reader*. Oxford: Berg, 2009.
"Meggings." *Lookbook*. https://lookbook.nu/collections/66316-meggings. Accessed October 02, 2020.
Merrill, Jane, and Keren Ben-Horin. *She's Got Legs: A History of Hemlines and Fashion*. Atglen, PA: Schiffer Publishing, 2015.
Miller, Monica. *Slaves to Fashion: Black Dandyism and the Styling of Black Diasporic Identity*. Durham: Duke UP, 2009.
Molloy, John T. *Dress for Success*. New York: Warner Books, 1975.
Monden, Masafumi. *Japanese Fashion Cultures: Dress and Gender in Contemporary Japan*. London: Bloomsbury, 2015.
"New Fall Collection from Eldridge de Paris." *Rolling Stone Magazine* (US) 197 (October 9, 1975): 65.
"Outfit – Hip und Klassisch: Meggings mit Sakko kombiniert." *Kaisers neue Kleider*. http://www.kaisers-neue-kleider.com/outfit-hip-und-klassisch-meggings-mit-sakko-kombiniert/. Accessed October 02, 2020.
Paoletti, Jo B. *Sex and Unisex: Fashion, Feminism, and the Sexual Revolution*. Bloomington, IN: Indiana UP, 2015.
Penney, Joel. "'We Don't Wear Tight Clothes': Gay Panic and Queer Style in Contemporary Hip Hop." *Popular Music and Society* 35, no. 3 (2012): 321–332.
Polhemus, Ted. *Fashion and Anti-Fashion: Exploring Adornment and Dress from an Anthropological Perspective*. London: Self-Publishing, 2011.
Rees-Roberts, Nick. "Boys Keep Swinging: The Fashion Iconography of Hedi Slimane." *Fashion Theory* 17, no. 1 (2013): 7–26.
Reynolds, Simon. *Shock and Awe: Glam Rock and Its Legacy*. London: Faber and Faber, 2016.
Sprenger, Ruth. *Die hohe Kunst der Herrenkleidermacher: Tradition und Selbstverständnis eines Meisterhandwerks*. Wien: Böhlau, 2009.
Steele, Valerie. "Anti-Fashion: The 1970s." *Fashion Theory* 1, no. 3 (1997): 279–296.
———. "Fashion: Yesterday, Today and Tomorrow." In *The Fashion Business: Theory, Practice, Image*, edited by Nicola White, 7–21. Oxford: Berg, 2000.
Stephens, Elizabeth, and Jørgen Lorentzen. "Male Bodies. An Introduction." *Men and Masculinities* 10, no. 1 (2007): 5–8.
Tulloch, Carol. *The Birth of Cool: Style Narratives of the African Diaspora*. London: Bloomsbury, 2016.
Turner, Alwyn. *Glam Rock: Dandies in the Underworld*. London: V+A Publishing, 2013.
Veblen, Thorstein. "The Economic Theory of Woman's Dress." *The Popular Science Monthly* 46 (1894): 198–205.

Vincent, Susan J. *The Anatomy of Fashion: Dressing the Body from the Renaissance to Today*. London: Phaidon, 2009.

Welters, Linda. "The Beat Generation: Subcultural Style." In *Twentieth-Century American Fashion*, edited by Linda Welters and Patricia Cunningham, 145–168. Oxford: Berg, 2005.

Welters, Linda, and Abby Lillethun. *Fashion History: A Global View*. London: Bloomsbury, 2018.

Wilson, Elizabeth. "Oppositional Dress." In *Fashion Theory: A Reader*, edited by Malcolm Barnard, 253–255. London: Routledge, 2007.

CHAPTER 13

"Isn't It Pretty to Think So?"—Disability and the Queering of Masculinity in Ernest Hemingway's *The Sun Also Rises* and D.H. Lawrence's *Lady Chatterley's Lover*

Martina Kübler

EXPERIENCING SURPRISE

"Oh, Jake," Brett said, "we could have had such a damned good time together."
Ahead was a mounted policeman in khaki directing traffic. He raised his baton. The car slowed suddenly pressing Brett against me.
"Yes," I said. "Isn't it pretty to think so?" (Hemingway 2004, 215–216)

This dialogue stands at the tail end of a star-crossed love affair. Ernest Hemingway's novel *The Sun Also Rises* follows Jake Barnes's and Lady

M. Kübler (✉)
Ludwig Maximilian University of Munich, Munich, Germany

C. Dexl and S. Gerlsbeck (eds.), *The Male Body in Representation*, Palgrave Studies in (Re)Presenting Gender, https://doi.org/10.1007/978-3-030-88604-2_13

287

Brett Ashley's failed romance, only to finally resolve that they cannot be together due to Jake's physical disability, an impotence incurred from a war wound. The "damned good time together" (215) thus remains hypothetical, and Jake's ability to perform as a sexual partner to Brett is fashioned as impossible due to his physical disability.

Focusing on Jake Barnes, the protagonist of Hemingway's *The Sun Also Rises*, and on Clifford Chatterley, one member of the love triangle at the heart of D.H. Lawrence's infamous *Lady Chatterley's Lover*, this article is concerned with two disabled heroes at the center of the literary canon of the early twentieth century. Published within two years of one another, in 1926 and 1928, respectively, the novels feature two men bound by a similar fate: both Hemingway's Jake and Lawrence's Clifford return from their respective engagements in World War I with injuries that have caused an irreversible impotence, and Clifford is even paralyzed from the waist down. In these paradigmatic texts, I argue, white male disability oscillates between several levels of signification. For one, impotence is presented as an overarching metaphor for 'masculinity in crisis', possibly even for the entire Lost Generation, as Gertrude Stein dubbed them: the disenchanted, directionless, and purposeless young people of the postwar years (Hutchisson 2016, 77). By being historically associated with femininity and homosexuality, disability furthermore works as a deconstructive moment against a supposedly stable hegemonic masculinity, which in the wake of World War I posited such hyper-masculine values as "leadership, physical prowess, competitiveness, and courage" (Tylee 2004, 304). Most importantly, however, I demonstrate how disability as a differential category interacts with constructions of masculinity in productive ways, allowing for new possibilities of fashioning masculinity. While this is merely hinted at in Lawrence's novel, the possibility of a reparative reading in Eve Kosofsky Sedgwick's sense comes into full play in *The Sun Also Rises*: rather than taking Lawrence and Hemingway for the sexist chauvinists they are often accused of being, I suggest to reveal and appreciate the ways in which their narratives let readers "experience surprise" (Sedgwick 2003, 146) by subverting then prevailing notions of masculinity, sexuality, and disability. Following Disability Studies scholars such as Sunaura Taylor, David T. Mitchell, and Sharon L. Snyder, I demonstrate that the material effects of impairment can foster non-normative, creative ways of knowing, being, and experiencing and that even a supposedly 'emasculating' impairment such as impotence allows for unprecedented ways of experiencing the male body in literary texts.

NARRATING DISABILITY

While the novels I discuss share some key characteristics on the level of the story, they could not differ more in how they narrate their heroes' respective disability on the level of discourse. In *Lady Chatterley's Lover*, Clifford's paraplegia is mentioned explicitly on the first page when the third-person narrator informs us that "the lower half of his body, from the hips down, [was] paralysed for ever [sic]" (Lawrence 2006, 5) and that he was "[c]rippled for ever [sic], knowing he could never have any children" (5). Hemingway's *The Sun also Rises*, by contrast, never explicitly mentions its protagonist's impotence. A conspicuous absence, Jake's 'wound' is only vaguely referred to. While the detrimental consequences it has for his love life are the pivotal point of the novel, his impotence is only alluded to symbolically, for example when the fish he catches are significantly "smaller" (2004, 105) than his friend's—"[t]hey're all about the size of your smallest" (105)—, or by way of paraphrase, for instance when Jake refers to it as "what happened to me" (23). The first-person narrator's silence regarding his disability is broken only once in the novel when Jake admits to a stranger, a prostitute, that sexual intercourse is out of the question for him because "he got hurt in the war" (14). Importantly, Hemingway is known for his 'iceberg theory'—his poetics of omission—, i.e., his minimalist style, its many gaps and allusions which often leave out the most relevant themes of his stories; in this respect, it is significant that Jake's disability, too, is omitted.

In *Narrative Prosthesis*, David T. Mitchell and Sharon L. Snyder theorize that disability can be used as an incitement for narrative, meaning that the plot can be inspired by bodily difference as a point of interest, a deviance that subsequently demands explanation or warrants rectification. They argue that the normalizing narrative objective pertaining to bodily difference is often such that the narrative explains the course of events that led to that impairment or ends in cure or acceptance (2000, 53). "In order to be disabled", Mitchell and Snyder claim, "one must narrate one's disability for others in sweeping strokes or hushed private tones" (xii). They summarize that "disability has functioned throughout history as one of the most marked and remarked upon differences that originates the act of storytelling" (54).

While I agree that the motif of disability functions as a plot device in both Lawrence's and Hemingway's texts, the two novels take very different routes in narrativizing their respective hero's disability. In *Lady*

Chatterley's Lover, Clifford Chatterley's paraplegia is a classic example of such an incitement for narrative. When Clifford returns home paralyzed and impotent, his wife must seek sexual fulfillment elsewhere, and his bodily difference literally sets off the plot of the novel. Jake, by contrast, presents readers with a more reluctant case of a disability narrative: his deliberate omission of it hints at the fact that narrating one's disability, and especially a man's impotence, is not an effortless enterprise. Rather, a genital disability such as impotence seems to be accompanied by feelings of shame and fear; hence Jake's silence. Evoking castration, impotence significantly counters hegemonic notions of masculinity and the virile male body, which ultimately causes Jake to remain silent about his status. Paradoxically, in the wake of World War I, physical impairments contracted during combat in some cases functioned as amplifications of masculinity. Joanna Bourke describes an "early sentimentalization of the war-wounded during the war and in the early 1920s" (1996, 56), which also speaks to the then prevailing norms of masculinity as predominantly virile and combative. Especially men with obvious, visible deformities and amputations became the objects of the most enthusiastic affections, as "public rhetoric judged soldiers' mutilations to be 'badges of their courage, the hall-mark [sic] of their glorious service, their proof of patriotism'" (56), which means that war-wounds were glamorized as signifiers of valor rather than signs of bodily failure. What is more, the soldier's wounded body was also attributed an increased sexual value, and "women were particularly fond of falling in love with the wounded" (56), especially those with obvious deformities. The veteran body and its relative physical integrity or lack thereof thus became a sign for a certain symbolic capital within the heterosexual matrix. While the body of the paraplegic Clifford Chatterley corresponds to this definition of the visibly impaired war hero, Jake Barnes, the secretly impotent veteran, fails to present a blatantly conspicuous wound that signals his masculine prowess. Jake's disability lacks visibility, and it is arguable whether Jake's impairment—even if it *were* disclosed—could function to amplify his masculinity.

In spite of its visibility, *Lady Chatterley's Lover* also registers Clifford's disability as an assault on contemporary notions of hegemonic masculinity as virile and aggressive. Notably, Clifford is described as "shy and self-conscious" (Lawrence 2006, 15) as a result of his recent paralysis. Upon closer inspection, he is endowed with a number of diametrically opposed attributes: "ruddy" yet hesitant, "often offensively supercilious, and then again modest and self-effacing, almost tremulous" (15). With this, Clifford's character combines several stereotypically masculine qualities, i.e., assertiveness and physical strength, with other, stereotypically more feminine attributes, i.e., shyness, self-consciousness, and passivity. Incidentally, this ambiguity is also addressed explicitly when the narrator remarks that Clifford "had never been one of the modern ladylike young men" (15) *before* his paralysis, adding that "his very quiet, hesitating voice, and his eyes, at the same time bold and frightened, assured and uncertain, revealed his nature" (15) as a now impotent and thus 'effeminate' man. What is at stake here is an identification of physical disability with femininity. The *Encyclopædia Britannica* fittingly describes the "Bath chair" Clifford uses as a "chair on wheels intended for use by ladies and invalids" (n. pag.), and the Chatterleys' gamekeeper Mellors reinforces this feminizing sentiment when he describes Clifford as "tame" and "a bit like a lady, and no balls" (Lawrence 2006, 196).

The discourse evoked here, i.e., the equation of disabled and female bodies, has a long tradition. As disability scholar Rosemarie Garland Thomson summarizes,

> many parallels exist between the social meanings attributed to female bodies and those assigned to disabled bodies. Both the female and the disabled body are cast as deviant and inferior; both are excluded from the full participation in public as well as economic life; both are defined in opposition to the norm that is assumed to possess natural physical superiority. (1997, 19)

These discursive similarities between female and disabled bodies culminate in the fact that historically, female bodies have often been *cast as* disabled bodies. As early as in Aristotle's *Generation of Animals*, for instance, female anatomies are described as "monstro[us]" (1943, 403) deviations from the male body by whom and in whose image they are conceived. Similarly, Sigmund Freud notoriously characterizes the female child as a deformed version of the male, discontent with the female genital organs considered to be only the atrophy of a penis (1967, 401). In addition, Freudian theory insists on what has been dubbed penis envy, suggesting that the girl mourns the penis she used to possess and is now lacking as a consequence of castration (397–400). Essentially, the female body is thus compared to and analogized with the castrated, disabled man.

The Sun Also Rises likewise connects male disability and notions of femininity. Reflecting especially on Jake's famous final line, "[i]sn't it pretty to think so?" (Hemingway 2004, 216), numerous critics have noted that "pretty" is a conventionally feminine word and that a 'real man' would never utter it. Jake's use of it in the final line of the novel thus supposedly underscores his lost and lacking claim of masculinity.[1]

POTENCY AND IMPOTENCE

In addition to its well-known association with femininity, disability also displaces men from hegemonic masculinity and marks them as 'Other' in terms of sexuality. This aspect is especially salient in Hemingway's novel and has been much remarked upon in critical scholarship. Jake's use of the adjective "pretty" has not only been read as a notion of femininity but also as signifying his association with homosexuality, i.e., as an indicator that Jake 'turns gay' because of his disability. Wolfgang Rudat, for instance, hypothesizes that "the gays [with whom Brett attends a party at the beginning of the novel] are like Jake himself" (1994, 173) in that they "are courting a woman although they know they will not go to bed with her" (173). Similarly, John S. Bak claims that "the gay men represent multiple versions of Jake himself – unmanned men, sexually [...] impotent with regards to feminine sexuality" (2009, 77). Undoubtedly, Hemingway's text suggests an unequivocal linkage between disability and (homo-)sexuality (Rudat 1994, 173) that puts the disabled, impotent man squarely in the realm of sexual Otherness and simultaneously outside of the then prevailing dominant form of masculinity which required men to be, above all, heterosexual.

The scenes in which Jake and his friend Bill go on a fishing trip to the Spanish Irati river illustrate this point. Michael Anesko notes that "[b]y this point in the novel, readers will recognize that Hemingway relies on phallic double-entendres and other kinds of bawdy humor both to generate and (nominally) to diffuse sexual tension, especially between men" (2015, 60). In one such humorous exchange, Bill teases Jake about his "lazy" expatriate lifestyle, adding: "You don't work. One group claims women support you. Another group claims you're impotent" (Hemingway 2004, 100–101). This joking banter occasions the

---

[1] For this line of argument see, for example: Rudat (1984, 33–36), Gladstein (1986), and Bak (2009).

only explicit—if jocular—mention of Jake's impotence in the entire novel. Most significantly, however, it also contains the only explicit reference to Jake's possible homosexuality which appears shortly afterward, when Bill suavely segues into a moving confession of his affection for his friend: "Listen. You're a hell of a good guy, and I'm fonder of you than anybody on earth. I couldn't tell you that in New York. It'd mean I was a faggot. That was what the Civil War was about. Abraham Lincoln was a faggot. He was in love with General Grant" (101). With this passage, the text ironically showcases its own homosexual suggestiveness: Bill addresses the fact that their homosocial fishing trip—saturated with phallic symbols such as comparing trout sizes—could be read as charged with homosexual desire. With this, the two crucial themes of the novel—disability and non-normative sexuality—surface explicitly within a single scene, embedded in jocularity. Bill's concession that he "couldn't tell [Jake] that in New York" (101) further attests to the difference in attitudes toward homosexuality between Europe and the USA in the early twentieth century: While homosexuality was often tolerated in larger European cities, it was still rigorously sanctioned in the USA. Furthermore, Bill's remark also points to the narrow confines within which permissible homosocial relations between men are policed, prohibiting male friends from confessing their affection to one another as it might compromise their heterosexuality as one of the most important pillars of their sense of masculinity. While Bill's affection for Jake is then deflected by his ludicrous hypothesizing about US-American history, Bill is just one example by which "the novel repeatedly emphasizes Jake's intrinsic ability to inspire affectionate regard in others, especially other men" (Anesko 2015, 61) as almost all of the book's male characters "respond to him with instinctive camaraderie" (61).

As Ron Picard notes fittingly, "Jake describes the entire celebration of traditional manhood in queer terms" (2004, 147), and the text's hypermasculine themes of all-male bonding, drinking, fighting, and violent sports are conflated with homosexual—which is what Picard's use of 'queer' refers to here—and thus non-hegemonic masculine undertones. The bullfighting aficionados Jake encounters are a particularly striking example of this: an exclusive circle, these men are "passionate about the bullfights" (Hemingway 2004, 115) because "[a]ficion [sic] means *passion*" (115; my emphasis), and amongst each other, they "often talked about bulls and bullfighters" (115), but they "never talked for a very long time. It was simply the pleasure of discovering what [they] each felt" (115). Next to a shared identity as bullfighting aficionados, Jake admits to his surprise that "nearly always there was the actual touching. It seemed as though they wanted to touch you to make certain" (115). This physical act of touching unsettles Jake, and he mentions the aficionado Montoya's "embarrassed putting the hand on [his] shoulder" (114–115) three times in the span of only two pages. Picard aptly remarks that "[t]hese men require physical intimacy to establish and maintain their unified worship of masculinity, but their embarrassment stems from the prohibition on such intimacy found in their masculine code" (2004, 147). To offset this predicament, he notes, "[t]he violent sacrifice of the bull washes away the guilt associated with transgressing this taboo and authenticates [the aficionados'] masculinity" (147) without violating then prevailing norms of heterosexual masculinity.

The bullfighting circles thus resemble "a closet for queer community" (147), similar perhaps to the period's underground gay clubs: a space within which behaviors become acceptable that would transgress the border of appropriateness when exercised outside. It becomes apparent that the supposedly hypermasculine, heterosexual masculinity presented through the sportsmen is queered. Inherent in this trope of "[t]he closet [as] the defining structure for gay oppression in this century" (Sedgwick 2008, 71) is, of course, a concomitant 'gay panic', i.e., an internalized fear of being—or being perceived as—homosexual. This proves to be a balancing act in which Jake continuously slips up due to his disability and resulting inability to sleep with women, a prerequisite to performing his heterosexuality. Due to the conflation of heterosexuality with masculinity, where the strong male body signals adherence to both gender and sexual norms, the aficionados manage to counterbalance their homosocial and homoerotic affection and body contact with their expertise on a masculine, sanguinary sport. Bak contextualizes this pattern:

> Specifically in America, homosexual panic [...] emerged on the national scene at the turn of the twentieth century, when homosexuality began to coalesce as a social identity and heterosexual American men were experiencing a crisis of masculinity [...]. [T]he popular image of the American male was becoming feverishly binarized, with gender often substituting for sexuality, and homophobia marking that distinction. (2009, 69–70)

He explains that while close, passionate homosocial relationships were common between men in the nineteenth century, "by the turn of the century, the growing legal, medical, and scientific literature on sexual inversion in Europe raised the 'specter of femininity' in American men" (70). This means that homophobia was not a problem until homosexuality was associated with femininity, and misogyny occasioned homophobia as a defense against the loosening of gender norms. With his particular disability, Jake thus embodies an ambivalence regarding both gender and sexuality, and that is on the one hand indicative, as Bak's quotation outlines, of this particular historical moment at the beginning of the twentieth century and, on the other hand, pioneering in the direction of a queerer, i.e., less heteronormative and homophobic, more fluid understanding of masculinity, as I will demonstrate shortly. Bak likewise summarizes that "[n]either concomitantly gay nor determinately straight, Jake represents one of Hemingway's finest expressions and subsequent criticisms of his time's emerging construction of the sexually binary male" (58–59). Hence, *The Sun Also Rises* critically evaluates norms of gender and sexuality, of masculinity and heterosexuality, by showing how inherently unstable they are and how precariously they hinge on the fleeting and constructed states of able-bodiedness and normative sexual potency and practice.

QUEERING DISABLED MASCULINITY

Jake's balancing act between masculine and feminine, between gay and straight evokes the figure of the queer. As mentioned above, Jake's queerness is invoked by his association with certain gay tropes, but the connection does not end there. Far from only denoting homosexuality, 'queer' has historically been understood in a variety of different ways, a discussion of which would exceed the scope of this article. Even though "to define what queer is [...] would be a decidedly un-queer thing to do" (2003, 43), as Nikki Sullivan stresses, the most important aspect of queerness for my argument is its opposition to the norm, more specifically its existence—however equivocal—outside of the heteronormative. As Sullivan emphasizes, queer "is constructed as a sort of vague and indefinable set of practices and (political) positions that has the potential to challenge normative knowledges and identities" (43–44). If we think of the queer as that which is "at odds with the normal, the legitimate, the dominant" (Halperin 1995, 62), then it denotes gender as well as sexual identities outside of the gender binary and outside of heteronormativity, i.e., the norm of monogamous heterosexual coupledom. Judith Butler calls this norm the "heterosexual matrix" (2006, 208), "that grid of cultural intelligibility through which bodies, genders, and desires are naturalized" (208) and in which it is assumed "that for bodies to cohere and make sense there must be a stable sex expressed through a stable gender (masculine expresses male, feminine expresses female) that is oppositionally and hierarchically defined through the compulsory practice of heterosexuality" (208). Queerness, then, is performed whenever a certain lifestyle, relationship, or identity does not adhere to these norms, when sex and gender do not match, and when sexual practices and relationship patterns deviate from the socially accepted monogamous arrangements, with sexual acts (at least theoretically) geared towards reproduction. It is my contention that disability routinely occasions such a break with normativity.

Disability scholars Mitchell and Snyder suitably term bodies with disabilities 'crip/queer' because "all bodies identified as excessively deviant are 'queer' in the sense that they represent discordant functionalities and outlaw sexualities" (2015, 3). Fittingly, Jake's lifestyle of travel, enjoyment, and seemingly constant alcohol consumption may be read as a queer sublimation of his desire for a heteronormative life. Measured against the paradigm of compulsory heteronormativity, this puts Jake in the realm of queerness because, as Halberstam explains, "we [can] try to think about queerness as an outcome of strange temporalities, imaginative life schedules, and eccentric economic practices" (2005, 1) which "develop, at least in part, in opposition to the institutions of family, heterosexuality, and reproduction" (1). The reckless lifestyle of the so-called Lost Generation of the postwar 1920s might therefore be characterized as queer in that it opposes a "reproductive temporality" (4) aimed at family formation which "create[s] longevity as the most desirable future, applaud[s] the pursuit of long life (under any circumstances), and pathologize[s] modes of living that show little or no concern for longevity" (4). Jake's disability registers this renunciation of a life dedicated to its own prolongation both by figuring a non-normative, non-healthy, non-whole body and through its inability to reproduce—or to be sexually active in reproductively significant forms.

Similarly, in *Lady Chatterley's Lover*, the impotent Clifford Chatterley is fashioned as queer in a society where, as Lee Edelman has argued, the figure of the child signifies futurity, and "we are no more able to conceive of a politics without a fantasy of the future than we are able to conceive of a future without the figure of the Child" (2004, 11). Far from only posing a problem for Clifford's own physical integrity, his inability to father a child is represented in political terms. The novel's very first page establishes Clifford's war wound as a hindrance to societal futurity when it reads that "[c]rippled for ever [sic], knowing he could never have any children, Clifford came home to the smoky Midlands to keep the Chatterley name alive while he could" (Lawrence 2006, 1). The pressure to create a future for him and his kind, to "produce an heir" (11) is registered several times over the course of the novel, and Clifford's fertility is a necessary prerequisite for this reproduction and perpetuation of the social order, which is underscored by a fixation on the penis as the symbol for procreation when it boldly reads: "[T]he bridge to the future is the phallus, and there's the end of it" (327).

Against this background, disabled bodies clearly interfere with this telos of futurity. Rather, as Alison Kafer stresses in *Feminist, Queer, Crip*, "disability is seen as the sign of no future, or at least of no good future" (2013, 3). From a reparative perspective, however, I argue that Clifford acts as a queer figure in his own right if 'queer' is conceived as an existence outside the heteronormative standard that includes the maxim of reproduction—and instead as "refer[ring] to nonnormative logics and organizations of community, sexual identity, embodiment, and activity in space and time" (Halberstam 2005, 6). Clifford's disability indicates a feasible lifestyle beyond heteronormative constrictions: in addition to renouncing sexual activity and procreation altogether, he eventually suggests to his wife Connie a non-normative, queer—possibly polyamorous—relationship and family model in which Connie is to have a child with another man while remaining married to Clifford. "If lack of sex is going to disintegrate you", he challenges her, "go out and have a love affair" (Lawrence 2006, 45). At the same time, he also implores her to stay in a relationship with him: "But only do these things so that you have an integrated life, that makes a long harmonious thing. And you and I can do that together... don't you think? ... if we adapt ourselves to the necessities" (45). Just as *The Sun Also Rises*, which celebrates the Lost Generation's vagabond lifestyle, Lawrence's novel also entertains the thought of queer alternatives to conventional family life by opening up the normative nuclear family—defined strictly by relationships of kinship—to include a third person to fulfill Clifford's lacking sexual and reproductive function. By suggesting that Connie have a love affair or even a child by another man while simultaneously main-taining an "integrated life" with himself, Clifford subversively toys with non-heteronormative alternatives, "other logics of location, movement, and identification" (Halberstam 2005, 1) than traditional family lineages, and his disability thus enables him to imagine systems of "affiliation" rather than biological "filiation" (Said 1983, 19). Hence, Lawrence's text suggests a reimagination of families as biological units of filiation centered around coupledom: by fashioning Clifford as a disabled man, it begins to imagine non-heteronormative family designs which can include more than two people and their offspring and which are not primarily characterized by kinship but instead by a shared network of commitment and care for each other.

In addition, Clifford's and Jake's respective disabilities not only queer them with regard to social norms but, as genital disabilities, affect their sexual practices as well. While both novels suggest a reparative reading of representations of disability, Hemingway's novel, even more than Lawrence's, not only attends to the challenges of impotence but also—and more significantly—underscores the affirmative and subversive potential of disabled bodies. It is helpful here to look at the ground-breaking study *The Sexual Politics of Disability: Untold Desires* conducted by Tom Shakespeare et al. in which they point to a "narrow notion of normal sexuality—which is focused primarily on the male erection" and the fact that this "is detrimental to the sexual and psychological health of both men and women" (1996, 98), especially when they are dealing with an impairment. However, by making some heteronormative sexual prac-tices impossible, disability might call for alternative, queer ways to have sex and to experience pleasure, a fact which both novels initially ignore when they posit the impossibility of having sex with a genitally disabled man. By contrast, as Shakespeare et al. have found, some disabled respon-dents in their survey "suggested that their sex lives may actually have improved as a result of impairment" (100) because their disabilities have given rise to greater "sexual adventurism" such as indulging in "sexual experimentation and alternative sexual acts" (100).

Upon closer examination, Hemingway's text registers multiple scenes in which Jake's and Brett's frustration at not being able to perform conventional sexual acts due to his disability becomes palpable. An espe-cially striking example occurs during one of Jake's and Brett's intimate shared taxi rides, which negotiates a number of queer themes in relation to Jake's disability. Initially, the kissing lovers are clearly eager to pursue sexual relations with each other, but soon the issue of Jake's disability is presented as a hindrance. For one, Brett refuses Jake's advances when she exclaims "[d]on't touch me" (2004, 22) repeatedly, and the irony of the phallic symbolism in her explanation—that she "can't stand it" (22)— is not lost on either Jake or the reader. At first glance, Brett's behavior reinforces the traditional stereotype of the disabled man as an asexual or at least inadequate sexual partner. Upon closer inspection, however, it is striking that Brett stresses her desire to keep seeing Jake, emphatically and paradoxically pleading: "But, darling, I have to see you. It isn't *all that* you know" (23; my emphasis). Whereas Clifford Chatterley proposes to Connie a celibate marriage in which she is free to pursue adventures with other men, Hemingway's text here also seems to challenge the primacy of heteronormative intercourse as a legitimation of intimate relationships when Jake is persistent in his advances and asks "[i]sn't there anything we can do about it?" (22). Could Brett's subsequent confessing to "turn all to jelly" (22) at Jake's touch possibly be interpreted as an alternative, queer, sexual practice? Dana Fore explains that Brett's admitting to "turn all to jelly" when touched "affirms the capacity to experience intense physical sensation from simple stimulation – which may translate into an ability to derive satisfaction from nontraditional sex" (2007, 80– 81). Similarly, I suggest that Jake's question "[i]sn't there anything we can do about it?" (Hemingway 2004, 22) refers to a momentary open-mindedness on his part toward alternative strategies for mutual pleasure. In spite of his realization that "there's not a damn thing we could do" (23) a few moments later, Jake seems to tentatively entertain the thought of sexual adventurism, a thought he subsequently discards after looking into Brett's eyes for a long time, assuming to see how "afraid" she was "of so many things" (23). Brett's resistance to queerness is further under-scored by her maintaining that she "[doesn't] want to go through that hell again" (23), possibly referring to an unsuccessful attempt at sexual intercourse with a disabled Jake.

The idea of a 'crip/queer' sexual relationship can be explored even further by considering the following incident, quoted in full to illustrate the suggestiveness of Hemingway's minimalism:

Brett came in the room, a glass in her hand, and sat on the bed.
"What's the matter, darling? Do you feel rocky?"
She kissed me coolly on the forehead.
"Oh, Brett, I love you so much."

"Darling," she said. Then: "Do you want me to send [the count] away?"
[...]
She was gone out of the room. I lay face down on the bed. I was having
a bad time. I heard them talking but I did not listen. Brett came in and
sat on the bed.
"Poor old darling." She stroked my head.
"What did you say to him?" I was lying with my face away from her. I did
not want to see her.
"Sent him for champagne. He loves to go for champagne."
Then later: "Do you feel better, darling? Is the head any better?"
"It's better."
"Lie quiet. He's gone to the other side of town."
"Couldn't we live together, Brett? Couldn't we just live together?"
"I don't think so. I'd just *tromper* you with everybody. You couldn't stand
it."
"I stand it now."
"That would be different. It's my fault, Jake. It's the way I'm made."
"Couldn't we go off in the country for a while?"
"It wouldn't be any good. I'll go if you like. But I couldn't live quietly
in the country. Not with my own true love." (2004, 48–49; emphasis in
original)

In this scene, Brett and the count call on Jake in his Paris apartment.
Plagued by a headache, Jake feels "rotten" and is "having a bad time"
(48) after his shower, and Brett sends the count away to get more champagne. During his absence, Jake seems to propose to Brett to engage in
a queer sort of relationship in that he urges her to live with him, even
without the heteronormative imperative of monogamous coupledom and
of sexual intercourse between the partners. Like Lawrence's Clifford, Jake
now desperately implores Brett to "just live together" (48), suggesting to
even tolerate Brett's inevitable affairs with other men just like he already
"stand[s] it now" (48).

Equally important, the fact that Brett sends the count "to the other
side of town" (48) in a taxi, and that the scene ends a few lines later
with "a ring at the bell-pull" (49) indicating the count's return, suggests
that—depending on the traffic situation in 1920s' Paris and on the liter-
alness of the expression "the other side of town"—at least one hour of
narrated time must have passed, likely more. The sparse dialogue quoted
above accounts but for a few minutes of narrative time, however, meaning
that a considerable amount of action must have gone unremarked upon

by the narrator, Jake. Especially the time-lapse indicator "[t]hen later:" (48) has been read as a suspicious omission during which narrative information must have been withheld. Kenneth Lynn, for example, believes that the pair engages in oral sex at various points in the novel, and claims that "the implication is fairly clear that, while the full extent of his injury is unspecified, Jake remains capable of achieving a degree of satisfaction through oral sex" (1987, 324). Michael Anesko takes this line of thinking even further by wondering whether "[p]erhaps it is Brett who performs anilingus? (Jake is fresh from the shower we know.) Or even sodomy? From the verbal patterning of the novel, we can at least infer that Jake's feeling 'better' presupposes sexual climax, however arrived at" (2015, 58). Similarly, Dana Fore proposes that Brett in this scene

> recognizes intuitively what recent work on the sexual development of disabled men and couples has confirmed, that it is possible for severely disabled people to achieve sexual satisfaction by re-training their bodies to feel erotic pleasure in different ways, through different erogenous zones. (2007, 80)

What these scholars fail to acknowledge is that a reconditioning towards other erogenous zones, be it different body parts or imaginary phantom limbs, is unnecessary because men—whether disabled or non-disabled, straight or queer—can receive sexual stimulation anally via the prostate. This heteronormative taboo, I suggest, might very well be explored in the scene above, cloaked in silence due to its shameful association with passive, 'un-masculine' gay sex, but not unlikely especially as Jake mentions his position of "lay[ing] face down on the bed" (Hemingway 2004, 48). Suggestions that sexual relief must have happened can be substantiated, as already mentioned, not only by the lapse of time but also if we consider the fact that Jake feels "rotten" initially but then later admits that he does "feel better" after Brett asks "[d]o you feel better, darling? Is the head any better?" (48).

Reading these scenes from a queer and reparative perspective suggests that disability incites both Brett and Jake to toy with the idea of engaging in nontraditional, adventurous, queer relations with each other, even if those advances are narratively concealed by silence and omission due to contemporary attitudes toward propriety and respectability, a fact that is reflected in the text by Jake's bashful "lying with [his] face away from her" and his "not want[ing] to see her" (48).

DISABILITY AS A CREATIVE ALTERNATIVE CORPOREALITY

Far from unambiguously positing the impotent man as a metaphor for lost masculinity, Hemingway's and Lawrence's novels allow for disability to be understood as an incitement for new, queer ways of being a man. With this in mind, I return to the allusive final lines of *The Sun Also Rises* quoted at the outset of this article. Brett and Jake reunite in Madrid after Brett has ended her affair with the young bullfighter Romero, and Brett now resolves to "go [...] back to Mike" (Hemingway 2004, 213), her fiancé. The final line, Jake's rhetorical question "[i]sn't it pretty to think so?" (216), has given rise to many different readings of the novel, many of which hinge on the word "pretty" and its feminine or homosexual connotation. Hemingway scholar Wolfgang Rudat concedes that he does "not mean that at the conclusion of *The Sun Also Rises* Jake Barnes turns gay, but [*does*] believe that Hemingway wanted the more adventurously speculative among his readers to at least *consider* such a possibility" (1990, 60; my emphases), and this line of argument already hints at the point I wish to make. What is equally interesting about the last line "[i]sn't it pretty to think so?" as the oft-discussed use of the word "pretty", I propose, is the "think so", which has never been addressed by critics. By suggesting to "think so", Jake stresses the *imagination* and thus bravely alludes to the possibility of stretching one's mind, of thinking possible alternative, queer ways of being. With his alcohol consumption reaching phenomenal levels in this final scene, even for a novel studded with characters well able to hold their drinks, Jake's language becomes increasingly frank and sexually suggestive. In response to Brett's question, "[w]hat do you like to do?", he seductively admits twice that he "like[s] to *do a lot of things*" (Hemingway 2004, 215; my emphasis), again hinting at possibilities of sexual activity beyond the realm of the heteronormative. Accordingly, Jake's "[i]sn't it pretty to think so?" prosodically stresses and hinges on the verb 'to think', i.e., Jake's capacity to *think* of the "damn good time" he and Brett *could* have had together, to *imagine* "a lot of things" he likes to do and *would* have done with Brett—had they not been restricted by a conventional, heteronormative understanding of sexuality, one precluded by his disability.

A last flicker of optimism—this is what Jake's question entails. By ending on a question, the narrative openness urges readers to reparatively imagine a joint life for Jake and Brett and to allow for a sexual relationship not predicated on the phallocentric idea of heteronormative sexual relations. With this, the subject position of the queer, disabled man is the very position which most urgently implores us to rethink limits, to imagine a more creative, less scripted, more interesting approach to sexuality, masculinity—and life. With this, as Dana Luciano and Mel Y. Chen confirm, "the figure of the queer/trans body does not merely unsettle the human as norm; it generates other possibilities – multiple, cyborgian, spectral, transcorporeal, transmaterial – for living" (2015, 187). Contrary to how it has been interpreted previously, then, the policeman's raised baton could signify not so much a symbol for an actual phallus and Jake's shortcomings in that regard, but rather a phallic symbol for a phallus-substitution, a tool—or toy?—that could be used as a substitute for a penis in queer sexual intercourse. Shakespeare et al. add accordingly that "a greater willingness to embrace diversity, experimentation and the use of sexual toys and other alternative techniques – [to 'do a lot of things'] would be of value to all sexually active people, not just to those who happen to have impairments" (1996, 99). Similarly, Fore agrees that Jake and Brett are ultimately hindered not by his disability itself but by prejudices surrounding his disability (2007, 86). The veritable impotence that Jake's disability symbolizes, then, is not that of the body, but of the mind. By suggesting alternative modes of intercourse beyond heteronormativity, his disability makes queerness thinkable; it engenders the necessity for queerness in order to move beyond the limitations of a heteronormative lifestyle.

In fact, this reparative potential of the disabled body to be a catalyst for divergent thinking and living has been stressed by a number of disability scholars and activists. Mitchell and Snyder assert that there is an "active transformation of life that the alternative corporealities of disability creatively entail" (2015, 2). They explain further that we must "revalu[e] the failures of crip/queer embodiments to fit within narrow normative frameworks" (77), suggesting instead to "read failure to normalize as the emergence of alternative strategies of nonnormative living in order to better speak to the political dilemmas of embodied vulnerability" (77). A similar notion is conferred more tangibly in Sunaura Taylor's insightful *Beasts of Burden: Animal and Disability Liberation*:

What do I find valuable about disability? I remember thinking. *How do I even begin to answer that?* [...] I searched my brain for reasons – things about interdependence and challenging normalcy. But before I could gather my bullet points in my head, the artist in me burst forth with a reply.

'I'm an artist, and so I think about creativity a lot. Being disabled gives you a completely new way of having to interact with the world... For instance, I was never taught by anyone how to use my mouth to do things. There is a certain level of creativity and innovation that goes into every single thing, which some people might find really frustrating, but for many of us who are actually living it, it's a very liberating thing to not have every aspect of your body already defined...' [...] I think there are many disabled people who value disability for the ways it gives a different perspective on the world.' (2017, 134–135; emphasis in original)

What Taylor's account underscores is that disability, when viewed from a reparative or 'crip' perspective, cannot just reach the status of being accepted or 'tolerated' by an able-bodied society. Rather, in the bodily singularities lie unexpected, productive, subversive, and infinitely creative opportunities for living. Where "[t]he project of queer theory seeks to resist heteronormativity by revealing its instability, by finding the nonstraight, antistraight, or contrastraight desire implicit in every heteronormative discourse" (Dennis 2004, 383), Crip Theory likewise challenges the stability of able-bodiedness and finds the power in living a disabled life. Precisely *because* it challenges the 'normal', the 'heterosexual', and the 'masculine', and *because* it forces people into non-normative, less conventional ways of navigating the world, disability echoes Halberstam's notion of the "queer art of failure" in that "[w]e can also recognize failure as a way of refusing to acquiesce to dominant logics of power and discipline and as a form of critique" (2011, 88). Halberstam adds that "[a]s a practice, failure recognizes that alternatives are embedded already in the dominant and that power is never total or consistent; indeed, failure can exploit the unpredictability of ideology and its indeterminate qualities" (88). I have illustrated that impotence in particular—a conspicuously 'emasculating' impairment and perceived failure—thus turns out to be the pivotal element from which to read disability reparatively. Instead of signifying emasculation, it can be regarded as an incipience, a starting point from which to imagine new, queer ways of being (masculine). Disability works to unearth alternatives already present within the dominant heteronormative ideology, and it is only through disability that Jake Barnes and Clifford Chatterley are forced to reevaluate existing hegemonic ideas of sex and masculinity. I have attempted to show that when read in light of Disability and Queer Theory, these canonical novels can be seen to negotiate how the material effects of impairment can foster non-normative, creative ways of knowing, being, and experiencing—isn't it pretty to think so?

References

Anesko, Michael. "The Torments of Spring: Jake Barnes's Phantom Limb in *The Sun Also Rises.*" *Literature and Medicine* 33, no. 1 (2015): 52–69.
Aristotle. *Generation of Animals.* Translated by A.L. Peck. London: William Heinemann/Cambridge, MA: Harvard UP, 1943.
Bak, John S. *Homo Americanus: Ernest Hemingway, Tennessee Williams, and Queer Masculinities.* Madison: Farleigh Dickinson UP, 2009.
"Bath Chair". In *Encyclopædia Britannica, inc.* https://www.britannica.com/topic/bath-chair. Accessed September 18, 2019.
Bourke, Joanna. *Dismembering the Male: Men's Bodies, Britain and the Great War.* Chicago: U of Chicago P, 1996.
Butler, Judith. *Gender Trouble: Feminism and the Subversion of Identity.* New York and London: Routledge, 2006 [1990].
Dennis, Jeffrey P. "Heteronormativity." In *Men and Masculinities: A Social, Cultural, and Historical Encyclopedia*, edited by Michael Kimmel and Amy Aronson, 382–383. Santa Barbara: ABC Clio, 2004.
Edelman, Lee. *No Future: Queer Theory and the Death Drive.* Durham and London: Duke UP, 2004.
Fore, Dana. "Life Unworthy of Life? Masculinity, Disability, and Guilt in *The Sun Also Rises.*" *The Hemingway Review* 26, no. 2 (2007): 74–88.
Freud, Sigmund. "Der Untergang des Ödipuskomplexes." In *Gesammelte Werke. Band 13: Jenseits des Lustprinzips, Massenpsychologie und Ich-Analyse, Das Ich und das Es*, edited by Anna Freud et al., 395–402. Frankfurt a. M.: S. Fischer Verlag, 1967 [1924].
Garland Thomson, Rosemarie. *Extraordinary Bodies: Figuring Physical Disability in American Culture and Literature.* New York: Columbia UP, 1997.
Gladstein, Mimi Reisel. *The Indestructible Woman in Faulkner, Hemingway, and Steinbeck.* Ann Arbor: UMI Research P, 1986.
Halberstam, Judith. *In a Queer Time and Place: Transgender Bodies, Subcultural Lives.* New York: New York UP, 2005.
———. *The Queer Art of Failure.* Durham and London: Duke UP, 2011.
Halperin, David. *Saint Foucault: Towards A Gay Hagiography.* Oxford: Oxford UP, 1995.
Hemingway, Ernest. *The Sun Also Rises.* London: Arrow Books, 2004 [1926].
Hutchisson, James M. *Ernest Hemingway: A New Life.* University Park, PA: Pennsylvania State UP, 2016.

Kafer, Alison. *Feminist, Queer, Crip*. Bloomington and Indianapolis: Indiana UP, 2013.

Lawrence, D.H. *Lady Chatterley's Lover*. Edited by Michael Squires. New York: Penguin Books, 2006 [1928].

Luciano, Dana, and Mel Y. Chen. "Introduction: Has the Queer Ever Been Human?" *GLQ* 21, no. 2–3 (2015): 183–207.

Lynn, Kenneth S. *Hemingway*. New York: Simon and Schuster, 1987.

Mitchell, David T., and Sharon L. Snyder. *Narrative Prosthesis: Disability and the Dependencies of Discourse*. Ann Arbor: The U of Michigan P, 2000.

———. *The Biopolitics of Disability: Neoliberalism, Ablenationalism, and Peripheral Embodiment*. Ann Arbor: U of Michigan P, 2015.

Picard, Ron. "Dancing with the Bulls: Engendering Competition in Hemingway's *The Sun Also Rises* and Silko's *Ceremony*." In *Upon Further Review: Sports in American Literature*, edited by Richard Cocchiarale and Scott D. Weston, 143–153. Westport, CT: Praeger, 2004.

Rudat, Wolfgang E. H. "Jake's Odyssey: Catharsis in *The Sun Also Rises*." *The Hemingway Review* 4 (1984): 33–36.

———. "Hemingway's *The Sun Also Rises*: Masculinity, Feminism, and Gender-Role Reversal." *American Imago* 47, no. 1 (1990): 43–68.

———. "Hemingway on Sexual Otherness: What's Really Funny in *The Sun Also Rises*." In *Hemingway Repossessed*, edited by Kenneth Rosen, 169–179. Westport, CT: Praeger, 1994.

Said, Edward. *The World, the Text, and the Critic*. Cambridge: Harvard UP, 1983.

Sedgwick, Eve Kosofsky. *Touching Feeling: Affect, Pedagogy, Performativity*. Durham and London: Duke UP, 2003.

———. *Epistemology of the Closet*. Berkeley: U of California P, 2008 [1990].

Shakespeare, Tom, Kath Gillespie-Sells, and Dominic Davies. *The Sexual Politics of Disability: Untold Desires*. London and New York: Cassell, 1996.

Sullivan, Nikki. *A Critical Introduction to Queer Theory*. New York: New York UP, 2003.

Taylor, Sunaura. *Beasts of Burden: Animal and Disability Liberation*. New York: The New Press, 2017.

Tylee, Claire. "First World War Literature." In *Men and Masculinities: A Social, Cultural, and Historical Encyclopedia*, edited by Michael Kimmel and Amy Aronson, 304–306. Santa Barbara: ABC Clio, 2004.

CHAPTER 14

Coda: Rereading the Male Body—The Cultural Power of Representation

Carmen Dexl and Silvia Gerlsbeck

The conception of *The Male Body in Representation: Returning to Matter* was motivated by the following complex of questions: What is the particular benefit a Cultural Studies take on corporeality and materiality can offer? What is the added value a concern with cultural phenomena has for other disciplines' notions of the body? What is the cultural power of representation, i.e., how does it facilitate a more nuanced understanding of the body in terms of bodily matter and how bodies come to matter? What power structures is representation entangled in, or, what are the politics of representation underlying the subject matter? In Foucault's

C. Dexl (✉)
American Studies, University of Regensburg, Regensburg, Germany
e-mail: carmen.dexl@ur.de

S. Gerlsbeck
English Studies: Literature and Culture, Friedrich-Alexander-Universität
Erlangen-Nürnberg, Erlangen, Germany
e-mail: silvia.gerlsbeck@fau.de

© The Author(s), under exclusive license to Springer Nature
Switzerland AG 2022
C. Dexl and S. Gerlsbeck (eds.), *The Male Body in Representation*,
Palgrave Studies in (Re)Presenting Gender,
https://doi.org/10.1007/978-3-030-88604-2_14

307

terms, what regimes of truth are perpetuated or undermined in representational practice? And what conclusions—theoretically, methodologically, epistemologically—are scholars to draw from the observations presented in this volume?

The contributions assembled here understand the realm of representation as co-constitutive of social reality. To cite Stuart Hall's observation on the processes of cultural transmission at work in the context of diasporic subject formation, bodies, here, can function "as the canvases of representation" (1993, 109), i.e., concepts of bodies and discourses of representation mutually constitute each other. This implies that representation is "involved in the actual generation of attitudes, discourses, ideologies, hierarchies of norms and values, and structures of feeling and thinking" (Nünning 2012, 160). The collected contributions thus assert that the exploration of male bodies in cultural productions, which variously present us with images and narratives of specific bodies and their gendered, sexed, racialized, classed, or dis/abled experiences, inform our perception and the bodily practices we engage in, our embodied consciousness, as well as the social meanings we ascribe to bodies. Against this background, the following reflections will sketch critical insights the readings in this book have generated and highlight important points of convergence with an eye on the incentives they offer for further scholarly thought.

Considering that representation involves "the power to represent someone or something in a certain way [...] [, which] includes the exercise of *symbolic power* through representational practices", most of the contributions raise questions regarding particular 'regimes of representation' (Hall 1997, 259; emphasis in original) their case studies are implied in. Attending to portrayals of bodies that are either complicit with hegemonic ideals or construed in terms of 'otherness' and thus faced with acts of social exclusion, these readings show how representation is implicated in generating social acceptance of existing power relations or fostering resistance against it.

The introduction to this volume as well as contributions, for example, by Ana Stevenson and David Patrick, as well as Jay McCauley Bowstead, which look at body images produced by and circulated through advertisements, reality TV, and social media, engage this concern and outline ideological implications of cultural representations as well as discursive continuities in this regard. They observe that the male body has gained increased visibility, particularly in form of portrayals that generate

Western-centric body norms as idealized images of white muscular men. They also draw attention to the workings of body politics in media representations from the 1950s and 1960s through the 2020s, which—by means of a similar rhetoric of self-improvement—ascribe responsibility for health, success, and attractiveness to the individual. The continuous proliferation of supposedly desirable bodies underscores how media representations are implicated in consumers' embrace of bodily practices and techniques of the self that comply with logics of policing and concomitant fashionings of 'docile' bodies, i.e., bodies that correspond with and subscribe to the dominant social, economic, and political order.

Picking up this line of thought, some contributions on representations of fashionable men, such as John Finkelberg's analysis of caricatures of the Dandy or Alla Myzelev's exploration of what could be termed the 'dandyesque figure' of the *Stiliagi*, illuminate the entanglements of cultural productions and historical and political contexts and outline the socio-political purposes of satirical depictions of fashionable men: Construed as liminal figures, which emerge at times of social and political change and serve to police male bodies, they work to either maintain an existing order or urge for political change.

Continuing the focus on 'fashionability', but from a different theoretical and methodological perspective, Melanie Haller's fashion-historical and body-sociological contribution on the meggings also underlines the enmeshment of cultural phenomena and social realities. Its historical trajectory urges us to recognize processes of transcultural exchange, the influence of marginalized styles, and acts of cultural appropriation. The article can be understood as a call for approaching this volume's subject matter from an Area Studies perspective that ponders the impact of transnational influences and processes of intercultural exchange in the context of globalization on body images and concepts.

Adding to these insights into representation's political and ideological functions, some contributions specifically emphasize the affective power of the politics of representation. The discourse of the sentimental, which Christian Krug identifies as a central strategy in *Violent Playground*, can mobilize affect for political purposes. Appealing to the viewers' feelings and eliciting emotional responses—that can also manifest on the body, e.g., in physical reactions such as tears or shudders—, sentimental aesthetics can serve to install the 'right feelings' in audiences and are thus often didactic and moralistic. Jonathan A. Allan also draws attention to representation's implication in generating feelings, particularly showing that a too affirmative, reparative take on the genre of the popular romance novel—i.e., a reading with the grain—contains its risks: constructions of the disabled male hero as desirable according to the genre's normative standards can make disability 'invisible', or at least ameliorate it in such a way that it negates the specificities of disabled social experience. Affect in itself as well as the mobilization of affect through representation, these contributions suggest, is discursively structured and ideologically charged. Further inquiries into representations of male bodies from the perspective of Affect Studies promises relevant insights into the political power of affect, its gendered dimensions, and—responding to new materialist demands—affect's positioning in between culture and biology or discourse and matter, as well as its role for embodiment.

Many contributions highlight how literature can work as a counter-discourse by using specific frames of representation to "challenge our usual ways of seeing, to startle us out of the torpor of habitual perceptions and received ideas" (Felski 2008, 114–115). Alla Myzelev's contribution, for instance, foregrounds the function of self-representational practices as 'safe spaces' for providing a counter-document to denigratory portrayals of bodies as corrupted and corrupting. Sandra Dinter's article on portrayals of cross-dressing and *flânerie* in nineteenth-century century women's literature shows that the subversive potential of these depictions was not necessarily predicated on women engaging in the cultural practice of cross-dressing and male walking itself, but rather on the *representation* of these acts in their memoirs and these books' circulation. The male disguise that is necessary for women to freely walk in the city and the *Stiliagi*'s necessary retreat into private homes as 'safe spaces' shielded from public denigration underscores the implication space has for body and gender politics. Space constitutes no neutral realm but is discursively shaped and—as these examples suggest—inscribed into dominant ideologies.

The particular significance that the concept of a 'safe space' has for discriminated groups is also emphasized by Michael McMillan. As transpires in his work, performance can function as a laboratory for exploring affects and bodies in motion and can thus anticipate new understandings of embodiment and masculinity. This suggests that Spatial Studies and Performance Studies constitute highly relevant fields of research for further studying constructions of space in interrelation with conceptions of the body, materiality, and performativity. In this regard, it might be beneficial to also consider the experience of cultural practitioners and draw on their embodied knowledge for adding to scholarly research on the body—a point that the fashion-oriented contributions make as well.

Yet, while always being implicated in the workings of discourse, representations of bodies can also emerge as vehicles to trouble ontologies and fixed categories of knowledge: In this respect, rl goldberg's article on a photographic project illustrates how the interrelation of queer and black representation in the book leads to questioning the linearity of Western historiography by disturbing notions of beginnings, embracing fragmentation and fabulation, and conveying historical interminability. Contributions like Martina Kübler's queer reading of the disabled body or Carmen Dexl and Silvia Gerlsbeck's inquiry into the function of the posthuman in a postcolonial context push in the same direction by questioning beginnings: This is foregrounded either by how the disabled body 'queers' notions of continuity and linearity, particularly by using the trope of 'impotence' and thus disturbing hegemonic narratives of heteronormativity, or by how the texts reframe historiographic processes that underlie the allegedly stable and coherent 'grand narrative' of colonialism. These significations of representations urge us to return to and re-read familiar stories, be it the so-called canonized classics, European fairytales, or examples of science fiction, for the purposes they were made to serve.

In highlighting the many facets of representation and its cultural power for co-constituting bodies and constructions of gender, *The Male Body in Representation: Returning to Matter* wishes to contribute to scholarly discussions of the body and provide an incentive to return to matter for its manifold significations.

References

Felski, Rita. *Uses of Literature*. Malden, MA and Oxford: Blackwell Publishing, 2008.

Hall, Stuart. "What Is This 'Black' in Black Popular Culture?" *Social Justice* 20, no. 1/2 (1993): 104–114.

———. *Representation: Cultural Representations and Signifying Practices*. London: Sage, 1997.

Nünning, Ansgar. "Narrativist Approaches and Narratological Concepts for the Study of Culture." In *Travelling Concepts for the Study of Culture*, edited by Birgit Neumann and Ansgar Nünning, 145–183. Berlin and New York: de Gruyter, 2012.

Index

© The Editor(s) (if applicable) and The Author(s), under exclusive license to Springer Nature Switzerland AG 2022
C. Dexl and S. Gerlsbeck (eds.), *The Male Body in Representation*, Palgrave Studies in (Re)Presenting Gender,
https://doi.org/10.1007/978-3-030-88604-2

313